The Souls of Black Folk

One Hundred Years Later

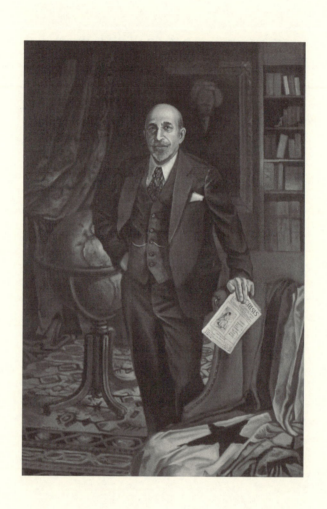

The Souls of Black Folk

One Hundred Years Later

Edited with an Introduction by Dolan Hubbard

University of Missouri Press
Columbia and London

Library of Congress Cataloging-in-Publication Data

The souls of Black folk one hundred years later / edited with an
introduction by Dolan Hubbard.
    p. cm.
  ISBN 0-8262-1433-9 (alk. paper)
  1. Du Bois, W. E. B. (William Edward Burghardt), 1868–1963.
Souls of Black folk.   2. Du Bois, W. E. B. (William Edward
Burghardt), 1868–1963—Criticism and interpretation.
I. Hubbard, Dolan, 1949–
  E185.6 .D79733 2003
  973'.0496073—dc21   2002154450

∞™ This paper meets the requirements of the
American National Standard for Permanence of Paper
for Printed Library Materials, Z39.48, 1984.

Designer: Jennifer Cropp
Typesetter: Bookcomp, Inc.
Printer and binder: Thomson-Shore, Inc.
Typefaces: Palatino, Berkeley Book, Aquinas

Frontispiece: *Portrait of W. E. B. Du Bois,* by Arnold Thielman,
courtesy of James E. Lewis Museum of Art, Morgan State University.
    The Du Bois Circle believed that the ninetieth anniversary of its
founding, inspired by the vision of Dr. Du Bois, was an appropriate time for the Circle to honor the memory of this great leader.
The Circle commissioned Mr. Arnold Thielman to paint the portrait of Dr. Du Bois that now hangs in the Morris A. Soper Library
and Information Technology Center on the campus of Morgan
State University in Baltimore, Maryland.
    Arnold Thielman is a citizen of Bonaire, in the Dutch West In-
dies. He received a Master of Fine Arts degree in the Mount Royal
School of Art from the Maryland Institute–College of Art in Baltimore in 1995.

Dedicated to the Du Bois Circle, the oldest Black women's organization in Baltimore, founded on January 5, 1906, as an auxiliary of the men's segment of the Niagara Movement, a forerunner of the NAACP.

———————————————

The Du Bois Circle continues to have active concern for theory and practice in politics, for poverty in a land of plenty, for immigration and population problems, for education as the stepping stone to employment and progress, for careers in occupations hitherto closed to men and women of color, and for the acceleration of the integration of the masses of Blacks into the mainstream of American society.

—Mission Statement of the Du Bois Circle

Contents

Acknowledgments

W. E. B. Du Bois became a part of my mental make-up, my intellectual exemplar, since I first taught a portion of *The Souls of Black Folk* at Winston Salem State University in the late 1970s. I was at once struck by the lyrical quality of his language, keyed to the cadences of the King James Bible. I wove his words and ideas into my teaching and even my attitude toward life, for he made me feel secure intellectually and emotionally in a world where I was not construed as a full citizen. Du Bois provided me with a grammar for articulating the self and for understanding what it means to be black in the United States. He used "words as a weapon," in the apt language of Richard Wright, and he intrepidly blended a concern for the poetics and politics of language, and their influence on how we perceive the world around us. Finally, I bonded with Du Bois because he put his tremendous intellect to use in improving the quality of life for all in our beloved community.

It is especially apt that I edit this book in Baltimore, a city that ranks next to Atlanta and New York in being where Du Bois chose to spend much of his time. Du Bois once lived in Morgan Park, a residential area adjacent to Morgan State University, and his legacy to the institution included one of his best students, Irene Diggs, who taught in the Department of Sociology and Anthropology for many years. Thus it is my pleasure to present this collection of essays celebrating his groundbreaking work.

I wish to thank my colleagues who read parts of this manuscript. They include Thelma B. Thompson, Ruby V. Rodney, Patrick Murphy, Betty Plummer, and Otto Begus.

I also extend my appreciation to the following individuals for their contributions to my work: Michelle Baliff, Rosemary Franklin, Barbara McCaskill, R. Baxter Miller, Hugh Ruppersburg, and Anne Williams, my former colleagues at the University of Georgia; Burney J. Hollis, Dean of the College of Liberal Arts, Otto Begus, Chair of Philosophy and Religious Studies, Karen A. Robertson, Director of Library Services, and Gabriel S. Tenabe, Director of Museums at Morgan State University; Sundiata Cha-Jua, Director of African American Studies, and Vera Mitchell, at the African-American and Africana Library, at the University of Illinois at Urbana-Champaign; M. Elaine Hughes at the William Russell Pullen Library at Georgia State University; Karen Jefferson, of the Archives and Special Collections at the Robert W. Woodruff Library in the Atlanta University Center; Judy Cooper, Johnnie Fields, and Vivian Fisher of the Enoch Pratt Free Library in Baltimore; James J. Davis, Chair of Modern Languages and Literature at Howard University; Leonard A. Slade, Jr., Chair of Africana Studies at the University of New York at Albany; Kweise Mfume, President and CEO of the NAACP; Edmonia Yates, President of the Du Bois Circle; Chester J. Fontenot, Jr., Chair of English at Mercer University; Joe Weixlmann, Interim Provost, St. Louis University; Dennis Vernon Proctor, Pastor of Pennsylvania Avenue A.M.E. Zion Church; and Emily Stipes Watts, George Hendrick, Frances Alston, Ruth Antoine, Adnee Bradford, Don Burness, Frank Dexter Brown, Linda Carter, Grace Coffey, Hazel A. Ervin, Jim Estepp, Sharynn Owens Etheridge, Clay Goss, Karl Henzy, Elwanda D. Ingram, Milford Jeremiah, Meena Khorana, Marvin A. Lewis, Charles H. Long, Monifa Love, Lois McMillan, Tiffany McMillan, Keith Mehlinger, Anita Pandey, Ralph Reckley, Margaret A. Reid, Ruthe T. Sheffey, Maxine Thompson Smith, Ella Stevens, Minnie Washington, Judy White, Jeffrey R. Williams, and the late Mildred White Barksdale, whose indefatigable spirit sustained me throughout this project from its inception.

I am especially grateful to Wendell Jackson, our department's Renaissance man and editor deluxe, and Caroline Maun, for their advice and encouragement throughout. The constructive comments of the two anonymous reviewers were especially helpful. I should also like to express my gratitude to all my students, who over the years have engaged me in spirited dialogue when I taught Du Bois.

My assistants, Tayari A. Jones, Erica L. Griffin, and Michael D. Hill, then at the the University of Georgia, and Tiffany Boyd Adams, Robert Matunda, Kara Janelle Scott, and Scott A. West, of Morgan State University, completed every task without complaint. The book would not have been published without the editorial foresight, patience, and perseverance of Beverly Jarrett and Jane Lago and their coworkers at the University of Missouri Press.

Finally, Ruth, Aisha, and Desmond weathered my excitement and disappointments, consoled only by their comprehension of the subject's importance.

Grateful acknowledgment is made to the Du Bois Circle and to Morgan State University for permission to use the portrait of Du Bois by Arnold Thielman. It now hangs in the Morris A. Soper Library and Information Technology Center. We also wish to thank The Crisis Publishing Co., Inc., the publisher of the magazine of the National Association for the Advancement of Colored People, for the use of two of their images.

Centurion

Thelma B. Thompson

for Dr. W. E. B. Du Bois

From sparkling stars of sun-swept Africa's Womb
He burst born brave.
Black comet come to commit to same.
Heir of Hadrian, brother of broken boys
Endowed, yet not bowed to intellect nor sect
Extraordinary man for extra ordinary times.

>Timekeeper of a race set pace
>Olympian in his right.
>Right of wrongs left.
>Speak, man of finest letters, prime thinker
>Write, write of thoughts thought.
>Unrecorded by silent suffrage souls.

>Centurion
>Dreamed old dreams of history's hate
>Of old mothers' eternal birth pains sold
>Of frail fathers' faith found lost to gold.
>Middle passage, message,
>Massage doubloons and fears
>America's bounty, bargain blocks, Black
>Tears
>Stubborn slave triangle,
>Indelible saga
>Nightmare of that visionary
>Radical, root of wrongs.

>Prophet, relentless relay-runner
>In man's Marathon race for race,
>Sprinter, sole splinter

Of the Black Soul's soul sold silent
Erudite, forthright forefather.

Centurion
Dreamed new dreams of talent bent,
Burnished
Upon gold and medals.
Bearer of society's bad news

And Views:

Content of whose character?
Washed by the Blood
Pressed, clean by selectivity,
Monticello,
Means and
Mama's meager memories made maid?

Centurion
Blessed with longevity, cursed with profundity
Outward going on his inward, lonesome sail
In a shallow world wallow with scholars,
Ships,
Doing time in America's hot pot melting.

Centurion
Purified in lava lavish
From his cortex, centrosphere,
Goes granite gray stone corner
Of his great gran' people folk.
Centurion's mighty pen, his sword, rapier,
Long lances
Lacerate a century's life
And pregnant brain bags
Burst.
Dormant duffel sacks of Blackness—
Congress Pan-African Babel unified,
A mere moment's silence in Eternity
In respect and retrospect, African accord
The temporary truce.

Magnificent master of Time's tree
Misunderstood, stands free.
Centurion of the color line, barrier and borderline
Of centuries and of love,

Bread and dread of armies
(Genes' gifts, unreturnable).

Centurion
Survivor of our Long March from ancient Africa,
Arrived triumphant, tired, midst thousands.
At King's homeward horizon's side
His monument, his mountaintop

In Washington's rainbow tide,
Yes, we gathered at the river
Our black Souls all aquiver.

> On that great day, words dumb to say
> Our hearts' hot, deepest sorrow
> Centurion ran, passed his baton
> Was gone,
> From us
> Forever.

Note: This poem was first read at the Middle Atlantic Writers Association Conference in Frankfort, Kentucky, in 1991.

The Souls of Black Folk

One Hundred Years Later

Introduction

Dolan Hubbard

The Occasion

On the eve of the one-hundredth anniversary of *The Souls of Black Folk* (1903), it is appropriate that the students of W. E. B. Du Bois (1868–1963) pause and assess the influence of the Old Testament of twentieth-century African American letters. This centennial is the occasion for this collection of essays that treats various aspects of a book that has been a keystone in twentieth-century thought. *The Souls of Black Folk* is a book for all seasons. Both its title and language suggest the idea of a revelation that is only partial; Du Bois, Picasso-like, is only able to "sketch in, in vague, uncertain outline, the spiritual world in which ten thousand thousand Americans live and strive" (5). Du Bois, thus, in the forethought to *The Souls of Black Folk,* hints of a deeper interpretation.

Like all classics, *The Souls of Black Folk* must be reinterpreted by each generation; the reinterpretation renews our appreciation of a work that has redrawn the boundaries of a cultural universe. The fact that *The Souls of Black Folk* still stirs our imagination raises the question, however, of how and why this collection of fourteen essays published at the dawn of the twentieth century continues to resonate at the dawn of the twenty-first. At the beginning of the twentieth century, Du Bois predicted the debate on multiculturalism that surfaced at the end of the century. He saw ethnic mixing, blending, as a strength and not a weakness.

Knowledge of *The Souls of Black Folk* helps one understand the historical background and character of American society. Despite Reconstruction, the New Negro, the New Deal, the Great Society, the War on Poverty, and Compassionate Conservatism, blacks in the United States still remain largely "faces at the bottom of the well," as Derrick Bell reminds us. *The Souls of Black Folk* strikes the ears with the welcome sound of a familiar song wafted down from a carillon. It awakens a heroic spirit in those for whom the story of black struggle never grows old.

In 1900, the Chicago publishing firm A. C. McClurg and Company invited the thirty-two-year-old Du Bois to assemble a manuscript that collected his recent essays for *Atlantic Monthly* and other journals. From more than three dozen articles and addresses already written or published, Du Bois "selected eight for adaptation or reprinting as nine chapters of *The Souls of Black Folk.*"[1] He transformed his "fugitive pieces" into "an integrated narrative" that drew on the "development of a proudly self-conscious (as opposed to 'double-conscienced') racial voice" to underscore the extent to which the black presence had enriched America.[2] Blacks made their contributions in spite of "the contradiction of double aims" that prevented them from realizing their full human potential. When Du Bois published *The Souls of Black Folk* in 1903, he effectively ended the Berlin Wall that excluded the black subject from history. It propelled him to national prominence.[3]

The response to its publication by readers from diverse backgrounds has been electric. James Weldon Johnson grasped its almost ecclesiastical hold on the imagination when he observed that it had "a greater effect upon and within the Negro race in America than any other single book published in this country since *Uncle Tom's Cabin.*" Jessie Fauset praised Du Bois for voicing "the intricacies of the blind maze of thought and action along which the modern, educated colored man or woman struggles." Three weeks after its publication, Ida Wells-Barnett, in the face of a spirited debate within the black intelligentsia over the merits of Du Bois's book, wrote: "We [she and her husband] are still reading your book with the same delighted appreciation." From the Gold Coast, West African author and nationalist Casely Hayford congratulated Du Bois after having "the pleasure of reading your great work *The Souls of Black Folk.*" Langston Hughes singled out *The Souls of Black Folk* in reminiscing that "my earliest memories of written words are those of Du Bois and the Bible." And literary historian Benjamin Brawley felt in its cadences "the passion of a mighty heart" and considered it the most important work "in classic English" produced by a black writer.[4]

1. Arnold Rampersad, *The Art and Imagination of W. E. B. Du Bois* (New York: Schocken, 1990), 69.

2. Robert B. Stepto, *From behind the Veil: A Study of Afro-American Narrative*, 2d ed. (Urbana: University of Illinois Press, 1991), 53.

3. W. E. B. Du Bois, *The Souls of Black Folk*, ed. Henry Louis Gates Jr. and Terri Hume Oliver (New York: Norton, 1999), 11. Subsequent page references in this essay are to this edition. On the publication history of *The Souls of Black Folk*, see David Levering Lewis, *W. E. B. Du Bois: Biography of a Race, 1868–1919* (New York: Henry Holt, 1993); Rampersad, *Art and Imagination*; and Stepto, *Behind the Veil.*

4. James Weldon Johnson, *Along This Way* (1933; reprint, New York: Viking, 1968), 203; Jessie Fauset to W. E. B. Du Bois, 1903, in *The Correspondence of W. E. B. Du Bois,*

Peter Abrahams, the South African "colored" writer best known for his autobiography *Tell Freedom,* was not alone when he said, upon first reading this book in 1948, that until then he had had no words with which to voice his Negro-ness. It had, he wrote, "the impact of a revelation . . . a key to the understanding of my world." For the critic J. Saunders Redding, the work "is more history-making than historical, so profound has been its impact on a variety of men." Extending the observation of Abrahams, Redding judged its impact to be incalculable because it fixed "that moment in history when the American Negro began to reject the idea of the world's belonging to white people only, and to think of himself, in concert, as a potential force in the organization of society."[5]

The historian Herbert Aptheker has declared that the book is "one of the classics in the English language." Darlene Clark Hine praises the book for Du Bois's "compelling prose" that "captured well his perception of the dichotomous nature of black identity." David Levering Lewis observed that it was "one of those events epochally dividing history into a before and an after."[6]

The Theater of the Intellect

William Edward Burghardt Du Bois (February 23, 1868–August 27, 1963), one of America's most distinguished intellectuals and social activists, wrote twenty volumes on history, sociology, anthropology, political science, and literature and more than one hundred articles that were both critical and scholarly. He was the only black person among the twenty-nine original founders of the NAACP, and he served as its director of publicity and research. He edited its official organ the *Crisis.* His Harvard dissertation, *The Suppression of the African Slave Trade to the United States of America,* was published as the first volume in the Harvard Historical Series (1896). His second volume, *The Philadelphia Negro* (1899), which documents in interviews the lives of five thousand African Americans trapped in poverty,

ed. Herbert Aptheker (3 vols.; Amherst: University of Massachusetts Press, 1973–1978), 1:66; Ida B. Wells-Barnett to W. E. B. Du Bois, May 30, 1903, *Correspondence,* 1:55–56; Casely Hayford to W. E. B. Du Bois, June 8, 1904, *Correspondence,* 1:76; Langston Hughes, *Black Titan,* ed. John Henrik Clarke et al. (Boston: Beacon Press, 1970), 8; Benjamin Brawley, *The Negro in Literature and Art* (New York: Duffield, 1918), 18.

5. J. Saunders Redding, introduction to *The Souls of Black Folk* (Greenwich, Conn.: Fawcett, 1961), ix; Peter Abrahams quoted on same page.

6. Herbert Aptheker, *Annotated Bibliography of the Published Writings of W. E. B. Du Bois* (Millwood, N.Y.: Kraus-Thomas Organization, 1973), 551; Darlene Clark Hine, " 'In the Kingdom of Culture': Black Women and the Intersection of Race, Gender, and Class," in *Lure and Loathing: Essays on Race, Identity, and the Ambivalence of Assimilation,* ed. Gerald Early (New York: Allen Lane/Penguin Press, 1993), 338; Lewis, *Biography of a Race,* 277.

is the first sociological study of American blacks by an American of African descent. He is generally accorded the title "Father of Pan-Africanism." He stands at the forefront of those who articulate what it means to be black in the modern Western world. Much of the subsequent thought and exposure by readers, both sympathetic and unsympathetic, to the sweeping vision of this radical democrat rests upon the foundational text of his critical vision, *The Souls of Black Folk* (1903).

Du Bois, in his prefatory "forethought" to the volume, explicates his intent to "show the strange meaning of being black here at the dawning of the Twentieth century" (5). He keeps this point before his reader in the book's first chapter, "Of Our Spiritual Strivings," with the arresting question: "How does it feel to be a problem?" The question serves as the leitmotif for the entire volume. Du Bois articulates the concerns of a community that called into question the epistemological foundations of the republic: What does freedom mean? Does history have any positive meaning for black people? If we are all made in the image of God, then why is it that black people have a special cross to bear? Does the moral order bend toward justice? Would America have been America without the contribution of New World Africans? Because Du Bois grapples with these basic questions that black people have asked themselves since their forced arrival in the New World, *The Souls of Black Folk* carries historical and spiritual weight.

In his highly lyrical narrative, Du Bois evinces the rhythms that govern black life in his transgenerational scripture. Du Bois transforms historical time with mythical timelessness. The language as well as the messages of *The Souls of Black Folk* convey for us the continuum in which we live, familiar and circumscribed, which we must come to grips with if we are to understand fully what it means to be black in the modern Western World.[7]

The Souls of Black Folk contains in broad outline themes that Du Bois would revisit again and again in the pages of the *Crisis,* in his scholarship, and in his imaginative literature, culminating in his magnum opus, *Black Reconstruction: An Essay toward a History of the Part Which Black Folk Played in the Attempt to Reconstruct Democracy in America, 1860–1880* (1935). The most prominent themes are the nature and meaning of freedom, the phenomenology of racism and the inscription of difference, economic inequality and the illusion of progress, squandering of resources, natural and human, and the spiritual resilience of black people in the face of overwhelming odds.

The Souls of Black Folk contains history, autobiography, elegy, threnody, philosophy, and, in the instance of his "twice-told tale," fiction. Du Bois,

7. See Robert Alter and Frank Kermode, eds., *The Literary Guide to the Bible* (Cambridge: Harvard University Press, 1987), 1.

who anticipated the cultural awakening known as the Harlem Renaissance, draws on a storehouse of black expression—spirituals, folklore, slave narratives, and speeches, to show white America how this rich cultural production made possible the histories, literature, and art that were emerging at the turn of the twentieth century. Using black expression as an organizing principle, Du Bois shows how blacks transgress the boundaries of definitional certainty and reclaim their consciousness, as evident in "Of the Faith of the Fathers" and "The Sorrow Songs." They are "the singular spiritual heritage of the nation and the greatest gift of the Negro people" (155). With the possible exception of the sorrow songs (or spirituals), *The Souls of Black Folk* is as close as many black people in the United States come to having a national scripture. Its texture is woven of a rich, black, oral, expressive literature held in dynamic tension with a Euro-American tradition.[8]

The Souls of Black Folk is one of the most significant documents in American intellectual history. Like the words of Thomas Jefferson, Thomas Paine, and Ralph Waldo Emerson, the words of *The Souls of Black Folk* are woven into the discourse of America. Like these architects of American thought, Du Bois invests the theater of the intellect with a new energy that inspires people to action. Explicitly, *The Souls of Black Folk* echoes Lincoln's call for a "more perfect union."

True to his post-Enlightenment roots, Du Bois raises questions about the sublime, ideology, aesthetics, freedom, and identity, especially American identity. As he struggles to derive answers to the problems of being, Du Bois dissects the epistemology of identity and the epistemology of racism. He sees both as intertwined with the New World struggle for self-definition. Placing Africans at the center of the New World experience, Du Bois provides an alternative reading of the text called America.

Defining the "Souls" of Black Folk

The title and composition of the book are of extreme importance. Du Bois signals to the reader that he will provide him or her with an index to understanding the character and humanity of black people whom the nation refuses to see. He lifts the veil on the experience of blacks in America. As Rampersad notes in *The Art and Imagination of W. E. B. Du Bois,* "The 'souls' of the title is a play on words, referring to the 'twoness' of the black American." In using the word *souls,* Du Bois opens an interpretive space. *Soul* means the immaterial essence, animating principle, or actuating cause of an individual life; it means a person's total self, an active or essential part, a

8. See Rampersad, *Art and Imagination;* Stepto, *Behind the Veil,* 62–64; and Donald B. Gibson, introduction to *The Souls of Black Folk* (New York: Penguin, 1989).

spiritual or moral force, or a fervor. Du Bois uses *souls* to present prototypes of the central figures in the black community: the preacher, the teacher, the intellectual, the laborer, and the bourgeois black. Du Bois digs into the "souls" or essence of these prototypes to show the roles these individuals play in an organic society that the larger world fails to see. Through his commanding rhetorical skills and his sociological training, Du Bois leads the reader to infer that, minus full participation in American society, each black person is one step removed from being a criminal.

The black woman is absent from his list of prototypes. The normative premise of Du Bois's trenchant discussion is a world that is black and male; women are subsumed under the prototype "teacher" and relegated to the domestic sphere. For Du Bois, the black woman as racial, rather than as gendered subject, provides him with a strategy for interrogating the construction of patriarchy and sexuality within America. One recalls the defeated optimism of Joise in chapter 4, "Of the Meaning of Progress." This "thin, homely girl of twenty, with a dark-brown face and thick, hard hair," dared to dream "to be a student in the great school in Nashville" (48) in the face of overwhelming odds. History and patriarchy consigned her to be "the centre of the family" (47) with little tangible reward. In the background "Of the Meaning of Progress," Du Bois links criminality and the collapse of the patriarch as a logical extension of the enslavement of Africans in the New World. Through these prototypes, Du Bois reached down and uncovered the essence of black life in the United States, what the members of the community faced and would face in the twentieth century.[9]

In the use of the term *folk*, Du Bois was "making a strong claim for the recognition" of the "dignity and separate identity" of Afro-Americans.[10] Taken together, the text, as Manning Marable observes, "blends the main themes that comprised Du Bois' emerging social theory": "double-consciousness"; the beauty and originality of Negroes' "sorrow songs" and black religion; the unique spirituality of the Negro people; the necessity to develop black educational institutions; and the division of the modern world along "the color line."[11] Du Bois frames his discussion of black folk in the stately language of the King James Bible, not only to draw on its rhetorical flourishes, such as referring to the Georgia Black Belt as "the Egypt of the Confederacy" or blacks trapped in a "house of bondage," but also to reflect the ethical and religious character of black people. Du Bois

9. Marcellus Blount and George P. Cunningham, eds., *Representing Black Men* (New York: Routledge, 1996), ix–xv; Hine, " 'In the Kingdom of Culture,' " 338. See also Hazel Carby, *Race Men* (Cambridge: Harvard University Press, 1998); Carby deconstructs the ideologies of gender in *The Souls of Black Folk*.

10. Rampersad, *Art and Imagination*, 74–76; Gibson, introduction to *Souls*, xi–xv.

11. Manning Marable, *W. E. B. Du Bois, Black Radical Democrat* (Boston: Twayne Publishers, 1986), 48.

implicitly aligns himself with the prophets of the Old Testament. Echoing them, he expresses fear for the salvation of his people and of America. He is afraid that the expanding capitalism that was sweeping across the South in the last decade of the nineteenth century would make people worship at the altar of the false god of "Mammonism," thereby undermining the higher platonic ideals of "Truth, Beauty, and Goodness" (57). While he supported black economic empowerment, Du Bois also looked to the university as a site to stem "a lust for gold" (57) and a place to elevate the soul. More than wealth, the South required "knowledge and culture. . . . The function of the university is not simply to teach bread-winning . . . it is, above all, to be the organ of that fine adjustment between real life and the growing knowledge of life, an adjustment which forms the secret of civilization" (60).

With a regal hauteur, Du Bois ignores the definitions of whites about a so-called "Negro Problem." He does not allow himself or those who would read him to believe that black people are a problem. Du Bois's charge to black intellectuals ("the talented tenth") is clear: They must dig up, search for, and analyze those problems and situations which imprison the community within the language. The black intellectual must free him- or herself and then the community from the efforts of whites to oppress them mentally and spiritually.

The Context

The bookends of Du Bois's life have been characterized as the U.S. Civil War and the modern Civil Rights Movement. Born in Great Barrington, Massachusetts, of Dutch, French, and African ancestry on February 23, 1868, five years after Abraham Lincoln issued the *Emancipation Proclamation* (January 1, 1863), Du Bois died in Accra, Ghana, on August 23, 1963, the eve of the March on Washington, where Martin Luther King Jr. delivered his stirring "I Have a Dream" Speech.

Du Bois's early life follows a familiar pattern, especially for the gifted "native intellectual." According to this script, a young man with a humble background, whose prodigious intellectual gifts presented themselves at an early age, would go to school, receive his education and training, and put his skills to use in maintaining the colonial hegemony over his people. At first glance, Du Bois would embody all the elements of this paradigm; however, on closer inspection, one could point to Booker T. Washington as the prototype. In this regard, Du Bois has as a narrative goal the wrestling of "a greater authorial control of what is, in effect, not simply a single volume but a major portion of [the American] canon up to that time."[12]

12. Stepto, *Behind the Veil*, 53.

An innocuous exchange of gifts gone awry prompted Du Bois to challenge the cultural script that rendered black and colored people invisible. A white female student, a newcomer to Great Barrington, introduced Du Bois, the only black student in Great Barrington High School, to the role assigned to blacks when she repelled his overtures of friendship: "Then it dawned upon me with a certain suddenness that I was different from the others; or like, mayhap, in heart and life, and longing, but shut out from their world by a vast veil" (10). Du Bois never got over this shock of recognition. This experience provoked him to pour into *The Souls of Black Folk* these stunning words that ever since have been quoted as summing up the African predicament in America: "It is a peculiar sensation, this double-consciousness. . . . One ever feels his two-ness—an American, a Negro; two souls, two thoughts, two unreconciled strivings; two warring ideals in one dark body, whose dogged strength alone keeps it from being torn asunder" (11). Henceforth, Du Bois would devote his prodigious intellectual gifts to deconstructing the colonial-industrial complex.

Du Bois broke with the narrative plot of his life as a gifted native intellectual at Fisk University in Nashville, Tennessee, where he graduated with a bachelor of arts degree in 1888. He then entered the junior class of Harvard College, where he graduated *cum laude* with a bachelor's degree in 1890; staying at Harvard, he received his master's degree in 1891. Shortly after he graduated from Harvard College, Du Bois, then a twenty-five-year-old University of Berlin graduate student, penned the following prophetic lines in his diary that recall the words of the Old Testament figure of Esther: "These are my plans: to make a name in science, to make a name in literature, and thus to raise my race. Or perhaps to raise a visible empire in Africa. . . . And if I perish—I PERISH."[13] These words formed the first commandment for black and colored intellectuals who have striven mightily to shift their communities from the margins to the center.

To understand the revolution in Du Bois's thought, one must understand the world in which he came to intellectual maturity. In the international arena, this world was defined by the mad scramble for Africa and the Berlin Conference (1884–1885), where the European powers "with great gusto carved up Africa." Motivated by the Industrial Revolution, they divided Africa irrespective of ethnic lines.[14] In the domestic arena, this world

13. Du Bois, "Celebrating His Twenty-fifth Birthday" (Feb. 23, 1893), in *Against Racism: Unpublished Essays, Papers, Addresses, 1887–1961* (Amherst: University of Massachusetts Press, 1985), 27–29. The autobiography omits the climactic part of the statement; see Du Bois, *The Autobiography of W. E. B. Du Bois: A Soliloquy on Viewing My Life from the Last Decade of Its First Century*, ed. Herbert Aptheker (New York: International Publishers, 1968), 170–71.

14. Roland Oliver and Anthony Atmore, *Africa since 1800* (Cambridge: Cambridge University Press, 1967), 108.

was defined by the Gilded Age, the Spanish American War, the war for the Philippines and the South Pacific, and the rise and collapse of Reconstruction and an almost complete disenfranchisement of African Americans. During what historian Rayford Logan called the "nadir" of black life in the United States, the color curtain was drawn so tightly around black people that this low point prompted Booker T. Washington to deliver what Du Bois bitterly termed the "Atlanta Compromise" (1895). Du Bois spoke truthfully to power that had enveloped the black and colonial world in a terrifying silence. In essence, *The Souls of Black Folk* was a single candle in the dark—a testament of hope.

We can then open up the critical lens and place Du Bois where he properly belongs, in a trans-Atlantic conversation with his contemporaries such as Charles Darwin, Herman Melville, Sigmund Freud, Joseph Conrad, Anna Julia Haywood Cooper, and Rudyard Kipling. In various ways, these thinkers raise the following questions: What does it mean to be human? What distinguishes mankind from animals? The genius of Du Bois is that he showed the world that the Imperial Imperative and American racism were not mutually exclusive. They are parts of a vast whole, in the rapacious competition for markets. He shows how they are mutually dependent or interrelated, much in the manner of Conrad in his narratives of modernity.

Du Bois challenges the prevailing orthodoxy that Africans were on the bottom rung of the great chain of being and that blackness was a badge of shame. He illuminates the nexus between color and economics in the global economy. To take but one example, Rudyard Kipling, the arch-representative of Empire and of the inscription of difference, was the pre-eminent advocate of the civilizing mission that required every Englishman, or, more broadly, every white man, to bring European culture to the heathens of the uncivilized world, as evident in his jingoistic paeans for European dominance, such as "The White Man's Burden" and *Kim* (1901). In 1907, he won the Nobel Prize for literature. Standing on a supposedly firm center, Kipling, as template for Empire, presented to the world his version of an orderly and rational portrayal of life. Kipling's imperial pastorals erased the contradictions, denying the humanity and epic complexity of black people, among others.[15]

A Kipling could not imagine a Du Bois, but a Du Bois knew that the Kiplings of the world must be dethroned if black and colored people were to reclaim their humanity. Armed with his wits and his pen, Du Bois rereads history and gives us a new historiography. He thematizes

15. For a gloss on one dimension of this trans-Atlantic conversation, see Michael North, *The Dialect of Modernism: Race, Language, and Twentieth-Century Literature* (New York: Oxford University Press, 1994).

blackness and makes the African relevant to the philosophical, political, economic, and cultural issues of the New World. As an exceptionally well-educated man, he was well aware of colonialism and the worldwide oppression of black people. Du Bois and the generation of largely African and Asian intellectuals—Mahatma Ghandi of India, Alain Locke, René Maran of Martinique, C. L. R. James of Trinidad, Ho Chi Minh of Vietnam, Langston Hughes, Aimé Césaire of Martinique, Léopold Sédar Senghor of Senegal, Léon Damas of Guyana, and the Nardal sisters, Jane, Paulette, and Andrée, of Haiti—who came of age in the 1920s and 1930s were "scholastic adornments of empire."[16] Du Bois represents that moment when these people from marginalized cultures—educated at the world's great universities to see themselves first as loyal citizens of the mother country and last as blacks—claimed intellectual independence. They were the product of a history and a way of life about which most whites knew very little. When he was writing *The Souls of Black Folk*, Du Bois really was searching for answers to the plight of blacks in America.[17]

The Souls of Black Folk is southern in character, northern in orientation, and global in implication. Du Bois sets up a trilogue among Europe, Africa, and the Americas. This conversation is designed to bring Africa affirmatively into the global conversation. The American South becomes the synecdoche for the colonial enterprise. With the rapid industrialization of the North, the South effectively becomes a colony within a colony, and blacks the ultimate outsiders within the body politic, so close to and yet so far away from the corridors of power.[18] Ralph Ellison, in *Invisible Man*, does a masterful exposé on this socioeconomic disjuncture. Du Bois rewrites the South in order to rewrite America. *The Souls of Black Folk* brings into sharper focus the relationship between the dominators and the dominated and makes clear how power is pivotally connected with the production of regional self-identity in "Of the Meaning of Progress," "Of the Wings of Atalanta," "Of the Black Belt," and "Of the Quest of the Golden Fleece." Du Bois illuminates the dialectical tension that exists between blacks and

16. David Levering Lewis, *When Harlem Was in Vogue* (New York: Vintage, 1982), 150.

17. I draw upon the following: Janet Vaillant, *Léopold Sédar Senghor* (Cambridge: Harvard University Press, 1990), 64–73, 89–95; Hazel Carby, "The Canon: Civil War and Reconstruction," *Michigan Quarterly Review* 28, no. 1 (winter 1989): 39–40; and Robert P. Smith Jr., "Rereading *Banjo*: Claude McKay and the French Connection," *CLA Journal* 30, no. 1 (September 1986): 46–58. For a response to how the Third World has been largely rendered silent under the heading "Minority Discourse," see the treatment of "The Nature and Context of Minority Discourse" in the two-volume issue of *Cultural Critique* (spring and fall 1987). In *Race Men*, Carby points out the contradiction between the theory and the practice of men who lead the fight for racial equality, but fall short of the mark in the area of gender equality.

18. Du Bois gives voice to the frustration of black America in "A Negro Nation within the Nation" (1935), in *W. E. B. Du Bois: A Reader*, ed. David Levering Lewis (New York: Henry Holt, 1995), 563–70.

whites and between the South and the nation, specifically the nation's un-acknowledged debt to the rich and diverse contribution of its citizens of African descent. In short, Du Bois brings new vigor to the interpretation of the culture and consciousness of the American South as he signifies on the routes, and roots, of American society.

Ultimately, Du Bois, through his new historiography, set in motion an oppositional discourse that contested the concept of culture as an ideologically charged semantic field used to justify European supremacy while systematically devaluing the contributions of Africans and Asians to world thought. Culture is the terrain of struggle *between* groups, "a continuous and necessarily uneven and unequal struggle," and "there is no whole, authentic, autonomous black culture which lives outside of these relations of cultural power and domination." The spatial juxtaposition in which Third World intellectuals found themselves in close proximity to the capitals of the Western world leads to the re-creation of self—a remembrance of things past that prompts them to read and reinterpret the metropolitan literatures whose central concern is with the formation of "a national subjectivity and ideology that constructs and simultaneously excludes a racialized other."[19]

The representation of the South as a frozen text often obscures the economic tension and the competition for resources, natural and human, between the North and the South. By means of his soaring rhetoric, Du Bois breaks through the "romance" of the South with its repressive history and engages the political economy of this region—the politics and economics of class relations—hidden behind the phenomenology of race. He presents a case study in underdevelopment and dependency. He leads the untutored white reader to surmise that if a region is dependent, then its development is retarded.

The South tells the naive reader something about America's "heart of darkness," and this telling is most revealed in the literature of the American South in general and in *The Souls of Black Folk* in particular. We see the ways in which the past shapes and continues to exert pressure on consciousness. We see the interrelated corporeal issues of race, class, and sex as Du Bois struggles to make a fractured psyche whole. We see most clearly the discrepancy between the promise and the practice of America, buoyed by humanity's stubborn hope, insistent search for truth, and love of beauty, and the triumph of the human spirit. Du Bois invites us to pay close attention to how the American South shapes the national character. He presents us with an alternative reading of America that is more comprehensive than the "fictions," or ideologically coded accounts of life in a romanticized South.[20]

---

19. Carby, "Canon," 43, 40.
20. See Sterling A. Brown, *The Negro in American Fiction* (1937; reprint, New York: Atheneum, 1969).

Further, Du Bois reveals the rhetorical incompatibility between the implicit and explicit plans of American discourse, as, for example, the disconnection between the promise and the practice of America—in the text called "America." Du Bois brings into sharp focus the competing utopian and dystopian readings of the South by its white and black native sons and daughters, trapped in a system rife with social claustrophobia. The former promotes an Arcadian existence, while the latter promotes a landscape of nightmare. These competing readings retard the growth and development of the region and of America. America would not be free until the South was free, as is evident in the chapters on the Black Belt.

The Souls of Black Folk anticipates William Butler Yeats's poetic epiphany "The Second Coming": "Things fall apart; the center cannot hold." Du Bois, as sign and symbol of the radicalized native intellectual, is the center that cannot hold. It is one thing for the margin to write to the center if one's name is George Washington, Thomas Jefferson, Thomas Paine, Cecil Rhodes, or J. C. Smuts; it is another if one's name is Alexander Crummell, Henry McNeil Turner, Anna Julia Haywood Cooper, José Martí, Ida B. Wells-Barnett, or W. E. B. Du Bois. The experience of colonialism combined with African enslavement and the sliding of the signifier *nigger* prompts a radical critique of the assumptions underlying Eurocentric notions of aesthetics, identity, history, and culture. From his decentered reality, fragmented self, and multiple identity, Du Bois, representing the marginalized, speaks through the rupture of his dislocation. As a ritual action, Du Bois in *The Souls of Black Folk* synchronizes the native intellectual with the motion of history.

The Legacy of *The Souls of Black Folk*

The Souls of Black Folk now belongs in the canon of American letters; that is, it is a book that has special authority. It provides us with a powerful interpretive scheme or point of view on black life that diverges from the orthodox reading of the social text of America. The telos or endpoint of *The Souls of Black Folk* is directed toward a pluralistic America where "two world-races" (16) can coexist in the "kingdom of culture" (11). Du Bois, like a prophet, holds center stage in his penultimate chapter, "The Sorrow Songs," where he reminds us that "Through all the sorrow of the Sorrow Songs there breathes a hope—a faith in the ultimate justice of things" (162). This New World Jeremiah states the contribution of blacks to the making of the New World: "Here we have brought our three gifts and mingled them with yours: a gift of story and song—soft stirring melody in an ill-harmonized and unmelodious land; the gift of sweat and brawn to beat back the wilderness, conquer the soil, and lay the foundation for a vast economic empire two hundred years earlier than your weak hands could have done it; the third, a gift of the Spirit" (162). He then appears to announce God's judgment on the American Eden, jerking the nation and its leaders back to righteousness. He warns a largely indifferent nation to recognize the humanity of black people, who *have* striven to maintain the principles of "Justice, Mercy, and Truth, lest the nation be smitten with a curse" (162). Through his emancipatory poetics, Du Bois enabled New World Africans to claim through their blackness their uniqueness, strength, pride, beauty, and dignity. They are the moral voice of the West.

The themes that Du Bois painted in broad brush strokes may be seen in the works of diverse writers such as C. L. R. James *(The Black Jacobins)*, Richard Wright *(Native Son* and *White Man, Listen!)*, Frantz Fanon *(Black Skin/White Masks)*, Eric Williams *(Capitalism and Slavery)*, Benjamin E. Mays *(The Negro's God)*, Howard Thurman *(Jesus and the Disinherited)*, Walter Rodney *(How Europe Underdeveloped Africa)*, Eugene Genovese *(Roll Jordan Roll)*, James Baldwin *(Notes of a Native Son)*, Amiri Baraka *(Home: Social Essays)*, Michel Foucault *(Discipline and Punish)*, Fredric Jameson *(The Prison House of Language)*, Samir Amin *(Unequal Development)*, Audre Lorde *(Sister Outsider: Essays and Speeches)*, and Toni Morrison *(Song of Solomon* and *Playing in the Dark: Whiteness and the Literary Imagination)*.

Toni Morrison, for example, recontextualizes the trope of the veil and the rhetoric of black invisibility to tell the black woman's story. In *Song of Solomon*, she replaces the "unconscious moral heroism" (47) of Josie, emblematic of the plight of too many black women, with the supporting garments of black women's subjectivity. Morrison unpacks the issue of truth and subjectivity in order that the reader may see the gender of history configured as black and female. She transforms the black woman from silent object (Toomer's unprotected Karintha, a "November Cotton Flower," and Hurston's black woman as "mule of the world") to speaking subject as she explores other dimensions of her character in *The Bluest Eye* (rape), *Song of Solomon* (race and class), *Sula* (friendship), *Beloved* (madness and healing), *Jazz* (sexuality), and *Paradise* (a towering outcast).

In certain segments of the black world, *The Souls of Black Folk* has become a cultural lingua franca. Irrespective of socioeconomic background or political ideology, progressive people continue a stream of interpretation, thereby providing a critical heritage for future generations. This volume has been written for scholars, as well as for lay and nonprofessional persons engaged in studying or teaching *The Souls of Black Folk* or African American creative forms generally.

The writers gathered here from divergent backgrounds and scholarly interests continue the process of interpreting an American classic that is read for its intellectual, cultural, and political implications. They contribute fresh, new interpretations of the ageless truth of a work that has achieved the status of a sacred text. It is in this sense that we can speak of their observations as ecumenical writings, for truth cannot be categorized according to geography, race, and gender.

The commentary is both timely and timeless. It is timely in that it builds on previous work, incorporates current critical methodologies, aids in discerning the meaning of key passages, and provides new insights into the relevancy of *The Souls of Black Folk* for the twenty-first century. It is timeless in that the commentators carry out Du Bois's criticism of compassion, treating eternal issues such as social justice, human dignity, and the search for the beloved community. They bring a variety of approaches to the interpretation of *The Souls of Black Folk:* historical, political, literary, feminist, and psychological. It is the intent of this work to enhance pedagogical approaches to the teaching of *The Souls of Black Folk,* as the writers offer us a comparative perspective on a book that helped redefine the way we read the Atlantic formation.

Thelma B. Thompson begins the volume with a poem in honor of Du Bois. Also, so that the reader may gauge the impact of *The Souls of Black Folk,* we have included early reviews of this landmark book, as well as Du Bois's response to his reviewers.

Any assessment of race relations in the United States must begin with the American South. One hundred years after the publication of *The Souls of Black Folk,* Reavis L. Mitchell, Jr., and James Daniel Steele revisit Alexandria, Tennessee, and Albany, Georgia, respectively. In these isolated communities, the latter of which is the center of the Black Belt, Du Bois feels "the awful shadow of the Veil . . . that hung between us and Opportunity" (48, 50). The failure of Reconstruction produced the death of a dream on a grand scale, as people were frozen in place by the plantation economy. In "Alexandria, Tennessee: Dusk and Dawn of the Rural Veil," Mitchell cuts through the rhetoric of the 1880s New South gospel and shows that the rise of Jim Crow laws effectively disbarred blacks from meaningful participation in the political, educational, and economic discourse of a community that time has now forgotten. In "The Souls of the 'Black Belt' Revisited," Steele illuminates the extent to which the long shadow of the plantation economy still hovers over Albany, Georgia, and by extension, much of the New South. His examination reveals that poverty, mortality rates, and unequal development made this region a Third World within the United States.

The next group of chapters provides us with keys to understanding Du Bois. The writers comment on the construction of an American identity, the controversy of leadership, and the issue of representation. In "Anna Julia Cooper, Pauline Elizabeth Hopkins, and the African American Feminization of Du Bois's Discourse," Barbara McCaskill discusses how the two writers add a missing feminist voice to the discourse of social and political change that characterizes *The Souls of Black Folk. Although The Souls of*

Black Folk was progressive for its day, Du Bois assigned "respectable black women" to traditional roles within the domestic sphere.

In "They Sing the Song of Slavery: Frederick Douglass's *Narrative* and W. E. B. Du Bois's *The Souls of Black Folk* as Intertexts of Richard Wright's *12 Million Black Voices*," Virginia Whatley Smith revisits the struggle for black leadership. She illuminates how the phototext, drawn on the spine of the slave narrative, played a pivotal role in the struggle for representation.

In "Du Bois's 'Of The Coming of John,' Toomer's 'Kabnis,' and the Dilemma of Self-Representation," Chester J. Fontenot, Jr., shows that black art is informed by black life. Specifically, he examines black bodies in white social space within the context of the dominant culture's desire to keep black people invisible.

In "W. E. B. Du Bois and the Construction of Whiteness," Keith Byerman examines four "moments" of construction of whiteness in *The Souls of Black Folk*. Byerman argues that in each of these "moments," Du Bois "reverses the gaze of racial domination so as to make whites the object rather than the subject of attention."

The next three chapters of this collection examine the visual and psychological paradigms that inform Du Bois's conception of "double consciousness." The influence of *The Souls of Black Folk* may be seen in Du Bois's impact on all segments of the black world, including the fine arts. Amy Helene Kirschke, in "The Intersecting Rhetorics of Art and Blackness in *The Souls of Black Folk*," demonstrates the influence of *The Souls of Black Folk* on the visual arts. She reminds us that Du Bois created the artistic space that enabled African American visual artists "to depict black subject matter in their work."

In " 'Looking at One's Self Through the Eyes of Others': W. E. B. Du Bois's Photographs for the 1900 Paris Exposition," Shawn Michelle Smith sees Du Bois as a visual theorist of art in the way he arranged his "American Negro" photographs that included 363 images of African Americans made by unidentified photographers. He subtly arranged the photographs to "contest the discourses and images of an imagined 'negro criminality' that were evoked to legitimize the crime of lynching in turn-of-the-century U.S. culture and to respond to the images of African Americans arranged by Booker T. Washington in 1895 with the Negro Building at the Cotton States International Exposition in Atlanta, Georgia. With Frederick Douglass at their back, both men were actively involved in shaping the history of African American social advancement in a world defined as "separate and equal."[21]

21. See the Library of Congress Prints and Photographs Online Catalog for additional pictures from the Paris Exposition of 1900. W. E. B. Du Bois and special agent Thomas J. Calloway spearheaded the planning, collection, and installation of the ex-

Shanette M. Harris, in "Constructing a Psychological Perspective: The Observer and the Observed in *The Souls of Black Folk*," draws upon psychology as a useful tool that helps us see *The Souls of Black Folk*, replete with its internal contradictions, as a map of the early phase of Du Bois's overall mission to integrate or heal conscious and unconscious divisions. She notes that the discipline of psychology has many theoretical models that help us understand the art and imagination of Du Bois.

The last essays focus on *The Souls of Black Folk* and the location of culture. In "W. E. B. Du Bois and *The Souls of Black Folk:* Generating an Expressive Repertoire for African American Communication," Carolyn Calloway Thomas and Thurmon Garner argue that a careful review of the literature on Du Bois shows that his insights have had incalculable influences on the way in which we interpret black expressive culture. For example, Du Bois advanced the then-revolutionary notion that "black communicative modes were generated from African Americans' experiences of and responses to their inhumane conditions in the New World, in their roles as slaves and free persons." Thomas and Garner then demonstrate how African American rhetorical strategies informed the Washington–Du Bois debate.

In "The 'Musical' Souls of Black Folk: Can a Double Consciousness Be Heard?" Christopher A. Brooks considers the double consciousness theory from a musical perspective and makes an argument for a musical double consciousness in Du Bois's work. He not only considers the double-voiced nature of the spirituals in their historical context, but also shows how Du Bois uses them to make a statement on the humanity of those "black and unknown bards" (James Weldon Johnson) that moved people to tears.

Carrie Cowherd, in "The Wings of Atalanta: Classical Influences in *The Souls of Black Folk*," shows how Du Bois reappropriates Latin and Greek references to illuminate what it means to be black in the modern Western World. His background in the classics of the Western World contributed to the totality of his thinking and to who he was.

My own essay, "W. E. B. Du Bois and the Invention of the Sublime in *The Souls of Black Folk*," examines a term, "the sublime," that is in theory rife with subjective evaluation, but in practice laden with objective implication. I approach this critique of the sublime in the firm belief that it is important to attend to both aesthetic and cultural questions as we examine the issue of representation, especially as it relates to the African presence in the modern Western world. In Du Bois's unceasing determination to recover the sublime and place Africans at the center of the New World, he gave black

---

hibit materials, which included 500 photographs. The LOC holds approximately 220 mounted photographs reportedly displayed in the exhibition (LOTs 11293–11308). See http://lcweb2.loc.gov/pp/anedubhtml/anedubabt.html. Shawn Michelle Smith prepared much of the text for an exhibit *Photography on the Color Line*, held at the Center for the Humanities at Oregon State University in 1999.

artists, writers, and intellectuals an accessible history, which they used to discuss their comparative American identities.

Finally, in "A Selected Publication History of *The Souls of Black Folk*," M. Elaine Hughes shows us that *The Souls of Black Folk* is a global text that has been translated into several languages.

History has looked favorably upon *The Souls of Black Folk*. Compared to the Herculean effort of single black men who "flash here and there like falling stars," Du Bois's landmark ideological statement did not die before the "world [had] rightly gauged [its] brightness" (11). Du Bois forces us to rethink world history in general and the history of the Americas in particular. The rethinking involves a deliberate revision of traditional perspectives and an acknowledgment that we must decenter existing authority.[22] Du Bois gave the world a new theoretical address that has had a far-reaching effect on politics and pedagogy, both domestically and internationally. *The Souls of Black Folk* stimulates serious discussion of subjectivity, ideology, aesthetics, and identity.

22. A. LaVonne Ruoff and Jerry W. Ward Jr., *Redefining American Literary History* (New York: MLA, 1990), 4.

Reviews of *The Souls of Black Folk*

Compiled by Erica L. Griffin

Review of *The Souls of Black Folk: Essays and Sketches,* by W. E. Burghardt Du Bois (Chicago: A. C. McClurg Company, 1903). By Anonymous Reviewer. *Nation* vol. 76, no. 5 (1903): 481–82.

Mr. Du Bois has written a profoundly interesting and affecting book, remarkable as a piece of literature apart from its inner significance. The negrophobist will remind us that Mr. Du Bois is not so black as he has painted himself, and will credit to the white blood in his veins the power and beauty of his book. But the fact is, that the features of Mr. Du Bois's mind are negro features to a degree that those of his face are not. They are the sensibility, the tenderness, the "avenues to God hid from men of Northern brain," which Emerson divined in the black people. The bar of music from one "Sorrow Song" or another which stands at the head of each chapter is a hint (unintended) that what follows is that strain writ large, that Mr. Du Bois's thought and expression are highly characteristic of his people, are cultivated varieties of those emotional and imaginative qualities which are the prevailing traits of the uncultivated negro mind. Hence one more argument for that higher education of the negro for which Mr. Du Bois so eloquently pleads. Such education of ten thousand negroes would be justified by one product like this.

The book will come as a surprise to some persons who have heard Mr. Du Bois speak upon his people's character and destiny, and, finding him coldly intellectual, have not been at all prepared for the emotion and the passion throbbing here in every chapter, almost every page. It is almost intolerably sad. "Bone of the bone and flesh of the flesh of them that live within the veil," the writer manifests throughout an aching sense of the wrongs done to his people, heretofore and still. But those will greatly misconceive who think that we have here merely an outburst of emotion. Back of this there is careful knowledge of past and present conditions in the South, clear insight into their meanings, a firm intellectual apprehension of their tendency, which is something to be reckoned with by every citizen who has at heart the welfare of his country, inseparable from the welfare of the colored people. The perfervid rhetoric will seem extravagant to the dull and cold, but, though it sometimes obscures what it would fain illuminate, it is the writer's individual form, it is not the substance of his protestation, which is compact of intellectual seriousness and moral truth.

The initial chapter is of a general character, setting forth the spiritual striving of the negro—to be at once a negro and an American; "to be a co-worker in the kingdom of culture, to escape both death and isolation; to use his best powers and his latent genius," which have heretofore been so wasted, dispersed, and forgotten. A second chapter takes more definite shape, telling the story of emancipation, what it meant to the blacks, and what happened in the days of the carpet-bagger and his co-adjutors in the Reconstruction period. The emphasis is on the Freedmen's Bureau, whose merits and demerits are considered in an impartial manner. There is an eloquent tribute "to the crusade of the New England schoolma'rm" in the South, which in one year gave instruction to more than one hundred thousand blacks. There is a fit rebuke for the cheap nonsense, of which we hear so much, concerning the enfranchisement of the negro. There was no choice, we are very properly assured, between full and restricted suffrage; only a choice between suffrage and a new form of slavery. It is conceded that a race-feud was the inevitable consequence of the choice the North was forced to make.

But the most concrete chapter in Mr. Du Bois's book is the third. "Of Mr. Booker T. Washington and Others." Mr. Washington's ascendancy is designated as "the most striking thing in the history of the American negro since 1876." Entertained with unlimited energy, enthusiasm, and faith, his programme "startled and won the applause of the South, interested and won the admiration of the North, and, after a confused murmur of protest, it silenced if it did not convert the negroes themselves." The merits of that programme are detailed with warm appreciation, while at the same time a criticism is made upon it so thoughtfully conceived that it deserves the attention of Mr. Washington's best friends and the best friends of the negro and the white people of the South. The criticism will be resented with bitterness by those for whom Washington's attraction is the concessions they suppose him to have made, and with hardly less by many who are convinced that he has solved the race problem in a completely successful manner. There are those who seem to regard any criticism of his programme as only a less malignant form of lese-majesty than criticism of the war programme of a President. But he is strong and wise enough to welcome any honest difference from his own views and aims. The criticism is that Mr. Washington asks the negro to surrender, at least for the present, political power, insistence on civil rights, the higher education. Advocated for fifteen years, triumphant for ten, this policy has coincided with the disfranchisement of the negro, his relegation to a civil status of distinct inferiority, the impoverishment of institutions devoted to the negro's higher education. That here is not merely coincidence, but effect, is Mr. Du Bois's contention. Also, that Mr. Washington's desired ends cannot be reached without important additions to his means: the negro may not hope to be a successful business man and property owner without political rights, to be thrifty and self-respecting, while consenting to civic inferiority, to secure good common-school and industrial training without institutions of higher learning. "Tuskegee itself could not remain open a day were it not for teachers trained in negro colleges, or trained by their graduates."

It is not so clear to us as it is to Mr. Du Bois that Mr. Washington has made the base concessions here ascribed to him. We recall passages in his books and speeches and letters that point a different moral. We recall his protests sent to the disfranchising conventions in Alabama and Louisiana. It may be that of late he has become more subdued than formerly to those he has worked with, some of whom have the habit of giving his programme the color of their own exaggerated caution and timidity. Then, too, Mr. Du Bois, while acknowledging that Mr. Washington's programme is provisional, does not make this acknowledgment with sufficient emphasis. But this third chapter as a whole, and the expansion of its prominent details in the succeeding chapters, deserve the carefullest consideration. Their large intelligence and their lofty temper demand for them an appreciation as generous as the spirit in which they are conceived.

Where all is good, it is invidious to select, but the chapters "On the Training of Black Men" and "Of the Sons of Master and Man" merit, perhaps, particular attention. The pathos of the chapter called "The Passing of the First Born" is immeasurably deep. It will appeal to all who have a human heart. It tells the story of a baby's life and death, the joy his coming meant; the "awful gladness" when he died: "Not dead, but escaped; not bond, but free." Clearly the burden of Mr. Du Bois's complaint, not explicitly, but implicitly at every turn, is made more grievous by the denial of social equality to himself and his people. In the urgency of this note is there not possibly a lack of the profoundest self-respect?

If Mr. Du Bois can sit with Shakespeare and Plato, and they do not wince at his complexion, why should he care so much for the contempt of Col. Carter of Cartersville? Why not trample on it with a deeper pride? A society based on money values may reject such a man as scornfully as one based on the tradition of slavery, but a society based upon character and culture will always welcome him though he were blacker than the ace of spades, not as showing him a favor, but as anxious to avail itself of his ability.

"The Negro Question: Essays and Sketches Touching upon It by a Colored Writer." Review of *The Souls of Black Folk*, by William E. Burghardt Du Bois (Chicago: A. C. McClurg Company, 1903). By Anonymous Reviewer. *New York Times*, April 25, 1903, p. 283.

It is generally conceded that Booker T. Washington represents the best hope of the negro in America, and it is certain that of all the leaders of his people he has done the most for his fellows with the least friction with the whites who are most nearly concerned, those of the South. Here is another negro "educator," to use a current term, not brought up like Washington among the negroes of the South and to the manner of the Southern negro born, but one educated in New England—one who never saw a negro camp-meeting till he was grown to manhood and went among the people of his color as a teacher. Naturally he does not see everything as Booker Washington does; probably he does not understand his own people in their natural state as does the other; certainly he cannot understand the Southern white's point of view as the principal of Tuskegee does. Yet it is equally certain that "The Souls of Black Folks" [*sic*] throws much light upon the complexities of the negro problem, for it shows that the key note of at least some negro aspiration is still the abolition of the social color-line. For it is the Jim Crow car, and the fact that he may not smoke a cigar and drink a cup of tea with the white man in the South, that most galls William E. Burghardt Du Bois of the Atlanta College for Negroes. That this social color line must in time vanish like the mists of the morning is the firm belief of the writer, as the opposite is the equally firm belief of the Southern white man; but in the meantime he admits the "hard fact" that the color line is, and for a long time must be.

The book is of curious warp and woof, and the poetical form of the title is the index to much of its content and phraseology. To a Southerner who knows the negro race as it exists in the South, it is plain that this negro of Northern education is, after all, as he says, "bone of the bone and flesh of the flesh" of the African race. Sentimental, poetical, picturesque, the acquired logic and the evident attempt to be critically fair-minded is strangely tangled with these racial characteristics and the racial rhetoric. After an eloquent appeal for a fair hearing in what he calls his "Forethought," he goes in some detail into the vexed history of the Freedman's Bureau and the work it did for good and ill; for he admits the ill as he insists upon the good. A review of such a work from the negro point of view, even the Northern negro's point of view, must have its value to any unprejudiced student—still more, perhaps, for the prejudiced who is yet willing to be a student. It is impossible here to give even a general idea of the impression that will be gained from reading the text, but the underlying idea seems to be that it was impossible for the negro to get justice in the Southern courts just after the war, and "almost equally" impossible for the white man to get justice in the extra judicial proceeding of the Freedman's Bureau officials which largely superseded the courts for a time. Much is remembered of these proceedings by older Southerners—much picturesque and sentimental fiction, with an ample basis of truth, has been written about them by Mr. Thomas Nelson Page and others. Here we have the other side.

When all is said, the writer of "The Souls of Black Folk" is sure that the outside interference of which the Freedman's Bureau was the chief instrument was necessary for the negro's protection from supposed attempts of his former masters to legislate him back into another form of slavery, yet he admits that "it failed to begin the establishment of good-will between ex-masters and freedmen." It is proper to place beside this, of course, the consensus of fair Southern opinion that the interference in question and the instrumentalities it employed were the cause of the establishment of an ill-will previously nonexistent. Here is a point where Booker T. Washington, as a Southern negro, has the advantage of his present critic in this that he knows by inherited tradition what the actual antebellum feeling between the races was. Du Bois assumes hostility.

While the whole book is interesting, especially to a Southerner, and while the self-restraint and temperateness of the manner of stating even things which the Southerner regards as impossibilities, deserve much praise and disarm harsh criticism, the part of the book which is more immediately concerned with an arrangement of the present plans of Booker T. Washington is for the present the most important.

In this matter the writer, speaking, as he says, for many educated negroes, makes two chief objections—first, that Washington is the leader of his race not by the suffrage of that race, but rather by virtue of the support of the whites, and, second, that, by yielding to the modern commercial spirit and confining the effort for uplifting the individual to practical education and the acquisition of property and decent ways, he is after all cutting off the negro from those higher aspirations which only, Du Bois says, make a people great. For instance, it is said that Booker T. Washington distinctly asks that black people give up, at least for the present, three things:

First, political power;

Second, insistence on civil rights;

Third, higher education for negro youth, and concentrate all their energies on industrial education, the accumulation of wealth, and the conciliation of the South. This policy has been courageously and insistently advocated for over fifteen years, and has been triumphant for perhaps ten years. As a result of this tender of the palm branch what has been the return? In these years there have occurred:

1. The disfranchisement of the negro.

2. The legal creation of a distinct status of civil inferiority for the negro.

3. The steady withdrawal of aid from institutions for the higher training of the negro.

These movements are not, to be sure, direct results of Washington's teachings, but his propaganda has, without a shadow of doubt, helped their speedier accomplishment.

The writer admits the great value of Booker Washington's work. However, he does not believe so much in the gospel of the lamb, and does think that a bolder attitude, one of standing firmly upon rights guaranteed by the war amendments, and alluded to in complimentary fashion in the Declaration of Independence, is both more becoming to a race such as he conceives the negro race to be, and more likely to advance that race. "We feel in conscience bound," he says, "to ask three things: 1, The right to vote; 2, Civic equality; 3, The education of youth according to ability" and he is especially insistent on the higher education of the negro—going into some statistics to show what the negro can do in that way. The value of these arguments and the force of the statistics can best be judged after the book is read.

Many passages of the book will be very interesting to the student of the negro character who regards the race ethnologically and not politically, not as a dark cloud threatening the future of the United States, but as a peculiar people, and one, after all, but little understood by the best of its friends or the worst of its enemies outside of what the author of "The Souls of Black Folk" is fond of calling the "Awful Veil." Throughout it should be recalled that it is the thought of a negro of Northern education who has lived long among his brethren of the South yet who cannot fully feel the meaning of some things which these brethren know by instinct— and which the Southern-bred white knows by a similar instinct; certain things which are—by both accepted as facts—not theories—fundamental attitudes of race to race which are the product of conditions extending over centuries, as are the some-what parallel attitudes of the gentry to the peasantry in other countries.

"The Case of the Negro." Review of *The Souls of Black Folk*, by W. E. Burghardt Du Bois (Chicago: A. C. McClurg Company, 1903). Pp. x, 264. By W. H. Johnson. *The Dial* 34 (1903): 299–302.[1]

No thinking man any longer contemplates the possibility of an offhand settlement of the Negro problem. With a Negro population approaching

1. Additional references, per original review, are Thomas Dixon Jr., *The Leopard's Spots: A Romance of the White Man's Burden* (New York: Doubleday, Page & Co., n.d.); Booker T. Washington, *Various Addresses and Papers* (Tuskegee Institute Steam Print, n.d.).

ten millions, and with the masses of both the white and the black race permeated by the prejudices growing out of slavery and the Civil War and enhanced by the blunders and crimes of the early years of emancipation, the best that can reasonably be hoped for now is a slow and steady progress in the right direction,—that is, in the direction of the highest possible freedom of opportunity for both white and black, unhampered by unfair legislation or administration, or by the no less galling methods of social oppression in walks of life where the law does not and should not enter.

In the countless attempts toward settlement, by far the most prominent at the present time is the work of Mr. Booker T. Washington, which has grown from its very humble beginning of twenty-two years ago until to-day the names of Harvard, Yale, and Princeton are scarcely more familiar than that of the Tuskegee Normal and Industrial Institute. The message which Mr. Washington feels it his duty to bear to his race is, *"Make yourselves industrially necessary, each man and woman of you, to the community in which you live.* Let the pursuit of art, literature, and politics wait, for the present, and train the mind directly to the guidance of the skilled hand. When you shall have learned to raise two or three bushels of corn or potatoes, two or three bales of cotton, on the ground where but one grows to-day, when you begin to pay heavy freights into the coffers of the railroads which now force you into 'Jim Crow' cars, when you figure as stockholders in the enterprises which now discriminate against you, then you will be rated simply as men and women, and neither hated nor pitied on the ground of color." Around this idea the work of the Tuskegee Institute has been built up, with careful attention to moral training, of course, hand in hand with the industrial. The idea has gained an immense popularity. It has seemed to justify itself by its results, and Mr. Washington has become, as Professor Du Bois well says, a leader both of the black race and the white.

No doubt the feature in Professor W. E. B. Du Bois's "The Souls of Black Folk" which will draw the most immediate attention is the fact that the writer takes determined and emphatic issue with Mr. Booker Washington's policy, and that too in its most salient point,—the insistence upon the industrial, and the elementary, in negro education. Professor Du Bois is perhaps the most scholarly man of his race in America today,—a man of high scholarship and culture in that broader republic of human attainment which knows no limitation of race, color, or clime. In his acquaintance with the art and literature of various lands and ages he finds the best solace for the peculiar troubles entailed upon him and his by race prejudice in this land and age. "I sit with Shakespeare and he winces not. Across the color line I move arm in arm with Balzac and Dumas, where smiling men and welcoming women glide in gilded halls. From out the caves of evening that swing between the strong-limbed earth and the tracery of the stars, I summon Aristotle and Aurelius and what soul I will, and they come all graciously with no scorn nor condescension. So, wed with Truth, I dwell above the Veil." One can readily see that such a spirit would scent the danger of low, materialistic ideals in the Tuskegee programme, so rigidly industrial. And we are not sure that there is not reason for his fear. To rely too solely upon worldly thrift is the great temptation of the age. It may be true, as Mr. Washington says, that the Negro who will pay $10,000 a year in freights will not have to ride in a "Jim Crow" car; but there are a great many white people who would rather ride in a "Jim Crow" with a Burghardt Du Bois or a Booker T. Washington on the other end of the seat than in a Pullman with either Negroes or white men whose consideration at the hands of the railway officials should grow only out of the amount paid to the road in freights. It is certainly possible to go too far in adjuring the Negroes to put away their ambition to enter the higher fields of literature and learning, and to forego their legitimate desire to avail themselves at will of the rights and privileges conferred upon them by the Constitution. Suppose that our colored millions should become industrious and prosperous, and fairly up with the average in personal morals, too, but entirely apathetic as to political rights and duties, and devoid of ambition toward the highest mental and spiritual development,—the present Negro problem would then be practically solved, but would it be an acceptable solution to anyone with a consistent belief in freedom and equality as the best basis for progress and permanence in human government and society?

Let no one assume, however, that Professor Du Bois and Principal Washington are hopelessly at variance. The divergence, at most, bears only upon present methods. Their ultimate aim is one,—the uplifting of their people physically and materially, mentally, morally, and spiritually. All that the latter can do to improve the material condition of their common people the former will gladly welcome. "So far as Mr. Washington preaches Thrift, Patience, and Industrial Training for the masses, we must hold up his hands and strive with him, rejoicing in his honors and glorying in the strength of this Joshua, called of God and of man to lead the headless host." And we are very seriously mistaken in Mr. Washington if he would knowingly put any obstacle in the path of any one of his race who has the ambition to climb to a place on the higher seats of mental culture by the Side of Professor Du Bois, at any rate when that ambition is coupled with evidence of sufficient mental ability to give a reasonable hope of results commensurate with the effort. Many of the white race are beginning to doubt whether we have not gone too far in pressing into the higher studies a class of youths who might readily make skilful and useful followers of some industrial pursuit, but have not the mental makeup for successful assimilation of the higher learning. We have not the statistics at hand by which to test Professor Du Bois's claim that Mr. Washington's work is drying up the fountains of support for the higher education of colored youths in other than industrial lines, but we feel quite confident that such a result would be contrary to his desire. We are not sure that Mr. Washington realizes the possible value of this higher learning to the very industrial training in which he is so deeply interested,—in fact but very few, white or colored, have realized it. It is true, however, that agriculture and the mechanical pursuits offer a fair field for the very highest type of trained intellect which the more distinctively cultural studies, Greek, logic, philosophy, etc., can produce. As the college graduate multiplies in the land, more and more will he be driven from sheer overcrowding elsewhere to devote his powers to these more fundamental means of livelihood, and the Negro will need his own trained leaders here as elsewhere. On the other hand we are not sure that Professor Du Bois, on more careful consideration, would feel himself justified in adding to the passage quoted above, the words: "But so far as Mr. Washington apologizes for injustice, North or South, does not rightly value the privilege and duty of voting, belittles the emasculating effects of caste distinctions, and opposes the higher training and ambition of our brighter minds,—so far as he, the South, or the Nation, does this,—we must unceasingly and firmly oppose them." Frank and full confidence between these two leaders of their race will surely enable them each warmly to aid the other in his chosen field, to the great advantage of their common aim.

We have placed among the material for this notice a work of a type far different from the writings of Professor Du Bois and Principal Washington,—"The Leopard's Spots," by Mr. Thomas Dixon, Jr. Though Mr. Dixon's book is thrown into the form of a novel, so far as it can be said to possess form at all, its aim is to justify to Northern readers the attitude of political and social suppression assumed toward the Negro by the dominant white sentiment of the South. As to the writer's method, he has chosen to set forth as vividly as possible the faults and crimes current among the Negroes of the South, culminating in an unflinching relation of a fatal assault by a brutal Negro upon an innocent white girl, and an equally unsparing description of the punishment swiftly visited upon the ravisher,—burning at the stake. Plainly the design is that the reader shall exclaim in his indignation, "I too would have helped to do the same, under the same circumstances!" And crude as the book is in most respects, it must be admitted that this portion of it is quite skillfully adapted to the end in view. And Mr. Dixon selected his time well, too,—the time when our unfortunate experiment in the Philippines has so generally deadened the public conscience toward any appeal to that finer regard for the rights of man simply as man, which was such an inspiration to the masses of the North in the initial years of our experiment with Negro freedom; when the eloquent Curtis could sway audiences at his will with the thought that now at length our government had been placed squarely upon its only consistent basis, the right of every citizen to a full participation in the government under which he was obliged to live. Mr.

Washington thought that he saw great reason for hope in the fact that white and black fought bravely together in the battles of the Spanish-American war. Professor Du Bois shows far truer insight into the tendencies resulting from that conflict when he speaks of "the silently growing assumption of this age that the probation of races is past, and that the backward races of today are of proven inefficiency and not worth the saving." But to go back to Mr. Dixon, it is only the unthinking man that can draw from his baleful picture the final conclusion which the writer desires. The Southern courts themselves, as Mr. Dixon would hardly have the hardihood to deny, can be depended upon absolutely to inflict the extreme penalty of the law upon any Negro identified as the perpetrator of such crime as he describes; and the Southern legislatures can as surely be depended upon to strengthen its laws for the suppression of such crime if in any case they are not sufficiently strong already. Under such circumstances no moral man in his right mind should allow his prejudices to lead him into the support, directly or indirectly, of lynching. We commend to Mr. Dixon the intelligent reasoning of Professor Du Bois and Mr. Washington on this subject. He has much to learn from either one of them. He will find, for instance, that the faults of their race which he has *passionately asserted* are by them *dispassionately admitted*,—on the whole, a rather more effective mode of presentation, if the end of presentation be the eradication of the faults in question.

Of course everybody reads more or less of Mr. Booker Washington, either from his books or from the frequent addresses occasioned by the prominence of his educational work. Professor Du Bois is known to a less extensive circle. We believe that a wide reading of the latter's new book will do much to promote a correct understanding of the problems of Negro education and citizenship. In style, it must be pronounced somewhat uneven,— always readily intelligible, rising now and then to a genuine eloquence, sometimes perhaps a little more flowery or figurative than the occasion demands, rather crude in certain instances in dealing with the great mysteries of human life; but all in all quite above the style of many who would be slow to admit that anything good in a literary way could come out of the African Nazareth. As to the tone of the book, we believe that the author would do well to imbibe a little bit more of the hopeful spirit of Principal Washington. He is distinctly right in the opinion that the cause of the Negro has for the present suffered a serious backset in many important particulars; but he does not accept the pessimistic conclusion that this lost ground is irrecoverable. This being so, perhaps he might find good working capital in a little more of the cheerful attitude. And yet one who stops to consider the essential bitterness of beating against closed doors which ought to be open will not condemn too severely the heart that cannot always show cheer under such circumstances. And it may be, too, that the most of us need this demonstration that the Negro is actually capable of intense mental suffering under unjust treatment. The recognition of human brotherhood is not a strong point with us at present.

Composed at different times and for different immediate purposes, the various chapters of Professor Du Bois's volume do not present a formal unity, and yet they all bear in one way or another upon the thought suggested by the collective title, "The Souls of Black Folk." On the historical side we find a very valuable sketch of the aims and failures, as well as the actual achievements, of the Freedmen's Bureau. Elsewhere the author's own experience as a country school teacher is related in an extremely interesting manner. Another chapter, essentially historical fact, to all appearances, though mingled with a certain amount of entirely consistent fiction, tells of the tragic end of a Negro youth who went away to college and educated himself beyond the possibility of contentment with his old environment (just as thousands of white boys are always doing, to the best interests of themselves and all concerned), and failed, upon returning, to accommodate himself adequately to the powers of prejudice around him. But it is not our intention to give a detailed exposition of the book's contents. Enough has been indicated to show that all who are, or ought to be, interested in the general subject should read it: to go further might tempt some such person into the belief that he had the drift of it sufficiently to excuse him from this duty.

Review of *The Souls of Black Folk*, by W. E. Burghardt Du Bois (Chicago: A. C. McClurg Company, 1903). Pp. x, 264. By Carl Kelsey. *The Annals of the American Academy of Political and Social Sciences* 22 (July 3, 1903): 230–32.

"Herein lie buried many things which if read with patience may show the strange meaning of being black here in the dawning of the twentieth century." With this sentence Professor Dubois, of Atlanta University, opens his book bearing the significant title of "The Souls of Black Folk." A more interesting book seldom comes into one's hands. The simple black cover with its gilt letters, the chapters headed with a few bars of some of the old negro melodies, the sorrow songs, seem in keeping with the theme. The interest in the subject matter is increased by the literary form in which it is couched. In the forethought the author says: "First, in two chapters I have tried to show what emancipation meant [to them, and what was its aftermath]. In a third [chapter] I have pointed out the slow use [rise] of personal leadership. Then[,] in two others I have sketched in swift outline the two worlds within and without the Veil, and thus have come to the central problem of training men for life . . . I have in two chapters studied the struggles of the massed millions of the black peasantry and have sought to make clear the present relations of the sons of master and man. . . . I have stepped within the Veil, raising it that you may view . . . the meaning of its religion, the passion of its human sorrow, and the struggle of its greater souls."

Though deserving of high praise, the book has its serious faults. As one reads there is not only a growing appreciation of the injustices to which attention is called, but also a growing protest against the spirit of the author. There is a tendency to snarl against social customs, an evidence of mental bitterness, natural perhaps, but one wishes Mr. Dubois could rise above it. Not until he ceases to go about with "chips on his shoulders" as it were, will he gain the influence to which his mental attainments entitle him. No doubt it is strange to "be a problem"; "an American, a negro, two souls, two thoughts, two unreconciled strivings." Yet, one who knows the educational opportunities afforded Professor Dubois, finds it hard to appreciate the statement that the soul-longing of the negro is that "He simply wishes to make it possible for a man to be both a negro and an American, without being cursed and spit upon by his fellows, without having the door of opportunity closed roughly in his face." The reader is sometimes inclined to think that the author might well have added to his other indications of a classical education another quotation: "Vergiftet sind meine Lieder."

To Professor Dubois the "problem of the twentieth century is that of the color line." He pleads for the extinction of race prejudice. We must seek its "abatement and not its systematic encouragement and pampering by all agencies of social power from the Associated Press to the Church of Christ." This he seems to feel is taking place to-day. To America of to-day the negroes do not come empty-handed. "There are to-day no truer exponents of the pure human spirit of the Declaration of Independence than the American negroes."

To many people the centre of interest will be in the attack on the policy of Booker T. Washington. Professor Dubois says this involves for the negro a giving up of (1) political power; (2) civil rights; (3) higher education of negro youth. "This policy has been insistently and courageously [courageously and insistently] advocated for over fifteen years and has been triumphant for perhaps ten years. As a result of this tender of the palm[-]branch, what has been the result [return]? In these years there have occurred (1) the disfranchisement of the negro; (2) the legal creation of a distinct status of civil inferiority for the negro; (3) the steady withdrawal of aid for institutions for the higher training of the negro" [44].

It is admitted that these changes have not been caused by Booker Washington, but it is charged that his influence has speeded their coming. Professor Dubois in opposition says, "On the contrary negroes must insist continuously [continually], in season and out of season, that voting is necessary to modern manhood." Washington is particularly criticized in that his influence has tended to withdraw the assistance of the whites and to make the negroes stand by themselves. I do not believe the attack on Washington is successful, although there may be a measure of truth in the charge that his educational program is too narrow.

Far more helpful, in my opinion, than the chapters of criticism are those devoted to the description of the psychical evolution of the negro; the work of the Freedmen's Bureau; the experiences drawn from life as a school-teacher in the chapter headed "Of the Meaning of Progress" and the description "Of the Black Belt"; "Of the Sons of Master and Man"; "Of the Faith of the Fathers." As Professor Dubois says, the South is a most fruitful field of social study. But the author is too much inclined to emphasize the bad; to chronicle the failures, the injustices and the wrongs. He feels that the whites "tamper with the moral fibre of a naturally honest and straight-forward people" and are teaching the youth that to succeed they must be sly and cunning, not open and honest. Thus arises an ethical dualism—the triumph of the lie. There is an interesting account of the career of Alexander Crummell, and a very able argument for negro colleges and universities. "Of the Coming of John" is a good story, but it ends in tragedy. The last chapter analyzes the sorrow songs.

While there is much in the book of great value, it may be emphasized again that bad as race prejudice is, it cannot be damned or bewailed out of existence. The negro is not the only victim of it. It will cease when the blacks can command and compel the respect and sympathy of the whites. The author who lives within the "Veil" of social prejudice will not accomplish his ends by such appeal as is found inserted in the afterthought: "Let the ears of a guilty people tingle with truth, and seventy millions sigh for the righteousness which exalteth nations, in this drear day when human brotherhood is mockery and a snare." There is more of good in the relationship of the two races than Mr. Dubois would have us believe.

Review of *The Souls of Black Folk: Essays and Sketches,* by W. E. B. DuBois, Professor of Economics and History in Atlanta University, Atlanta, Georgia (Chicago: A. C. McClurg Company, 1903). Pp. Viii + 265. $1.20, *net.* By Theophilus Bolden Steward. *American Journal of Sociology* 9 (1903–1904): 136–37.

In this volume of essays and sketches Professor DuBois approaches the many-sided negro question with the confidence and conviction of a master, and with the grace and beauty of a poet. The crux of the problem, as he views it, is the adequate training of the black man in the higher industrial and intellectual education. To him the all-important product of this education "must be neither a psychologist nor a brickmason, but a man"; and in this particular the efforts of the southern universities for the training of negroes are of great and far-reaching importance.

The author is at his best in an unbiased consideration of the negro's emotional nature. In the chapter "Of Our Spiritual Strivings" he outlines the struggles in which this emotionalism involves the black man. That there can be no doubt of the preponderance of misdirected emotionalism is evidenced in the rapidity with which the negro swings from love to hate, from laughter to tears.

But Professor DuBois most clearly comprehends that peculiar phase of interracial strivings which brings about the control of a man by the possession of those agents and forces which furnish him the means of subsistence. It appears that, through ignorance of conditions and lack of business foresight, the negro farmer is a ready victim for the white trader and cotton buyer. Being generally restricted by his landlord to the raising of cotton, he makes the crop either on shares or under a crop or chattel mortgage for provisions advanced during the period of cultivation. The chances of freedom from debt are thus the slightest, being dependent upon the success of a crop planted in an already over-worked soil and upon the price offered by the buyer. The relation which the white "furnisher" sustains to the black farmer thus becomes practically that of slaver and enslaved. The struggles and the unhopefulness of the negro under this industrial bondage are thoughtfully discussed in the two chapters which deal with the "Black Belt."

Under the caption "Of Booker T. Washington and Others" he gradually delineates the origin and evolution of negro leadership and the conditions incident to each cycle of change and progress. His attitude toward Mr. Washington is one dictated by radical difference of opinion. While tolerant of Mr. Washington's views and deeply grateful for his assistance in the efforts for racial uplift, he does not fail to emphasize the possible interpretation that Mr. Washington, by his silence in regard to the political activity of the negro, lends influence and confirmation to the advocates of negro disfranchisement.

The chapters "Of the Faith of Our Fathers" and "The Sorrow Songs" give a vivid picture of the credulity of the negro and the power of his soul to express in plaintive melody his soul-sorrows and strivings.

As a practical solution of the color-line problem, which is assuredly assuming national importance, Professor DuBois's book cannot be said to do more than offer the rich hints from a vast store of sympathy and knowledge. Yet it is, indeed, the best statement of the factors that greatly complicated the negro's life and destiny in America and which tend largely to segregate him as a "group within a group." The author feels intensely and expresses beautifully the soul-sighs and the spirit of unhopefulness, which are the heir-looms of slavery and oppression, of those "who dwell within the Veil," shut out from the greater and freer life by ignorance, oppression, ostracism, and infant strength of purpose and ambition. Although conscious of the fact that the negro is hardly self-effectual and that the future's sky is over-dark, he has shown a depth of sympathetic investigation and a seriousness of purposeful expression which everywhere strive with the reader and influence him to the thought that now we are coming to a systematic discussion and an intelligent striving from which shall ultimately be born that time, long written of and striven for, when all men shall enjoy the inalienable rights of "life, liberty, and the pursuit of happiness."

The Souls of Black Folk. By Professor W. E. Burghardt Du Bois, Atlanta, Georgia. *The Independent* 57 (November 17, 1904): 1152. [Du Bois responds to his critics.]

One who is born with a cause is pre-destined to a certain narrowness of view, and at the same time to some clearness of vision within his limits with which the world often finds it well to reckon. My book has many of the defects and some of the advantages of this situation. Because I am a negro I lose something of that breadth of view which the more cosmopolitan races have, and with this goes an intensity of feeling and conviction which both wins and repels sympathy, and now enlightens, now puzzles.

The Souls of Black Folk is a series of fourteen essays written under various circumstances and for different purposes during a period of seven years. It has, therefore, considerable, perhaps too great, diversity. There are bits of history and biography, some description of scenes and persons, something of controversy and criticism, some statistics and a bit of story-telling. All this leads to rather abrupt transitions of style, tone and viewpoint and, too, without doubt, to a distinct sense of incompleteness and sketchiness.

On the other hand, there is a unity in the book, not simply the general unity of the larger topic, but a unity of purpose in the distinctively subjective note that runs in each essay. Through all the book runs a personal and intimate tone of self-revelation. In each essay I sought to speak from within—to depict a world as we see it who dwell therein. In thus giving up the usual impersonal and judicial attitude of the traditional author I have lost in authority but gained in vividness. The reader will, I am sure, feel in reading my words peculiar warrant for setting his judgment against mine, but at the same time some revelation of how the world looks to me cannot easily escape him.

This is not saying that the style and workmanship of the book make its meaning altogether clear. A clear central message it has conveyed to most readers, I think, but around this center there has lain a penumbra of vagueness and half-veiled allusion which has made these and others especially impatient. How far this fault is in me and how far it is in the nature of the message I am not sure. It is difficult, strangely difficult, to translate the finer feelings of men into words. The Thing itself sits clear before you; but when you have dressed it out in periods it seems fearfully uncouth and inchoate. Nevertheless, as the feeling is deep the greater the impelling force to seek to express it. And here the feeling was deep.

In its larger aspects the style is tropical-African. This needs no apology. The blood of my fathers spoke through me and cast off the English restraint of my training and surroundings. The resulting accomplishment is a matter of taste. Sometimes I think very well of it and sometimes I do not.

The Souls of the "Black Belt" Revisited

James Daniel Steele

It seemed a curious choice. W. E. B. Du Bois selected Dougherty County, Georgia, to establish the context and explore the condition of African Americans in the South at the turn of the century. "Of the Black Belt" is one of the least heralded of the works included in *The Souls of Black Folk*.[1] It does not introduce the reader to dazzling concepts ("double consciousness"), or literary invention ("the veil"). Arnold Rampersad, in *The Art and Imagination of W. E. B. Du Bois,* offered only a passing reference to the chapter. Manning Marable, in *W. E. B. Du Bois: Black Radical Democrat*, discussed the importance of the chapter only as a contemporary description of the postslavery South. Marable chose however not to elaborate on the importance of the chapter to the social sciences or to its general importance as a work of propaganda for which Du Bois was also recognized.

Du Bois did not write "Of the Black Belt" to further construct his social vision. He wrote it not to create a world, but to see the present one clearly, and in some way to help white America see a world it either chose to ignore or refused to see. More than an afterthought, "Of the Black Belt" was the product of an evolving effort by Du Bois to examine the rural South. In *W. E. B. Du Bois: Biography of a Race, 1868–1919,* David Levering Lewis observed that "Of the Black Belt" could be traced to "The Negro as He Really Is," a 1901 article Du Bois wrote for the periodical *World's Work*. Lewis noted that with "Of the Black Belt," "Of the Quest of the Golden Fleece," and "Of the Meaning of Progress," Du Bois "succeeded in reconstructing a culture and its institutions in the rural South."[2]

---

1. W. E. B. Du Bois, *The Souls of Black Folk,* ed. Henry Louis Gates Jr. and Terri Hume Oliver (New York: Norton, 1999). References to this edition will be cited parenthetically in the text.
2. David Levering Lewis, *W. E. B. Du Bois: Biography of a Race, 1868–1919,* 278, 285. Both chapters 7 and 8 of *The Souls of Black Folk* are revisions of Du Bois's "The Negro as He Really Is," *The World's Work* (June 1901): 848–66.

Even in the 1900s, there would appear to have been many more important cities through which to evaluate the condition of African American life
in the South, including Atlanta, New Orleans, and Charleston. Yet it was
in Dougherty County—and the many other "Dougherty counties" of the
South—where the institutionalization of white supremacist ideology, with
its attendant political, economic, and social influences, were most brutally
applied and enforced. As Tom Dent has indicated in *Southern Journey,* many
of the memorable campaigns of the Civil Rights era did not take place in the
noted capitals of the South; instead, they were in the lesser-known towns
and cities of the South, such as Greensboro, North Carolina; Orangeburg,
South Carolina; Albany, Georgia; and Selma, Alabama.[3]

Census figures for 1900 indicate that 89.6 percent of African Americans
in the United States lived in the South, of which 83 percent populated rural
areas. African Americans have now become a predominantly urban people. Census data for 1994 show that 86.3 percent live in urban areas while
13.7 percent are classified as living in nonurban or rural communities.[4] This
is an almost complete reversal from the start of the twentieth century. In
many ways, the world of African Americans was considerably different at
the start of the twentieth century than it is at the start of the twenty-first—
but in many ways it is not. No valid understanding of African American life
and conditions in the South can be achieved without accounting for those
smaller jurisdictions and towns that are so central to the development and
history of southern life.

This chapter will explore the world of the "Black Belt" and identify the
extent and nature of political change in the region. Specifically, it is hoped
that this discussion of the "Black Belt" will be viewed as a critical component to the understanding of the objective conditions that African Americans confronted at that point in time and the extent that it formed the
foundation of future programs and activities by African Americans in the
twentieth century.

Central to the present essay is the importance of Du Bois to the span of
African American intellectual life through his pursuit of a thesis that the
issue of race in the postslavery period of the United States was the product of deep-rooted structural manifestations and not the flawed whims
and characteristics of racist individuals, groups, or their misguided min-
ions. W. E. B. Du Bois's essay not only provides us with an opportunity

3. See Thomas C. Dent, *Southern Journey: A Return to the Civil Rights Movement* (New
York: William Morrow, 1997).
4. U.S. Department of Commerce, Bureau of the Census, *Historical Abstract of the
United States, Colonial Times to 1970, Part 1* (Washington, D.C.: Bureau of the Census,
1976), series A172–194, p. 22; see also *Negro Population of the United States 1790–1915,*
1918: 134–35, table 13.

to examine the meaning of Dougherty County for its residents but also challenges us to see that the flaws of history, economics, and politics can only be repaired by attending to an understanding and response to institutions and their structural relations to society. It will be argued here that the importance of Du Bois's chapter 7 surpasses mere historical analysis or journalism; it is an insight into the social and institutional relations that have dominated the South.

The Black Belt Defined

Georgia is the focus of Du Bois's case study of the African American South, for "the Negro problem seemed to be centered in this State" (75). He also selected Georgia because "no other State fought so long and strenuously to this host of [one million] Africans" (75) in order to maintain the plantation economy. Specifically, Du Bois examines the area below Macon, where the "world grows darker; for now we approach the Black Belt" (76). Figuratively and literally, he departs from the "Jim Crow Car" of the train in the July sun and takes the white reader on a tour of Dougherty County and Albany, the center of the "Black Belt."

In the introduction to the 1900 U.S. Census supplement entitled *Negroes in the United States,* Walter Wilcox attempted to set parameters on what was known as the "Black Belt." He defined it as "the counties in which the Negroes are at least half the total population," and these lie "mainly south and east of the northern and western boundaries of the Austroriparian zone of plant and animal life" (11). By this definition, 254 counties from Maryland to Texas had an African American population of at least 50 percent, and 55 counties had an African American population of at least 75 percent (see Table 1).

For Wilcox, the concept of a "Black Belt" was descriptive. Data were interpreted to reveal concentrations of African Americans relative to a specified geographic region. The data collected on the region was also defined in relation to specified political jurisdictions (counties) with a majority African American population. The Black Belt also described conditions, for within this defined area were people who endured levels of poverty and death as severe as this nation has ever experienced.

Although the African American population has grown over the course of the twentieth century, the number of counties that have an African American population of 75 percent or more has diminished greatly. With social desegregation, the impact of industrialization, and the movement of people from rural to urban areas, the number of counties where African Americans constitute 75 percent or more of the population has been reduced from 55 to 7 (see Table 2).

Table 1
U.S. Counties with an African American Population of at Least 75 Percent, 1900

County	Percent	County	Percent
Issaquena, Mississippi	94.0	Leon, Florida	80.4
Tensas, Louisiana	93.5	Wilcox, Alabama	80.4
Madison, Louisiana	92.7	Madison, Mississippi	79.8
East Carroll, Louisiana	91.6	Wilkinson, Mississippi	79.6
Beaufort, South Carolina	90.5	Berkeley, South Carolina	78.7
Tunica, Mississippi	90.5	Adams, Mississippi	78.6
Washington, Mississippi	89.7	Phillips, Arkansas	78.6
Coahoma, Mississippi	88.2	Perry, Alabama	78.5
Leflore, Mississippi	88.2	Bossier, Alabama	78.2
Bolivar, Mississippi	88.1	Russell, Alabama	78.1
Sharkey, Mississippi	88.1	Claiborne, Mississippi	78.0
Concordia, Louisiana	87.4	Holmes, Mississippi	77.9
Chicot, Arkansas	87.1	Jefferson, Florida	77.9
Lowndes, Alabama	86.6	Lee, Arkansas	77.8
Green, Alabama	86.3	McIntosh, Georgia	77.7
West Feliciana, Louisiana	86.2	West Baton Rouge, Louisiana	77.1
Lee, Georgia	85.4	Yazoo, Mississippi	77.1
Noxubee, Mississippi	84.8	Marengo, Alabama	76.9
Crittenden, Arkansas	84.6	Quitman, Mississippi	76.9
Dallas, Alabama	83.0	Georgetown, South Carolina	76.6
Sumter, Alabama	82.7	Morehouse, Louisiana	76.5
Dougherty, Georgia	82.1	Warwick, Virginia	76.3
Bullock, Alabama	81.7	Fairfield, South Carolina	76.0
Burke, Georgia	81.7	Lowndes, Mississippi	75.5
Desha, Alabama	81.7	Hinds, Mississippi	75.2
Hale, Alabama	81.7	Houston, Georgia	75.1
Macon, Alabama	81.6	Sunflower, Mississippi	75.0
Jefferson, Mississippi	81.1		

Source: U.S. Department of Commerce and Labor, Bureau of the Census, *Negroes in the United States,* bulletin 8 (Washington, D.C.: U.S. Government Printing Office, 1904), table 9, p. 23.

The Nadir of Freedom

The final decade of the nineteenth century proved to be horrific for a people that in a short time had emerged from slavery to freedom. The acceptance of racist ideology as a justification for the denial and usurpation of basic rights and protections against African Americans became ubiquitous in U.S. institutional life, from the Supreme Court to the intellectual canon of "important" universities and "scholars" of the time. Under the cloak of legitimacy that the acceptance of racist ideology provided, the use of terrorist tactics by southern whites finally enshrined into national law the restoration of whites as the dominant force in southern institutions of power. Southern "customs" had been granted national acceptance as the

Table 2
U.S. Counties with an African American Population of at Least 75 Percent, 1990

County	Percent
Jefferson, Mississippi	86.2
Macon, Alabama	85.6
Claiborne, Mississippi	82.1
Greene, Alabama	80.6
Hancock, Alabama	79.4
Holmes, Mississippi	75.8
Tunica, Mississippi	75.3

Source: U.S. Department of Commerce, *County and City Data Book* (Washington, D.C.: U.S. Government Printing Office, 1994), xiii.

Supreme Court decision in *Plessy v. Fergusson* embraced racial apartheid to be compatible with the Constitution and its principles of democracy.[5]

The decline in African American electoral power was also due to the inaction and sometimes the design of the national and state governments. One prime example occurred in November 1898, when the city of Wilmington, North Carolina (which was then approximately two-thirds African American) exploded with violence when racist whites failed in their efforts to discourage African American voters and their candidates from participating in elections. In the aftermath, African American elected officials and businesses were forced to leave the city. Those who led and supported this coup of legally elected officials did not meet with resistance from state and national government troops of any kind. In the decade of *Plessy v. Fergusson*, the Wilmington massacre and the threat of lynching rendered the gains of the Fourteenth and Fifteenth Amendments ineffective. The use of terrorist tactics were not challenged successfully.[6]

Across the South and the nation, laws were passed to either prohibit or

5. See also John Hope Franklin and Alfred A. Moss Jr., *From Slavery to Freedom: A History of African Americans*, 7th ed. (New York: Alfred A. Knopf, 1994); Rayford W. Logan, *The Betrayal of the Negro, from Rutherford B. Hayes to Woodrow Wilson* (1965; reprint, New York: Da Capo Press, 1997); and Nell Irvin Painter, *Exodusters: Black Migration to Kansas after Reconstruction* (New York: Norton, 1992).

6. On the Wilmington, North Carolina, massacre, see H. Leon Prather, *We Have Taken a City: The Wilmington Racial Massacre and Coup of 1898* (Rutherford, N.J.: Fairleigh Dickenson University Press, 1984). On the pogrom against blacks in Wilmington, see Charles W. Chesnutt, *The Marrow of Tradition*, ed. Eric J. Sundquist (New York: Penguin, 1993). For insight into the use of force and terrorist tactics to support the aims of white supremacy, see Ida B. Wells, *A Red Record: Tabulated Statistics and Alleged Causes of Lynchings in the United States, 1892, 1893, and 1894* (Chicago: Donohue and Henneberry, 1895). Later Du Bois, as editor of the *Crisis*, would write a memorable editorial, "The Lynching Industry."

limit electoral activities by African Americans. With the exit of Congressman George Henry White of North Carolina in 1901, African Americans in the South were left without a single voice in Congress from the beginning of the twentieth century until the election of Oscar de Priest from Chicago in 1928. On the state level, no state legislature had an African American member.[7] As a result of the rampant spread of the ideology of white supremacy in the wake of Reconstruction, the South did not have a single African American representative to Congress until 1972, with the election of Andrew Young to Congress from the state of Georgia. Rayford W. Logan referred to this period of African American life as "the nadir."[8]

The ideological conquest of the South, leading to the period of redemptionist politics, made racism virtuous in the minds of many and was an important consequence to the lives of African Americans beyond electoral politics. Census figures for 1900 indicate that 89.6 percent of African Americans in the United States lived in the South, of which 83 percent were living in rural areas. Of the old cotton-producing states of the Confederacy, two had a majority African American population that approached 60 percent (South Carolina and Mississippi), while five other states had African American populations ranging from 40 to 50 percent (Florida, Georgia, Louisiana). The heavy concentration of African Americans in the region could not be localized to just a few localities, as African Americans averaged 38 percent of southern state population in 1900.[9]

The political and economic threat posed by African Americans to the old southern order was quite real to a great number of white southerners, most especially to those whites who lived in Black Belt counties, where whites constituted a minority of the population. V. O. Keys, in fact, argues that whites in Black Belt counties were a critical major factor in shaping the politics of white supremacy in the South. It would not be the first time that people would feel that any gain by "others" would mean a net "loss" to them.[10]

7. Harry Ploski and Roscoe Brown, *The Negro Almanac* (New York: Bellwether, 1971): 455, 463; it should be noted that White introduced the first antilynching legislation to Congress. Although unsuccessful, it did provide some measure of recognition of the level of concern by his direct constituents and his more general constituents in the African American community of the South. See also Peter Bergman, *The Chronological History of the Negro in America* (New York: Harper and Row, 1969), 330.

8. Logan, *Betrayal*.

9. *Historical Abstract of the United States, Colonial Times to 1970, Part 1*, series A172–194, p. 22. Ulrich B. Phillips gives more of a state-sanction reading of the Old South in his *Life and Labor in the Old South* (1929; reprint, Boston: Little, Brown, 1963). Du Bois offers a corrective to Phillips's defense of the Plantocracy in *Black Reconstruction: An Essay toward a History of the Part Which Black Folk Played in the Attempt to Reconstruct Democracy in America, 1860–1880* (1935; reprint, New York: Harcourt, Brace, 1992).

10. V. O. Keys, *Southern Politics in State and Nation* (New York: Alfred Knopf, 1950): 5–12. Paranoia over the idea of blacks and power has been with us for quite some time.

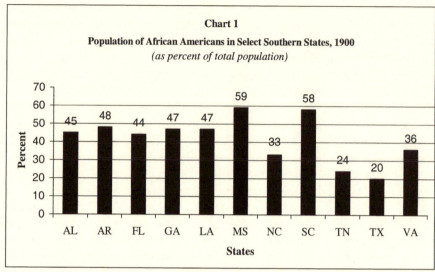

Chart 1

Population of African Americans in Select Southern States, 1900
(as percent of total population)

Source: U.S. Department of Commerce, Bureau of the Census, *Negro Population, 1790–1915* (Washington, D.C.: U.S. Government Printing Office, 1918), 43–44.

The term *minority* as it is used by pundits and analysts at the end of the twentieth century would have had little meaning to those African Americans at the end of the nineteenth century who lived in counties where they were the population majority. The true meaning of *majority* and *minority* with regard to politics rests in the idea that these concepts must be linked to power if they are to have any significance to the distribution of resources and the formation of public policy. Most African Americans knew that even when they were a population majority in a county, they had little authority over their own lives, much less their governmental institutions. The yearning for the restoration of the old order by whites was motivated by much more than simple nostalgia. In the wake of Reconstruction, the imposition of Jim Crow laws instituted a formidable challenge to the ability of African Americans to compete in every walk of life in the South.

By the time Du Bois began compiling *The Souls of Black Folk,* the social environment for African Americans was dire. The level of social inequality in the postslavery period would seem to be imaginary if not for the existence

---

Many have noted the additions to the Constitution to guarantee the support of the national government should there be a slave revolt. Reconstruction and the ascendancy of black elected officials were an anathema to southern whites, who viewed this as the embodiment of their gravest fears. One also recalls the reaction by many whites when Student Nonviolent Coordinating Committee activist Willie Ricks uttered the phrase *Black Power* during the Selma march in June 1966. Rarely had there been so many people taking to the nation's airwaves interpreting the meaning of those words to a fearful white audience in a manner that would ease their anxieties.

of the data. Should these rates be compared to the nations of the modern world, they would portray a grim picture of the severity of life for African Americans at that time.

The life expectancy, nationally, for African Americans in 1900 was an astoundingly low 33 years as compared to 47.6 years for whites; a difference of 38 percent.[11] One major factor for such a low life expectancy among African Americans was that infant mortality rates were mournfully high.

Census data indicate that at the beginning of the twentieth century, infant mortality for blacks was more than double that for whites. The infant mortality rate for African Americans was 344.5 per thousand as compared to 159.4 per thousand for whites. World Bank figures for 1997 indicate that Sierra Leone was the nation with the highest infant mortality rate (170 per thousand) nearly a century after Du Bois's study—and that is still less than half the rate for African Americans in 1900.[12]

There has long been considerable debate about the meaning of such a low life span during the immediate postslavery era of the late nineteenth century. Whether the figures represent a continuation of what had been the norm or a genuine improvement is still under dispute.[13] The high death rates actually provided ammunition for those who believed that freedom was detrimental to the survival of African Americans; predictions of the extinction of African Americans were rampant. These were desperate times.

Data from this period also indicate the percentage of African American women in the population was generally higher than that for men. Nationally, there were 878 men to every 1,000 women among African Americans, as contrasted to 991 to every 1,000 women among the white population. The disparity between men and women was greater for African Americans in several census regions, including the South Atlantic (817/1000), East South Central (863/1000), and West South Central (860/1000).[14]

There are several possibilities to explain the data: (1) infant mortality disproportionately affected African American males at infancy, especially in the South; (2) African American men migrated from the South to the northern and western states in numbers greater than their female counterparts; (3) their living and labor environments were uncommonly dangerous to their health, that is, they faced unsafe conditions at home, were worked to

11. *Historical Abstract of the United States, Colonial Times to 1970, Part 1,* series A195–209, p. 209.

12. World Bank, *World Development Report, 1999/2000* (Oxford: Oxford University Press, 1995), 343.

13. Denoral Davis, "Toward a Socio-Historical and Demographic Portrait of Twentieth-Century African-Americans," in *Black Exodus: The Great Migration from the American South,* ed. Alferdteen Harrison (Jackson: University of Mississippi Press, 1991), 2–19.

14. Jessie Smith and Carrell Horton, *Historical Statistics of Black America* (New York: Gale Research, 1995), 2:1476, table 1695.

death, or both; (4) they were the victims of violent attacks that led them to die in numbers that were disproportionate to all other groups; and (5) there might have been a census undercount.

While a complete answer to this question cannot be offered in this chapter, it can safely be said that it was some combination of these factors that resulted in the relatively low ratio of African American men to African American women. It is quite apparent that the South was an inhospitable place for African American men at, as well as before, the onset of the twentieth century.[15]

The Intellectual as Witness

Much of the critical work on *The Souls of Black Folk* tends to focus on Du Bois's operating at many levels, as essayist, historian, humanist, musicologist, public intellectual, and as an analyst on global and national politics. However, it is often forgotten that his work was grounded in his analysis of African American life in the South and an understanding of the relationship and importance of African labor leading to the slave trade and the perpetuation of southern planter interests. Du Bois knew that to understand the South a framework had to be developed that would account for broader economic and political forces of the nation.

As a sociologist and as a resident of the South, Du Bois was familiar with the appalling conditions experienced by African Americans in America and the importance of the South in that assessment. Perhaps the great importance that can be assigned to the work of Du Bois was his view that African Americans were in need of serious research. Many years later, in *Dusk of Dawn* (1940), Du Bois commented that "true lovers of humanity can only hold higher the pure ideals of science, and continue to insist that if we would solve a problem we must study it" (63). At a time when Social Darwinism was providing a "scientific" basis for the general disdain of African Americans, the need for African Americans to arrive at solutions based upon study was obvious. "Research" that was the product of anecdote or predetermined judgments was to be challenged. At the dawn of the twentieth century, Du Bois felt that the social sciences could fill this void.

His work on African Americans in the South was concurrent with his arrival at Atlanta University in 1897. Publications such as "The Negro in the Black Belt" (1899) and "The Negro Landowner in Georgia" (1901), and his leadership of the Atlanta University Studies Conferences, presaged his

15. See Stewart Tolnay and E. M. Beck, "Rethinking the Role of Racial Violence in the Great Migration," in *Black Exodus*, 20–35.

work in *The Souls of Black Folk* and focused needed attention on the region where most African Americans lived—the South.[16] The supplement to the 1900 Census, "Negros in the United States," includes a chapter written by Du Bois entitled "The Negro Farmer." Du Bois made accessible to a wider public the centrality of African Americans to the southern agricultural economy during and after slavery.

African Americans had what was at the time considered to be small farms. In *Negroes in the United States,* the Bureau of the Census described the average such farm as "an area of from 20 to 50 acres—the "one mule farm"—requiring the labor of a man and his family and one mule."[17] Du Bois wrote that close to half of all of the farms operated by African Americans were of this size. Although constituting 13 percent of the farms in the year 1900, African American–operated farms (which included owners and debtors, the latter by way of the sharecropping system) proved to be vital to the nation's agricultural activity (see Chart 2).

It was within the South that African American farm owners and operators were most prevalent. Du Bois further observed that:

> Over one-half the farms in Louisiana, Mississippi, and South Carolina are conducted by negroes; between one-third and one-half in Alabama and Georgia; and between one-fourth and one-third in Virginia, Arkansas, and Florida. Mississippi has nearly one-third of its total farm acreage under negro farmers and Alabama, Georgia, Louisiana and South Carolina have one-fifth to one-third of their acreage. Of the total value of farm property negroes control two-fifths in Mississippi, and more than one-fourth in Louisiana and Georgia. Of farm products measured by value negroes raise more than one-half in Mississippi, two-fifths in South Carolina, and one-fourth to one-third in Alabama, Georgia, Louisiana, and Arkansas.[18]

The paradox was that while African American farm operators (a term that included farm owners) were productive and essential to the South and the nation's agricultural sector, they were not the material beneficiaries of their own production. Du Bois summarized succinctly the answer to this paradox, "the white farmer invests principally his cash capital, land, and

16. Manning Marable, *W. E. B. Du Bois: Black Radical Democrat* (Boston: Twayne Publishers, 1986), 28. In chapter 13 of *The Souls of Black Folk,* Du Bois addresses the issue of the plantation economy of the Old South in "Of the Coming of John." Other African American writers who have engaged this issue include Jean Toomer, in "Blood Burning Moon," in *Cane;* Langston Hughes, in "Father and Son," in *The Ways of White Folk;* Zora Neale Hurston, in *Their Eyes Were Watching God;* Richard Wright, in *Uncle Tom's Children;* Alice Walker, in "The Child Who Favored Daughter," from *In Love and Trouble;* and Toni Morrison, in *Jazz.*

17. U.S. Department of Commerce and Labor, Bureau of the Census, *Negroes in the United States,* bulletin 8 (Washington, D.C.: U.S. Government Printing Office, 1904), 71.

18. *Negroes in the United States,* 91.

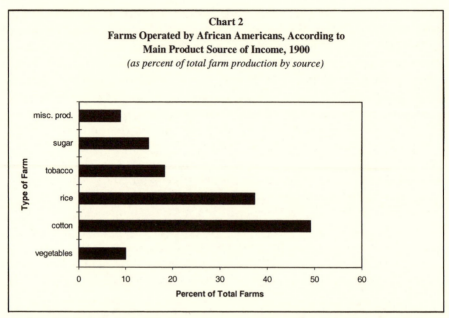

Chart 2
Farms Operated by African Americans, According to
Main Product Source of Income, 1900
(as percent of total farm production by source)

Source: W. E. B. Du Bois, "The Negro Farmer," in *Negroes in the United States,* bulletin 8 (Washington, D.C.: U.S. Government Printing Office, 1904), 69–98.

experience; the negro invests his labor, skill, and his capital as represented in his mule and seed."[19]

In *The Souls of Black Folk,* Du Bois decried that "a pall of debt hangs over the beautiful land; the merchants are in debt to the wholesalers; the planters are in debt to the merchants; the tenants owe the planters, and laborers bow and bend beneath the burden of it all" (84). African American farm operators found themselves in a seemingly endless cycle of poverty and debt, mainly to white landowners. The crop-lien system (of which sharecropping was a major part) and its attendant legal devices served as the most favored economic model to insure white economic domination in the South as the region and its economy moved from slave society to a postslavery order.

Laws aided and abetted the dependency of the newly freed upon the reconstituted plantation system. The imposition of the so-called Black Codes after the Civil War represented an entire set of laws dictating the activities of former slaves.[20] People were forced into the crop-lien system, for example, because laws threatened to imprison those without a permanent address. Laws were further expanded to create a new slave structure via the criminal justice system, as questionable arrests led to prison work farms in

19. Ibid., 95.
20. Richard Bardolph, "The Crop-Lien System," in *The Civil Rights Record: Black Americans and the Law, 1849–1970* (New York: Thomas Crowell, 1970), 35–41.

many states.[21] Du Bois wrote of the intimate relationship between the criminal justice and economic systems, and in the process he provides insight into the reasons for the relative absence of African American men in the South:

> After the war it [the land] was for many years worked by gangs of Negro convicts,—and black convicts then were even more plentiful than now; it was a way of making Negroes work, and the question of guilt was a minor one. Hard tales of cruelty and mistreatment of the chained freedmen are told, but the county authorities were deaf until the free labor was ruined by wholesale migration. (84)

Du Bois noted that the impoverishment, lack of education, and general oppression experienced by African Americans was due not to the individual activities of racist southern whites but was based on structural relations imbedded in the political, economic, and social order of the nation. If such inequality was the product of group decisions and codified into law and commerce, and was not the will of the Divine or the product of innate biology, then opposition could be mounted with strategies devised to overturn these structural relations. By asserting that oppression and impoverishment are the products of human beings and the systems they create, Du Bois provided the context for protest. He sought to counter the racial status quo by asserting that the African American condition was not due to a natural order but to a social order, and a social order could be opposed.

A Notch in "the Belt": Dougherty County, Georgia

When Du Bois visited Dougherty County, he reported on a place that was seemingly in transition from slavery to feudalism, not unlike many southern towns at the time. Dougherty County, as with the entire former Confederacy, had been humbled. Du Bois was of course aware of the high concentration of African Americans who lived in southern states, and he knew that they were more likely to live in places like Dougherty County than in the larger cities of the South. He also was acutely aware that there were important pressures that often kept African Americans in the South and on the land.

Who ruled, and who was ruled, was not determined by sheer numbers. Beyond his comments about the land and the people, Du Bois described the social systems that organized Dougherty County, "with [its] ten thousand Negroes and two thousand whites" (76). Politics and political par-

---

21. Barbara Eposito and Lee Wood, *Prison Slavery* (Washington, D.C.: Committee to Abolish Prison Slavery, 1982), 92–117.

ties are incidental to his observations about the county, however; Du Bois limited himself to an analysis that mainly was historical, economic, and social. The politics had long been decided, and those most struggling in the aftermath nevertheless formed the backbone of the county's economy and its pertinence to the outside world. Du Bois understood that the exclusion of African Americans in electoral politics had long been the status quo.

Dougherty County, "the west end of the Black Belt," was once known as the "Egypt of the Confederacy" (a term that modern-day African Centrists no doubt find disturbing) (81). By 1860, it was considered to have been "the richest slave kingdom the modern world ever knew" (82). "A hundred and fifty [cotton] barons" (82) had 6,000 slaves producing more than 20,000 bales of cotton per year to England and other destinations (86). For property owners (of both land and slaves) Dougherty County was heaven; for the slaves who worked the fields, it was as one ex-slave recollected, "a little Hell" (82). This witness recalled days when "I've seen niggers drop dead in the furrow, but they were kicked aside, and the plough never stopped" (82), a blues-toned description that recalls Paul D's harrowing experience on the chain gang in *Beloved* by Toni Morrison. The county was important for more than foreign trade as it also became known as the "granary of the Confederacy," a name it earned as a major producer of potatoes and corn. More than 90,000 acres of land were in production (tilled), valued at the then-astronomical sum of three million dollars (83).

The years of overintensive farming eventually eroded the topsoil and exposed its red clay foundation, making the land unable to produce the crops that farmers had so heavily relied upon. As before, cheap African American labor made the land profitable for white landowners. With its fertile soil base diminished and the Confederacy dead, landowners resorted to a new form of land tenure, tenant farming, including sharecropping, and related businesses to maintain cash flows. Field laborers, who commonly earned only thirty cents per day (without board), remained dependent upon the descendants of the old aristocracy that had existed during slavery. A generation had passed after the end of slavery, and those who worked the land were still generally unable to afford to purchase their own property to farm.

Dougherty County and the Era of Redemptionist Politics

Despite having a slim numerical majority, African Americans in Dougherty County remained a "minority" in terms of political and economic power. The rigid institutional racism of the county's past perpetuated the dominance of the major white landowners. This relationship was not effectively challenged until the 1960s, when the county seat, Albany, became the site of one of the more important confrontations in the Civil

Rights movement. Young leaders of the Student Nonviolent Coordinating Committee (SNCC) initiated a long series of protests against segregation and attempted to integrate the city's bus terminal. In a relatively short time, the participants expanded to include students attending Albany State College and local high schools in the area. After an early skirmish when the arrested protesters were beaten by the police, the black adults of the city and county set aside whatever differences and misgivings they had about the SNCC activists and openly supported the protests.

Dissension among the Albany Movement leaders ensued with the arrival and arrest of Dr. Martin Luther King Jr. and his cadre from the Southern Christian Leadership Conference (SCLC). Despite filling local jails to capacity and waging a period of protest from October 1961 to the fall of 1962, little was won in Albany and the county. While facilities were gradually integrated over time, the old power structure remained intact.[22]

What developed from this period of protest seemed to have had more immediate benefits for future Civil Rights campaigns than it did for the fortunes of African Americans in Albany and Dougherty County. The national leadership became aware that the youth could indeed organize adults and realized that young people were vital to sustaining a protracted campaign. The leadership also came to recognize the power of culture and learned to use the music of the Civil Rights movement to galvanize support and communicate their interests. For those who remained behind in Dougherty County, however, there were too many broken promises and wasted opportunities.

African Americans have now moved into a variety of important, visible positions across a wide spectrum of professions, but even though there have been important electoral gains, the county remains embroiled in a struggle for power that has reflected racial and class divisions.[23] Despite such visible change, the legacy of poverty and a substandard education system continue to haunt Dougherty County.

By the 1990 Census, this county in southwest Georgia can barely be described as the "Black Belt" county it was at the beginning of the century; the 1990 Census reports that Dougherty County, Georgia, is 50.15 percent

22. While there are many accounts of the events in Albany, Georgia, see particularly Dent, *Southern Journey;* Clayborne Carson, *In Struggle: SNCC and the Black Awakening of the 1960s* (Cambridge: Harvard University Press, 1981), 56–65; and Taylor Branch, *Parting the Waters: America in the King Years, 1954–1963* (New York: Simon and Schuster, 1988).

23. What has been defined as "minority-majority" electoral districts have been attacked as contrary to the equal protection clause of the Fourteenth Amendment and subsequently a violation of the Voting Rights Act. The irony of white conservatives claiming that districts drawn to reflect the interests and voting strength of racial minorities discriminate against whites ignores history. The case that reverses the establishment of minority-majority electoral districts designed to remedy historic discrimination can be found in *Shaw v. Reno* (113 S. Ct. 2816) 1994.

African American.[24] The 1990 Census indicates that 41.2 percent of African Americans in Dougherty County live below the poverty line, well in excess of an already high 30.3 percent for African Americans in the state of Georgia. The median income for households is also similarly below state levels ($18,689) at $14,252. In its 1994–1995 report, the Georgia Department of Education found that Dougherty County has a public school enrollment that is 73.9 percent African American, although African Americans make up little more than one-half the population; this is the result of a retreat by whites to private schools in the area, rather than be subjected to integration.[25] African American students, however, are more likely than whites to be retained (82.9 percent) yet are less likely than whites to receive a diploma (66 percent). The elementary and middle schools are little better than their high school counterparts, as Dougherty County students overall (all races) score below state averages in basic reading and math (as tested in third, fifth, and eighth grades). While the "New South" is a phrase that has been often used to suggest a departure from an often brutal past, there is much to indicate that the legacy of the "Old South" still lingers.

Du Bois did not write a requiem for a people. Beyond the assembly of data or recollection of historical fact to describe the "Black Belt," Du Bois tells the story of a people who had weathered the inhuman storm of slavery, its memory and its misery. He provides the reader with a sympathetic view of African Americans that contradicts the stereotype of them as happy, lazy souls who long for the paternalism of whites. Despite the harsh, oppressive conditions for African Americans at the start of the twentieth century, it must be remembered that the people were themselves not overwhelmed by the odds against them. Accordingly, the "Negro as he really is" did more than survive. Like the cotton roots that dig deep into the soil in search of water during a drought, the black people of Albany and Dougherty County, Georgia, at midcentury also reached down to their cultural roots when they began to challenge the entrenched attitudes of the Old South. Led by their youth in the 1960s, blacks in Dougherty County harvested the seeds of rebellion and resistance that were sown by their ancestors to make the walls come tumbling down in this "Egypt of the Confederacy."

24. U.S. Department of Commerce, Bureau of the Census, *1990 Census of the Population, Social and Economic Characteristics, Georgia* (Washington, D.C.: Government Printing Office 1992), 22, table 6.

25. Ibid., table 9; Georgia Department of Education, "1994–95 State of Georgia Education Report Card; Dougherty County Schools," 1.

Alexandria, Tennessee

Dusk and Dawn of the Rural Veil

Reavis L. Mitchell, Jr.

Of Alexandria at the end of the nineteenth century, W. E. B. Du Bois asked, "How shall men measure Progress there where the dark-faced Josie lies? How many heartfuls of sorrow shall balance a bushel of wheat? How hard a thing is life to the lowly, and yet how human and real! And all this life and love and strife and failure,—is it the twilight of nightfall or the flush of some faint-dawning day?"[1]

His sadly musing questions came in response to his return to Alexandria's African American settlement in 1897, ten years after he had been engaged as the teacher of the seasonal "colored school" in rural DeKalb County, Tennessee. His pilgrimage revealed bittersweet changes in Alexandria's white agrarian community and its sister settlement of black farmers.

When Du Bois spent the hot summers of 1886 and 1887 teaching rural black youngsters, he was an undergraduate student at Nashville's Fisk University. Being young, idealistic, and self-confident ("Fisk men thought that Tennessee—beyond the Veil—was theirs alone" [46]), his unwavering belief in higher education for future economic improvement of all African Americans, whether urban or agrarian, reflected the spirit of optimism in African Americans, who were confident they were participants in the surrounding white-shaped world. And that spirit of optimism was justified as post-Reconstruction Tennessee, historically more liberal than her Deep South sister states, had embraced the pro-industry "New South" gospel espoused since the mid-1870s by Henry Grady (1850–1889), editor of the

1. W. E. B. Du Bois, *The Souls of Black Folk,* ed. Henry Louis Gates Jr. and Terri Hume Oliver (New York: Norton, 1999), 53–54. Subsequent references to this work appear as page citations in the text. The book's fourth chapter, "Of the Meaning of Progress," was first published as an essay entitled "A Negro Schoolmaster in the New South," in *Atlantic Monthly* 83, no. 495 (January 1899): 99–105.

Atlanta Constitution. According to Grady's gospel, through the American-ization of the South via industrialization and the infusion of northern capi-tal, southerners would rise in material comfort, level of education, and self-respect, with the African American man "to get a return on his investment through education and participation in the political process."[2]

The New South doctrine was at work in Tennessee in the mid-1880s, with seven African Americans elected to the state House of Representa-tives. They followed in the footsteps of six earlier black representatives, who had broken through the veil of racism to win seats in the legisla-ture: Sampson W. Keeble (c. 1832–post-1886), R—Davidson County, 1873–1875; Thomas A. Sykes (1835–post-1893), R—Davidson County, 1881–1883; John W. Boyd (1857–1932), R—Tipton County, two terms, 1881–1885; Is-ham F. Norris (?–post-1891), R—Shelby County, 1881–1883; Thomas Frank Cassels (c. 1843–post-1899), R—Shelby County, 1881–1883; and Leonard Howard (?–?), R—Shelby County, 1883–1885.[3]

In 1886 and 1887, the seven black legislators serving in the state House of Representatives, who were role models for young Du Bois, were David Foote Rivers (1859–1941), R—Fayette County, two terms, 1883–1887; Sam-uel Allen McElwee (1857–1914), R—Haywood County, three terms, 1883–1889; Greene E. Evans (1848–post-1875), R—Shelby County, 1885–1887; William A. Fields (c. 1852–post-1888), R—Shelby County, 1885–1887; Wil-liam C. Hodge (c. 1846–post-1889), R—Hamilton County, 1885–1887; Styles Linton Hutchins (?–post-1905), R—Hamilton County, 1887–1889; and the sole Democrat, Monroe W. Gooden (1848–1915), D—Fayette County, 1887–1889.[4]

As the decade of the eighties drew to a close, earlier "Jim Crow" laws (named for the imaginary black street beggar personified by Thomas

2. Grady's famous "New South" oration is quoted in H. Brandt Ayers, "You Can't Eat Magnolias," in H. Brandt Ayers and Thomas H. Naylor, eds., *You Can't Eat Magnolias: A Publication of the L. Q. C. Lamar Society,* 6–7. See also C. Vann Woodward, *Origins of the New South, 1877–1913* (Baton Rouge: Louisiana State University Press, 1971).

3. For more on these legislators, see Robert M. McBride and Dan M. Robison, eds., *Biographical Directory of the Tennessee General Assembly, Volume 2, 1861–1901* (Nashville: Tennessee State Library and Archives and Tennessee Historical Commission, 1979) (hereafter cited as *Directory 2*), 484–85. See also Ilene J. Cornwell, "Addenda to Vol-ume 2," in *Biographical Directory of the Tennessee General Assembly, Volume 6, 1971–1991* (Nashville: Tennessee Historical Commission, 1991), 259; and Mingo Scott Jr., *The Ne-gro in Tennessee Politics and Governmental Affairs, 1865–1965: "The Hundred Years Story"* (Nashville: Rich Print, 1964), 48–49.

4. For more on these seven state representatives, see *Directory 2,* 276, 290, 342–43, 423, 448, 572, 771–72. See also Linda T. Wynn, "Samuel A. McElwee (1857–1914)," in *Profiles of African Americans in Tennessee,* ed. Bobby L. Lovett and Linda T. Wyan (Nashville: Annual Local Conference on Afro-American Culture and History, 1996), 85–87; Arna Bontemps, *Chariot in the Sky: The Story of the Jubilee Singers* (New York: Holt, Rinehart and Winston, 1951), 180, 182, 186, 187; and Joe M. Richardson, *A History of Fisk Univer-sity, 1865–1946* (Tuscaloosa: University of Alabama Press, 1980), 25–27.

"Daddy" Rice in his 1828 vaudeville act and burlesque song, "Jump, Jim Crow") enacted by the Tennessee General Assembly continued to shape the state's social fabric. The 1870 law prohibiting interracial marriages, followed by the segregation act of 1875 and the 1881 act segregating blacks in separate railroad cars, were strengthened by the Supreme Court's 1883 ruling as unconstitutional the Federal Civil Rights Act of 1875 and by its *Plessy v. Ferguson* decision in 1896 upholding a Louisiana law directing railroads to provide equal but separate accommodations for the white and colored races. These reinforced discriminatory laws exacerbated the solidity of racism's veil between the white and black populations. The white-mandated veil also blocked the African American male's path to the polls, since he could not pay the exorbitant poll tax nor risk losing his small farm or sharecropper's position and income.

Thus, during the Progressive Era of the 1890s, there was no African American representation in the Tennessee General Assembly—although in 1896 Jesse M. H. Graham (1869–1930; R—Montgomery County), a black resident of Clarksville, was elected to the Fiftieth Assembly; he was seated on January 4, 1897, subject to investigation by the House Committee on Elections. On January 20, Graham was disqualified by the House of Representatives when it determined that the duration of his "residence in Tennessee [following his pre-1895 residence in Louisville, Kentucky, was] less than the three years required by constitution." The voiceless status of Tennessee's African Americans would continue until the modern civil rights movement and reforms of the 1960s, when Archie W. Willis Jr. (1925–1988; D—Shelby County), a black Memphis attorney, was elected in 1964 to the Eighty-fourth General Assembly, then reelected in 1966 to the Eighty-fifth Assembly.[5]

In 1886, however, the veil-rending election of Archie Willis lay seventy-eight years in the future, and seven African Americans represented their constituents in the state House of Representatives as eighteen-year-old W. E. B. Du Bois, imbued with a youthfully optimistic "Progressive sense of the possible,"[6] arrived in Lebanon, Wilson County, to begin summer training sessions at the Teachers' Institute. There he discovered that the "awful shadow of the Veil" was omnipresent in both urban and rural Tennessee: White teachers attended training sessions in the morning and Negroes attended the same sessions at night. Then, when he and a white teaching candidate rode horseback to the county school commissioner's house to secure employment in late July, the veil's shadow fell once more as the two white men sat down together to share dinner, and, as Du Bois sadly

5. For more on Graham, see *Directory 2*, 350–51; for more on Willis, see Ilene J. Cornwell, ed. *Biographical Directory of the Tennessee General Assembly, Volume 5, 1951–1971* (Nashville: Tennessee Historical Commission, 1980), 476–77.

6. Ayers, "You Can't Eat Magnolias," 17.

observed, "they ate first, then I—alone" (48). His youthful life as a free black in New England had not given Du Bois the experience to comprehend that beneath the professed ideals of mutual respect and equality among whites and blacks in the South lay an omnipresent chasm filled with more than two and a half centuries of mistrust, fear, and accumulated evils rooted in the enslavement and exploitation of the black race.

For the black sharecroppers and independent farmers living on the hilly countryside in rural Tennessee, memories of the accumulated evils inflicted upon African Americans during enslavement had been indelibly burned into their collective consciousness and heritage. Those middle-aged parents of Du Bois's nearly thirty students—the Dowells, the Burkes, the Lawrences, the Neills, the Hickmans, the Thompsons, and the Eddingses— had experienced fewer than twenty-five years of freedom from enslavement. Those tradition-bound agrarians, whom Du Bois would describe retrospectively as sharing "a common hardship in poverty, poor land, and low wages" (50), could not envision any path to earning a livelihood (albeit scarcely subsistence) except the established one through the precarious praxes of agricultural and manual labor. Thus, while the young schoolmaster Du Bois educated his students in the log schoolhouse—previously used by local landowner and Confederate veteran Captain J. D. Wheeler for corn storage, then converted during Reconstruction into the Wheeler School for Blacks[7]—the students' parents stifled their doubts about book learning and briefly tolerated the absence of their offspring from domestic chores and family-farm or sharecrop labor.

As Du Bois would soon discover, however, all the parents shared the pragmatic philosophy of Mun Eddings, "who worked Colonel Wheeler's farm on shares" and never hesitated to keep his sons Mack and Ed from school when "the crops needed the boys" or to detain daughter Lugene at home to "mind the baby" (49). Even quasi-independent older students were hard-pressed to attend school regularly. Twenty-year-old Josie— whose "longing to know, to be a student in the great school [Fisk University at Nashville] hovered like a star above this child-woman amid her work and worry" (48)—was frequently absent from classes as she tended her younger siblings, helped with household chores, and created family apparel on the sewing machine she had bought one winter through her four-dollars-a-month domestic employment. For the offspring of the tenant and independent farmers, the leisure to obtain formal education was

7. *Tennessee Historical Markers Erected by the Tennessee Historical Commission*, 8th ed. (Nashville: Tennessee Historical Commission, 1996), 32. The historical marker commemorating the Wheeler School for Blacks stands at the junction of Goose Creek Road and U.S. Highway 70 on the northern outskirts of Alexandria. The marker, funded by the Sons of Confederate Veterans and the Black Student Alliance of Tennessee Technological University, Cookeville, was erected in 1995.

a luxury unfeasible; their labor was a vital component of the family units struggling to eke out marginal subsistence in the rough hills north and northeast of Alexandria.

The center of this hardscrabble "little world . . . and so its isolation made it" (50), Du Bois noted, was the town of Alexandria, established by deed on April 15, 1820, from Daniel Alexander in what was then part of Smith County. Alexander, born in 1773 in Maryland, apparently settled in the area before 1800, for by 1801 he had built his dwelling; in 1802 he was granted a license to keep a tavern in his house. "The tavern business evidently did well, and Alexander was wealthy enough by 1820 to own ten slaves," according to DeKalb County Historian Thomas G. Webb. "He was a prominent man in the affairs of his community. A few years after founding Alexandria, in 1829 Daniel Alexander moved to Rutherford County," Tennessee.[8]

The town named for Alexander continued to flourish without his presence. Alexandria was listed in Eastin Morris's *Tennessee Gazetteer* of 1834 on the stage route from Knoxville—via Sparta, Alexandria, and Lebanon—to Nashville and as containing "250 inhabitants, one doctor, five stores, three groceries, two taverns, two tailors' shops, two blacksmiths' shops, one shoe shop, two saddlers' shops, two carpenters, one tanyard, and two churches." The *Gazetteer* also included statistics from the Census of 1830, the first complete census of Tennessee, and the figures for Smith County recorded a total of 21,492 inhabitants: 9,391 free white males; 7,723 free white females; 83 free people of color; and 4,294 slaves.[9]

Antebellum Alexandria appeared destined to become a major city in the late 1830s. "Before the Civil War, Alexandria was the largest town in DeKalb County [created from portions of Smith and Cannon counties in 1837 and named for the Revolutionary War Continental Army major general, Baron Johann DeKalb], as well as the wealthiest," wrote historian Thomas G. Webb. "Alexandria citizens were the leaders in establishing the Lebanon-Sparta Turnpike in 1838, and Alexandria had DeKalb County's first newspaper and first bank." The town was incorporated in 1848, and by 1860 there were "29 farms in the county valued at $5,000 or more. Seventeen farms of the 29 were in the first district near Alexandria."[10]

8. February 6, 1998, letter from DeKalb County Historian Thomas G. Webb, Smithville, Tenn., with article, "Alexandria Celebrates 150th Birthday in 1970," published in the *Smithville Review,* April 30, 1970. Webb also is the author of *DeKalb County, Tennessee* (Memphis: Memphis State University Press, 1986), and *A Bicentennial History of DeKalb County, Tennessee* (Smithville: Smithville–DeKalb County Chamber of Commerce, Taylor Publishing, 1995).

9. Robert M. McBride and Owen Meredith, eds. *Eastin Morris' Tennessee Gazetteer, 1834, and Matthew Rhea's Map of the State of Tennessee, 1832* (Nashville: Gazetteer Press, 1971), 60, 62, 103, 303.

10. Thomas G. Webb, "DeKalb County Fair," *Smithville Review,* June 3, 1976.

The town's incorporation lapsed during the Civil War and Reconstruction era, and not until the early 1880s did Alexandria's progressive spirit resurface. By 1888, the local *Liberty Herald* newspaper waxed enthusiastically that a "spirit of improvement has taken hold upon Alexandria, the most since the war. New buildings are going up almost daily; everyone is full of faith in the future prosperity of our town. Of 15 stores in town, only one is vacant." In August of the following year, in keeping with this progressive spirit, Alexandria's active African American community served as host to the three-day, twenty-first-anniversary convention of the United Benevolent Societies (Colored) of Tennessee. After several days of internal business and programs, the group "had a big daylight procession and picnic. They marched through the principal streets, then to the fairgrounds."[11]

Alexandria's fairgrounds were established near Hickman Creek in 1856 for the DeKalb County Fair, operated by the DeKalb County Agricultural and Mechanical Association, and became an important gathering place for both Alexandria and the surrounding county. In keeping with Alexandria's custom begun in the antebellum era, a "Black Fair" was held during the two final days of the annual (white) fair. "Although Blacks had access to all rides, concessions, and exhibits, they were required to sit in a reserved area located on the south of the grandstand. A wall between the two sections was solid, so the occupants could not see each other," according to Alexandria's local historian Frances Lawrence. "The Black Fair was operated by Dib Burks of Alexandria [who also served as fireworks specialist for the fair and for the Tennessee State Fair in Nashville] and his cousin Henry Belcher of Nashville. The Black Fair was held the Friday and Saturday following the DeKalb Fair and had entries and picnics. A dance was held in the women's building with a live band."[12]

By the end of the decade, the "Progressive sense of the possible" was tangible in Alexandria. The town's population stood at 640 (80 more inhabitants than were recorded in the 1880 Census), with tangible assets of "133 dwellings, 2 hotels, 3 school buildings, 6 churches, 1 roller mill, 1 saw and planing mill, 1 carriage manufactory, 5 dry goods stores, 4 grocery stores, 2 drug stores, 1 hardware store, 1 furniture store, 2 large ware houses, 5 blacksmith shops, 2 barber shops, 2 undertaking and cabinet shops." As in the previous decade, "most of the black men were still hiring out to do farm labor, but three of them were blacksmiths," related Thomas Webb. "Most of the black women who worked outside the home were household servants, cooks (usually excellent and generally preferred over white

11. *Liberty Herald,* October 31, 1888, and August 14, 1889, furnished by Thomas G. Webb, February 6, 1998.
12. Frances Lawrence, ed., *The History of the DeKalb County Fair, the Grandpa Fair of the South, 1856–1996: The 140th Consecutive Exhibition, Alexandria, Tennessee* (Alexandria: DeKalb County Fair, 1996), 5, 10.

cooks), or did washing and ironing for white families. Essentially, the same was true in 1900 in Alexandria, except that there were among the black men four blacksmiths, a barber, three ministers, a stone mason, and a wagoner. The black population of DeKalb County was never large [the 70 percent in 1860 had dwindled to 7 percent by 1900] and it has steadily decreased, primarily from out-migration."[13] Today, most blacks reside in the three larger towns of Smithville, Dowelltown, and Alexandria.

The changes wrought by progress in Alexandria were obvious to W. E. B. Du Bois when he made his pilgrimage back to the town in 1897,[14] fresh from his 1896 graduation by Harvard University, as the first African American to earn the institution's Ph.D. degree, and a decade after his student-teaching experience prior to his 1888 graduation from Fisk University. His description of Alexandria, however, as "a straggling, lazy village of houses, churches, and shops . . . [and] cuddled on the hill to the north was the village of the colored folks, who lived in three- or four-room unpainted cottages . . . [which were] centred about the twin temples of the hamlet, the Methodist and the Hard-Shell Baptist churches" (50) does not accurately record the geographical location of the town's elements, according to county historian Webb:

> Alexandria's black community was located primarily right in town, just east of the square on the street ["Cemetary" Road, according to the present street sign] leading up to the [East View] cemetery. Beside the cemetery is Seay's Chapel Methodist Church, U.S.A., which [has been] used by the black community from 1869. The school was just behind the church, and the black cemetery beside that and adjoining the white cemetery (a rock fence between them). . . . Some of the blacks also lived on the upper (south) end of High Street, where the Walker's Chapel Primitive ("Hard-Shell") Baptist Church was built about 1882 and the Mt. Zion Missionary Baptist Church about 1894.[15]

Despite his errant sense of direction, Du Bois's other senses were honed to razor-sharp precision as he investigated "how life had gone with my school-children" (51) over the previous decade. He discovered that the black agrarians' hardscrabble existence, with poverty's attendant malaise of malnutrition and disease, had eliminated any possibility of advanced educational opportunity for his former students. For them, opportunity beckoned through the slightly ajar door of the New South industrialism's

13. Letter from Thomas G. Webb, February 6, 1998, with copies of figures from the 1880 and 1890 U.S. Censuses of Alexandria.

14. Progress described by Du Bois included the old log schoolhouse being replaced in 1897 by a "jaunty board" schoolhouse. This schoolhouse was renovated and moved in the fall of 1997 to the Lebanon Fairgrounds for use in a turn-of-the-century village display, according to Alexandria's local historian Frances Lawrence, February 21, 1998.

15. Letter from Thomas G. Webb, February 6, 1998.

demand for manual labor, despite the wages being "depressed by the availability of free or nearly free labor under the convict-lease system . . . [so that the average working man] could labor for an entire month without seeing daylight and make only $8–$14."[16] Du Bois's former students, in pursuit of a modicum of material wealth to enable their rise above marginal living, had joined the black exodus from exhausted farmland to industrialized cities. In addition to several of his students having "gone to work in Nashville" (53), one student had taken up the carpenter's trade and another had become the community's Baptist preacher. His older student, Josie, had helped her parents sell their farm and move nearer to town, then "toiled a year in Nashville, and brought back ninety dollars to furnish the house and change it to a home. . . . Josie shivered and worked on, with the vision of school-days all fled . . ." (51). Her dreams expired with her in premature death at age thirty.

And the collective dream of Alexandria's African Americans to attain agrarian affluence also died, despite the efforts of debt-ridden black farmers and laborers unified into the Working People's Labor and Art Association during the depression years of the early 1890s; the last record of the association would be in 1905.[17] As Alexandria's economic focus shifted from general agriculture to livestock breeding to commerce and manufacturing, the town's population diminished with each passing year (to reach its lowest ebb in 1950 with 372 inhabitants).[18] As the century came to an end, black ownership of small farms in DeKalb County continued to dwindle, and a decade later there would be only 59 black farmers and 33 black owners of farms, compared to 2,541 white-owned farms and 2,482 white farmers, recorded for the county's total farmland of 197,912 acres.[19]

In April of 1917, New South boosterism and the wave of progressive reforms benefiting both rural and urban African Americans were swept away by America's entry into the First World War. The "shadow of the Veil" remained an impenetrable barrier for all black Tennesseans who, although they were in the forefront of young volunteers enlisting in the armed ser-

16. Ayers, "You Can't Eat Magnolias," 7. Tennessee's convict-labor-lease law was not repealed until 1936.

17. Working People's Labor and Art Association (Alexandria, Tenn.), "Constitution of the Working People's Labor and Art Association; revised Aug. 28–30, 1905, at Alexandria, Tennessee," copy on file at the Tennessee State Library and Archives, Nashville. An overview of Tennessee's agrarian movement is included in "A Troubled Decade, 1886–1896," in Stanley J. Folmsbee, Robert E. Corlew, and Enoch L. Mitchell, eds., *Tennessee: A Short History* (Knoxville: University of Tennessee Press, 1969) (hereafter cited as *Tennessee: A Short History*), 397–401.

18. *Tennessee Blue Book, 1957–1958* (Nashville: Tennessee Secretary of State, 1958), 151.

19. Letter from Gene Danekas, State Statistician with U.S. Department of Agriculture, Tennessee Agricultural Statistics Service, Nashville, February 5, 1998; data extracted from the *Thirteenth Census of the United States taken in 1910*.

vices to fight overseas, discovered that the general white attitude toward them had not changed. "As late as 1917, after nearly two decades of 'progressivism,' aroused Shelby Countians [in West Tennessee] could lynch a Negro accused of rape and murder and in the same week listen to a prominent Memphis lawyer and civic leader urge them to support the war effort to prevent Germany from turning back 'the hands of Civilization . . . a hundred years.' "[20] When African Americans returned to American soil after the 1918 armistice, they found few fissures in the South's veil of racism, thus the majority of young black veterans were carried by the tide of out-migration to industrial jobs in northern factories.

For the grandchildren of the handful of African Americans remaining in Alexandria, a new opportunity for improved education was created in the late 1930s. As a result of the National Conference on Fundamental Problems in the Education of Negroes, held in 1934 in Washington, D.C., and publication of its proceedings, *Child Health Problems*, by the Southern Office of the Julius Rosenwald Fund,[21] Alexandria's black children were beneficiaries of a Rosenwald School for Negroes. The large, weather-boarded schoolhouse was built on the hilltop south of the 1897 schoolhouse and above the narrow valley bisected by Shady Lane. Two teachers taught about fifty pupils in the Rosenwald School. "Around 1957, the number of pupils had declined until there were only enough for one teacher, with thirty or more pupils," stated county historian Thomas Webb. "Mrs. Daisy Tubbs stayed as the teacher at Alexandria, and Mrs. Zella Rutland League [who had begun teaching in the school in 1944] came to Smithville to teach at the black school (which was not a Rosenwald school). At the end of the 1962–1963 term, both schools were closed, and the DeKalb County schools were integrated."[22]

Despite improved educational opportunities for Tennessee's African Americans, the out-migration of blacks continued steadily, and the black population declined from 23.8 percent of the total population in 1900 (with

20. Folmsbee, Corlew, and Mitchell, "Social and Intellectual Developments in the Twentieth Century," in *Tennessee: A Short History*, 574.

21. Alfred A. Moss, "Philanthropy, Northern," in *Encyclopedia of Southern Culture*, ed. Charles Reagan Wilson and William Ferris (Chapel Hill: University of North Carolina Press, 1989), 651–53. Julius Rosenwald, president of Sears, Roebuck and Company, was a northern philanthropist guided by educator Booker T. Washington to support—within the context of segregation and vocational training—public education for blacks in the South. As early as 1910, Rosenwald began donating funds for social service and educational institutions to benefit southern blacks. In 1917 his largesse was institutionalized in the Julius Rosenwald Fund. Before the fund was liquidated in 1948 (sixteen years after Rosenwald's death), approximately $63 million had been utilized in the South to improve rural blacks' education, black health education, and racial relations. See the periodical published by the Rosenwald Fund, *Julius Rosenwald Fund: Review of Two Decades, 1917–1936*, by Edwin R. Embree (Chicago: The Fund, 1936).

22. Letter from Thomas G. Webb, March 1, 1998.

7 percent in DeKalb County) to 16.5 percent by 1960 (with 2.6 percent in DeKalb County). The population movement accelerated during the second half of the twentieth century, and the 1990 Census recorded DeKalb County's black population as 1.5 percent of the 14,360 inhabitants.[23] The handful of blacks remaining among Alexandria's 730 inhabitants were employed as laborers in the thirty manufacturing plants in the county or in construction and mining. By 1992, there were 75,000 farmers in Tennessee, but only 900 were African Americans. None among the black farmers were classified as principal operators (defined as producing one thousand dollars in products). There were no active black farmers among Alexandria's 697 inhabitants nor in DeKalb County.[24]

The answer to W. E. B. Du Bois's plaintive questioning of Alexandria's progress in 1897—"is it the twilight of nightfall or the flush of some faint-dawning day?"—hovered above the distant horizon even as he posed the question (54). It was both. It was the nightfall of the younger generation's blindly following the traditional praxes of their parents to lead marginal lives as hardscrabble farmers, who live and die in the shadow of one blue hill. Yet it also was the flush of a faint-dawning day offering hope for new opportunity over the rolling blue hills to the north, far beyond Tennessee's rural veil.

23. DeKalb County black population figures furnished by Thomas G. Webb, February 6, 1998.

24. Letter from Gene Danekas, State Statistician with U.S. Department of Agriculture, Tennessee Agricultural Statistics Service, Nashville, February 5, 1998; data extracted from U.S. Department of Commerce, *U.S. Census of Agriculture* (Washington, D.C.: U.S. Government Printing Office, 1993).

1. The north side of Alexandria's town square containing the post office, barber shop, and grocery store was photographed circa 1900, when horse-drawn buggies and wagons were preferred modes of rural transportation. Photograph from the collection of Frances Lawrence, Alexandria.

2. The north side of Alexandria's town square (shown at right, looking west from the junction of High Street and Tennessee 26) in February 1998. The buildings now contain a real estate agency, a hardware and variety store, an insurance company, a video store, and offices for a physician and a dentist. Photograph by Ilene J. Cornwell, Nashville.

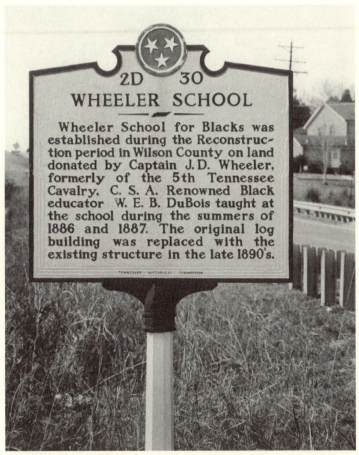

3. In 1995, a state historical marker was erected at the junction of U.S. 70 and Goose Creek Road on the northern outskirts of Alexandria to commemorate the log Wheeler School for Blacks. Photograph by Ilene J. Cornwell, Nashville.

4. The 1897 "jaunty board" schoolhouse, which replaced the log Wheeler School for Blacks, stood in Alexandria until autumn 1997, when the structure was moved to the Lebanon Fairgrounds for use in a turn-of-the-century village display. Photograph by Frances Lawrence, Alexandria.

5. The third school for blacks was the Alexandria Rosenwald School, built in the late 1930s through a rural education program established by the Julius Rosenwald Fund. The school operated until the DeKalb County schools were desegregated at the end of the 1962–1963 school year. Photograph from the collection of Frances Lawrence, Alexandria.

6. By February 1998, the massive fieldstone foundation and collapsed, rotting wood were all that remained of Alexandria's Rosenwald School for Negroes. Photograph by Ilene J. Cornwell, Nashville.

7. The fieldstone Seay Methodist Church, U.S.A., sits on a hill east of Alexandria. The site has been used by the black Methodists since 1869. Alexandria's local historian Frances Lawrence (left) guided the author (right) to the site on February 21, 1998, and related the church's history. Photograph by Ilene J. Cornwell, Nashville.

8. The "white" East View Cemetery was established shortly after Alexandria's founding in the early 1800s and sprawls along the hill (east) above Seay Methodist Church; the tin roof of the church can be seen against the foliage in the center background. Photograph by Ilene J. Cornwell, Nashville.

9. The south boundary of East View Cemetery is marked by a fieldstone wall, which separates the "white" burial ground from the adjacent cemetery for Alexandria's African Americans. The vantage point is looking west, toward the front fieldstone wall and entrance. Photograph by Ilene J. Cornwell, Nashville.

10. Walker's Chapel Primitive Baptist Church was built circa 1882 on the south end of High Street in Alexandria. Du Bois described it in 1897 as the "Hard-Shell Baptist" church. Photograph by Ilene J. Cornwell, Nashville.

11. The shell of Mt. Zion Missionary Baptist Church, built circa 1894, stands next to Walker's Chapel on High Street; services ceased in the 1950s. Since this church had not been built in 1886–1887, Du Bois's description of the village being centered around "the twin temples of the hamlet" must have referred to Walker's Chapel and to the circa 1869 Seay Methodist Church, situated about a mile to the east at the end of "Cemetery Road." Photograph by Ilene J. Cornwell, Nashville.

Anna Julia Cooper, Pauline Elizabeth Hopkins, and the African American Feminization of Du Bois's Discourse

Barbara McCaskill

I.

> Woman, Mother,—your responsibility is one that might make angels tremble and fear to take hold! To trifle with it, to ignore or misuse it, is to treat lightly the most sacred and solemn trust ever confided by God to human kind. The training of children is a task on which an infinity of weal or woe depends. Who does not covet it?[1]

At the turn of the century, it cannot be disputed that, alongside W. E. B. Du Bois and other African American male luminaries, African American clubwomen and opinion leaders (such as Anna Julia Cooper quoted above) were codefenders of an insouciant nationalist program. Defined by the Pan-African Conference of 1900, Du Bois's nationalism asserted that there were cultural distinctions that united peoples of African descent across geographical, national, and linguistic borders. He stopped short, however, of attempting to implement a separate African American nation-state. Writing on the construction of African American identity, Judith Stein states that Du Bois's nationalism at this time was not dominated by eschatologies of a separate African statehood. Rather, he assigned "a moral and metaphysical significance" to the idea of nation-building on the basis of

I am grateful for a Fall Quarter 1994 Sarah H. Moss Fellowship from the University of Georgia, which enabled me to travel to research issues of the *A.M.E. Church Review* at Howard University's Moorland-Spingarn Research Center. With a 1989 Summer Faculty Research Award from the State University of New York–Albany, I visited Fisk University for Pauline Hopkins's manuscripts.

1. Anna Julia Cooper, "Womanhood a Vital Element in the Regeneration and Progress of a Race," in *A Voice from the South: By a Black Woman of the South* (1892; reprint, New York: Oxford University Press, 1988), 22.

racial distinctiveness,[2] and he elected to emphasize and actualize African Americans' entitlement to white America's economic, educational, medical, and legal attainments.

Du Bois's nationalistic project combined the American ex-colonist's character of material self-sufficiency and moral accountability with the American ex-slave's commitment to striving for black pride and stridently interrogating the binary of America as the "light of democracy" and Africa as the "dark continent." It would be recorded for posterity as nothing short of a sophisticated conjunction of intellect, activism, and enthusiasm. It endeavored to put such prior philosophical movements as Europe's Enlightenment and America's Great Awakening to shame.

Within this shift of attitude, however, an exception to the climate of change persisted. This was an old, vexing position on African American womanhood—one more fantasy than fact—which even Du Bois's progressive *The Souls of Black Folk* maintained. This position—the assignation of respectable African American women to functions as wives, mothers, daughters, and sisters in the exclusive sphere of the home—now occupied contested terrain. Where America had reached consensus about 1900 at the dawn of the "new century," African American men and women debated the condition and claims of the black "new woman."

Anna Julia Cooper and fellow writer Pauline Elizabeth Hopkins, both staunch allies of Du Bois, fantasized new versions of home life that had been prohibited by outworn assumptions of women's capacities. Their portraits of African American women anticipate the metaphor of home in Du Bois's *The Souls of Black Folk,* and they are attempts to disturb it. While holding on to a familiar language that credits African American spirituality, indeed "soul," to woman's influence in the home, Cooper and Hopkins nevertheless set out to enlarge the scope of her role within and without this private sphere. Thus, they add a missing feminist voice to the discourse of social and political change that characterizes Du Bois's agenda.

In his long, illustrious career as a philosopher, sociologist, educator, editor, and Pan-Africanist, Du Bois did much to challenge the assumption that African American women had not contributed intellectually or artistically to African American and American culture. In his chapter "Of the Sons of Master and Man," it is the eighteenth-century poet Phillis Wheatley whom he selects as avatar of the civilized African American masses— masses who are treated like the most criminal caste of their race, "simply *because*" (118) they happen to be black. In his "Negro Art and Literature," a chapter from his *Gift of Black Folk* (1924), he lionizes many African American women writers: Wheatley, the nineteenth-century poet and novelist

2. Judith Stein, "Defining the Race: 1890–1930," in *The Invention of Ethnicity,* ed. Werner Sollors (New York: Oxford University Press, 1989), 84.

Frances Ellen Watkins Harper, the late-nineteenth-century A.M.E. journal-
ist Gertrude Bustill Mossell, and the Harlem Renaissance women of letters
Georgia Douglas Johnson and Jessie Redmond Fauset.

Had twentieth-century scholars read more Du Bois, they perhaps would
have noted his recognition of Linda Brent (a pseudonym for Harriet Brent
Jacobs) as an African American slave narrator. As a consequence, they
possibly might have avoided a raucous debate over the authorship of her
narrative, *Incidents in the Life of a Slave Girl* (1861), which raged until the
historian Jean Fagan Yellin meticulously documented and published confirmation of Jacobs as the author.[3]

On the political front, Du Bois stood alongside others on the podium
to decry the exploitation of African American women in the South who,
"without protection in law and custom," were vulnerable to rape, concu-
binage, and lynching in their roles as sharecroppers or domestic servants.[4]
And to unjust allegations that African American women's sexual promis-
cuity compromised their moral respectability, Du Bois's rebuttal was un-
ambiguously swift and impassioned:

> Out of [slavery], what sort of black women could be born into the world
> of today? There are those who hasten to answer this query in scathing terms
> and who say lightly and repeatedly that out of black slavery came nothing
> decent in womanhood; that adultery and uncleanness were their heritage and
> are their continued portion.
>
> Fortunately, so exaggerated a charge is humanly impossible of truth. The
> half-million women of Negro descent who lived at the beginning of the 19th
> century had become the mothers of two and one-fourth million daughters at
> the time of the Civil War and five million granddaughters in 1910. Can all
> these women be vile and the hunted race continue to grow in wealth and
> character? Impossible.[5]

3. For her presentation of evidence establishing Jacobs's authorship, see Jean Fagan
Yellin, introduction to *Incidents in the Life of a Slave Girl. Written by Herself,* by Harriet
Jacobs (1861; reprint, Cambridge: Harvard University Press, 2000), xv–xli. Yellin also
discusses how she traced Jacobs's life and the authorship of *Incidents* in the first section
of her "Texts and Contexts of Harriet Jacobs' *Incidents in the Life of a Slave Girl: Written
by Herself,*" in *The Slave's Narrative,* ed. Charles T. Davis and Henry Louis Gates Jr. (New
York: Oxford University Press, 1985), 262–82. Other literary productions in which Du
Bois imprints African American women's cultural contributions include his essays "The
Propaganda of History" (1935) and "Phillis Wheatley and African American Culture"
(1941), both in *The Oxford W. E. B. Du Bois Reader,* ed. Eric J. Sundquist (New York:
Oxford University Press, 1996), 328–42, 438–54.

4. Quoted in David Levering Lewis, *W. E. B. Du Bois: Biography of a Race, 1868–1919*
(New York: Henry Holt, 1993), 415. This originally appeared in a three-page leaflet, written by Du Bois on behalf of the NAACP, entitled "An Appeal to England and Europe."
Signed by thirty-two African American men, the leaflet was published in the December 1, 1910, *New York Sun* during the same year that Du Bois initiated publication of the
first issue of the *Crisis.*

5. Quoted in Lewis, *Biography of a Race,* 164. See also, for example, the discussion of
Du Bois's coordinated efforts with Fisk University alumni to diminish what he saw as

In addition to this vindication, Du Bois joined the leadership of African American women—Mary Church Terrell, the founding president of the National Association of Colored Women; Addie Hunton, founding president of the Southern Federation of Colored Women; Adella Hunt Logan, the "lady principal" of Tuskegee University; and others—to shout from the proverbial rooftops that prejudice and class snobbery, or what Anna Julia Cooper would call "the provincialisms of women who seem never to have breathed the atmosphere beyond the confines of their grandfathers' plantations," neutralized the progressivism and exposed the hypocrisy of white suffragettes.[6]

In addition, his *Crisis: A Record of the Darker Races,* issue by issue and in firm, direct terms, bore his imperative that, as they campaigned for the vote, white women must include and represent African American women as well as African American men—or be vilified as antisuffragist. Finally, in his capacity as editor of the *Crisis,* Du Bois enjoined African American men to resist emulating the gender oppression of those white men who dismissed women as their inferiors.[7] If African American womanhood were threatened, then at stake was the survival of the darker race itself.

In spite of this feminism, Du Bois was a by-product of his times. Within the elite middle and upper classes, enlightened African American men were chary of creating authoritarian, male-dominated relationships with those female peers of theirs who had suffered with them in enslavement. Yet these were times when race advancement demanded (to cite a popular phrase from uplift discourse) that the "better classes" of respectable African American women subscribe to a restrictive femininity imagined more for urban, literate, privileged white women than for the greater proportion of rural, semiliterate, impoverished African American ones.

Paradoxically, African American men were impressed into a patriarchy that disclaimed women's equality to men in the political and professional spheres while simultaneously mythologizing this same sisterhood's moral and domestic superiority over their brothers. Scholars have traced this impulse of the early-twentieth-century African American male bourgeoisie

---

an agenda to keep blacks "in their place" via a racial caste system facilitated by funding from paternalistic white southerners and northern industrial philanthropists, in James D. Anderson, *The Education of Blacks in the South, 1860–1935* (Chapel Hill: University of North Carolina Press, 1988), 263–71. A similar account of the tensions between Booker T. Washington and white donors to Tuskegee is in Robert G. Sherer, *Subordination or Liberation? The Development and Conflicting Theories of Black Education in Nineteenth Century Alabama* (Tuscaloosa: University of Alabama Press, 1977).

6. Cooper, "Woman versus the Indian," in *Voice from the South,* 83.

7. See "Votes for Women," in the *Crisis* special issue on women's suffrage (4 [September 1912]: 234) featuring critical commentary by Du Bois, Terrell, Logan, Fanny Garrison Villard (daughter of *Liberator* editor William Lloyd Garrison and wife of the philanthropist and railroad baron Oswald Villard), and Martha Gruening, a white *Crisis* staffer.

in dictating the status of African American women to many factors, such as anxieties about maintaining racial purity and controlling class mobility, and desires to correct social perceptions, deriving from enslavement, which infantilized and feminized black men and indicted them for their own victimization by American racism.[8]

A constant among Du Bois's early writings is an essentialist, reductive view of African American women possibly arising from these tensions. An apparent exception to this pattern, his "Damnation of Women" (1920) might stand as yet another example of what the critic Mary Helen Washington calls a "compassionate and generally progressive essay,"[9] that is, one written in resistance to the oppression of African American women and on behalf of their equality with African American men, white men, and white women. Even here, however, he paints African American women either as "daughters of sorrow" (passive pawns of American racism); or, for all of his pan-Africanism, as sub-Saharan "primal . . . All-Mother[s]"; or as virginal race matriarchs of tomorrow.[10] He honors African American women, even as he homogenizes African American womanhood. He extols African American womanhood, even as he fronts programs that expurgate or outright exclude African American women.

II.

> Three things American slavery gave the Negro—the habit of work, the English language, and the Christian religion; but one priceless thing is debauched, destroyed, and took from him, and that was the organized home.[11]

A scrutiny of *The Souls of Black Folk* confirms a presentation of African American womanhood that reinforces Victorian assumptions of respectable femininity that African American men like Du Bois—and numbers of their African American sisters—were accustomed to inserting in their projects for race advancement. As the quotation above reminds us, the volume stood as Du Bois's attempt to add a multiplicity of African American experiences, issues, and voices to the narrow construction of black consciousness and identity that he felt Washington's *Up from Slavery* (1901)

8. See Kevin K. Gaines, *Uplifting the Race: Black Leadership, Politics, and Culture in the Twentieth Century* (Chapel Hill: University of North Carolina Press, 1996), 12–13, 42–43, 122–123; and Hortense J. Spillers, "Moving on Down the Line: Variations on the African-American Sermon," in *The Bounds of Race: Perspectives on Hegemony and Resistance*, ed. Dominick LaCapra (Ithaca: Cornell University Press, 1991), 59–60.

9. Mary Helen Washington, introduction to Cooper, *Voice from the South*, xli.

10. Du Bois, "The Training of Negroes for Social Power," in *Oxford Du Bois Reader*, 354–62.

11. Ibid., 360.

had normalized two years earlier. "Without the existence of *The Souls of Black Folk*," writes Donald B. Gibson,

> interested people, and, indeed, the nation at large, could easily have believed that Washington's version of how things stood between black and white was the true and only one. . . . The book offered a candid black voice, rather than a weak voice simply echoing what the society in general, the white South in particular, and especially those northern entrepreneurs turned philanthropists, wanted to hear.[12]

However, whereas *The Souls of Black Folk* may have redressed *Up from Slavery*'s perceived racial monolithism, Du Bois himself homogenizes African American womanhood.

There is an absence in his book of women who are modeled as publicly prominent, politically powerful members of African America to be reckoned with—the female equivalents of the Crummells and Washingtons whom Du Bois does mention. Though this absence certainly reflects the reality of African American women's relationship to public culture, that Du Bois is hard-pressed even to imagine its alternative seems based on his premise of their disinvolvement, invisibility, and silence in these affairs. To talk of the women in *The Souls of Black Folk*, in fact, is to talk of very few women. When referencing African Americans collectively, Du Bois's gender of choice in the book is the masculine one. And when women do appear, the potential for their revolutionary involvement in political struggle is neutralized by their preordained functions as mothers, wives, daughters, and sisters. In these appearances, their corporate role seems largely that of serving as a metaphor for the orderly, moral African American home life that, Du Bois insisted, was a casualty of enslavement. To him, the black home stood in dire need of healing at the nineteenth century's end.

Dorothy Gale's well-known *Wizard of Oz* sentiment, "There's no place like home!" sags next to the poignancy of the idea throughout four centuries of African American creative expression. In the African American literary tradition, writers define femininity in relationship to the home. In her *Incidents*, for example, Linda the slave girl gauges her womanhood on how effectively she can sneak her children out of enslavement and establish a secure, nuclear household for them up North. She concludes her narrative still unresolved in her quest for "a home of my own," one she desires "for my children's sake far more than for my own." Similarly, in the story of evangelist Jarena Lee, it is only when she can entrust her sickly son to her own mother's tender care—that is, only when she can confirm her femininity by demonstrating her commitment to her home life—that she may

---

12. Donald B. Gibson, introduction to W. E. B. Du Bois, *The Souls of Black Folk* (New York: Penguin, 1989), xxxiv.

challenge church patriarchy by investing full-time in itinerant preaching and healing.[13]

In the Harlem Renaissance novels of passing, it is an old saw that the mulatto woman bears the potential of corrupting the purity and sacrosanctity of white bloodlines. Yet writers such as Nella Larsen and Jessie Redmond Fauset also make the mulatto woman's disappearance in the white world threatening, in part, because her departure from African American society means a consequent loss of her steadying influence in its Christian, albeit patriarchal, homes. In contrast, with their women characters who prioritize independence, sexual freedom, and a career over monogamy and motherhood, or who place self-fulfillment ahead of self-sacrifice, Terry McMillan's five wildly popular, contemporary novels—*Mama* (1987), *Disappearing Acts* (1989), *Waiting to Exhale* (1992), *How Stella Got Her Groove Back* (1996), and *A Day Late and a Dollar Short* (2001)—problematize whether domesticity is the only rightful place for women. For all of its much-heralded feminism, however, the 1996 film version of McMillan's *Waiting to Exhale* returns to an ideology predicated upon the assumption that matrimony and family are the ideal loci of femininity. In a gesture of female self-determination, Angela Bassett's character stages the now-legendary burning of her adulterous husband's clothes and car, swiftly followed by a court decision which vindicates her postponement of her own career and investment of sweat equity to attain his material success and social prominence. We viewers applaud all this, but her story does not end with her at home alone and happy. Instead, we watch her waltz into the foothills of marriage to a man presumed much worthier of her charms than the previous cad.

This near-fetishization of the monogamous African American mother and wife can be traced, as Du Bois insists, to the collision of enslavement and post-Reconstruction racism with the American Dream. In slavery, the African American home was a site of constant, spontaneous intrusion and control by the white master and mistress or by posses of white vigilantes self-elected to spread terror and violence. The father's authority in the slave family was nullified by his owners' ability to sell, abuse, or move his wife and children at whim. The enslaved mother's love was soured by the reality that, so long as she is their biological mother, her children, too, are chattel. And her monogamous sexual partnership with her husband could be usurped at any time by her master's promiscuous desires for her body. The African American home in enslavement was thus a far cry from the mother-guided, father-led household, depicted in such nineteenth-century

13. Jacobs, *Incidents in the Life of a Slave Girl*, 201; Jarena Lee, *The Life and Religious Experience of Jarena Lee, a Coloured Lady, Giving an Account of Her Call to Preach the Gospel. Revised and Corrected from the Original Manuscript, Written by Herself*, in *Sisters of the Spirit: Three Black Women's Narratives*, ed. William L. Andrews (Bloomington: Indiana University Press, 1986), 46.

engravings as "The Light of the Home" from *Godey's Lady's Book and Maga-zine* (1859–1887), which popular culture held out to all Americans as ideal and attainable.

The July 1860 issue of the influential *Godey's*, edited by Sara Josepha Hale, includes an illustration that shows a normative (white) middle-class fam-ily in the parlor of their residence. The mother cuddles an infant on her lap; at her feet, a young girl mirrors her mother by gently seating a doll in the doll-sized chair. To the left of the mother, infant daughter, and doll, the school-aged son erects a house of cards on a side table. The symbol-ism of this engraving is obvious. The son and daughter are modeling the respective roles that the members of their sex are socialized to assume in adulthood. It is the husband and father who places his mark, his creativity, on the material world around him; the wife and mother stamps her imprint, her "light," through her intercession in the spiritual and emotional lives of the family she nurtures. That no adult male inhabits this domestic sphere heightens the adult woman's power here. At the same time, the adult white male's ubiquity and agency can be read in the eye contact all the women make with the son, who substitutes for the master of the house in lieu of a real master's absence.

As a corrective to the propaganda of failed African American mother-hood that the *Godey's* illustration assisted in installing, Du Bois offers *The Souls of Black Folk*. In his thirteenth chapter, "Of the Coming of John," moth-erhood and sisterhood symbolize the idea that the integrity and courage of African American men in a racist, public world controlled by whites must rely upon the virtues women tender in the "organized" African American home. John is a young African American Everyman studying teaching at one of the many eastern "institutes" for the edification of African American youth. He enacts the traditional masculine script of making an imprint on the world by leaving his segregated Georgia community for the ungodly, liberal North. There, he is inspired through hard times by his mother's and sister's quiet examples and support.

When his "tardiness and carelessness, . . . poor lessons and neglected work" result in his suspension from school, for example, John pleads with his dean: "But you won't tell mammy and sister,—you won't write mammy, now will you?" (145). When he is discouraged about his prospects as an educated African American man in the "Egypt of the Confederacy" (Du Bois's metaphorical name for Georgia), his worries are soothed by thoughts "of a far-off home" (147). And he remembers his southern home not as hearth and bedside but as "the great eyes of his sister, and the dark drawn face of his mother" (147). When John returns South and his progres-sive ideas are met with scorn, it is his sister who embraces him and, with this cynosure of gentle persuasion, encourages him to hold fast against his opposition. Home—the inspiration and encouragement of his mother and sister—has sustained John during his northern education, and, thus, his sister's embrace is a gesture both symbolizing his return and affirming the brighter future for which he left them in the first place. This final scene is a trope of female assurance that Du Bois anticipated in his eleventh chapter, "Of the Passing of the First-Born." Here, Du Bois credits the disappearance of his anxieties about fathering a newborn son to his wife, "[t]hrough [whom] I came to love the wee thing" (131). Woman again is active in making peace hold within the domestic space, and, again, she assures that tranquility by championing a man's abilities and staving off his self-doubt.

If the women of "The Coming of John" and "Of the Passing of the First-Born" were described solely in terms of their maternity, then Du Bois would have been remiss. His argument that African American women assert conventional feminine influences in the home pivots, too, upon the abilities of African American men to wield traditional male power outside it. The maternity of Du Bois's women characters is connected to how his male characters succeed in defining their maleness in a hostile, antagonistic white world. The African American men of *The Souls of Black Folk* must debunk the Reconstruction's stereotypes of themselves as ne'er-do-wells, philanderers, and rapists. Then, they must restore themselves to the roles that it precluded: responsible breadwinners, loving fathers, and passionate defenders of their women's virtue.

"As part of a patriarchal U.S. culture," writes Kevin K. Gaines, "African Americans understandably regarded conformity with patriarchal gender norms as the crucial standard of race progress. . . . To be patriarch, the master of one's family, was ardently desired by African American men, who considered this an essential prerequisite of respectability, civilization, and progress."[14] Thus, "The Coming of John" must conclude with the young title character's tragic, inevitable attempt to define his sister as virtuous, and himself as patriarchal, by protecting her from rape—for which he is bitterly rewarded by a lynching. Raised in a household with an absent father, John's struggle with the white rapist demonstrates a romantic maturity. He exemplifies William Wordsworth's famous claim that "the Child is father of the Man," even as his martyrdom interrupts these words with the reality of how racism retards such evolution and perpetuates a cycle of fractured families.

Implicit in the outcome of "The Coming of John" is that the African American woman's viability and power in the great national debates about race and gender may be limited by the vulnerability of her physical body, however strong her intuition and ethics may be. As Cooper reminded her readers in her essay on "The Status of Woman in America," a woman's "kingdom is not over physical forces. Not by might, nor by power can she

14. Gaines, *Uplifting the Race*, 169.

prevail. . . . If she follows the instincts of her nature, however, she must always stand for the conservation of those deeper moral forces which make for the happiness of homes."[15]

Where much of "The Coming of John" is a positivistic blueprint for how African American women can influence racial progress from the domestic sphere, other chapters in *The Souls of Black Folk* measure the cost of racism by the failure of African American women to transcend poverty and ignorance and, thus, sustain strong homes. Josie is "a thin, homely girl of twenty" (47) whom Du Bois encounters in the Tennessee backwoods in his chapter "Of the Meaning of Progress." His description of her is a page direct from domesticity. He writes:

> She seemed to be the centre of the family: always busy at service, or at home, or berry-picking; a little nervous and inclined to scold, like her mother, yet faithful, too, like her father. She had about her a certain fineness, the shadow of an unconscious moral heroism that would willingly give all of life to make life broader, deeper, and fuller for her and hers. (47)

Yet the conditions Josie shares with many African American women of 1903—malnutrition, undereducation, impoverishment, prejudice—lead to her death and the disintegration of her family. Her slow wasting under the weight of these perils reminds the reader that gender and race discrimination, coupled with the disadvantages of struggling as a single woman wage earner in a patriarchal marketplace, preclude African American women from conforming to cultural models of home. This is what consigns African American women to the dustbins of femininity, not "adultery and uncleanness"[16] or any other moral deficiencies that may linger from enslavement.

III.

> Fifty years ago woman's activity according to orthodox definitions was on a pretty clearly cut "sphere," including primarily the kitchen and the nursery, and rescued from the barrenness of prison bars by the womanly mania for adorning every discoverable bit of china or canvass with forlornly looking cranes balanced idiotically on one foot. The woman of to-day finds herself in the presence of responsibilities which ramify through the profoundest and most varied interests of her country and race.[17]

Like Dante's Virgil, African American men at the nineteenth-century's end were perhaps identified the better masters in comparison to African

15. Cooper, *Voice from the South*, 133.
16. Lewis, *Biography of a Race*, 164.
17. Cooper, "Woman versus the Indian," 142.

American women. It would seem axiomatic that the achievement of African American women in the nationalist project of uplift would be judged on their facility in two categories. They had better 1) mouth male mantras, or else 2) settle for smiling demurely in the women's wings (such as the ladies' departments of African American newspapers or the ladies' auxiliaries of African American churches), for there—and only there—it was appropriate for them to carry out those mantras.

For example, setting about its own ambivalent policy towards the African American woman's position in Black Nationalism, the *Crisis* ran a column called the "Women's Club." This could be read as a disclaimer of sexism among the African American male fraternity, or as an assumption that African American women's voices were more legitimate if heard emanating from a strictly (and subordinately) female ghetto where they would not rival those of men, or both. Just as African American women feminist-intellectuals made dismantling gender biases and gender-based hierarchies an urgent task, so, too, did they find themselves "usually situat[ing] their appeals for women's independence within the rhetoric of female domesticity."[18]

In the annals of African American history, literature, and letters, the names of Wells-Barnett, Harper, Hopkins, and Cooper have become synonymous with influential teaching, polished public advocacy, messianic activism, and piercing insight. Yet all of their accomplishments on behalf of Black Nationalism might be read as transparencies of the gender politics that I have identified. Although Ida B. Wells-Barnett used her two companion pamphlets *Southern Horrors* (1892) and *Red Record* (1895) in order to dramatize the lynching issue on the international stage, many African American ministers publicly opposed her campaign, and both Du Bois and Booker T. Washington branded her "a woman who refused to adopt the 'ladylike' attitudes of compromise and silence."[19]

In "Woman's Political Future," her 1893 address to the World's Congress of Representative Women at Chicago's Columbian Exposition, Frances Ellen Watkins Harper wrote of a new generation of women who would share "freedom, an increase of knowledge, the emancipation of thought, and a recognition of . . . brotherhood with men."[20] Yet if, as one of these new women, she aspired to preach the gospel from the A.M.E. pulpit, then Harper would probably find that those very same church fathers who welcomed her oratory nevertheless would veto her ordination. The African Methodist Episcopal and African Methodist Episcopal Zion denomina-

18. Gaines, *Uplifting the Race*, 137.

19. Hazel V. Carby, *Reconstructing Womanhood: The Emergence of the Afro-American Woman Novelist* (New York: Oxford University Press, 1987), 108.

20. Frances Ellen Watkins Harper, "Woman's Political Future," in *Words of Fire: An Anthology of African American Feminist Thought*, ed. Beverly Guy-Sheftall (New York: New Press, 1995), 40.

tions had a long history of suppressing popular, charismatic women ministers such as Jarena Lee, Julia Foote, and Amanda Berry Smith.[21]

Similarly, to Booker T. Washington, Hopkins's pro–Du Bois stance in the *Colored American Magazine* merited silencing. Washington ultimately accomplished this in 1904 through agents of his ubiquitous Tuskegee Machine. They purchased the project—and summarily dispatched the heterodox Hopkins from it.[22] And to Du Bois (to be blunt, no stranger to projects such as the American Negro Academy, which excluded African American women from membership), an uneasiness caused by Anna Julia Cooper's combination of intellect and womanhood may explain his failure to credit her in public for her literary suggestions, even though he appropriated them behind closed doors. For example, according to Mary Helen Washington, Du Bois's *Black Reconstruction in America: An Essay toward a History of the Part Which Black Folk Played in the Attempt to Reconstruct Democracy in America, 1860–1880* (1935) was a response to a letter that Cooper wrote him in 1929, requesting that he publish a rebuttal to a racist revisionary history of Reconstruction entitled *The Tragic Era*. Also, in his earlier essay "The Damnation of Women," continues Washington, "Du Bois quotes Cooper's brilliant observation that 'only the black woman can say when and where I enter' and attributes that statement *not* to her but *anonymously* to 'one of our women.' "[23] Ironically, Cooper had shared the dais with Du Bois at London's Pan-African Conference of 1900.

African American nationalism at the turn of the century managed delicately to negotiate what have long been misperceived as exclusive or oppositional paths. One was represented by Washington's classic, assimilationist command to "Cast down your bucket where you are" in his 1895 Atlanta Exposition Address; the other, by Du Bois's aristocracy of "leaders of thought and missionaries of culture," which he proposed in his 1903 essay "The Talented Tenth." And another contradiction also complicated this nationalist ideology, and dared to expose its motives as fraudulent. "Black women," as Kevin K. Gaines writes, were "placed in the subordinate position of sacrificing gender consciousness and their reproductive self-determination in the name of race unity."[24]

21. C. Eric Lincoln and Lawrence H. Mamiya, *The Black Church in the African American Experience* (Durham: Duke University Press, 1990), 279–85.

22. Richard Yarborough calls Hopkins "the single most important black woman writer at the turn of the century" in his introduction to *Contending Forces: A Romance of Life North and South,* by Pauline Elizabeth Hopkins (New York: Oxford University Press, 1988), xxviii. Hopkins (1859–1930) served as literary editor of the Boston-based *Colored American Magazine* from mid-1903 through mid-1904.

23. See Washington, introduction to Cooper, *Voice from the South,* xli–xlii. See also Mary Helen Washington, "Anna Julia Cooper: The Black Feminist Voice of the 1890's," *Legacy* 4, no. 2 (fall 1987): 3–15.

24. Booker T. Washington, "The Atlanta Exposition Address," in *The Norton Anthology of African American Literature,* ed. Henry Louis Gates Jr. and Nellie McKay (New

A masculinist discourse assigned even university-educated African American women to a position of wardship and subordinacy and deference vis-à-vis African American men, even as Du Bois himself identified the "uplift of women, next to the problem of the color line and the peace movement, our greatest modern cause."[25] Tied as it was to patronizing notions of African American femininity, this discourse militated against African American women intellectuals' constructive involvement with Du Bois in theorizing Black Nationalism. It threatened to colonize a politics of gain by the politics of gender.

The words of one of the century's self-described "new" women, the Washington, D.C.–based educator Anna Julia Cooper, affirm how activist rhetoric of public, professional African American women was inflected by such old scripts of femininity, even as it championed new ones. Cooper begins her essay "The Status of Woman in America" by borrowing from the received discourse of true womanhood. She figures her sex as home-based, sentimental, angelic Marah Rockes ministering "the sympathetic warmth and sunshine of good women, like the sweet and sweetening breezes of spring, cleansing, purifying, soothing, inspiring" to the grasping, capitalist Gabriel LeNoirs of commerce. Several pages later, she adds a long complaint:

> While the women of the white race can with calm assurance enter upon the work they feel by *nature* [emphasis mine] appointed to do, while their men give loyal support and appreciative countenance to their efforts, recognizing in most avenues of usefulness the propriety and the need of woman's distinctive co-operation, the colored woman too often finds herself hampered and shamed by a less liberal sentiment and more conservative attitude on the part of those for whose opinion she cares most. That this is not universally true I am glad to admit. There are to be found both intensely conservative white men and exceedingly liberal colored men. But as far as my experience goes the average man of our race is less frequently ready to admit the actual need among the sturdier forces of the world for women's help or influence. That great social or economic questions await her interference, . . . that her intermeddling could improve the management of school systems, or elevate the tone of public institutions, . . . that she could contribute a suggestion on the relations of labor and capital, or offer a thought on honest money and honorable trade, I fear the majority of "Americans of the colored variety" are not yet prepared to concede.[26]

York: Norton, 1997), 514; W. E. B. Du Bois, "The Talented Tenth," in *W. E. B. Du Bois Writings*, ed. Nathan I. Huggins (New York: Library of America, 1986), 861; Gaines, *Uplifting the Race*, 134.

25. Du Bois, "The Damnation of Women," in *Oxford Du Bois Reader*, 574.

26. Cooper, "The Status of Woman in America," in *Voice from the South*, 131, 134–35. The seminal article on "true womanhood" is Barbara Welter, "The Cult of True Womanhood," *American Quarterly* 18 (1966): 151–74. See also Barbara Welter, *Dimity Convictions: The American Woman in the Nineteenth Century* (Athens: Ohio University Press, 1976).

Eliding business sphere and home, Cooper makes African American women's desires to exercise their much-lauded civilizing influence in "problems of national import" sound as natural and proper as their attending to
illness or other distresses within their families.

The reception of her essay collection, *A Voice from the South,* in the African
American sacred and secular press reinforces Cooper's ambivalence
towards the African American woman's public and private roles. A notice
in the "Book List" section of the April 1893 *A.M.E. Church Review* clearly
celebrates her volume as one of race advancement's finest productions,
one that "will at once take its place among the very best productions of
the Afro-American." There is an implied association of her intentions with
those of her hero Du Bois, as her book is also described as "a standing
argument in favor of the capability of our people."[27]

Yet the limits of a woman's ability to make such public arguments are
evidenced by how the notice inscribes Cooper within gendered rhetorical conventions. She is described as "a lady of culture," and, almost an afterthought (surprising in a magazine where women published frequently),
as one "who thinks, reads widely, and writes well." It is as if thinking,
reading, and writing stand as exceptions to the activities of African American ladies—or, at least, such doings on their part are not as important as
other ones. In addition, where a Du Bois may use reason and persuasion
to argue his case for African American enfranchisement to skeptical white
audiences, Cooper's cognition and logic are presented here, predictably
attired, as womanly emotion and sentiment. Cooper, writes the *Review,* "is
the voice of a woman pleading for justice to women and to humanity—and
she pleads well." Small wonder that in 1894 a columnist for the *Woman's Era*
"Notes" would lament that, notwithstanding "a few inquiries concerning
it," *A Voice from the South* "has never been put on sale in Boston."[28] Before
they could take their voices for granted in public debates, African American women's social roles still remained up for grabs.

In Hopkins's work, however, we see how Du Bois's nationalism and
African American women's feminism may harmonize. To her, home itself is
the fretful, politicized space where African American women must initiate
reproductive, fiscal, and matrimonial control. Like Du Bois, her teleology
of the household begins with the history of enslavement and, especially,
with the fictional and actual mammy's place in that picture.

As early as her 1879 drama, *The Slave's Escape* (retitled as *Peculiar Sam;
or, The Underground Railroad*), Hopkins replaces the matriarchal stereotype

27. Book list, *A.M.E. Church Review,* April 1893, 416.
28. Ibid.; *Woman's Era* 1, no. 5 (August 1894): 8. See also Elizabeth Alexander, " 'We
Must Be about Our Father's Business': Anna Julia Cooper and the In-Corporation of
the Nineteenth-Century African American Woman Intellectual," *Signs* (winter 1995):
336–56.

that the mammy image reinforced with the reality of African American women's struggles to assert self-determination within the slave family. In *Peculiar Sam* she presents Virginia, a slave, as a dignified character whose husband's attempts to replicate white patriarchy ("[Y]ou're my wife now," he says, "an' you's got to do as I says") are ridiculous, violent, and self-destructive.[29] Then, in her short fiction of the early 1900s published in *The Colored American*, Hopkins refabricates the mammy herself. Turbaned and hefty though she may be, Sister Maria Nash, the mammyish figure of "Bro'r Abr'm Jimson's Wedding" (1901), chooses her lovers, dispenses her mother-wit, and invests her savings in a manner that discards the notion of female subservience as a prerequisite for domestic bliss.[30] It is not as if Hopkins is suggesting that African American women cannot win the battle for parity with African American men in the public sphere. Rather, she proposes that there is no fitter ground than the home for women to launch the initial salvos of their offensive.

For both Cooper and Hopkins, to reason for African American women's political involvement necessitates revisiting the home. It is ironic that their feminization of Du Bois's discourse implicates a territory so humble and so easily brushed aside. The legacy of their voices endures in twenty-first-century African Americans' return to home as the foundation for strong generations—and in our collective recognition of parlor and podium as equally viable stages for male and female power.

29. Pauline Elizabeth Hopkins, "Peculiar Sam; or, The Underground Railroad," manuscript in the Fisk University Library Special Collection, folder no. 4, 1880.

30. Pauline Elizabeth Hopkins, "Bro'r Abr'm Jimson's Wedding," in *Short Fiction by Black Women, 1900–1920*, ed. Elizabeth Ammons (New York: Oxford University Press, 1991), 107–25. See also my discussion of Sister Nash in my essay " 'To Labor . . . and Fight on the Side of God': Spirit, Class, and Nineteenth-Century African-American Women's Literature," in *Nineteenth-Century American Women Writers: A Critical Reader*, ed. Karen L. Kilcup (Oxford: Blackwell, 1998), 164–83.

They Sing the Song of Slavery

Frederick Douglass's *Narrative* and W. E. B. Du Bois's *The Souls of Black Folk* as Intertexts of Richard Wright's *12 Million Black Voices*

Virginia Whatley Smith

The rise of a nation, the pressing forward of a social class, means a bitter struggle, a hard and soul-sickening battle with the world such as few of the more favored classes know or appreciate.

W. E. B. Du Bois's concluding remarks in chapter 8 of his 1903 text *The Souls of Black Folk* became the banner cry for Richard Wright to stage a class war against Du Bois for Negro leadership in his 1941 photographic text *12 Million Black Voices: A Folk History of the Negro in the United States*. Ironically, the struggle for Negro leadership over black culture and its subsequent trope of battle had been introduced much earlier by Frederick Douglass in his 1845 autobiography, *Narrative of Frederick Douglass, an American Slave, Written by Himself*.[1] The narrative delineates Douglass's dehumanizing experiences as a slave in the American South from his birth in 1818

A version of this paper first appeared as "Image, Text, and Voice: Oppositions of Meanings in the Wright-Rosskam Photographic Text," *OBSIDIAN II* (fall/winter 1993): 1–27.

1. W. E. B. Du Bois, *The Souls of Black Folk*, ed. Henry Louis Gates Jr. and Terri Hume Oliver (New York: Norton, 1999): 104; Richard Wright, *12 Million Black Voices: A Folk History of the Negro in the United States* (New York: Viking, 1941); Frederick Douglass, *Narrative of the Life of Frederick Douglass, an American Slave, Written by Himself*, ed. William L. Andrews and William S. McFeely (New York: Norton, 1997). All future references to these texts will be to these editions and will be abbreviated *Souls*, *12MBV*, and *Narrative*, respectively. At times, additional references to song titles and interpretive modes will refer to Donald B. Gibson's introduction and notes to the Penguin edition of *The Souls of Black Folk* (New York: Penguin, 1989).

to his escape to freedom in the North in 1838 and his rise to Negro leadership after his discovery at an abolitionist convention in New England
in 1841.[2] Upon Douglass's death in 1895, Booker T. Washington became
his replacement, after which tropes of war concerning the mantle of race
leader became a recursive cultural metaphor. In 1903 Du Bois publicly contested Washington's position of leader, and the bitter debate continued until Washington's death in 1915, which left Du Bois in power. He remained
relatively unchallenged as leader until Wright's ascension in 1940. Wright
repeated history by staging a class war against Du Bois for the title of Negro
spokesperson. This battle took place both overtly and covertly in *12MBV*
because Wright skillfully designed his photographic text in the mode of
a revolutionary slave narrative, parodying or appropriating, through intertextual revoicings, the literary styles and rhetoric of both Du Bois and
Douglass. All three slave narrativists disparately explore the range of sociological problems hindering the Negro in the United States, from times preceding American slavery in 1619 up to 1941. And of those issues, all three
leaders interrogate the role of slave music in terms of cultural preservation
and liberation. The rhetorical trope of "voice," as signified by Wright's book
title, remarks upon speech acts of slave singers and songwriters previously
noted by W. E. B. Du Bois in *Souls* and Frederick Douglass in *Narrative*. In
essence, Richard Wright adds another vocal dimension to a southern slave
musical trope already provided by Douglass and parodied by Du Bois to
upgrade the hues and cries of oppressed blacks to 1941. These prominent
Negro spokespersons ultimately sing a cultural song of slavery because
each one supplies an aspect of a musical performance, namely the lyrics
(Douglass), musical scores (Du Bois), and chorus of singers (Wright), to
show Negro Americans the path to freedom.

I. Master/Apprentice Writer Relations

Richard Wright's linkage to both Douglass and Du Bois is located in
a labyrinth of revealed or concealed rhetorical devices that speak to his
predecessors' texts by indirection. To discern these connections, Wright's
photo text must be deconstructed to recover not only the war trope but also
other submerged codes illuminating how Wright converges on a musical
paradigm with Douglass and Du Bois. His network of interlocking rhetorical strategies is dense and, for this essay, will be discussed by means of four
main sections: 1) master/apprentice writer relations; 2) the slave narrative
genre as a tool of revolution; 3) the South as a site of the Negro problem in
parts 1 and 2 of *12MBV*, and 4) the role of southern slave music as a cop-

2. William Lloyd Garrison, preface to *Narrative*, 3.

ing device for or revolutionary mechanism against dehumanizing social conditions.

A master/apprentice struggle for intellectual domain is behind Wright's conflict with Du Bois. Indirection is Wright's technique, however, and deconstruction of *12MBV* must begin on this master/apprentice "war of words" initiated by the author when Wright says:

> This text, while purporting to render a broad picture of the processes of Negro life in the United States, intentionally does not include in its considerations those areas of Negro life which comprise the so-called "talented tenth," or the isolated islands of mulatto leadership which are still to be found in many parts of the South, or the growing and influential Negro middle-class professional and business men of the North who have, *for the past thirty years or more,* formed a sort of liaison corps between the whites and blacks. (*12MBV,* 5; italics mine)

Both "talented tenth" and "mulatto leadership" are key words relating to the Negro race and the rise of the middle-class, black bourgeoisie and were probably familiar to the average reader of the 1940s, who would immediately conjure up a mental picture of W. E. B. Du Bois and his book *The Souls of Black Folk.* However, that reader might not have known that five years after that book's publication, America's next leading Negro writer and spokesperson was born into the lower class in 1908. The copyright page of *12MBV* indicates that Richard Wright is the writer of "text and captions" for this picture-word project. His power to name the object or interpret its meaning is not surprising, considering Wright's prestige as a writer with Marxist/Proletarian leanings. One assumes that Edwin Rosskam, the codirector, is responsible for the pictures. In the index, entitled "About the Photographs," Rosskam lists eighty-eight photographs, including their titles, photographers, and pictorial sites. To show his colleagiality with Wright, Rosskam does *not* include a photograph of Du Bois, a physical marker of the one who had impelled Wright to declare a class war against the "talented tenth." Nonetheless, Wright does "signify upon" W. E. B. Du Bois by calling out his name by indirection, according to the theory proffered by Henry Louis Gates Jr.[3] Wright places the burden on the reader to conjure up a mental picture of Du Bois, since no image appears in the volume.

There is another mode by indirection, however, to uncover Du Bois's absent image in *12MBV* and to expose the Du Bois/Wright, master/apprentice writer relationship. This link can be detected by means of semiotic theories of language related to photography. In "The Photographic Messages," Roland Barthes uses the press photograph to illustrate how pictures have linguistic substructures arising from the intersections of the sign (the

3. Henry Louis Gates Jr., *The Signifying Monkey: A Theory of Afro-American Literary Criticism* (New York: Oxford University Press, 1988) 106–10.

written or spoken word), the signifier (the image), and the signifieds (the meanings). He declares that the press photograph conveys two levels of messages, which he labels the "photographic paradox." The first level involves the literal or denotative structure that transmits a "message without a code." The figurative or second-order structure, he argues, emanates from the coded message or connotation, and this message depends upon the objects, their artistry, their treatments, and the writing or rhetoric (titles or captions) on the photograph. Says Barthes:

> Connotation is not necessarily immediately graspable at the level of the message itself (it is . . . at once invisible and active, clear and implicit) but it can already be inferred from certain phenomena which occur at the levels of production and reception of the message: on the one hand, the press photograph is an object that has been worked on, chosen, composed, constructed, treated according to professional, aesthetic, ideological norms which are so many factors of connotation, while on the other hand, this same photograph is not only perceived, received, it is *read* connected more or less consciously by the public that consumes it stock of signs.[4]

On the literal level, says Barthes, a press photograph is just a piece of paper with things such as "images or shadows" imprinted on it, thereby constituting a "message without a code." But at the figurative level, the photograph conveys a coded message to the receiver about its meaning. The icon, or signifier, has been "staged," meaning that it has been posed, treated, lighted, or inscribed by writing or rhetoric.

These dual levels of language constitute the picture/word structure of *12MBV* and, in particular, the manner by which Wright's words attain power at the secondary level of reinscription. Since the phrasing of the blurb with Rosskam's name in "About the Photographs" is parallel to that of Wright's text and captions, we can assume that Wright also wrote the blurb. In it, Wright states: "The photographs in this book—with the exception of a few otherwise credited—were selected from the files of the Farm Security Administration, U.S. Department of Agriculture." He also points out that "None of the photographs here reproduced was made for this book; they were taken by Farm Security photographers as they roamed the country during the past five years" (*12MBV*, 149). According to Wright, Rosskam incorporated eighty-two FSA, four non-FSA, and two personal pictures by Richard Wright and Louise Rosskam in the album. The FSA and non-FSA photographs taken by field photographers for both government and nongovernment agencies also were deliberately borrowed for this photo-text project. They function as Barthes's "press photographs";

4. Roland Barthes, "The Photographic Message," in *A Roland Barthes Reader*, ed. Susan Sontag (New York: Hill and Wang, 1982), 196, 199.

however, the two "personal" photographs by Wright and Louise Rosskam do not.

One press photograph is of particular interest, since it connotes the "twin-rooted" relationship between author and codirector, and parodies or signifies upon Du Bois's phrase as well as sections of his text. On page 104 of *12MBV*, Wright's personal photographic exhibit entitled "Sign, Brooklyn, New York" appears on the left, facing Rosskam's FSA reprint entitled "Entrance to an apartment house, Chicago, Illinois," on page 105. The twinned exhibits not only connote the Negro-Jewish alliance to fight racism during this era, but also some key rhetorical strategies germane to language, literature, and photography. Edwin Rosskam, it should be noted, had previous experience as a photojournalist, and his old FSA reprint on page 105 perfectly exemplifies the dual denotative and connotative levels of meanings according to Barthes's photographic paradox. On a literal level, the FSA picture is just a piece of paper conveying "traces" of objects. But on a secondary level, it has been staged or inscribed with writing or rhetoric to transmit a specific message to the viewer at the time of filming and captioning of this scene. This photograph appears in part 3, "Death on City Pavements," and connects image and text, the verbal and the visual, for it fits into a section in which Wright's text repeats the word *kitchenette* to connote squalid urban housing; meanwhile, Rosskam's picture, a physical signifier, is only one visual example among many. Wright's style of repetition illustrates his power with words and how it takes language to "describe" an image or object.[5]

It must be recalled, however, that Rosskam's photograph has been prestaged and preprinted for another project, but here it appears in a new context. In essence, this picture has been restaged, recontextualized, and recoded by language, Wright's venue, at the secondary level of connotation, acquiring new meanings in 1941. Rosskam's picture "Entrance to an apartment house, Chicago" illustrates also how this image functions as a connotator, a lexical unit housing a chain of meanings in its writing and rhetoric. On the one hand, it connotes the trope of autobiography relating to Rosskam's prior experience as a photographer for both the FSA and *Life* magazine during the 1930s. On the other hand, it connotes the trope of biography regarding Wright's knowledge of photojournalistic techniques popularized in the 1930s. The breadth of experience that each one brings to this verbal/visual project conforms to that of other photojournalist teams during this 1940s era of Wright's high visibility as the famous author of *Native Son*. Their combined autobiographical and biographical experiences connoted by Rosskam's Chicago picture on page 105 further indexes the rise of the photo-text genre inaugurated in 1888 by Jacob Riis, particularly

5. Roland Barthes, "Photographic Message," 98.

with his documentaries of urban slum life, *How the Other Half Lives* (1899) and *The Battle with the Slum* (1902).[6] Both releases coincided with the publication of Du Bois's sociological studies *The Philadelphia Negro* (1899) and *The Souls of Black Folk* (1903). Both Riis's and Du Bois's publications signify upon the rising social consciousness of whites and blacks in America as they focused on the dispossessed classes of Americans. Riis, especially, influenced the sudden popularization of documentary writing in the 1920s that also was extensively used as a genre by proletarian writers and photojournalists during the Great Depression, when Wright, a young Communist, was an aspiring writer. In 1940, the Wright-Rosskam team again reprised the photo-text genre, owing to Rosskam's recent experience as a photo-text editor and his proposal to Wright that they collaborate on a photo-text project specifically about "Negro life." Their acquisition of the New Deal's large bank of FSA and non-FSA pictures was not uncommon for documentary writers of this period. To illustrate, Wright acknowledges Arthur F. Raper and Ira De A. Reid's *Sharecropper's All* in his foreword, since the picture-word assemblage served as a model for *12MBV* (5).[7]

Nonetheless, the team's selection of *specific* photographs was inordinate and indicates Wright's guiding hand, although both Edwin Rosskam and Horace Cayton assisted him. For example, Rosskam's Chicago picture also connotes the team's behind-the-scene restaging techniques associated with photographic trick effects. The picture on page 105 is no accident in the structural formation of the photo text, even though Rosskam had inserted an exhibit of his work in a previous 1940 project on Native American life for Oliver LaFarge entitled *As Long as the Grass Shall Grow*. But Michel Fabre, Wright's biographer, reports that Wright and Rosskam had pictorial assignments for the project. It was Wright's task to provide a "For Rent" sign of a *Chicago* apartment house; however, one quickly notes that Wright's exhibit, on page 104, preceding Rosskam's, is entitled "Sign, Brooklyn, New York" in the index (*12MBV*, 152). This alteration of locations exemplifies how Wright, the controlling figure over text, captions, *and* photographic selections, obfuscates the distinctive relationships between an object, its name, and its meaning. Wright directs the team's effort, overtly or covertly, to recode Rosskam's prestaged press photograph (as well as the other exhibits) in order to provide a new context for an old meaning. The word *Chicago* designating the site of Rosskam's picture, for instance, connotes

6. Jacob A. Riis, *How the Other Half Lives*, ed. David Leviatin (1899; reprint, Boston: St. Martin's, 1996), 60; Jacob A. Riis, *The Battle with the Slum* (1902; reprint, Montclair, N.J.: Patterson Smith, 1969), 104.

7. Michel Fabre, *The Unfinished Quest of Richard Wright* (New York: William Morrow, 1973), 232. See also Arthur F. Raper, and Ira De A. Reid, *Sharecroppers All* (Chapel Hill: University of North Carolina Press, 1941).

the trope of biography linked to Wright's residence in Chicago from 1927 to 1937 after his relocation from the South.

For example, Wright acknowledges in his foreword and in his statement in "About the Photographs" the contributions of Horace R. Cayton, who authenticated the accuracy of Wright's textual statements and Rosskam's pictorial representations.[8] A Chicago sociologist, Cayton did not know Wright during the latter's hungry years of living in a Chicago kitchenette while struggling to become a writer. However, in his autobiography *Long Old Road*, Cayton notes that Wright later reminded him of their meeting at the University of Chicago while Cayton was serving as a research assistant to esteemed sociologist Louis P. Wirth, whom the young Wright had come to visit.[9] Ironically, Wright's social worker at the welfare agency came to be Mary Wirth, wife of the sociologist. Both Louis and Mary Wirth became Wright's invaluable friends because of his needs for government subsidies for his family and research data for his writings. Thus in his foreword, Wright names Wirth as a contributing sociologist, along with E. Franklin Frazier and Cayton.

Cayton's name, allied to Rosskam's picture, however, is what enables the reader to recover Du Bois's absent signifier/image and bring it just above the surface in *12MBV*. Cayton directly links Wright to Du Bois; he wrote a little-known, unpublished biography of Wright that was short-circuited by his untimely death from a heart attack while he was researching Wright's life in Paris. In 1970, Cayton had acquired a copy of a list of books Wright had checked out during his Chicago period from the George C. Hall Branch of the Chicago Public Library located on the South Side, where Wright lived.[10]

Between 1927 and 1937, Wright's reading list included *The Souls of Black Folk* and *The Philadelphia Negro* by Du Bois; three biographies on Frederick Douglass, by Charles W. Chestnutt (1899), F. M. Holland (1891), and Booker T. Washington (1907); two works by Washington, the autobiographical *My Larger Education: Being Chapters From My Experience* (1911) and the biographical *The Story of the Negro, the Rise of the Race from Slavery* (1909);

8. Horace R. Cayton, "Wright's Book More Than Just a Study of Social Status," in *Richard Wright: The Critical Reception,* ed. John M. Reilly (New York: Burt Franklin, 1978), 105.

9. Horace R. Cayton, *Long Old Road* (New York: Trident Press, 1964), 246.

10. Horace R. Cayton, "Richard Wright: Bibliography on Negro in Chicago," and "Richard Wright Biography," both in the Horace Cayton Files, Special Collections, Carter G. Woodson Public Library, Chicago, Illinois. Cayton was the coauthor with George S. Mitchell of *Black Workers and the New Union* (Chapel Hill: University of North Carolina Press, 1939), cited by Wright, and also coauthor with St. Clair Drake of *Black Metropolis: A Study of Negro Life in a Northern City,* rev. ed. (Chicago: University of Chicago Press, 1993).

the *Autobiography of Oliver Otis Howard* (1907); and E. Franklin Frazier's *The Negro Family in Chicago* (1932), which Wright masks when he switches to *The Negro Family in the United States* (1939) in his foreword (*12MBV*, 5). Hence, as late as 1940–1941, Wright parodies the trope of Du Bois the master writer in *Souls* when he revoices it as Wright the master writer in *12 Million Black Voices.*

However, Wright's sparring relationship with Du Bois had begun much earlier in his writing career, when Wright the apprentice writer was looking to Du Bois the master writer for guidance. Wright's reading of the autobiography of Oliver O. Howard during his years in Chicago extends the chain of signifieds related to Rosskam's picture to read temporally and spatially as "kitchenette; Richard Wright; Chicago; 1927–1937; Wirth; Cayton; George C. Hall Library; Du Bois, and *Souls.*" And by means of this latter text, *Souls* subsequently releases another chain of names and meanings to include Oliver O. Howard, Booker T. Washington, and Frederick Douglass as well as data pertinent to their writings and historical significances. In chapter 2 of *Souls*, "Of the Dawn of Freedom," Du Bois explains Howard's roles in the organizing of the Freedman's Bureau after the Civil War and then his establishing of schools for blacks. In recognition of his service as commissioner of the Freedmen's Bureau, Howard University in Washington, D.C., was named in his honor. He served as its president from 1869 to 1873 (*Souls*, 21).[11] In chapter 3, Du Bois also provides a full analysis of the social conditions enabling Booker T. Washington's rise to power (*Souls*, 34). Cayton's research directly links Wright, the past apprentice/present master writer, to *Souls*, and Rosskam's picture is a signifier of these biographical linkages. Wright's foreknowledge of Du Bois's sociological studies brings up the Du Boisian/Douglassian connections to the slave narrative in *12MBV.*

II. The Slave Narrative as a Trope of Revolution

The word *imitatio* should be added to the concealed inscriptions attached to Du Bois's name connoted by Rosskam's picture. Du Bois, too, practices linguistic techniques of parody by the revealing and concealing of his signifiers. In chapter 3 of *The Souls of Black Folk*, Du Bois speaks of "Frederick Douglass" as "the greatest of America's Negro leaders" because his political policies of "self-assertion" were the means by which blacks could assimilate into American culture and thereby acquire their human and civil rights (*Souls*, 39). It can be assumed that Du Bois, whose birth (1868) was closer to the eve of slavery and dawn of freedom than Wright's, and who

11. Gibson, notes to *Souls* (Penguin edition), 222.

won acclaim by being the first African American to earn a Ph.D. from Harvard University, would be more familiar with Douglass's life and autobiography. Conversely, however, Du Bois himself inserts no icon/object in *Souls* as a representation of the sign "Frederick Douglass" and its meaning of "self-assertive leader" in *Narrative of the Life of Frederick Douglass*. Instead, Du Bois signifies upon Douglass's "image" through indirection by citing the name of a "Lloyd" plantation in South Georgia that revoices the name of the Lloyd plantation where Douglass served as a house and field slave (*Souls*, 82). Douglass's narrative functions as an infrastructure of *Souls* and ultimately accounts for Du Bois's iconic representations of southern slave music in his work.

By indirection, Rosskam's signifier of "Entrance to an apartment house, Chicago" does project an "image" of both W. E. B. Du Bois and Frederick Douglass below the shadowy objects on the surface of picture 105, but their clear images are too deeply submerged for the average reader's eyes to see. And Wright alternately names or indirectly signifies upon words and other meanings relating to these absent pictures in counterpoint to Rosskam because Wright has imitated Du Bois's art of indirection.

For example, language theft connects Douglass and Du Bois to Wright. In Baltimore, Maryland, Douglass steals the master's language by learning clandestinely to write between the spaces of letters in his young master's school workbook (*Narrative*, 35). Du Bois then repeats but surpasses Douglass's mere copying by taking the art of stealth to a higher, intellectual level of competition. In Great Barrington, Massachusetts, he appropriates the master's language by taking all the academic prizes away from his white classmates (*Souls*, 10).[12] And Wright extends the deft craft one step further by stealing the master's words and Du Bois's and Douglass's expressions as well (*12MBV*, 40). His encoded message, once deconstructed to the lowest substructure of Rosskam's picture, reveals the practice of language theft among these black writers. The author's deft act of repetition by difference thereby pushes Frederick Douglass's image and his *Narrative* of 1845 to the forefront as the precursor model for both *Souls* and *12MBV*. Moreover, in its position as the exposed master narrative, Douglass's poem in the appendix entitled "Parody," his tropes of slave music and "voice," and his rhetorical modes pertinent to slavery discourse, are by extension more easily traceable as repetitions of sameness or difference in Du Bois's *Souls* and in Wright's *12MBV*. Ultimately, *12MBV* is a parodic, but modern, slave narrative.

In *From behind the Veil*, Robert Stepto makes several observations about

12. Du Bois, who graduated with high honors in a class of thirteen at Great Barrington High School, was encouraged to attend college by several of the white people in his western Massachusetts hometown; see Arnold Rampersad, *The Art and Imagination of W. E. B. Du Bois*, (New York: Schocken, 1990), 8–12.

the fluid nature of the slave narrative. On the one hand, it can be viewed as a "generic text" integrating forms such as autobiography, essay, fiction, or history. On the other hand, any one of these forms presented separately can function as an "authenticating narrative" for the basic slave narrative. Both representations illustrate the eclectic nature of the slave narrative. For example, Stepto contends that a "call-response" relationship exists between Douglass's precursor model and its response texts in different formats of essay, autobiography, fiction, or history by W. E. B. Du Bois and Booker T. Washington.[13] All three of these authors appear on Wright's reading list, and all three influenced his construction of *12MBV* as a slave narrative. This point becomes especially apparent when Frederick Douglass's text is positioned as the precursor model for responding texts by Du Bois and Wright.

Douglass's narrative of revolution (escape to freedom) is short—eighty pages including the appendix—but it nonetheless influences Du Bois's construction of *Souls* as an authenticating narrative revoicing Douglass's analysis of the South as the site of the Negro problem, the sociological conditions of slavery, and its dehumanizing effects upon Negroes. These tropes are evident when one notes the full title and subtitle of the 1903 edition of Du Bois's *The Souls of Black Folk: Essays and Sketches*. Du Bois's upgrading and revoicing of Douglass's slave narrative consists of a series of disparate essays concerning Du Bois's sociological studies of the Negro in the United States, in general, and the South, in particular, that are integrated by a musical score appearing as an epigraph to each chapter. Appropriately, the work incorporates various literary forms, thereby enabling it to function as a literary history of slavery not only from 1619 to 1900 but from as far back as continental African slavery, owing to Du Bois's narrative of family slavery. Also Du Bois's "Forethought" and "Afterthought" signify upon Douglass's preface/letter and his appendix.

On the other hand, Wright's slave narrative of *12MBV* is not only shorter than *Souls*—152 versus 164 pages (Norton edition; 217 in the Penguin edition)—but also simpler in having only four main divisions: part 1, "Our Strange Birth"; part 2, "Inheritors of Slavery"; part 3, "Death on City Pavements"; and part 4, "Men in the Making." Like Du Bois, Wright also conducts a sociohistorical analysis of the dehumanizing effects of slavery, the Negro problem in the United States that at this point is in both the South and the North, and the ontology of Negro identity as it is constructed in these regions. Wright's foreword, "tale," and "About the Photographs" simulate the Douglass/Du Bois slave narrative design.

13. Robert B. Stepto, *From behind the Veil: A Study of Afro-American Narrative*, 2d ed. (Urbana: University of Illinois Press, 1991), 4–5.

III. The South as a Site of the Negro Problem

Common to all three of these slave narratives, however, is the role of the narrator-speaker of the text. This aspect of narration concerning themes of time and space illuminates the slave worlds described by Douglass, Du Bois, and Wright. In "Space, Ideology, and Literary Representation," W. J. T. Mitchell reminds us of the functions of time and space in their oppositional representations as narration/description, animus/corpus, life/death, soul/body, spirit/flesh, dynamism/stasis, and so on. He says, "Space is static, visual, external, empty, corporeal and dead. It is only redeemed from these essential, natural conditions by some intervention or violence; it must be pushed into motion, temporalized, internalized, filled up, or brought to life by time and consciousness."[14] Time is associated with life, consciousness, and movement, and space is associated with death, corporeality, and stasis in picture-word theories. And because of his parodies of both Du Bois and Douglass, Wright inserts these contradictions in *12MBV* owing to his revoicing of their slave narrative techniques.

Douglass, for example, illustrates the liveness or animus associated with time as he constructs his autobiography in chronological sequence beginning with his southern birth, undated but circa 1818; escape from the South to the North in 1838; residence in the North and discovery as an abolitionist speaker in 1841; and final remarks as the successful orator, author, and narrator of his *Narrative* in 1845. As the escaped slave narrator of the present, he speaks predominantly in the first person in order to provide an eyewitness account of slavery for his targeted white audience. On the other hand, he presents his life as a representation of the southern slave experience endured by others who are still captive or less articulate. Douglass construes his testimony as a collective experience that is central to the group identity of the slave community. At one point in his narrative, he speaks about his involvement in leading a slave plot with five other men. This event occurs before the eyes of the reader, who observes the evolution of Young Fred from a nimble survivor on the streets of Baltimore to the seventeen-to-twenty-year-old fieldhand on the eastern shore. Though "broken in" by an infernal system, Douglass vowed to escape down "the pathway from slavery to freedom" (*Narrative*, 29). In forging a bond of love with his fellows, he speaks of a year's experience as a fieldhand and a leader of a conspiracy, and he describes his social relationship with them as "we were one" (56). Through this perception of oneness, Douglass identifies himself as a member of a collective body of slaves, and this membership justifies his election

14. W. J. T. Mitchell, "Space, Ideology, and Literary Representation," *Poetics Today* 10 (spring 1989): 93.

by abolitionists as a cultural spokesperson for and collective consciousness of the black race whenever Douglass asserts his predominant first-person-singular "I" or uses his rare "we."

In parodying Douglass, Du Bois, the sociohistorian, invokes his pre-decessor's alternating I/we, personal/collective consciousness. In assem-bling his essays as a unified literary history of slavery, Du Bois alternates between minimal autobiographical accounts, of his teaching experiences (chapter 4) and the death of his firstborn (chapter 9), in order to mag-nify his predominant biographical accounts, of a race (chapter 1) and of individuals (chapters 12 and 13). Although using this first-person, autobi-ographical "I" or third-person, biographical "he," Du Bois often takes his narrative cues from Douglass and amplifies the "we," the collective expe-rience of the enslaved Negro (*Souls*, 15). His sociological study of slavery in the South concerns that collective "we," inclusive of the problems of the enslaved, freed, and reenslaved Negro in the South as well as in the North of the United States. Between chapters 1 and 8, for instance, Du Bois examines the history of slavery from its African roots through its American practice, from 1619 to 1900, supporting his dates with immense statistical data. His study focuses on the South, and particularly southern Georgia, in chapters 7 and 8. In these two chapters, which were adapted from a "long article" previously published in *The World's Work*,[15] he covers narra-tive time from Old South slavery to Emancipation and concludes with the post-Reconstruction era, 1900. Du Bois uses a different alternating I/we narrative technique because he is accompanied by a traveling companion (who remains unidentified) and asserts this duality when he says, "Out of the North the train thundered, and we woke to see the crimson soil of Georgia stretching away." (*Souls*, 74).

Du Bois reports his personal research trip in these two chapters, during which he is additionally accompanied by a "talkative little storekeeper" who is his local guide (88). Du Bois, an outsider, a middle-class educator, differs from the lower-class Negro subjects of his study in outlook and orientation. Yet Du Bois claims his cultural identity in the "we" slave expe-rience by way of his matrilineal heritage of African slavery, which he relays in chapter 14, and by means of his common ties to the folk as a grassroots teacher in Tennessee, which he describes in chapter 4. Both of these per-sonal experiences justify Du Bois's "outsider-within" status as signified by his metaphor of "the Veil" that enables him to identify with his grassroots subjects although he comes from higher, middle-class leanings. Hence, these southern slave and neoslave experiences validate Du Bois's claims of having compassion for the "folk" of his study. But, unlike Douglass, Du

15. David Levering Lewis, *W. E. B. Du Bois: Biography of a Race, 1868–1919* (New York: Henry Holt, 1993), 285.

Bois injects a separateness of narrative perspective as he switches points of view throughout these two chapters from that of his personal, first-person, "I" viewpoint of outsider, tourist, and researcher to that of an insider, first-person "we" perspective drawn firsthand from the voices of these fellow victims of slavery. Du Bois's symbiotic chapters not only structurally mimic Douglass's narrative techniques, but also prefigure Wright's parody of his style in like manner.

Wright, by repetition and difference, suppresses his "I" personal voice implied by photographic exhibits 104 and 105, but he noticeably opts only for speaking in the first-person-plural of "we." By using this narrative strategy, he inverts Douglass's predominant "I" and magnifies his minimalist "we" references instead. As such, Wright, like Du Bois, is attempting to update the history of American slavery by beginning his review on the shores of seventeenth-century Africa, then extending his study beyond Du Bois's closing date of 1900, and concluding his observations on current neoslavery in America at 1941. Therefore, Wright, too, provides a sociological study of the Negro problem in the United States. He gives an analysis of the dehumanizing social conditions in the South and in the North, speaking in the collective "we" as the authoritative guide and fellow victim of slavery for the reader "touring" his verbal and visual slave narrative. Wright also organizes his text by region, with parts 1 and 2 pertaining to the South and parts 3 and 4 pertaining to the North, parodying the regional tropes established by Du Bois and Douglass. Using Du Bois's statistical data as a guide, he directs his focus on the South and also provides a historical analysis of past and present slavery in parts 1 and 2. In scene after scene, he displays familiar images of Negro fieldhands at work: plowing, picking cotton, facing the bosses, or recuperating in their cabins. These conditions culminate in Negro unrest and the black migration from farm to city. Wright says in Du Boisian language: "From 1890 to 1920, more than 2,000,000 of us left the [southern] land" (*12MBV*, 89). Du Bois records in chapter 8 the 1880–1900 movement from country village to town as the "rush" to migrate (*Souls*, 99).

Wright's dual position as present speaker and past actor throughout *12MBV* and specifically in parts 1 and 2 speaks to other complex distinctions of time and space in the narrative. Following patterns of Douglass and Du Bois, Wright presents himself as occupying an intermediate position between past slavery and present neoslavery. As the *"living* past living in the present," or living narrator speaking about the past (the dead), Wright shows that it takes the mobile qualities of life, animus, and the "violence" of his consciousness to enliven the deadness of space associated with corporeality, the external, and the dead (*12MBV*, 146). As such, the subjects that Wright presents to his audience through verbal imagery or iconic representation are literally, denotatively, the "resurrected" dead, and yet mere "shadows" or "traces" on paper.[16] It takes the consciousness of "living" time, the present, to enliven the inertia of space, the dead of the past. In picture-word theory, the photograph signifies this pastness, this deadness, and verbal, descriptive imagery serves a similar function of spatial reimaging of deadness. In *12MBV,* Wright illustrates how the verbal and visual imagery of space metaphorically enslaves time in a "stilled, stilling movement" of time and creates an ekphrastic juncture in which the "mute picture speaks" through the consciousness of the voice of time—the metaphorical cultural spokesperson.[17] Wright has assumed his position as the "voice of time" owing to his borrowing of the phrase from Du Bois and his application of it to photography (*12MBV,* 147). But Du Bois, while using his phrase of the "voice of Time" to describe human art in contrast to nature's sounds, illustrates his consciousness of contemporary poetical techniques of ekphrasis in which space intersects with and slows down time to a still, stilling movement, thereby causing the "mute picture to speak" (*Souls,* 50).[18] This "speaking picture" derives from Douglass's strategy of depicting timeless "slave time" in continuous "slave space."

For instance, Douglass functions dually as narrator of the present and actor of the past that he describes. As the distanced, escaped northern narrator, he resorts to his memory of his southern slave past. He does so in chapter 1, demonstrating the power of words to "describe" and thus to enslave time, in order to show the continuing horror of timeless, unending slave life and its brutal sociological conditions. He starts his narrative on unnumbered time, noting his birth without citing a date, which, consequently, forces the reader to concentrate on the illicit union of a white master with his slave mother, Harriet Bailey. Between birth and the age of about seven, when he physically moved from the country, Tuckahoe County, Maryland, to the city of Baltimore, his narrative reflects the "stilled, stilling movement" of timeless slave life. Douglass proceeds to describe his position in the context of space and how his chattel identity at birth had been preordained by white society. He was deigned subhuman property and treated accordingly, complete with the denial of maternal bonding that caused his dysfunctional detachment from his siblings and kinsmen. His struggle as a socially constructed slave child was to survive the daily terror of living under constantly punitive conditions. Douglass first broadly positions the "site" of his birth in context of the Upper South state

16. Roland Barthes, "Rhetoric of the Image," in *Image, Text, Music,* ed. Stephen Heath (New York: Hill and Wang, 1977), 32.

17. Murray Krieger, "The Ekphrastic Principle and the Still Movement of Poetry; or, *Laokoön* Revisited," in *The Play and Place of Criticism* (Baltimore: Johns Hopkins Press, 1967), 107–9.

18. Jean Hagstrum, *The Sister Arts: The Tradition of Literary Pictorialism in English Poetry from Dryden to Gray* (Chicago: University of Chicago Press, 1948), 20.

of Maryland and then narrows the point of his study to Tuckahoe County, twelve miles from the township of Easton. He illuminates how systemic racism, oppression, and slavery operate by attaching their meanings more specifically to the "country village setting" of his birth, the huge manorial holdings of Colonel Edward Lloyd (*Narrative*, 16–20). Contrasting with this opulent country manor, he describes his early years as a dehumanized, underfed, ill-clothed house slave, tended by a "mammy" (his grandmother) in infancy, and then, as a young child slave, being processed into such work as herding cows or acting as playmate to the master's young son.

In the four pages of chapter 2, Douglass provides detailed descriptions of how the southern slave manor operated through a chain of judicial commands from the master on downward to his sloop operators. The orders extended by reduction to the overseers, with each white ruler administering a form of discipline and punishment to keep the slaves controlled. At this home seat of government, slaves got their monthly rations of food or yearly rations of clothing, work assignments or sales, and administrations of punishments. The home seat also had its central operations manned by slaves performing jobs such as blacksmithing, weaving, shoemaking, and so on (*Narrative*, 18). Douglass's analysis includes examples of slaves enduring beatings, being deprived of food and clothing, performing assigned domestic or agrarian labor according to house or field status, and experiencing the limits of their mobility according to slave laws. The Lloyd Plantation is a southern slave "business," according to Douglass. He also introduces the trope of "two-in-one" when he discusses how the physical layout of the opulent, one-thousand-slave Lloyd Plantation sets up class distinctions between house and field slaves. These class divisions between the twenty-two outfarms and central Great House Farm account for the dual symbolism innate to the single-owner manorial plantation that influences Du Bois's thinking.

Du Bois, too, functions as the dual narrator of the present and actor of the past that he describes in *Souls*. Like Douglass, Du Bois resorts to memories of his earlier trip to Dougherty County, Georgia, which he relays in chapters 7 and 8. He demonstrates here his German education and knowledge of theories of the doppelgänger or "double" that preceded modern psychology.[19] These two chapters function as one "twin-rooted unit," mirroring Douglass's description of the Lloyd manor's home base/outfarm dual network. Du Bois also appropriates the "fieldhand" symbolism from Douglass's experiences and makes this labor class the major subject of his twin chapters. Du Bois, in effect, expands Douglass's limited experiences as a field laborer. In chapters 7 and 8, Du Bois temporally begins where

19. Lewis, *Biography of a Race*, 282.

Douglass ends his text in 1845. He verbally "fills in" the historical gap between slave time and emancipated time in order to expose, through his lower-class labor subject, the debilitating effects of slavery on each generation of black people. He also shifts the slave site of study about ongoing neoslavery from Douglass's Tuckahoe County, Maryland, to his own state of residence and the specific target area of Dougherty County, Georgia, the capital of the Cotton Kingdom.

For example, Du Bois starts chapter 7 by reminding his reader that "360 years ago," early Spaniards wandered the lands of Georgia. Riding in the Jim Crow car of the train, Du Bois makes his reader aware of his movement through space. He connotes his consciousness of time's passage by remarking upon names of cities or noting their settlements by race. He tells his reader when the train passes the land of the Cherokees below Atlanta and leaves the red clay and pines of North Georgia, describing the changes in color as the "world grows darker" in racial makeup below Macon. He dubs Albany the "heart of the Black Belt." But in observing his target of research, Dougherty County, he describes it in general-to-specific terms like Douglass, remarking that it is "two hundred miles South of Atlanta, two hundred miles west of the Atlantic Ocean, and one hundred miles west of the Great Gulf, . . . [and] contains ten thousand Negroes and two thousand whites" (*Souls*, 76). Providing dense statistics surpassing Douglass, Du Bois then introduces the rhetoric of stasis germane to the region and associated with the stillness of slave time. He begins by describing Dougherty County as once being the "Egypt of the Confederacy," when cotton was King in the 1860s, and then proceeds to connect its past with its present by dubbing it the "center of the Negro Problem."[20] Georgia was a major slave state, renowned for its importation of fifty thousand African slaves, of which some two thousand had come from Virginia—the Upper South. But, out of all of Georgia's regions, Dougherty County is the most infamous for its unrelenting, timeless slave and neoslave practices (*Souls*, 75–77, 81).

Using time as a symbol not only for stasis (regional stagnation) and kinesis (movement by transport) during his train ride from Atlanta to Dougherty County via Albany, Du Bois next brings his reader with him on a tour of Dougherty's Negro population. In *Double-Consciousness/Double Bind*, Sandra Adell observes that Du Bois's "descent into the Black Belt describes a symbolic space that would later become very important for writers like Jean Toomer, Zora Neale Hurston, and Toni Morrison."[21] This

20. Also compare the observations of Carrie Cowherd on the "Egypt of the Confederacy" in this volume, "The Wings of Atalanta: Classical Influences in *The Souls of Black Folk*."

21. Sandra Adell, *Double-Consciousness/Double Bind* (Chicago: University of Chicago Press, 1994), 21.

remark is true in terms of Du Bois's contact with the folk. He announces the start of his tour in the context of time when he says, "Finally we started. It was about ten in the morning, bright with a faint breeze, and we jogged leisurely southward in the valley of the Flint" (*Souls*, 78). Over two days, he travels by carriage southward; he turns west along the county lines where one can see the hills of Baker, turns at the western boundaries of Dougherty County and goes northward, turns northwest, and finally turns eastward back to lodging (*Souls*, 80, 87). As the tour progresses *temporally*, Du Bois registers an immediate change from optimism to depression as he observes the timelessness of slave time still informing the county. He views scene after scene of phantom gates, dilapidated slave cabins, abandoned, gutted big houses, failing crops, and dispossessed, poor Negroes. Time slows to a stilled, barely discernible movement when Du Bois stops to visit with a fieldhand and his family.

In this chapter Du Bois also provides direct accounts of his interactions with rural and town neoslave community members. Instead of paraphrasing or diluting the words of his agrarian subjects, he allows their "pictures to speak" in first-person testimonies. Although Du Bois engages in a dialogue with a local during an informal interview, he generally provides a one-sided "picture" by focusing only on their responses to his inquiries. In essence, he stages his pictures like a photographer, and in the process, artistically treats the desired "image" by foregrounding the fieldhand subject as well as the family. By excising his own portrait, Du Bois acquires the desired "picture" in which the interview subject directly recounts his own experiences of poverty and suffering rather than having them translated through Du Bois's expressions. Oddly, while Du Bois the data-gatherer notes the labor production of women and children under his gaze, he does not elaborate upon their gender or age differences, even in chapter 8, during which Du Bois examines the variety of jobs performed by fieldhands in his effort to classify them according to income level. Invariably, Du Bois's study focuses on male subjects because of the historian's precise interest in updating the labor experiences of his model, Frederick Douglass.

In fact, Douglass is never far from Du Bois's thoughts. In chapter 7, he revisits Douglass's life by taking his reader to a version of the old Lloyd Plantation, in a Deep South setting and showing the ravages of time, post-Emancipation, with the change of ownership and white flight. Just like the parks and groves of Douglass's Maryland plantation, this Georgia plantation, Du Bois muses, reflects the debacle that occurred when the "masters moved to Macon and Augusta, and left only the irresponsible overseers on the land" (*Souls*, 82). Du Bois perceives an estate, the "Lloyd 'home-place' "—a ghost of Douglass's past—as a site of "ruin." By Du Bois's description, it seemingly vies in size with the large plantation holdings of Douglass's era:

> . . . great waving oaks, a spread of lawn, myrtles and chestnuts, all ragged and wild; a solitary gate-post standing where once was a castle entrance; an old rusty anvil lying amid rotting bellows and wood in the ruins of a blacksmith shop; a wide rambling old mansion, brown and dingy, filled now with the grandchildren of the slaves who once waited on its tables; while the family of the master has dwindled to two lone women, who live in Macon and feed hungrily off the remnants of an earldom. So we ride on. . . . (*Souls,* 82–83)

As with many other cases cited by Du Bois, the remnants of the earldom have passed from absent landlord and master to the present neoslave occupants.

For Wright, revisiting cultural memory through the lives of Douglass and Du Bois is important in terms of his own reconstruction of history through time and space. He, too, uses the trope of the timelessness of slave time in order to report unchanging, transhistorical slave conditions in his southern section of *12MBV*. In parts 1 and 2, "Our Strange Birth" and "Inheritors of Slavery," Wright appends fifty-two of the total eighty-eight pictures with verbal descriptions that replicate Du Bois's verbal and visual stylistics. Du Bois also had inserted physical icons signifying corporeality in *Souls*, choosing musical emblems of printed slave music before chapters. However, Du Bois leaves off the names of the songs conveyed by the bars of music, although he explains their names and meanings in chapter 14, "The Sorrow Songs." The musical icons work in the same manner as Wright's pictures accompanying his written text. In chapter 14, Du Bois cites the title for chapter 7 as "Bright Sparkles," which he describes as a "maze-like medley" and a "primitive" song (158); for chapter 8, he identifies the melody as an unknown Negro folk song (157–58). These songs, though distant by time from slavery and the images of suffering slaves they capture, still anchor thematically the subject matter discussed in the chapters they introduce. In chapter 7, Du Bois portrays Dougherty County as still vested in primitive slave customs; in chapter 8, he provides a close-up view of this "Negro peasant life" led by the typical fieldhand.

Wright's parodying and expanding of Du Bois's chapters 7 and 8 can be recovered, first, by tracking the method by which Wright replicates Du Bois's verbal and visual style of foregrounding his southern subjects while simultaneously excising his own image. The technique used by Du Bois goes back to Douglass. To comprehend Wright's revoicing strategies does, however, require acknowledgment of Wright's skill with photographic techniques. For example, Wright and Rosskam reprise Douglass's broad/narrow trope, distinguishing Maryland the state from the Upper South region, and Tuckahoe County's specific locale near the township of Easton. Wright and Rosskam recapitulate this paradigm by using photographic trick effects that connect language and photography. In Wright's blurbs in the foreword and "About the Photographs," he uses descriptive language to convey how he and Rosskam adopted the poses of 1930s field photographers in the process of taking pictures with a wide-to-narrow-angle telephoto camera. Starting in his foreword, Wright adapts the wide-angle pose when he states that "This text, while purporting to render a *broad picture* of . . . Negro life in the United States, intentionally does not" (italics mine). Then, in "About the Photographs," Wright uses opposite terminology to describe how Rosskam achieved a vertical perspective by tilting the camera. Wright says, "The photographs in this book . . . form *part* of a document on contemporary America which at this writing has reached a *total of 65,000 pictures*" (*12MBV*, 5, 149; italics mine). With the conjoining of Wright's wide, horizontal shot with Rosskam's narrow, vertical view, their dual perspectives intersect to form a cross.

At this junction, Wright and Rosskam replicate Du Bois's technique of cropping or foregrounding his southern subjects while omitting his own image. Wright and Rosskam, however, use this strategy as a weapon against Du Bois. The moment the team intersects at the cross, they simultaneously zoom in on their combined, central image of the Negro peasant captured in their telephoto lenses' "stenope"—the little hole "through which the [camera] operator looks, limits, frames, and perspectives the object."[22] Then Wright and Rosskam switch their lenses to wide-angle, horizontal shots of this particular Negro proletariat, in order to achieve a "*broad picture* of the entire" Negro peasant class in the southern (as well as northern) United States. While snapping their shutters on the Negro peasant, the team simultaneously crops the image of Du Bois and his middle-class disciples from the combined picture by using Du Bois's own strategy to erase himself from vision. The team's recapitulation of the verbal and visual strategies of both Douglass and Du Bois now captures the image of Du Bois's and Douglass's fieldhand subject, who signifies upon the multifaceted portraits of his lower-class, southern community and its conditions circa 1900. This past-time emphasis seemingly contradicts Wright and Rosskam's purpose of including up-to-date textual data as well as FSA and other pictures dating from the last five years up to "current times." Wright and Rosskam deliberately illuminate the nonprogressive nature and stillness of neoslave time circa 1890–1900 in order to dismantle myths of Negro progress implied by their recent images taken between 1936 and 1941.

To show the stillness of slave and neoslave times, Wright, too, opens his narrative with the human subject instead of the landscape, parodying

---

22. Roland Barthes, *Camera Lucida: Reflections on Photography* (New York: Hill and Wang, 1981), 10.

Douglass and Du Bois by naming part 1 "Our Strange Birth." Douglass had not described his physical image except once, in relating the story of his being discovered as the leader of a slave conspiracy. Mrs. Freeland, the wife of the Maryland plantation owner to whom Douglass was hired, points out his strangeness. She feeds the other captured conspirators, whom he had led astray, but refers to Douglass as *"You devil! You yellow devil!"* implicating Douglass's mulatto skin coloring and mixed-race heritage as the cause of Douglass's mental aberrancy and rebelliousness (*Narrative*, 60). To correct Mrs. Freeland's misrepresentation of Douglass as a social deviant, Du Bois calls out the name of Frederick Douglass, bestowing on him black culture's connotation of "the greatest of American Negro leaders" (39). And, to pay additional tribute to black America's cultural hero, Du Bois then inserts a landscape "image" of a Lloyd plantation in Dougherty County. Du Bois, by allusion, transfers Douglass's "spirit" of enslavement to the Deep South site, to illustrate the timelessness of Douglass's slave experience as the contemporary sufferings of Deep South blacks. Black progress has been minuscule or arrested in Dougherty County. For example, before arriving at this site, Du Bois recalls meeting a rare farmer in South Georgia whom he describes as a "tall bronzed man" with a "sober face that smiles gravely." Du Bois surmises that he "walked too straight to be a tenant" farmer (*Souls*, 79), and notes that he owns a neat cottage, a store, a gin mill, and 240 acres of land. He is a rarity, for on the next page, Du Bois recounts meeting a more typical fieldhand. He describes encountering a "kindly old man, black, white-haired, and seventy," who had spent the last forty-five years eking out a living and who had now become destitute and a charity case (*Souls*, 80). Here is an aged fieldhand left over from Douglass's era, one who has never known economic freedom.

To emphasize and illuminate the demeaning effects of neoslavery and its relentless and timeless hold on southern black laborers, Wright and Rosskam attack the evil of miscegenation. To do so, Wright returns to Douglass and Du Bois to create a surreal portrait using trick effects conjoining words with pictures. He first draws upon Mrs. Freeland's description of Douglass as a "yellow devil" for use in his section pertaining to southern life and its peculiarities of black and white sexual relations. Wright begins part 1 with a frontispiece showing a partial human subject, a portrait of a decapitated, fair-skinned man in overalls who is holding a hoe. On the following page, he depicts the enlarged head of a dark-skinned, white-haired old man. Du Bois's two seemingly unrelated pictorial representations now become a "twin-rooted," body/head shot of a white/black man in Wright's text to show the "still unimaginable," the surreal "monstrous" personage created by the master's rape of his black female slave. Wright's critics have charged him and Rosskam with sloppy editing because the decapitated sharecropper is a white man.[23] However, Wright and Rosskam deliberately chose and placed the body of a white man as foreground to the image of the enlarged Negro head on the next page to illustrate the dilution of the "pure," dark-skinned African who originally fell into American slavery. Douglass, the mulatto, represents the diluted, aberrant product of illicit sex.

In part 1, Wright also points out the long-term effects of this initial sexual violation as being among a chain of transcendent aberrancies extant in American culture today, which still were motivating white society's racial treatment of Negroes in 1941. Wright says, "We black men and women in America today, as we look back upon scenes of rapine, sacrifice, and death, seem to be children of a devilish aberration, descendants of an interval of nightmare in history." Below, he anchors his statement with a picture of a teenage male, again signifying upon Douglass, by way of Wright's choice of the word *devilish* and his insertion of a picture of a black youth as its Douglassian, Satanic representation (*12MBV*, 17, 27).

By revoicing portions of the texts of Douglass and Du Bois, Wright also makes transhistorical thematic links composing the multifaceted life and personality of "the Negro" for a contemporary white audience unfamiliar with the lives of African Americans. Wright turns to epistemological theories of Douglass and Du Bois deriving from studies of the fieldhand subject. Remarking upon Douglass's opening page and Du Bois's chapter 1, Wright starts his first scene in *12MBV* with the argument that the first element of "the Negro problem" is rape, and then makes a visual indictment of hegemony, master/slave relations, white male power, Negro subordination, and the bottom-rung powerlessness of black women to exert control over their bodies. To help his naive, contemporary white reader to "know" the "Negro" and the monstrous, biracial human product begat by errant slavery, Wright delves into philosophy, inserting the trope of epistemology, the "knowing" of a subject as addressed by Douglass and Du Bois (*12MBV*, 10–11, 30). Douglass, the escaped slave narrator, had initially inserted this trope of epistemology in context of his remembrances of slave music as a representation or signifier of the dehumanizing conditions of slave life. In doing so he provided an example of a two-line refrain of a sorrowful song frequently sung by fieldhands in transit from the outfarms to the home seat: "I am going away to the Great House Farm! / O, yea! O, yea! O!" (*Narrative*, 19). Douglass attaches an epistemological meaning to the lyrics, which he allies to the collective history of Negro slavery as well as to his own condition: "To those songs I trace my first glimmering conception of the dehumanizing character of slavery." And as a member "within

23. Smith, "Image, Text, and Voice," 14; see also William Stott, *Documentary Expression and Thirties America* (New York: Oxford University Press, 1973), 30.

the circle" of slavery, Douglass recalls arriving at a meaning in context of his social position as a slave among other captive peoples:

> They told a tale of woe which was then altogether beyond my feeble comprehension; they were tones loud, long, and deep; they breathed the prayer and complaint of souls boiling over with the bitterest anguish. Every tone was a testimony against slavery, and a prayer to God for deliverance from chains. The hearing of those wild notes always depressed my spirit, and filled me with ineffable sadness. I have frequently found myself in tears while hearing them. (*Narrative*, 19)

Douglass attributes the discursive formation of the spirituals to the "soul-killing effects of slavery" (*Narrative*, 19). He provides the reason for Du Bois's enlargement of Douglass's historical study of the Negro problem and slavery by beginning his study in the United States at 1619 and ending it in his own present time of 1903. Douglass also provides the rationale as to why Wright repeats but varies the pattern by extending his timelines to Africa, pre-1619, and to America, in 1941. Both Du Bois and Wright were seeking new ways to educate their white audiences about "the Negro problem." To do so, Du Bois appropriates and then updates Douglass's epistemological statement about the "soul-killing effects of slavery" to current times. One reason for Du Bois's tour is that he discerns a gap emerging between his educated "talented tenth," whom he sees as the solution to the Negro problem, and the submerged, lower-class fieldhand of his study. Moreover, Du Bois envisions the few leading the many, for he tells his reader that one can only learn about such a racial-social problem by means of "intimate contact with the masses, and not by wholesale arguments covering millions in time and space, and differing widely in training and culture" (*Souls*, 90). Du Bois is responding to the quandary of time as an ever-changing trope.

Previously, Douglass, as preeminent American Negro leader, had addressed the nation in hindsight in his riveting "What to the Slave Is the Fourth of July?" speech, delivered in Rochester, New York, on July 5, 1852. He asserted that "We have to do with the past only as we can make it useful to the present and the future" (*Narrative*, 123). Inside slave history (the "within-the-circle" reaction), Douglass indicates that his ability to comprehend reality becomes so stunted by the sufferings of himself and other slaves that his capacity to fathom a free world of kindness from a surreal world of barbarity is subsequently warped (*Narrative*, 19). Only as a person removed from his own pain is Douglass able to develop a theory of temporal distinctions as exemplified by his Fourth of July speech. Du Bois not only responds to the issue of temporality raised in Douglass's benchmark speech, but also engages the idea of a useable past. Hence, Du Bois the outsider embarks on a tour to assess the economic and social growth of the Negro firsthand, and thereby he rejects the limited stereotypes of criminal, idolatrous, and contented Negroes in the past as informing the current image of millions of neoslaves in the present. Du Bois, instead, is only concerned with the improvements of the Negro within the present-ness and futurity of that past. His preoccupation with Negro progress, in large part, explains Du Bois's emphasis on the present and the rationale behind his visit to Dougherty County. He intends to gauge Negro progress and uncover the reasons for the widening gap emerging between the lettered and unlettered.

Wright rejects Du Bois's class snobbery and goes directly to the heart of Douglass's epistemological statement about the "soul-killing effects of slavery" and gauges his interrogation on the sociological problems of the Negro fieldhand at the depths of society. This lower-class subject is the reason that Wright follows his reconstructed white body/black head arrangement with a general overview of three hundred years of slavery that is supported by visual shots of the 1936–1941 Negro in a variety of servant's uniforms: "the black maid," "the black industrial worker," "the black stevedore," "the black dancer," "the black waiter," and "the black sharecropper" (*12MBV*, 18–23). He repeats the definite article, creating a drumming "syntactical concatenation" of sounds familiar to the modern viewer, North and South, that corroborates their assumptions about the visual objects of the uniformed Negro servants that the words confirm.[24] But Wright is only creating a photographic illusion for his reader, for next he warns that beneath these familiar garments "lies an uneasily tied knot of pain and hope whose snarled strands converge from many points of time and space" (*12MBV*, 11). This rootedness in past time and space is the reason that Wright, contrary to Du Bois, sees the past of slavery in the present of modern neoslavery, and he proceeds to recall that past in Douglass's lower-class slave world, beyond its representation in Du Bois's 1898–1900 time frame. Wright synthesizes both Douglass's slave and Du Bois's neoslave accounts in order to write the futurity of the time in which he inhabits. Wright purposefully makes his contemporary readers feel discomfort, beginning with the monstrous body/head image, presented first in order to destroy his audience's assumptions about the word *Negro*—its image and its alleged meanings.

In part 2, especially, Wright and Rosskam provide images of the Negro slave community in the broad context of the whole southern region, not narrowed to the county level as in the case of Du Bois. In addition, they expand gender and age representations in their verbal and visual representations. Wright's southern terrain upon which the freed slave was released includes "Arkansas, Missouri, Tennessee, Kentucky, North Carolina, South

24. Barthes, "Photographic Message," 203–4.

Carolina, Louisiana, Alabama, Mississippi, Georgia, Virginia, and West Virginia" (*12MBV*, 36), all of which had been referred to by Du Bois throughout *Souls*. Wright's southern landscape, nonetheless, still revoices elements of the antebellum and postbellum plantation landscapes of his models and reflects the unchanged, rigorous house and field work and the sparse leisure activities of slaves and neoslaves.

Moreover, Wright constructs their activities in the context of Douglass's formerly intact plantations of slave times and Du Bois's abandoned southern lands and Big Houses of the 1890s that characterized the migration of Negroes from country to town. Wright's text on page 36 regards this altered topography of the New South, and on the opposite page he flashes a transcendent picture of a "mammy" figure sitting on the porch of a timeless, dilapidated neoslave cabin to reinforce his assertions. The image of women cotton pickers in part 1 reflects the illusion of time passing but points to unchanged time in part 2, which depicts the image of an elderly couple sitting in front of a sharecropper's cabin as the frontispiece. These pictures of Douglass's timeless slave world, unidentified by state, are images that Du Bois also found in Dougherty County, and Wright recapitulates them in his neoslave photographic text.

For the reader/viewer, the image of the Negro fieldhand is the means by which to extrapolate meanings of and visual representations for "the Negro" that connects Wright to Douglass and Du Bois. Slave music, on the other hand, provides a concise, thematic approach. Douglass, in chapter 2 of his *Narrative*, Du Bois, in chapters 7 and 8 of *Souls*, and Wright, in parts 1 and 2 of *12MBV*, all interrogate this issue in their efforts to explain how the Negro, in spite of continuous disfranchisement, is able to sustain a modicum of hope or sense a glimmer of freedom while living in a captive state in America.

IV. Slave Music as a Coping or Liberating Device

For Douglass, Du Bois, and Wright, slave music in its temporal or transhistorical repetitions and transformations, and its capacity as a revolutionary tool, offers both solace for and a solution to the Negro problem. However, these three race leaders do not necessarily agree on the methodology or approach to the solution. It is thus understandable that Wright, being the son of an illiterate sharecropper and avowed Marxist in 1941, would disagree with Du Bois's bourgeois class ties and "talented tenth" platform of privileging the upwardly educated few to lead the multitude of the masses. His response to Du Bois on the first page of *12MBV* makes Wright's position clear regarding their class differences. But it is surprising that Wright also quarrels with his hero, mentor, and fieldhand guide, Douglass. The reasons for Wright's class war, even against Douglass, stem from Wright's different definitions of literacy and education as the answer for the Negro problem of inequity. The rhetoric of slave music does tie Wright to Douglass and Du Bois, but Wright's valuation of slave music in its normal secular and sacred manifestations takes on a whole new dimension. There is a common agreement on political discourse among Douglass, Du Bois, and Wright. But Wright's stance is that slave music must evince a more politicized text in the stead of the earliest primitive and pre-literate slaves forcefully removed to America who immediately commenced to plot revolution. Wright's message is not easily detected, however, and must be decoded like a "maze medley" slave song with all of its hidden connotations.

In fact, it is the paradoxical quality of slave music with its dual meanings that enabled slave composers, singers, and auditors to plot insurrections, even if they were not successful. For example, at the end of part 2, "Inheritors of Slavery," in *12MBV*, Richard Wright positions the trope of "flight" that signifies upon the action of Douglass when he escaped from Maryland in 1838 by means of the *"uppergound railroad"* (*Narrative*, 65). Wright, too, presents his readers with an image of Douglassian field workers in flight from the South, but ironically these are modern neoslaves. The author's purpose is to challenge claims of slave music as a solace for dehumanization. Its "ephemeral" quality of orality, in fact, only provides temporary but not permanent comfort from the harsh realities of slave or neoslave conditions daily informing the lives of these lower-class southern escapees.

Wright positions this trope of short-term relief in order to show the true "pathway from slavery to freedom," later, at the end of *12MBV*. To illustrate the ephemeral and thus illusionary nature of traditional slave music, Wright returns to historical memory of Douglass and to the significance of the slave song of "Great House Farm" that Douglass reports in chapter 2 of *Narrative*. Douglass recalls listening to slave music sung by fieldhands when he was a child on the Lloyd Plantation in Maryland. Even now the escaped slave hears these songs as he writes, and he tells his white readers that, contrary to myth, "Slaves sing most when they are most unhappy" (*Narrative*, 19). Douglass now is unhappy owing to recollection of his dehumanizing experiences as a slave. By speaking to his audience in the present tense, however, Douglass brings the dead locked in his memory alive by means of their music. Thus, through song, Douglass enables the past to become alive in the present.

The significance of the presentness of the past as an informational guide is also the reason that Wright appropriates Du Bois's Latin imperative to whites at the end of chapter 10 of *Souls* concerning the Negro church, *"Dum vivimus, vivamus,"* which translates as "Why we live, let us live" (*Souls*, 129). Du Bois, too, lets his reader know how the slave and emancipated

Negro field workers in *Souls* live stressful lives, and throughout the book he emphasizes a system of twoness to define the similarities and differences of the stress endured by the conflicted Negro American. One example in which Du Bois demonstrates his binary system is his linking chapters 7 and 8 together as a twin-rooted unit, since they both pertain to Du Bois's studies of the Negro field worker in Dougherty County, Georgia, and his scrupulous assessments of the different class levels of his model in positions of paid or unpaid laborer. Wright, then, revoices Du Bois's symbol of twoness to reveal the conflicted consciousness of southern men, women, and children in his photographic text to show how all Negroes are caught between the dichotomous worlds of the *"living* past in the living present" (*Souls*, 87; *12MBV*, 146).

Douglass initially provides his reader with a working definition of slave music and even appends an emotional connotation to its meaning. He says that "The songs of the slaves represent the sorrows of the heart" and demonstrates how personal an experience they represent when he adds that "I have frequently found myself in tears while hearing them" (*Narrative*, 19). He responds emotionally to his recollection because the slaves, whom young Douglass himself had seen daily on the plantation, would place an emotional emphasis on and meaning to the songs during their performances, whether the songs were old or new compositions. The same old suffering incessantly remains, and the blues refrains or laments by these slave singers reflect their sorrow over the endlessness of their life sentences to enforced captivity. Douglass only recalls the Lloyd slaves singing one song consistently as they walk from the outfarms to the big house: "I am going away to the Great House Farm! / O, yea! O, yea! O!" On the one hand, the "Great House Farm" song itself is locally specific about the site of their pains and sufferings; on the other, it transmits a contradictory message of permanency and ephemerality. The song indexes the changeless nature of their lifelong position as captives, but it also symbolizes that the occasion for their singing derives from their short-term respites from the rigorous field labor. The journey to the Great House main site buoys their spirits, for it briefly halts their labor time. Their euphoria simulates the feelings of joy felt by many slaves, like Douglass, who eventually traveled from country to city.

Douglass also indicates how the song "Great House Farm" remarks upon class conflicts among the slaves. Like the privileged house slaves, the fieldhand delegate who is elected to go to the home site to pick up monthly or yearly rations for other slaves attains a higher class status among the fieldhand laborers. The delegates feel a sense of "joy" unshared by the nondelegates left behind to work. Even in this submerged class there are, according to Douglass, class distinctions among them that keep the thousands of slaves owned by Colonel Lloyd divided and incapable of staging a mass revolt because they are disunified. The master's sectioning of slaves into house or field statuses or sublevels of messengers or nonmessengers causes competition among the slaves and becomes another meaning of divisiveness attached to Douglass's statement that "To those songs I trace my first glimmering conception of the dehumanizing character of slavery" (*Narrative*, 19). There is an ontological implication associated with identity formation and self-esteem in this intraracial class system. The singers of "Great House Farm" indicate that the slave community's system for evaluating self-worth, internalized and practiced by the slaves, is one socially constructed by the master. This divisive mechanism of creating class conflicts among slaves is another cause for sorrow. The "Great House Farm" song, with its abstract meaning of sorrow, carries additional connotations of ephemerality, classism, and divisiveness reflecting the real hardships of slave life, and it serves as a prototype for similar representations of slave life through music revoiced and differentiated by both Du Bois and Wright. Douglass invariably sets up the pattern of secular slave musical discourse to be repeated and transformed by Du Bois and Wright. He provides the first component of a slave musical composition—the lyrics—and encodes its meanings, although its originary fieldhand composer or innumerable fieldhand singers remain unidentified.

Douglass's work, however, is not done. His lyric of "Great House Farm" also has a primary function to fill a "void." This trope of emptiness has a time and space component related to musical theory. Robert Morgan, who has conducted a study of the linkages between music and space in his essay "Musical Time/Musical Space," begins with the uncontested notion that "there is no question, of course, that music is a temporal art." That music is a temporal art is clear because of the diachronic movement of a composition from beginning to ending. But Morgan further argues for the existence of spatial boundaries in music. He points out that "sounds fill up to a greater or lesser degree—some sort of available space" because variations of texture in the sounds "produce an effect that is unmistakably spatial in quality." Douglass already unconsciously notes such spatial segments in "Great House Farm" as it was being sung by the slaves. He locates the high and low notes of the song, which suggest the "textures" of the song at specific spatial points when the singers change the pitch of their tonal ranges. These high and low points are features of the unfolding composition and signify specific spatial moments in a "system of interrelations" within the entire composition that are "independent of the time when the [entire] composition unfolds."[25] Douglass, moreover, pinpoints the moment when the slaves would connect time to space, stating that the

25. Robert P. Morgan, "Musical Time/Musical Space," in *The Language of Images*, ed. W. J. T. Mitchell (Chicago: University of Chicago Press, 1980), 259–60.

fieldhands "would compose and sing as they went along, consulting neither time [time] nor tune [space]. The thought that came up, came out—if
not in word, in sound" (*Narrative*, 18). The slaves would compose at a moment's urging, and their thoughts would erupt from their lips in a burst of
words or sounds to "fill up" the empty space of their lives. Music, with or
without words, serves as psychotherapy for the unhappy slaves.

Du Bois, too, illustrates how temporal slave music "fills up" space, but
he also does several things differently from Douglass when he positions
slave music directly with the slaves and neoslaves under his study. He
does not foreground a musical lyric, but switches to presenting iconic representations of formal, printed sheet music. Du Bois replicates the musical
fragment as a historical signification of slavery, but he also multiplies the
number and then places them as epigraphs to his fourteen chapters. Only
at the final chapter, "The Sorrow Songs," does Du Bois provide the words
for the music—the name of a tune or a fragment of its lyrics—because he is
simulating Douglass's exercise in semantics of interpreting the meaning of
"Great House Farm." By separating images from their words (lyrics or song
titles), Du Bois introduces the trope of narrative distance of his being separated by time (the discursive formation of a song) or space (the exact site)
that Douglass could situate within slave time and slave space. As a child
in the South, Douglass was trapped in slave time and space; as an escaped
narrator in the North, Douglass is still living under the fear of slave time
and remandment to slave space. As an outsider "within" slavery, Douglass
correlates this continuity of slave time with the song "Great House Farm"
to situate it as an exemplum of the presentness of his slave past.

To resolve his time/space problem and to link the slave past to the
neoslave present, Du Bois inserts a physical icon of his examples of vocal,
intangible slave music to connote the alliance, as Eric Sundquist notes, between "speech and music."[26] And by this double representation of so many
slave songs through words and music, Du Bois problematizes Douglass's
one lyrical representation by extending reenactment of his sorrow songs
in a recontextualized musical space and musical time. Du Bois attaches a
post-Reconstruction signification to his slave music examples by situating
the collection in an industrial world in which migration of southern field
workers from country to town had begun by the 1880s. They, in turn, influenced the rise of the music industries (and, later, recording industries in
1914) owing to the commercialization of the slave composer or singer and
his being no longer able to provide sole, unremunerated entertainment
for one person or a few but now being able to serve a wide audience at
tent shows and circuses throughout the South at which the entertainer is

26. Eric Sundquist, "Swing Low: *The Souls of Black Folk,*" in *To Wake the Nations: Race
in the Making of American Literature* (Cambridge: Harvard University Press, 1993), 529.

paid. This migration also accounts for the upsurge of printed sheet music that became more widely accessible after the 1890s, fulfilling the demands of a growing, literate audience to whom "these spirituals were widely known by the turn of the century."[27] Douglass's premise that literacy is the pathway to freedom is confirmed by the commercial success of sheet music at this time. Du Bois merely reaffirms Douglass's premise visually, and presents written "proof" of a present, literate class of black people, his "talented tenth," to whom the music would appeal, as well as to a few white audiences in turn-of-the-century America. To Du Bois, the icons signify the painful, educational strides of a race just emerging from slave bondage.

Du Bois's emblems of slave songs in print as notated music have additional temporal/spatial significations that revoice Douglass's style in terms of music theory. As Sundquist notes, "the music and words of [Du Bois's] sorrow songs form a hidden, coded language in *The Souls of Black Folk,* one that recapitulates the original cultural function of the spirituals themselves." Robert Morgan also makes this temporal/spatial connection. He points out distinctions between ephemeral sounds and their tangible representations on paper. He says that "the score, the physical embodiment of a work, transcends the essentially ephemeral nature of its events as sounds. In score form the work becomes a time-less object, capable of consideration apart from its temporal sequence."[28] Unlike Douglass's vocal music, which is ephemeral, Du Bois's notational music is enduring, permanent. With its notes positioned graphically on staves and contextualized by clefs, measures, and time and key signatures, each musical score forms a visual "kind of picture" whose "graphic qualities are as important as its auditory results." Morgan additionally remarks that "Traditional Western notation is two-dimensional: it is read left to right, which presents the unfolding sequence of the composition, and a space dimension, read vertically (i.e., simultaneously), which reveals the temporal coincidence of the different textural components."[29] This intersection of space and time enables the musicologist to "see" the different textural levels of song as opposed to just being able to "hear" it; therefore, he or she can isolate specific areas of notational space to study its textural traits.

Du Bois provides this physical image of a musical score in order to enable his reader to scan some exhibits of slave music which are part of longer segments. Morgan observes that written music allows the musician to see the "whole" product, but he also notes that few musicians rehearse a composition in its entirety at once or necessarily in its full,

27. Thomas J. Hennessey, *From Jazz to Swing: African American Jazz Musicians and Their Music, 1890–1935* (Detroit: Wayne State University Press, 1994), 492.

28. Sundquist, "Swing Low," 470; Morgan, "Musical Time/Musical Space," 260.

29. Morgan, "Musical Time/Musical Space," 269, 260.

temporal sequences. The conductor often starts to rehearse at any point in the composition. This truncated performance option is why Morgan defines a specific spatial zone in a temporal work as a "notational space." Du Bois presents fragments of slave songs to function as epigraphs, and some of the musical inscriptions contain more than one bar of "notational space." These notational spaces are individual "pictures," and each bar has its own textural features within the domain of the full composition. By tone and mood, these musical fragments containing up to three notational spaces signify upon the moods of the "dead" slave composers and singers who either invented the tunes or repeated the lyrics in another era. As printed documents, Du Bois's textured musical pictures bear another connotation of permanency associated with corporeality, or the body, as opposed to the ephemeral or "soul" signification attached to the intangible sounds through the words and music of Douglass's slave song. Du Bois thus adds a dual, material/immaterial connotation to the sorrow songs that he has reproduced at this point in time.

To illustrate, Du Bois achieves the body/soul nexus affiliated with vocal music in forms of words and sounds by collapsing his written music with Douglass's vocal music for the purpose of capturing the immortal "soul," "essence," or "spirituality" of suffering slaves of the past. In chapter 14, Du Bois explains that he is classifying nearly all of the slave music under discussion as "Sorrow Songs," saying that "Of nearly all the songs . . . the music is distinctly sorrowful." As a time-distanced auditor, he feels no ambiguity about their emotional connotation contrary to dualities of "joy" and "sorrow" expressed by Douglass. He also implies differences between and among the examples that he is presenting, and notes that he considers some contemporary music, such as white minstrel songs, gospel songs, and coon songs, as impure forms of the "original," "primitive" slave music affiliated with early African slaves in the Americas who inspired these songs. These purist representations are those grouped as the "ten master" songs, which Du Bois defines as those songs of "undoubted Negro origin . . . peculiarly characteristic of the slave" (*Souls*, 157–59). They serve as epigraphs to ten of the fourteen chapters. Noticeably, Du Bois omits inclusion of any lyrics with the iconic musical epigraphs, including chapters 7 and 8, although he provides the known titles and words within chapter 14.

And Du Bois innovates again, to signify upon Douglass's life by indirection, but now through slave music. In chapter 14, he inserts a short musical score for "Great House Farm," entitled "My soul wants some thing that's new, that's new" (*Souls*, 159–60).[30] This time, the spiritual song has both body and soul, icon and lyrics, picture and words, permanency and ephemerality. The tune not only has a repetitive refrain, but also signifies,

---

30. Gibson, notes to *Souls* (Penguin edition), 247.

according to Du Bois's interpretation, a "soul-hunger" of the oppressed slave or freed neoslave for a better life (*Souls*, 159). Du Bois also parodies Douglass by starting all his chapter titles with the preposition *Of*, thereby creating a "syntactical concatenation of sounds," a pattern later repeated by Wright. He then switches at chapter 14 to the definite article, *the*, in order to magnify and localize the transcendent conditions of oppression that inspired the slave songs, and the musical, iconic representations that signify the sufferings of blacks thereafter. On a literal level, these bars, like Wright's photographs, are mere traces, shadows, of the past on paper. And it is because of this very "spirituality of dead Space," the musical bars, that Du Bois, by his use of written music, is able to amplify and enliven this phantom quality, this soulness of the dead, by means of his role as the present voice of time and consciousness who speaks for the otherwise mute pictures.

In an ekphrastic juncture involving time and space, Du Bois collapses moving time with inert space to achieve a "stilled, stilling movement" as he describes each slave song and interprets its meaning for his reader. In order to emphasize the musical representation of black subjectivity, in chapter 14 Du Bois deviates from his routine of inserting an epigraph of a poem by a white poet. Here, the anonymous Negro song lyrics to "Lay This Body Down," anchored by the musical notation for the sorrow song "Wrestling Jacob," announces this chapter's topic of black subjectivity.[31] Together, these twin-rooted expressions of music reinforce the subject matter of race and racial injustice to be discussed by means of the discourse of slave music being explicated. "Lay This Body Down" achieves primacy over all of the poems by white poets quoted in the preceding thirteen chapters. While Sundquist considers the epigraphs by white poets as representing the "trap of divided identity in which Du Bois himself was caught," Keith Byerman not only echoes this observation but additionally states that the "pairing" of poetry by whites with songs by slaves "symbolizes common humanity, despite racial difference."[32]

Du Bois constructs his text so that the Negro song of "Lay This Body Down" also links the beginning to the ending of *Souls* to corroborate Du Bois's assertion that "there is no true American music but the wild sweet melodies of the Negro slave." Appropriating a "wild trope" voiced by Douglass in his description of slave music, Du Bois associates primitivism with the lives of slaves to buoy his assertion that, because of the dehumanizing slave experience, the Negro "to-day" represents the "pure human

31. See William Francis Allen, Charles Pickard Ware, and Lucy McKim Garrison, *Slave Songs of the United States: The Classic 1867 Anthology* (1867; reprint, New York: Dover, 1995), 19, 4.

32. Eric Sundquist, introduction to *The Oxford W. E. B. Du Bois Reader* (New York: Oxford University Press, 1996), 15; Keith E. Byerman, *Seizing the Word: History, Art, and Self in the Works of W. E. B. Du Bois* (Athens: University of Georgia Press, 1994), 35.

spirit of the Declaration of Independence." Du Bois also says that the majority of old sorrowful songs signify sacred music and remarks that few under his review represent secular music because "many were turned into hymns by a change of words" (*Souls,* 16, 159). One sees this distinction in Douglass's "Great House Farm," a secular song anonymously authored and sung by a "chorus" of field slaves (*Narrative,* 19), and Du Bois's epigraphic, eight-line stanza, "Lay This Body Down," a sacred hymn also authored anonymously but sung in church (*Souls,* 154).[33] Like Douglass, Du Bois attaches an emotional connotation to these songs born under secular circumstances but reborn as hymns in times distant from slavery. Initially, a song could be inspired by slaves plotting to escape, such as "Steal Away," or it could be born of circumstances, such as the bleak weather conditions that motivated a field worker to sing, "Dere's no rain to wet you. . . ." Du Bois envisions the man plowing tediously "in the hot, moist furrow" and being moved by the absence of rain to create these lyrics (*Souls,* 158). Overall, Du Bois's epigraphic segments of notational music recall the trope of emptiness used by Douglass; here, they function to "fill up" a void or rather "fill in" the "pictorial space" left vacant by Douglass's immaterial lyrics. In print, these notational segments provide an "image" or a concrete picture of an art form symbolic of the musical talents of slaves. They, as physical objects, also serve as a second link in the staging of a slave musical composition begun by Douglass when he supplied the lyric of "Great House Farm." The last component remaining in this collective endeavor is the physical representation of the human subjects—the "image" of the chorus of singers never identified by Douglass and left to be provided by Richard Wright.

The task of "filling up" the space in the slave image that sits between the name and its meaning falls to Wright when he joins the Douglass–Du Bois collective. Wright, in this instance, supplies images of the missing "chorus of [fieldhand] singers." He also manages to enliven these technically and photographically dead images as he presents the "*living* past in the living present," or more importantly, as Du Bois's "voice of Time." And Wright's representation of his twin-rooted position as the living/dead occurs also in context of his slave and neoslave musical examples. He inserts verbal expressions associated with "voice" in forms of songs, ditties, refrains of poetry, and a long sermon in *12MBV* in order to depict the "living spirituality" associated with theories of time, its traits of consciousness, animus, and mobility, in his role as a Du Boisian "voice of Time." Wright thus privileges Douglass's oracular performance even though Douglass's text emerges at the end as an index of written literacy. As Sundquist observes, "The *Narrative* is, in fact, something of a memorized lecture performance transferred to paper . . . and Douglass's language . . . corresponds to the oratical codes and literary conventions" expected by a white audience during Douglass's

---

33. See also Gibson, notes to *Souls* (Penguin edition), 245.

era.[34] Because of this emphasis on oration, Wright discerns the difference between Douglass's seeing the sorrow songs as a signification of pure, oral literacy as opposed to Du Bois's perception of seeing them as transformed expressions synthesizing both oral and written literacy. This trope of literacy is why Wright returns to the "pure," primitive oracular quality of slave music, as first observed by Douglass of the slave songs he witnessed during his early years (*Narrative*, 18–19), and secondarily revoiced and valorized as the epigraphic ten master songs signifying true American music identified by Du Bois (*Souls*, 16, 157–59).

Wright's revoicing of the oral literacy trope of purity/primitiveness has not been arbitrarily selected. His temporal regression to examine the child's status of purity allows Wright to reinforce his premise that uncontaminated, unpoliticized slave music is only an ephemeral flight from reality and to rewrite a script from this point that says politicized revolutionary slave music is the permanent pathway to freedom. This premise means that Wright, at this junction a former Communist but still practicing Marxist, believes that revolution against the white capitalist or black bourgeoisie class of Du Bois is the salvation for the masses of black Americans. For example, Douglass intimates the anonymity of the fieldhand composers, but never supplies a verbal "picture" of their physical features. They are a faceless collective, and Douglass only elaborates upon their voices. Echoing Douglass, Du Bois, too, separates the human image from the written music; moreover, he problematizes the construction of a physical image, for Du Bois sits at a greater temporal distance from slavery. Both Douglass and Du Bois manage, nevertheless, to capture the inward souls of faceless black folks through their singularly immaterial or combination immaterial/material representations of the folk through slave music. Wright agrees by disagreeing with both Douglass and Du Bois. In his book, he, too, represents the dead "folk" as shadowy objects on photographic paper. But by revoicing Du Bois's ekphrastic juncture of time with space in his kinetic role as the "voice of Time" and consciousness that thereby animates Wright's own spatial descriptions, Wright enables his mute, photographically dead "souls" of black folk to speak through him at the secondary level of connotation. His black subjects receive spatial "life" by means of Wright's position as the present consciousness of time, as in similar feats performed by Douglass and Du Bois.

Wright thus enlivens the dead, photographic "image" of his black human subjects or landscape objects and keeps these images partially contained within the stillness of neoslave time during his analysis of southern Negro peasant life. Moreover, by collapsing past slave time with present, neoslave time, Wright truncates the distance between past and present, unlike Du

---

34. Eric Sundquist, "Signs of Power: Nat Turner and Frederick Douglass," in *To Wake the Nations*, 89.

Bois. Wright revisits the childhood of his model Douglass to emphasize the nearness of "primitive" slave music in the recontextualized spaces and times that Wright reenacts. A significant difference is that Wright broadens his neoslave community representations to include images of women and young children. In eight short pages, simulating Douglass's short chapter 2 as opposed to Du Bois's longer, more densely packed chapter 14, Wright devotes a small section of part 2, pages 65–73, to sacred music, in order to illustrate how slave music has moved from the fields outside to the inside of a building. This interior focus echoes Du Bois's remarks that, by a change of words, secular music became sacred; Wright, by contrast, chooses to emphasize how, by a change of site, secular music became sacred by being moved into a church.

Using Douglass's history as well as Du Bois's chapter "Of the Faith of the Fathers" as his models, Wright adapts this whole section on the preacher, the church, and sacred music to focus on the oracular nature of slave culture in part 2 of *12MBV*. He starts out with a transitional picture of a "preacher/teacher" standing in a dilapidated schoolhouse that has been converted for Sunday services (*12MBV*, 66). This picture signifies upon Douglass's yearlong, secretive position as a Sunday school teacher during his hiring-out period to the slaveowner Mr. Freeland. He says that he started the class in order to teach other slaves how to read and write. His sessions lasted until the school was raided, and Douglass was forced to transfer his classroom to the home of a "free colored man" (*Narrative*, 55). Du Bois later makes a similar observation about social activities in Dougherty County, in which the "Preacher and Teacher" used to be the solidifying agents in the old slave community. But rising urban popularity has eroded their power to keep the black community unified (*Souls*, 15, 99, 109). Wright then echoes Du Bois's remark about the power formerly held by these community leaders so that he can emphasize the diminished role of the teacher and the magnified role of the preacher. He signifies upon Du Bois's analysis of a typical Sunday routine by first presenting a picture of a black family all dressed up and on their way to church for its day-long activities. On the next page, Wright begins his analysis of the church setting by emphasizing the role of Du Bois's preacher and how he mesmerizes his audience with powerful oratory (*12MBV*, 68). To simulate the enlivening force of the preacher's voice, Wright's text appears in italics to underscore the preacher's oratorical power. Over the course of four pages, he presents the preacher's sermon on God, heaven, and Lucifer, which corresponds to Du Bois's expurgation of the topics of "Sin, Redemption, Heaven, or Hell" that are typically covered in a sermon (*12MBV*, 69–72; *Souls*, 122).

The antiphonal, call-and-response relationship rooted in secular slave music replays itself in a religious setting through the interactions between the preacher and his audience. Wright's sermon anchors four scenes expressing the emotional reactions of the parishioners: a group of mesmerized women, a choir singing, a group of men praying, and a woman throwing up her hands. These scenes signify upon Du Bois's observation about the performative nature of a religious service consisting of the "Preacher, the Music, and the [audience's] Frenzy" (*Souls*, 120). The image of the woman in the last scene connotes the emotional response of "frenzy" by her throwing up her hands and "shouting." Her releasing of pent-up emotions recapitulates Douglass's notation of similar reactions displayed by fieldhand singers. The high and low notes of their song signifies upon this gush of emotion, particularly at the point where whatever "came up, came out." This exclamation also connotes spontaneity and improvisation. Most slaves, though they had been musicians in Africa, lacked Euro-American formal musical training and, according to Douglass's assessment of descendant slaves, created their own "tradition," consulting neither "time nor tune" (*Narrative*, 18). In *12MBV*, the woman's "shout" inside the church is, by contrast, at a sacred place but her utterance replicates the "primitive" field holler initially emitted by African fieldhands in the secular, outdoors setting where the roots of slave music and the blues laments began.[35] This nameless black woman, a time-distanced African slave descendent herself, considering the decade of Wright's exhibit, is feeling the existential moment of the urge to act and to express her feelings of "emotional intensity" or spiritual relief (*12MBV*, 73).

In this section, too, Wright provides the missing image of the chorus of singers, but he only insinuates their aliveness by means of his voice. He varies from Douglass's representations of direct discourse coming from the mouths of his fieldhands and Du Bois's replications of the Atlanta University Jubilee Singers at the end of chapter 14. But there is an explanation for this variation. Wright speaks for his mute subjects—or rather he "sings for" them—in his capacity as spokesperson for twelve million black voices. By inserting the group image of church choir members lifting their voices in song, Wright completes the chain of a slave musical composition consisting of the lyrics (Douglass), printed music (Du Bois), and chorus of singers (Wright). However, the question still remains: Is Wright, as a Marxist, bestowing the power of direct speech and its capacity to move an audience upon a chorus of dead religious singers? The answer is no—he bestows that power upon a second group of singers, whom he reveals at the end of *12MBV*.

Douglass, Du Bois, and Wright, among others, do much to illuminate the link between black music and a community's ability to survive the horrors

35. Hennessey, *From Jazz to Swing*, 15–16.

and traumas of slavery. In illustrating the evolution of secular field music from Douglass's era to hymns sung inside of a church in Du Bois's time, Wright extends this historical memory of music from its context in the stillness of slave time, circa 1818–1838, associated with Douglass, to its recursive, modern expressions, circa 1936–1941, associated with his life. Wright fills a gap normally occupied by a live preacher with his own sermonic voice, which Sundquist noticed had been a flaw in Du Bois. Sundquist reminds us that it "would be a mistake moreover, to confuse Du Bois's formal rhetorical style and narrative structure in *The Souls of Black Folk* whatever its unusual generic accomplishment, with the cadences of the black preacher. If black religion did not provide him a language, however, it did provide the central matrix of his reconstruction of African culture."[36]

However, even having replicated the cadences of the preacher's voice, Wright still emphasizes the fact that the sacred world is insufficient to sustain the neoslave community. Like Du Bois, Wright follows his images of the sacred rites of a Sunday morning with images of the secular activities of a Saturday night. Wright shows the rise of leisure activities formerly limited in slave life, but now amply available and assertively commanded owing to the migration of Negroes to town in the 1890s, the impact of phonograph music in 1914, and the rise of popular dance halls in response to this music craze. Wright's picture signifies upon this historicity and shows a scene of dancers cavorting to music in a dance hall. His lyric of "Shake it to the East" also reflects the rising popularity of ragtime, blues, and jazz music subsequently inspired by country fieldhands between 1890 and 1935 (*12MBV*, 74).[37]

Moreover, in this secular section, Wright returns to informal poetry, which Du Bois would condemn as "doggerel," but which Wright deliberately cultivates as a response to Du Bois's "nonsensical," indecipherable family slave song "Do bana coba" from an aboriginal African tongue (*Souls*, 157).[38] Wright also signifies upon two other representations of secular and sacred music that are cited by Du Bois in his final chapter. Where Du Bois includes both the music and lyrics to "Poor Rosy" to serve as a rare example of a secular love song—"Poor Rosy, poor gal; . . . Rosy break my poor heart" (*Souls*, 160)[39]—Wright provides a counterpart ditty which contains the words of "I love you once / I love you twice. . . ." He assigns this song to love-struck preteens innocently wandering, "singing" and "whistling," through the backwoods of the South. The scene is reminiscent of the musical performances in words or tunes by Douglass's fieldhands, but which now is being performed by children in other rustic settings.

36. Sundquist, "Swing Low," 458–59.
37. Hennessey, *From Jazz to Swing*, 30–32, 19.
38. Sundquist, "Swing Low," 528.
39. See also Allen, Ware, et al., *Slave Songs*, 7.

Similarly, the song of "I'm a stranger / Don't drive me away . . ." is a tune to be "hymned," according to Wright's definition (*12MBV*, 75), suggesting it has a sacred significance, like its model, "The Weary Traveller," which Du Bois provides in words and notational score: "Let us cheer the weary traveller . . . (*Souls*, 163). Wright decreases the number of speakers. In his song, the narrator expresses a plea in the first-person singular of "I"; in Du Bois's song, a collective voice of "we" is implied by the phrase "Let us." In both cases, the object person is requesting or being given a communal welcome.

In tribute to Douglass's life, Wright devotes many scenes in *12MBV* to children and their reactions to living under oppressed conditions. An emotional response of depression is felt by Douglass the captive fieldhand as symbolized by his apostrophe to Chesapeake Bay (*Narrative*, 46). Du Bois also conveys this emotional response in his reactions to the depressing environment of Dougherty County. Wright likewise captures the psychological reactions to oppression of black children. He inserts a pair of images showing two black youths to reinforce this emotional connotation. The caption under a picture on the left begins "There are times . . . ," and staring at the reader is the face of a depressed-looking, black teenage girl in a doorway; the caption for the right picture says, " . . . when we doubt our songs" and shows a black boy lying on a cot with a distant look on his face (*12MBV*, 81, 76–77). Recalling Douglass's account, Wright situates the "sorrow" of neoslave life in the early identity formation of children in order to illustrate that the reality of depression is their normative response after enjoying the brief euphoria of church. Children, Wright argues, are the real "sorrow songs" of neoslavery.

Overall, neither sacred nor secular music is a permanent solution to southern white or even bourgeois black capitalistic oppression. The resolution must come from the labor-based fieldhand model prototypical of the mass members making up the black community, and from a political leader with a "voice" announcing the time of revolution. Wright's last church and dance hall settings connote two contradictory connotations relating to "seeing" and associated with the illusory nature of slave music. The church setting of Wright's labor subjects only provides an ephemeral release from oppression; the same, short-lived reaction occurs while the dance hall is in action. Immediately after these diversions end, the respondents feel reality settling quickly upon them. And the realism of such daily suffering is what impels Wright's fieldworkers to revolt and flee the South similar to Wright's mentor, Douglass. Du Bois—reluctantly—returns "north" by train to the safe haven of the city and the academic towers of Atlanta University, but he leaves behind the subjugated of Dougherty County still locked within the country walls of neoslavery. Wright recapitulates Du Bois's northern journey and shows activist, class-bound southern labor

subjects, who, deciding to endure no more, also take modern transportation north by means of trucks, cars, or buses instead of expensive trains.

To Wright, political discourse is also a necessity in fighting freedom. He
thus revamps a political connotation at the ending of *12MBV* that signifies upon his indebtedness to the texts of Douglass and Du Bois in finding a resolution to the Negro problem in America. This political connotation illustrates Douglass's, Du Bois's, and Wright's disparate perceptions
of what permanent versus ephemeral solutions are needed to resolve an
ongoing problem. Slave music is proffered by each as a politically inspired
music that inaugurates this revolutionary process. Douglass, for instance,
imposes a distinction between speech and writing that functions as a stamp
of his theoretical premise as a race leader on how to resolve the Negro
problem in the United States. This differentiation can be grasped through
another theory, related to poetry and painting, by Michel Foucault, who
integrates the temporal relationships between the past, present, and future
in time/space theories. Foucault distinguishes the "original" temporal or
spatial object in nature from its first reproduction, the "semblance," and
then from the reprints or "simulacrums" of the reproduction. In painting,
says Foucault, a simulacrum is a reproduction which itself has a "model . . .
that orders and hierarchizes the increasingly less faithful copies that can
be struck from it." The first reproduction of the original is called the "semblance," and those secondary reprints thereafter are known as the "simulacrums" or "less faithful copies."[40] The rendition of "Great House Farm"
reported by Douglass is an example of a simulacrum. It is a "less faithful
copy" at least twice removed from the absent "original" of the past and is
equivalent to multiply reproduced art reprints. The repeated performances
of "Great House Farm" by a number of Lloyd plantation slaves give this
tune an impure quality. Adding to the dilution process is their habit of ap-
pending new lyrics to the old tune during their performances while walking to town.

Douglass does, on the other hand, provide a "semblance" representative
of "current," present-time slave life only once removed from the "original." Douglass inserts a mark of his representation, his mock hymnal of
"Parody" at the conclusion of *Narrative* in the appendix. It is a first-order
semblance of his oral, but absent, performance in nature, and thus functions as a reproduction within *Narrative* in place of the real, reciting author.
The mock hymnal is Douglass's response to the sacred hymn "Heavenly
Union" frequently sung at white churches (*Narrative*, 78). His lyrics serve
as a vocal announcement that this escaped slave is providing an exposé
about the real, hypocritical, religious practices of slaveholders at southern

40. Michel Foucault, *This Is Not a Pipe*, trans. James Harkness (Berkeley and Los Angeles: University of California Press, 1983), 143.

churches. Douglass shows contempt for the pious guises that white Christians assume while in the sanctuary of the church but renounce once they leave church or private prayer. At home, these slaveholders revert to their "natural selves"—brutish, whip-wielding murderers.

"Parody," however, is not the only personal mark or semblance that Douglass uses in *Narrative* to stand for a first-order reproduction of his unseen physical image in nature. "Parody" has a tenuous reign in its position of primacy over "Great House Farm," the simulacrum, for Douglass takes a strong political stance to privilege reading and writing over speech. His "self-subscription" of "Frederick Douglass" denotes a written signature that is Douglass's parting semblance or image in the text. Thus, Douglass deliberately positions his written name to anchor his oracular representation of "voice," the mock hymnal "Parody," in order to make a political statement that written literacy is the pathway to freedom for the Negro in America (*Narrative*, 80).

Similarly, Du Bois reaches a writerly conclusion as the solution to the Negro problem. Throughout chapter 14, he establishes a hierarchy of sorrow songs and classifies the ten master songs as having the highest rank of those slave songs under his study. At the same time, he dismisses the recent diluted representations of gospel hymns, minstrel songs, and coon music as the most impure forms. However, the master songs and all other songs are musical expressions distantly removed from their "originals," are altered in lyrics, and are now relocated to a new sacred site away from the open field where they had arisen as secular music. In 1880–1900, they had become ever-repeating simulacrums, representations of the horrors of slave life in the past, and also present symbols of slave music being mass reprinted to appeal to a literate audience. It is notable that Du Bois inserts his own "personal mark" of vocal music in repetition of Douglass, and presents his "grandfather's grandmother's" personal song "Da bana coba" as the only African "original" song unquestionably linking the past, primitive roots of Afro-Dutch slavery to anyone, but here specifically to him as the present, post-Reconstruction, fourth-generation descendant of this mixed-race lineage.

Du Bois's family song, printed in *Souls*, technically has two significations. In words, it is an often-repeated simulacrum distantly removed from its unknown African composer, with four generations separating Du Bois from his Afro-Dutch slave foremother who introduced the song to his family. In musical notation, it is a printed semblance, a "picture," freshly transcribed by Du Bois, yet it is also a family simulacrum now mass-reprinted for a consuming public because of its unique disbursement in multiple issues and editions of *Souls*. Because of its known kinship link to if not authorship in Du Bois's family and the purity of the words retained, this slave song is technically the urtext, the master song of *Souls*, even exceeding the

temporal ranking of the ten master songs. But because it is also a transformed oral song, "diluted" by writing, since Du Bois has appended its
formal notational elements, Du Bois has decided not to foreground his family song representing his "personal voice" in this concluding chapter 14.
Instead, he privileges another, spiritual past, also a simulacrum, to assume
the role of primacy and to represent the collective "we" spirit of the academic struggle against post-Reconstruction neoslavery. With "The Weary
Traveller," Du Bois conveys a dual message: The song represents the re-
cursiveness of the oracular slave past, and it represents the transformation of the neoslave present into a new domain of academic writing. The
old spiritual of "The Weary Traveller" emitting from the lips of Du Bois's
"children," the Atlanta University Jubilee Singers, signifies upon the slave
songs' movement from outside, in the secular slave field, to inside, in the
secular yet sacred walls of Du Bois's institution of higher learning. He en-
dorses the primacy of this anonymous musical simulacrum over his own
family song in order to foreground the present-time, collective strides of
the race, the literate, freed Negro men and women of his talented tenth.
His endorsement of "The Weary Traveller" thus connotes Du Bois's ongoing attempt to imitate Douglass in his rise to race spokesperson. Du Bois is
the leading spokesperson of intellectual life from his station at Atlanta University, but he does not hold the primary position of political spokesperson
for black culture. He does not attain such position until after Washington's
death in 1915.[41]

Like a preacher "calling" to his responsive audience, Du Bois stages a
call-and-response interaction with his "children" at the conclusion of *Souls*.
As a conservative academic, Du Bois is not naturally inclined to play the
role of a grassroots preacher. This informal, grassroots approach would not
transmit Du Bois's indelible stamp to Washington's nine million black souls
that written literacy is the proper route for Negroes to attain freedom. This
need for corporeality or a visual marking is why Du Bois imparts a second,
personal mark as the final, permanent image for his present and future
readerships. To lead his broad audience along the Negro pathway to freedom, Du Bois devises a second "twin-rooted" set of slave songs. He begins
by privileging a second vocal mark, his "Afterthought," an invocation to a
higher, spiritual leader of "O God the Reader"; he now relegates to second
position the slave song of "The Weary Traveller" meant primarily for an
academic audience.

His second personal signature of "I," not a family song but here Du
Bois's own spiritual invocation, is a first-order "new semblance" freshly
"coming up, and coming out" of Du Bois's own lips, the unseen "original" in nature. But even this newly composed slave lyric still ends up

41. Gibson, introduction to *Souls* (Penguin edition), xxxiii.

totally removed from the open fields of slave labor owing to Du Bois's location at his office at Atlanta University. Ultimately, he anchors his personal "I-mark" of spiritual voice with a new, visual "we-mark" of writing in the stead of Douglass. This sanctioning of written literacy over oracular literacy (speech) is indexed by Du Bois's final plea in his invocation that "infinite reason [may] turn the tangle [of slavery and neoslavery] straight, and these crooked marks on a fragile leaf [his book] be not indeed" misunderstood (*Souls*, 164). Du Bois does not sign his name, but he validates its presence through *Souls*, his freshly minted mark of writing. By indirection, this newly appended manuscript signifies his personal image as the author of the text, but it also indexes the collective voice of nine million black souls, the subjects of his chapters, whose voices have been retransmitted through Du Bois's consciousness in his role as the voice of time. The majority of Du Bois's essays had been previously published and would be familiar to some members of his audience. As a collection, however, they have become another version in a new time. Here also, Du Bois's twin-rooted metaphor recurs to define his text. *Souls* is, on the one hand, a simulacrum housing Douglass's history and the histories of thousands of slaves; on the other hand, it is a semblance containing the present neoslave history as of 1900. Thus, when Du Bois refers to "crooked marks" in his last statement, he is referring to the cursive, academic letters indelibly transmitting the image to his readership in the form of the published slave song of *Souls*. He upgrades Douglass's penmanship for the political purpose of conveying to Washington's and thus Du Bois's seventy million black and white American readers that the only solution to the Negro problem in America in 1900 is through the doors of higher education.

Wright, too, inserts his personal, politically oriented mark at the conclusion of *12MBV*, but it differs from both Douglass's and Du Bois's messages that printed letters (Douglass's) and cursive writing (Du Bois's) are the ways to resolve the Negro problem of slavery and neoslavery in America. Unlike his models, Wright provides no poem at the conclusion of *12MBV*. Rather, he constructs another scenario of the escaped southern Negro having now reached the North, only to discover that he or she is still bounded by modern neoslave migration laws and, therefore, without anywhere else in America to run. This time, Wright portrays Du Bois's two slavemongers of the "Lords of the Unfenced" (South) and "Wizards" (North) as the "Lords of the Land" and the "Bosses of the Buildings" still regionally in commerce to keep the Negro economically disenfranchised. But Wright, on the final page, offers his stamp of writing to resolve this Negro quandary.

Like Douglass and Du Bois, Wright has provided a hierarchy of visual representations with varying ranks involving time/space theory. Rosskam's photograph on page 105 of "Entrance to an apartment house, Chicago," for example, is an FSA reprint and falls into the category of the other mass-produced simulacrums of the past, all eighty-six of the "less faithful copies" of FSA and non-FSA reprints. And like Du Bois's pairing of oral and written slave songs competing for positionality as stamps of Du Bois's present-time mark, Wright follows his mentor but in the more simplistic manner of Douglass.

In another trick effect, Wright and Rosskam insert an eighty-seventh photograph on page 149 by Louise Rosskam entitled "At the Savoy, Harlem" to represent "current" Negro life. It vies for contemporaneous placement with the eighty-eighth picture of Wright's personal exhibit on page 104, "Sign, Brooklyn, New York." Michel Foucault reminds us, however, that "Resemblance predicates itself upon a model it must return to and reveal."[42] This revealed model or "original" must be representative of the problem Negro (as in the case of Douglass the escaped slave), be the only current picture of Negro life, and, most importantly, be from a black perspective. This "insider" status is why Wright's picture 104 dislodges Louise Rosskam's picture of "At the Savoy, Harlem" from its precarious station as the highest-ranking pictorial representation of Negro life in America, circa 1941. "Sign, Brooklyn, New York" is a first-order semblance, a reproduction one step removed from the "original" Negro model, Richard Wright, the object of the camera's eye, and functions as a personal mark for his absent image.

Even with this photograph connoting Wright's invisible presence, he inserts a permanent political stamp of his "image" by means of writing in order for it to act as his final visual message to his audience. Wright, the preacher, insinuates his living presence into the text again by means of an X, replicating the mark of the preliterate, oracular, primitive African slave of Douglass's era, who used his wit to survive the painful existence of American slavery. Wright's point is that slave wit has not evolved into Du Bois's academic wit, but has been transformed into Wright's Douglassian, street-level wit, upgraded and changed into a Marxist-style, political wit that philosophically rejects Western Christianity and formalized, Eurocentric education. Considering his grammar-school education and his being a self-taught writer, Wright's solution should not be surprising. In *Black Boy*, his autobiography, which came out in 1945, Wright details how he joined the Chicago, Illinois, branch of the John Reed Club in 1934 as an apprentice writer, but he severed ties with the Chicago Communist Party in 1936.[43] But in 1941 and until the time of his death in 1960, Wright was a practitioner of Marxist philosophies of class struggle through revolution, and his Marxist message is signified in *12MBV*. His revolutionary orally educated model is the pure, primitive African prototype whose index of literacy is

42. Foucault, *This Is Not a Pipe*, 144.

43. Richard Wright, *Black Boy* (1940; reprint, New York: Harper/Perennial, 1991), 373, 452–53.

his signature of X. And this symbol, as Wright's personal mark, resurfaces on the last photograph in *12MBV*, of a contented Negro male with his face in the sunlight (*12MBV*, 147). Wright's X is formed by the intersecting shadows of a roofline and a clothesline. This mark of Wright is gradually moving to erase the familiar face of the "contented Negro," whom Douglass had suggested as Sandy Jenkins (*Narrative*, 59), whom Du Bois had identified as "Scars" in Dougherty County (*Souls*, 86), and whom Wright now shows as an extant stereotype in 1941. Wright proffers to replace this type with the rare image of the "Angry Negro," who had been a resistant member of Douglass's group of exposed slave conspirators (*Narrative*, 55), and a rebel also identified by Du Bois in Dougherty County (*Souls*, 86).

The image of this New Negro is now being processed as photograph number 89 taken by Rosskam. It is the "permanent" angry face of the grassroots revolutionary who represents the future Negro in America. He recalls the trope of disciples allied to Douglass's followers after his premiere as an orator at a New Bedford abolitionist meeting,[44] and Du Bois's disciples, whom he calls "children" at the ending of *Souls*. And it is by means of Wright's transcendent past, italicized voice of the preacher in his pulpit now upgraded to the present, not-italicized voice of the street-level, Marxist revolutionary that has propelled this young fieldhand recruit into action. Moreover, a musical tenor still exists by way of Wright's bellicose voice rising in varying textures of high and low pitches to sound a warning to white America of an impending slave revolt. He foresees a new world for Negro Americans, as signified by Wright's chanting of a modified "Great House Farm," a menacing, two-bar political lyric warning his reader that "Men are moving! And we shall be with them . . ." (*12MBV*, 147). Wright's use of present tense indicates a slave revolt in process. Like Douglass and Du Bois, Wright uses patriarchal discourse privileging black males as leaders of Negro America. However, he departs from Douglass and Du Bois by providing wider exposure of the roles of women and children in fieldhand life and explicated in *12MBV*. And as the live representation of the "*living* past in the living present," Wright has acted as the past consciousness of twelve million black men, women, and children. Here, then, is the location where Wright positions his representations of a chorus of Douglass's fieldhand singers, and by means of his voice. In the present, he acts as both the speaker and the revolutionary mobilizer of millions by way of one, new male recruit functioning symbolically as the emerging collective, and, therefore, as black America's future.

The force behind this mobilization is Wright's oracular performance. His newly forged, political slave song is transmitted by means of Wright's high-pitched, urban, "street holler." His message of "Men are moving!" to his

44. Garrison, preface to *Narrative*, 3.

reader/viewer is about a Marxist revolution in process against white cap-
italists as well as Du Bois's Negro bourgeois. Wright follows the stead of
his fieldhand mentor, Douglass; therefore, Wright's X merely functions to
anchor his primary, oracular voice, and signifies, contrary to the conclusion of Douglass the adult, that the oral wit of the preliterate, African field
slave is still the revolutionary pathway to freedom for Negroes in America.
And in acting out the ubiquitous roles of the preacher denoted by Du Bois,
Wright the preacher reveals himself to be both singularly and collectively
a chameleon-like political figure: a leader (anarchist/radical), a politician
(Marxist), an orator (street hawker), a boss (overseer of Negro letters), an
intriguer (head of a slave revolt), and an idealist (visionary of a submerged
tenth, free Negroes in America). And in this multifaceted role of Negro
spokesperson, Wright breaks the shackles not only of white America but
also of Du Bois's talented tenth of middle/upper class bigots as well. The
oral literacy of song, not the written literacy of printed music, Wright argues, is the permanent musical pathway to freedom for the millions of Negroes still mired in the lower depths of American society in 1941.

   To Wright, Du Bois's words that "the rise of a nation" depends upon a
"bitter" class war with the world to prove its worth includes two battle-
ments: interracial and intraracial war (*12MBV*, 104). To enact such a war
for Negro freedom, Wright synthesizes both Douglass's and Du Bois's
accounts in order to seize control of Negro leadership and to illuminate
the ongoing, dehumanizing social conditions into the futurity of neoslave
time that he inhabits. His technique of parody or signifying through the
second-order of connotation leads to his recovery of "original" and transformed slave songs, as noted by the "wild" lyric of Douglass's "Great
House Farm," and pure, African primitive master songs and expanded or
diluted song narratives, as recovered and reprinted as iconographic representations by Du Bois. Through slave music in its most primitive form
and political implications, Wright's parody of *Narrative* and *Souls* enables
the author to position and reject both secular and sacred nonresolutions
to the Negro problem as symbolized by his representation of a chorus of
fieldhand singers for his contribution to a collective musical refrain on
the African American experience. The short-term relief afforded by secular
slave music in Douglass's agricultural fields or by sacred slave music in Du
Bois's sanctuary are not apt resolutions for the Negro problem in America.
Similarly, Douglass's self-subscription, symbolizing written literacy as the
pathway to freedom, and Du Bois's cursive marks, symbolizing an elevation in academic settings, do not provide the answers, either. Wright says
that black Americans must return to their uncorrupted purity, the state
of unpolluted slave wit expressed by the African primitives removed to
America's shores, but who still retained a modicum of pure, revolutionary spirit. But the staging ground for such a politicized revolution is no

longer regionally bound as the South, but inclusive of the entire United States. Since there is no other place for blacks in America to run in order to escape oppression, Wright argues that they must look to the "origin" and to African "purity" and "primitiveness," as indexed by the "wildness" of the African souls preceding the lyric of "Great House Farm" in Douglass's day and recovered as "master songs" in Du Bois's text. This type, unencumbered by material baggage, stands his ground and makes the urban streets the new site of revolution.

Thus, Wright illustrates that transhistorical slave music serves a historical purpose: It recovers the "twin-rooted" relations of Du Bois to Douglass that influences Wright's similar homage to Du Bois as a writer. The musical "team" of Douglass, Du Bois, and Wright provides a complete history of Negro slavery and neoslavery in America to 1941, starting with the captivity of Africans on their own shores, their falling into the confines of American bondage, and their being sociologically recontextualized as chattel slaves. The prototype of the fieldhand labor class in all three works enables Douglass, Du Bois, and Wright to sing a collective song of slavery, transcending time and space. By means of Wright, however, all three race leaders illuminate how slave music captures the homogenous theme of pain and suffering timelessly endured by black people throughout the history of America. Richard Wright, who has the last word of this trio, appropriates, changes, reveals or conceals, and buries the rhetorical codes of Douglass and Du Bois, but his final message is strong. He warns that history will repeat itself, and thus he transmits the modern, political, musical message that the new Negro leadership in America will come from the "primitive" fieldhand class of revolutionaries signified by young Frederick Douglass, connoted by Du Bois's term for the rustic group as the "submerged tenth," and figured by himself and the New Angry Negro disciple standing at Wright's side.

Du Bois's "Of the Coming of John," Toomer's "Kabnis," and the Dilemma of Self-Representation

Chester J. Fontenot, Jr.

Some time ago I was in a hotel lobby in Washington, D.C., talking with a friend from another university. The occasion that brought both of us and eighty-two other scholars to the nation's capital was the annual competition for the Ford Foundation Dissertation and Post-Doctoral Minority Fellowships Program, hosted by the National Research Council. After two days of intense review sessions of proposals from qualified minority scholars, we had fulfilled our responsibilities and were taking a moment to reflect on the many fine proposals that deserved funding but which—due to limited moneys—would only receive "honorable mention." While we were engaged in conversation, a middle-aged white male approached my friend and me and asked if either of us was the bellman. We were both taken aback at this man's query, since although both of us are African American males, neither was dressed as a bellman. In fact, my friend had been teasing me about my dapper style of clothing, complete with a 100 percent virgin wool Kango hat and matching topcoat, accented by Stacey Adams shoes, an expensive suit, French-cuffed white shirt, and tie. I, in turn, had been "signifying" on his more than casual style of dress, for he had chosen to "dress down" after the sessions by donning the garb of the hip-hop generation, with a baseball cap, Air Jordan tennis shoes, jeans, casual shirt, and a trendy athletic warm-up jacket. We responded to this man's query by telling him that not only was neither of us the bellman, but also that a bellman traditionally distinguishes himself from others by wearing a particular uniform, which neither of us wore. As the man walked away, we continued to comment that not only did we not look like bellmen, but each of us carried a briefcase, usually a signifier of professional status.

Now that I have achieved distance from this event, I think there was more to this man's question than one might first suspect. While he was certainly trying to locate the bellman so that he could get some help in signaling a cab and carrying his luggage, his inability to differentiate between myself, my friend, and the bellman—three African American males—may reflect his unwillingness to allow my friend and me the privilege of sharing with him the public space usually reserved for white males, except in the subservient role of bellman. Even though both of us hold faculty rank at our respective institutions and were in Washington, D.C., at the invitation of the National Research Council—which is usually perceived as a sign of a national scholarly reputation—this man's question collapsed the difference between us as black intellectuals and the bellman as a service worker into a homogenized black other, the black subject.

This confrontation was even more problematic since we were aware that this man meant us no harm—he simply wanted to locate the bellman. But his representation of a bellman was nonspecific. For him the bellman was a social construct that represented the black subject, the African American male, irrespective of class, social status, or physical appearance. When he looked at us, the man actually saw a bellman, a formless black body. W. E. B. Du Bois, writing in *Dusk of Dawn*, recalls a similar experience while attending college at Harvard. Even though Du Bois embraced the small black student body at Harvard and attempted to "forget as far as was possible that outer, whiter world," he found that

> naturally it could not be entirely forgotten, so that now and then I plundered into it, joined its currents and rose or fell with it. The joining was sometimes a matter of social contact. I escorted colored girls, and as pretty ones as I could find, to the vesper exercises and the class day and commencement social functions. Naturally we attracted attention and sometimes the shadow of insult as when in one case a lady seemed determined to mistake me for a waiter.[1]

Perhaps Ralph Ellison expressed our conundrum best in the prologue to *Invisible Man:* "I am invisible, understand, simply because people refuse to see me. Like the bodiless heads you see sometimes in circus sideshows, it is as though I have been surrounded by mirrors of hard, distorting glass. When they approach me they see only my surroundings, themselves, or figments of their imagination—indeed, everything and anything except me." Indeed, my friend and I felt like Ellison's nameless protagonist, who complains about being "bumped against by people of poor vision."[2]

This sensation of being "bumped against" by "people of poor vision" expresses the dilemma of self-representation for African Americans. The culture of dominance that initially produced slavery, and later, a racial hierarchy, constructed black people as a race of bodies valued only for its market value as a commodified physical subject. These tropes of the

1. W. E. B. Du Bois, *Dusk of Dawn: An Essay toward an Autobiography of a Race Concept* (1940; reprint, New Brunswick, N.J.: Transaction, 1984), 35.
2. Ralph Ellison, *Invisible Man* (New York: Modern Library, 1952), 7.

body substantially influenced the ability of African Americans to represent themselves from the point of view of their own culture that sought to
assert the primacy of the totality of subjecthood. It restricted their representation to tropes that corresponded with the dominant hegemony. These
fragmented tropes became fixed within the cultural texts of the Western
world, and divided the black subject into two separate selves: mind and
body. Racist discourse emphasized the representation of African Americans as material bodies and delimited the mind as a signifier of black
identity.

This mind/body binary is grounded in Christianity since it first evolved
from the Apostle Paul's assertion that Christians must mortify the flesh
in order to achieve spiritual purity and was later refined by St. Augustine
who, in his *Confessions*, argues that the body is sinful and must be negated
in order to reach spiritual communion with God. This body/spirit binary
gives rise to the body/mind paradigm, since the European Enlightenment,
heavily influenced by Christianity, held that the intellect endowed Europeans with the ability to deny the body, resist its natural carnal nature, and
impose the order of human agency on an object that resists such restric-
tions. Conversely, the balance of mind and body indicated the inability to
control the body as material subject; it was perceived as a sign of intellectual weaknesses, cultural backwardness, and savagery.

W. E. B. Du Bois, utilizing double-voiced discourse that signifies on the
submerged mind/body binary in nineteenth-century American life, expresses the dilemma of self-representation for African Americans in his
seminal text *The Souls of Black Folk*, when he writes

> Between me and the other world there is ever an unasked question: un-
> asked by some through feelings of delicacy; by others through the difficulty
> of rightly framing it. All, nevertheless, flutter round it. They approach me in
> a half-hesitant sort of way, eye me curiously or compassionately, and then,
> instead of saying directly, How does it feel to be a problem? they say, I know
> an excellent colored man in my town; or I fought at Mechanicsville; or, Do
> not these Southern outrages make your blood boil?[3]

Similarly, Jean Toomer writes

> Generally, it may be said that the Negro is emergent from a crust, a false
> personality, a compound of beliefs, habits, attitudes, and emotional reactions
> superimposed upon him by external circumstance. . . . First, there are those
> factors which arise from the condition of being a black man in a white world.
> Second, there are those forms and forces which spring from the nature of our
> civilization, and are common to Americans . . . [4]

3. W. E. B. Du Bois, *The Souls of Black Folk*, ed. Henry Louis Gates Jr. and Terri Hume
Oliver (New York: Norton, 1999), 9. All citations in this essay refer to this edition.
4. Jean Toomer, in Frederik L. Rusch, ed., *A Jean Toomer Reader: Selected Unpublished
Writings* (New York: Oxford University Press, 1993), 87.

The common thread that runs through my experience of being "bumped against" by the man's question, Du Bois's reference to the "unasked question" by those of the "other world," and Jean Toomer's analysis that "blackness" is the social construct of "whiteness" is the inability of African Americans to represent themselves from the perspective of their own cultural traditions or, in other words, in other than mind/body binaries. Surely, Du Bois and Toomer were aware that this was not a new problem. In 1841, the abolitionist movement published *The New England Anti-Slavery Almanac for 1841*, a "how to" book that directed abolitionist editors of slave narratives to "speak for the slave" and "write for the slave," since "they [the slaves] can't take care of themselves."[5] This idea of slaves as subjects and abolitionist narrators as their authenticating narrative voice belies the implicit goal of eighteenth- and early-nineteenth-century slave narratives—to justify slavery—and expresses a hegemonic relationship between the silenced slave and empowered narrator. It begins, within American cultural texts, a tradition that is a trope against the self representation of the African American personality. The inability of African Americans to represent themselves publicly, however, can be traced back as early as the late eighteenth century, with the controversy surrounding the authenticity of Phillis Wheatley's poems, and throughout the nineteenth century, in its emphasis on the minstrel tradition as an authentic representation of black life. Indeed, Eric Lott, in *Love and Theft: Blackface Minstrelsy and the American Working Class*, demonstrates admirably both the construction of "blackness" through the minstrels and the tendency of white working-class males to insist that the white minstrels accurately represented African Americans. The performance language created for minstrel characters, dialect, was in fact a way of representing the belief of many whites that African Americans were less intelligent, barely human, and incapable of grasping even the most basic concepts of the English language. Later in the nineteenth century, the plantation era attempted to justify slavery through revising tropes of the mind/body binary, in which black subjects were represented as black bodies deprived of minds and rational intellects who actually enjoyed their experience of slavery.

While this cultural assault on the personalities of African Americans rendered impotent their attempts to represent themselves from the point of view of their own cultural traditions, political legislation insured that they would not gain control of their own social narratives by insisting that the African American was a fractured, incomplete, inauthentic person, less valuable than his or her white counterparts, and suitable only to be hewers of wood and drawers of water. The underpinnings of both processes were centered in the beliefs, first, that African Americans were not citizens, but property, and thus enjoyed only the advantages guaranteed to them by

5. *The New England Anti-Slavery Almanac for 1841* (Boston, 1841), 1.

laws that governed property rights, and second, that if African Americans were to exist as free men and women, they could not share the same social, political, and economic space as whites, but instead had to be relegated to that space ascribed to them by those who had initially constructed "blackness" to represent the racialized other.

In *The Souls of Black Folk,* Du Bois attempts to represent what he calls "the world within the Veil," the spiritual world of African Americans by articulating, from the perspective of African Americans, an identity that is fixed rather than permeable. His often quoted statement on "double-consciousness" expresses, for Du Bois, the otherness that lies at the core of black identity. Although Du Bois's statement has been criticized as overly simplistic, in that it is primarily a male construct that fails to acknowledge class and gender, this double identity is central to twentieth-century racial discourse, including Jean Toomer's *Cane* (1923), because he also attempts to fix racial identity through the construct of doubleness. Du Bois deconstructs the trope of bodies, derived from the mind/body binary, by fixing black identity in the mind/spirit binary and privileging the spirit. While Du Bois locates the problem of self-representation in the African American's struggle to merge his twoness—American and Negro—Toomer identifies this problem in African Americans' psychological and material difficulty in embracing their spirituality.

Both Du Bois and Toomer, however, though physically distant from the actual existence of black people, find that in the South, they first locate what Donald Gibson calls their "bodies," their social essence. In a sense, both writers locate the "black essence" through what Paul Gilroy calls "routes," not "roots."[6] That is to say, they both find that geographical routes, the black South, allow them to represent African Americans accurately. Reflecting about his experience in Georgia, Toomer wrote in "Outline of Autobiography":

> There, for the first time, I really saw the Negro, not as a pseudo-urbanized and vulgarized, a semi-Americanized product, but the Negro peasant, strong with the tang of fields and the soil. It was there that I first heard folk-songs rolling up the valley at twilight, heard them as spontaneous with gold, and tints of an eternal purple. Love? They gave birth to a whole new life.[7]

"Of the Coming of John," chapter 13 in *The Souls of Black Folk,* and "Kabnis," the ending narrative in *Cane,* are Du Bois's and Toomer's linguistic representations of racial doubleness, in which they claim the privilege of representing black identity from the point of view of their culture.

6. Donald Gibson, introduction to W. E. B. Du Bois, *The Souls of Black Folk,* ed. Donald B. Gibson (New York: Penguin, 1989), xiii; Paul Gilroy, *The Black Atlantic: Modernity and Double Consciousness* (Cambridge: Harvard University Press, 1993), 11.

7. Toomer, "Outline of Autobiography," in Rusch, *Jean Toomer Reader,* 2.

In "Of the Coming of John," a story set at Wells Institute, an academy for racial uplifting in Johnstown, Du Bois engages in linguistic play in representing two Johns, one white, the other black. The academy is a preparatory school whose black students "have few dealings with the white city below." Using tropes that anticipate Jean Toomer's *Cane,* Du Bois constructs foreboding images of the city and students. He writes, "When at evening the winds come swelling from the east, and the great pall of the city's smoke hangs wearily above the valley, then the red west glows like a dream-land down Carlisle Street. . . ." Similarly, he refers to the "forms of students in dark silhouette against the sky. Tall and black, they move slowly by, and seem in the sinister light to flit before the city like dim warning ghosts. Perhaps they are . . ." (143).

Du Bois says that John Jones, the "black John," is

> one dark form that ever hurries last and late toward the twinkling lights of Swain Hall,—for Jones is never on time. A long, straggling fellow he is, brown and hard-haired, who seems to be flowing straight out of his clothes, and walks with a half-apologetic roll. He used perpetually to set the quiet dining-room into waves of merriment, as he stole to his place after the bell had tapped for prayers; he seemed so perfectly awkward. And yet one glance at his face made one forgive him much,—that broad, good-natured smile in which lay no bit of art or artifice, but seemed just bubbling good-nature and genuine satisfaction with the world. (143)

Here, Du Bois's language suggests that John embodies the representation of nineteenth-century black males—undependable, innocent, happy, and lacking responsibility and purpose. In fact, the white folks of Altamaha, Georgia, his hometown, "vote" him a "good boy," "a fine plough-hand, fool in the rice-fields, handy everywhere, and always good-natured and respectful." The representation of John is set against the pastoral imagery of the community, "away down there beneath the gnarled oaks of Southeastern Georgia, where the sea croons to the sands and the sands listen till they sink half drowned beneath the waters, rising only here and there in long, low islands" (143).

This depiction of a harmonious community in which John is commodified as a black subject is reinforced when his mother sends him off to Wells Institute to study. While the black community proudly follows him to the train station carrying his baggage, the white folks reject higher education for blacks and exclaim: " 'It'll spoil him,—ruin him,' . . . and they talked as if they knew" (143). Here Du Bois appropriates the language of nineteenth-century racist discourse that asserted that higher education for blacks was not only improper and unfitting for them, but also was disruptive to the racial hierarchy that insisted on the superiority of whites and the servile nature of blacks.

In spite of the potential disruption in this racial paradigm, John leaves Altamaha bound for Wells Institute, while a blues refrain resounds as a cultural subtext within "they that stood behind." The refrain to which I refer here is the line in a blues song that is repeated throughout. It serves both as a structuring mechanism for the composition—since it centers the lyric discourse by calling the speaker and hearer back to it repeatedly— and as a central theme for the song. As the temporal sequence of the blues song unfolds, the language of the speaker begins a descent into a world of problems. The refrain prevents the blues structure from collapsing under its own weight of discourse that problematizes human experiences by returning the speaker and hearer to the ethical center of the blues narrative. This allows the blues narrative to function as a cultural catharsis for the hearers, since no matter how bad the experience rendered in the song is, the blues refrain allows both the speaker and hearer to exit the seemingly endless abyss of human problems and return to the ethical center of the lyric. The narrator in Du Bois's short story identifies this refrain as "one ever-recurring word," "When John comes," suggesting its musical nature. This refrain embodies the logos of the community; they expect him to return from the institute prepared to teach. Upon his return, "then what parties were to be, and what speakings in the churches; what new furniture in the front room, —perhaps even a new front room; and there would be a new schoolhouse, with John as teacher; and then perhaps a big wedding; all this and more—when John comes." The utopian discourse of the black community is balanced against the foreboding disposition of the white people who "shook their heads" (143–44).

While this refrain initially structures the cultural narrative that gives voice to the black community's logos, it is transformed into a "legend" during the seven years of John's absence. The narrator tells us that at first, John expected to come back for Christmas, but that he does not because his vacation time was too short. Later, he had no money during the summer, and since the school was so costly, he worked, instead, in Johnstown. The community, once solidified through adherence to the "one recurring word" of the refrain, is transformed: "playmates scattered, and mother grew gray, and sister went up to the Judge's kitchen to work" (144). Although the refrain had once given voice to the community's attempt to represent itself as upwardly mobile through the symbolic act of John going away for training and returning a teacher and race leader, the phrase loses its cultural power: It "lingers" as a legend, and it suggests the community's difficulty in countering the negation of their self-worth by the "white folks," who continue to represent them through nineteenth-century racist discourse.

The refrain is even more problematic since it is double-voiced, multivocal. The judge, a powerful white man, is introduced through a powerful image—"the Judge's house." The narrator tells us that while the black community finds it difficult to sustain the refrain as both the ritualistic repetition of the anticipated return of John, and the cultural glue that holds the community together, people in the judge's house—suggesting the Bahktinian notion of hearing one's discourse reflected in the speech of the other—like the refrain; the judge also has a John, his son, who has been accepted to Princeton University. This John is the racial double of John Jones. He is "a fair-haired, smooth-faced boy, who had played many a long summer's day to its close with his darker namesake" (144). Here the word "played" signifies the nature of the racial hierarchy, for while both the white and black Johns are allowed to "play" as children, their child's "play" does not defer meaning; they are unequal and alienated from each other as adults. The language the judge uses to represent his expectation for his John is oppositional to the white community's judgment of John Jones as he leaves the town for the institute. While the judge commodifies John Jones as a black subject who will be spoiled by higher education and unfit for the subservient role of servant, the judge proudly says, " 'Yes, sir! John is at Princeton, sir. . . . Showing the Yankees what a Southern gentleman can do. . . . It'll make a man of him . . . college is the place' " (144).[8]

There is a multivocal discourse between the white John, who is in the process of becoming a man at Princeton, as the embodiment of Southern manhood, and the black John, who is expected to accept the role of the racialized other, as one "fixed in a consciousness of the body as a solely negating activity," as Bhabha put it. This dynamic argues against the judge's attempt to depoliticize and domesticate race relations under the rubric of racial homogeneity. It embodies what Bhabha calls a "simplification because it is an arrested, fixated form of representation that, in denying the play of difference (which the negation through the Other permits), constitutes a problem for the representation of the subject in significations of psychic and social relations."[9] The play of difference requires the white community—the judge—to recognize the multiple community mirrored in both Johns. The village awaits the "coming" of the Johns, although "neither world thought the other world's thought, save with a vague unrest . . . it was singular that few thought of two Johns,—for the black folk thought of one John, and he was black; and the white folk thought of another John, and he was white" (144).

Du Bois constructs a binary opposition between the white John's evolving into manhood through success at Princeton and the black John's initial failure at the institute. The faculty sees him as "the clay" that "seemed unfit for any sort of moulding. He was loud and boisterous, always laughing and singing, and never able to work consecutively at anything. He did not know how to study; he had no idea of thoroughness; and with his tardiness,

8. In "Father and Son," Langston Hughes treats the issue of the black subject whose black body invades public white space, where the plantation economy and the racialized double is a source of unending enmity; *The Ways of White Folks* (New York: Knopf, 1934).

9. Homi K. Bhabha, *The Location of Culture* (London: Routledge, 1994), 75.

carelessness, and appalling good-humor, we were sore perplexed" (144). In response to his refusal to conform to the representation of race leadership that is promoted at the institute, the faculty vote that he, " 'on account of repeated disorder and inattention to work, be suspended for the rest of the term' " (144). The language used here to describe "Jones" constructs another binary in this narrative; it is opposite to that of racial uplifting embedded in Booker T. Washington's *Up from Slavery* (1901).[10]

Upon being told by the dean that he is being suspended, Jones strikes a bargain with him not to tell his mother and sister: " 'But you won't tell mammy and sister,—you won't write mammy now will you? For if you won't I'll go out into the city and work, and come back next term and show you something' " (145). The suspension not only causes Jones to assume the posture of humility, the necessary prerequisite for racial uplifting, but it also transforms him from the nineteenth-century carefree minstrel archetype to a man with "sober eyes and a set and serious face" (145). Jones's physical appearance reflects his psychological and spiritual change: "he grew in body and soul, and with him his clothes seemed to grow and arrange themselves; coat sleeves got longer, cuffs appeared, and collars got less soiled. Now and then his boots shone, and a new dignity crept into his walk" (145). When he passes out of the preparatory school into college, the narrator tells us the experience "almost transformed the tall, grave man who bowed to us commencement morning" (145).

Jones's transformation into a new kind of man, a new genus, is centered in his awareness of the need to represent himself from the perspective of racial leadership. His previous failure, which the narrator attributes to a "queer thought world," is supplanted by a racialized identity that forces him "back to a world of motion and of men" (145). This perspective, distinguished by its difference from "blackness" as the social construct of "whiteness," brings Jones to the awareness of the "Veil." Jones

> grew slowly to feel almost for the first time the Veil that lay between him and the white world; he first noticed now the oppression that had not seemed oppression before, differences that erstwhile seemed natural, restraints and slights that in his boyhood days had gone unnoticed or been greeted with a laugh. He felt angry now when men did not call him "Mister," he clenched his hands at the "Jim Crow" cars, and charged at the color-line that hemmed in him and his. (145–46)

While Du Bois uses the term *veil* to signify the social separation of blacks and whites, he also believes that one's sense of race comes from the expe-

---

10. See Robert B. Stepto for a discussion of *The Souls of Black Folk* and *Up from Slavery*, in his *From behind the Veil: A Study of Afro-American Narrative,* 2d ed. (Urbana: University of Illinois Press, 1991).

rience of depersonalized group oppression. In spite of Du Bois's insistence that African Americans are "born with a veil," he does not feel that racial consciousness is inborn. In *The Autobiography of W. E. B. Du Bois* (1968), in the chapter "My Birth and Family," he discusses his racialized self as a construct that is estranged from his social identity. The veil with which African Americans are born is, for Du Bois, a caul, the inner fetal membrane that, at times, emerges from the womb wrapped around the head of a newborn child. Within the dialogic system of the black South, the caul or veil is a sign of difference that points to a special divine dispensation of gifts or purpose as human agency.

The meaning of the veil, however, becomes inverted; though it begins as a fixed indicator of divine favor, it becomes what Stuart Hall would call a "floating signifier" that denotes the curse of racial consciousness, blackness. Jones's awareness of the "Veil that lay between him and the white world" generates what Frantz Fanon calls the need for violence, however symbolic, as the cleansing agent for his damaged psychology.[11]

Just as his racial awareness creates within him anger, it also alienates him from the black community in his hometown. Jones manifests the characteristics of Frantz Fanon's newcomer in that he "otherizes" his indigenous community in spite of his initial desire to return to it and assume the role of race leader. After weighing his options, he "seize[s] with eagerness the offer of the Dean to send him North with the quartet during the summer vacation, to sing for the Institute" (146).

The spatial movement here, from rural South to urban New York is, of course, symbolic of one strand of thought within nineteenth- and early-twentieth-century black thought for racial uplift. The northern cities were a trope within the African American dialogic system against the delimited nature of southern social, economic, and political life. Jones attempts to appropriate this route by enthusiastically accepting the dean's offer, but he neglects to realize that the role he will play is that of an entertainer, a singer, probably for the purpose of raising funds for the institute, and not that of a potential race leader as teacher. This trope is against the attempts of whites to commodify black art. The singer, rather than teacher, represents Wells Institute in New York because northern whites are more likely to accept African American males when they restrict their public representation to the social spaces circumscribed for them. Needless to say, this "black space" does not include intellectual pursuits; it is delimited to performance for the delight of whites. In this way, Jones's representation of the institute commodifies him as the black subject for the purpose of deconstructing racial-

11. See Frantz Fanon, *The Wretched of the Earth*, trans. Constance Farrington (New York: Grove Press, 1966); see also Stuart Hall's videotape, *Race: The Floating Signifier* (New York: Media Education Foundation, 1996), for his discussion of race as a floating signifier.

ized paradigms that differentiate between public space for white males and private space for black males.

Unaware of his restricted public representation, Jones casts the city of New York in the romantic images characteristic of the pastoral nature of rural Georgia: The men remind him of the sea, an image of the vitality of life. Invigorated by this construct, Jones declares, "This is the World." His utopian vision is centered in entertainment. After purchasing a ticket for five dollars to enter "he knew not what" (146), he is depersonalized by the white John with whom he played as a child. John Henderson's un-named companion tells him,

> "you must not lynch the colored gentlemen simply because he's in your way. . . . You *will* not understand us at the South. . . . With all your professions, one never sees in the North so cordial and intimate relations between white and black as are everyday occurrences with us. Why, I remember my closest playfellow in boyhood was a little Negro named after me, and surely no two,—*well!*" (146)

The white John's language here is interesting. Although he chides his female companion for taking offense at Jones's attempt to share her public space, he appropriates racist southern discourse that deconstructs his romantic paradigm of "intimate relations between white and black" which he characterizes as "everyday occurrences." On one hand, his idea of intimate relations maintain the structure of southern race relations through the perspective of the plantation era that sought to offer an apology for slavery by constructing harmonious images of social relationships between blacks and whites. On the other hand, his vision of racial intimacy is demystified by the metaphor of childhood play between himself and the black other whom, he insists, was named after him. The racial doubling created by the white John's belief that John Jones was named after him is striking here; it suggests that John Jones's social identity is constructed through a naming process in which he is cast as the racialized double of the white John but without the privilege of sharing his racial double's public space.

Further, at the white John's urging, Jones is escorted out of the hall; the manager tells him he is sorry he made the mistake of selling him a seat that was unavailable and offers to refund his money. But Jones's inability to assert his identity as an upwardly mobile black leads him to rush away, telling himself, "John Jones, you're a natural-born fool" (148). In an act that recalls the refrain, now legend, he pens a note: "Dear Mother and Sister—I am coming—John." His "coming" signals the fulfillment of the community's hopes. On the train back to Altamaha, Jones resolves that his duty is to "help settle the Negro problems there." After a seven-year hiatus, John's "coming" reunites the black community; "dark Methodists and Presbyterians were induced to join in a monster welcome at the Baptist church" (148).

In spite of the optimism of both John and the community in anticipation of his "coming," upon his arrival, John perceives the people in the town, including his own family, as the other:

> An overwhelming sense of the sordidness and narrowness of it all seized him; he looked in vain for his mother, kissed coldly the tall, strange girl who called him brother, spoke a short, dry word here and there; then, lingering neither for hand-shaking nor gossip, started silently up the street, raising his hat merely to the least eager old aunty, to her open-mouthed astonishment. (148)

The community responds to John's inability to locate his own mother's "body," his estrangement from his sister, whom he identifies only because she calls him brother, and the psychological and physical distance he places between himself and the people in the town by speaking to them in "a short, dry word here and there," and refusing to linger "neither for hand-shaking nor gossip," with confusion. His transformation from the jovial, warm, and friendly person to a distant, unemotional man causes them to ask, "This silent, cold man,—was this John? Where was his smile and hearty hand-grasp? ' 'Peared kind o'down in the mouf,' said the Methodist preacher thoughtfully. 'Seemed monstus stuck up,' complained a Baptist sister" (148). The contrast between the community's expectations of John's "coming" and his physical presence suggest that John represents a mind/body binary of the community. The community's memory of John is that of a man who embodies their logos and whose black body gives voice to their self-representation. The material presence of John, however, indicates that he has privileged his mind over the emotiveness attributed to the black body.

The difference between the community's representation of John and the person whose material essence—"silent, cold," unsmiling, with a cold handshake, and "monstus stuck up"—they greet at the train station is expressed in nature's response to John's "coming." The cultural glue that unites the community through John's return is countered with the binary response of the natural environment. The meeting at the Baptist church fails. The sharing of a communal meal, which is the center of the social fabric of the religious community, is aborted, since "rain spoiled the barbecue, and thunder turned the milk in the ice-cream" (149). These naturalistic tropes suggest impending tragedy in the relationship of John to his community. Later, at the church service, the spontaneity in the religious fervor of the community, set against the preparedness of the three preachers, is silenced by the presence of John, who

> seemed so cold and preoccupied, and had so strange an air of restraint that the Methodist brother could not warm up to his theme and elicited not a

single 'Amen'; the Presbyterian prayer was but feebly responded to, and even
the Baptist preacher, though he wakened faint enthusiasm, got so mixed up
in his favorite sentence that he had to close it by stopping fully fifteen minutes
sooner than he meant. (149)

John as the speaking black subject no longer voices the logos of the community but instead speaks in a manner that alarms his hearers. He differ-
entiates himself from other black leaders by calling for a new age of leadership, of what he terms "new ideas" that consciously establish difference
from the seventeenth, eighteenth, and nineteenth centuries' self-effacing
representation of blacks. He focuses on the "broader ideas" (148) of human brotherhood, destiny, and the rise of charity and popular education,
in particular the spread of wealth and work. While John's initial speech
causes his audience concern, the question he raises evokes wonderment:
"What part the Negroes of this land would take in the striving of the new
century" (149).

Moreover, his vision of his representation as race leader in the community lacks a historical trope that will allow his listeners to appropriate and
bring it into fruition. His vision includes a new Industrial School, organizing charitable and philanthropic work, saving money to establish banks
and businesses, and ending the divisiveness among religious denominations. Revising Booker T. Washington's model for racial uplifting, he asserts
that blacks will not be ushered into the fullness of American life because
of denominations or even their adherence to Christianity, but depending
upon whether they are "good and true" (149).

The community members' response to John's visionary discourse indicates both their embrace of their cultural logos and the pain caused by
aborting racialized essentialism. Once John ends his speech, "a painful
hush seized the crowded mass," for they had not understood much of what
he had said. The narrator tells us that, except for a reference to baptism,
John spoke, from the community's perspective, "an unknown tongue," a
biblical trope that usually signifies divine inspiration but here, in a secular
usage, suggests the alienation of John from his community. In response
to John's discourse, an old man ascends to the pulpit, Bible in hand, and
speaks in a manner that moves the crowd to emotional frenzy. Just as his
hearers did not understand John's speech, John did not understand what
the old man said; "he only felt himself held up to scorn and scathing denun-
ciation for trampling on the true Religion, and he realized with amazement
that all unknowingly he had put rough, rude hands on something this little world held sacred" (149). The old man's speech is a corrective to that
of John's. It voices the community's distrust in and disapproval of John
as the representation of a black man who challenges their historical fabric
that is undergirded by their adherence to difference in religious practices.

John's perception that he "had put rough, rude hands on something this little world held sacred" indicates his awareness that he has violated the community's ethos without demonstrating cultural empathy, and demonstrates his tendency to otherize them.

John attempts to insulate himself from the antagonism that is represented here as a class division within a racial paradigm by leaving the church and, accompanied by his little sister, walking to the sea. As they talk, John and his sister attempt to establish a community of hearers that are responsive to his discourse.

> "John," she said, "does it make every one—unhappy when they study and learn lots of things?"
> He paused and smiled. "I am afraid it does," he said.
> "And, John, are you glad you studied?"
> "Yes," came the answer, slowly but positively.
> She watched the flickering lights upon the sea, and said thoughtfully, "I wish I was unhappy,—and—and," putting both arms about his neck, "I think I am, a little, John." (150)

The relationship here between happiness and formal education is the subtext that structures the community's rejection of John's material "coming." Here it seems that happiness is the product of limited insights resulting from inadequate education. It echoes the perspective toward the involvement of blacks in higher education voiced by the white postmaster on John's return to the community: "That damn Nigger . . . has gone North and got plum full o' fool notions; but they won't work in Altamaha" (148–49). The "fool notions" here that are derived from higher education and experience in the North deconstruct happiness, since the necessary prerequisites for this happiness are the denial of educational pursuits and the correct assessment of the cultural signifiers as indicators of black space. Higher education, when combined with the northern experience, moves the black subject as material body from black space to white space without the comfortable tropes that buffer this shifting racial paradigm.

John's presence as a black body in white space decenters him within the community. When he goes to the Judge's house to ask for permission to teach at the Negro school, the Judge stares at him "a little hard" and brusquely tells him to "go round to the kitchen door . . . and wait" (150). When Judge Henderson finally gives John an audience, he does not invite John to sit down but instead lectures him that while he "likes colored people," John's going away led him not to help him and his family more because

> "the Negro must remain subordinate, and can never expect to be the equal of white men. In their place, your people can be honest and respectful; and

> God knows, I'll do what I can to help them. But when they want to reverse nature, and rule white men, and marry white women, and sit in my parlor, then, by God! we'll hold them under if we have to lynch every Nigger in the land." (151)

We should notice here that John's privileges, as the black subject whose black body invades public white space—the judge's house—are circumscribed through the trope of private black space: the kitchen door; remaining subordinate; staying in his place; and not reversing "nature" by trying to rule white men, marry white women, or sit in his parlor. The black person whom the judge likes is the "colored" person who acquiesces to fill the black space to which he is assigned; the ones whom the judge abhors and wants to lynch are those who seek equality with white men, in other words, those who attempt to share public white space. The judge asks John if he is going to teach "the darkies to be faithful servants and laborers as your fathers were,—I knew your father, John, he belonged to my brother, and he was a good Nigger . . . are you going to be like him, or are you going to try to put fool ideas of rising and equality into these folks' heads, and make them discontented and unhappy?" (151). John's awareness of the nature of racial hierarchy in Georgia leads him to deconstruct the judge's desire for him to fulfill the historical role of "good Nigger" by voicing his status as the black subject—he responds that he is going to accept subservient status.

In spite of having struck a "fool's bargain," so to speak, with the judge, Jones opens the school only to find that his work is more difficult than he first anticipated. In language that revises the trope of racial uplifting constructed by Booker T. Washington, the dispassionate narrator tells us that the "Negroes were rent into factions for and against him, the parents were careless, the children irregular and dirty, and books, pencils, and slates largely missing" (152). Once he decides to persevere, he finds that the "attendance was larger and the children were a shade cleaner this week. Even the booby class in reading showed a little comforting progress. So John settled himself with renewed patience this afternoon" (152). The language here not only reflects the discourse of racial upliftment through higher education, but it also signifies on the dialogic system of nineteenth-century black educators who believed that the indicator of racial betterment was adherence to the demands of formal education.

John Jones's "coming" and the opening of the Negro school is paralleled by the return of his racial double, the white John. Much like the black community's response to the coming of John Jones, the white people respond with pride and gladness. The "other John came home, tall, gay, and headstrong. The mother wept, the sisters sang. The whole town was glad. A proud man was the Judge, and it was a good sight to see the two swinging down Main Street together" (151). But while the judge had hoped his son might become mayor of Altamaha, a representative to the legislature, and maybe even governor of Georgia, his son, much like John Jones, sets himself at odds with both his father and the town, "for the younger man could not and did not veil his contempt for the little town, and plainly had his heart set on New York" (151). Although the narrator insists that he is "not a bad fellow,—just a little spoiled and self-indulgent, and as headstrong as his proud father," John casts the town as a symbolic prison where "there isn't even a girl worth getting up a respectable flirtation with" (152). When his father tells him that he expects him to settle down and work in the town, John responds, "you surely don't expect a young fellow like me to settle down permanently in this—this God-forgotten town with nothing but mud and Negroes?" (151). The linguistic construct equating John's displeasure with the town with its two dominant characteristics—mud and Negroes—is obvious. Suffice it to say that while the earthy quality of his discourse suggests the humanity of blacks, it also indicates the strong racial and class hierarchy.

The deconstruction of the white John's "coming" is mirrored in the Judge's report from the postmaster that John Jones is " 'livenin' things up at the darky school,' " with " 'his almighty air and uppish ways. B'lieve I did heah somethin' about his givin' talks on the French Revolution, equality, and such like. He's what I call a dangerous Nigger' " (151). The binary representation of John Jones, first as a "good Nigger," when he voices to the judge that he will accept the subservient status to which he and other blacks have been assigned, and later as a "dangerous Nigger," who has an "almighty air," "uppish ways," and dares to engage in public discourse about the French Revolution and equality, is striking. Jones's self-representation as race leader disrupts the comfortable construct for black education that both the black and white communities have accepted as the social norm.

Upon hearing of Jones's rebellious behavior, the white John asks the identity of the John who is " 'livenin' things up at the darky school' " (151). When the judge tells his son that the dusky fellow is " 'little black John, Peggy's son,—your old playfellow,' " the white John reveals to his father that " 'it's the darky that tried to force himself into a seat beside the lady I was escorting—' " (152). The judge and his son use different language to represent Jones; the Judge characterizes Jones in words that recall the custodial relationship of whites to blacks, the black childish body frozen in time, the "little black John," his son's "playfellow," and the white John speaks of Jones in language that signifies the representation of the adult black other by "whiteness." The representations, however, share a common origin: nineteenth-century racist discourse. In an attempt to control the "dangerous Nigger" that Jones had become, the Judge abruptly closes the school because "the white people of Altamaha are not spending their money on black folks to have their heads crammed with impudence and lies" (152).

Du Bois's racial doubling is best expressed in the "great black stump" (153), a revised trope from nineteenth-century slave narratives. The "great black stump" signifies both a whipping place for blacks who were judged incorrigible and the site of impending judgment for black males who dared violate white space. Both the white and black Johns' tragedies are centered in this trope. While pondering his fate in the prisonlike village, the white John sits on the "great black stump" and concludes that the village offers no desirable females with whom he would like to become involved, or have "a respectable flirtation with." John settles for a disrespectable one by pursuing Jennie, Jones's sister, the racialized black other, the black fragmented erotic body who works for the judge as a kitchen maid. He tells her, "Why, you haven't kissed me since I came home" (153). When she resists his advances and runs, John chases her through the tall pine trees, catches her, and tries to force her to acquiesce to his sexual demands.

This scene, revised from historical narratives that voice the rape of black women at the hands of white men, reflects the relationship of black men and women to powerful white men that leads to Jones's double tragedy. Just as he attempted to buffer the old man's rebuke in the black church by walking to the sea, Jones goes to the water after the Judge closes the Negro school and resolves within himself to shield his failure from his mother, find a job elsewhere, and send for her and his sister. The naturalistic tropes signify against John's attempt to bring a harmonious resolution to his quandary: "The great brown sea lay silent. The air scarce breathed. The dying day bathed the twisted oaks and mighty pines in black and gold. There came from the wind no warning, not a whisper from the cloudless sky" (153). If the first part of Jones's tragedy is concluded with the closing of the Negro school, the second part is initiated when he sees his sister fighting the white John, grabs a fallen limb, and strikes him "with all the pent-up hatred of his great black arm; and the body lay white and still beneath the pines, all bathed in sunshine and blood" (153). Here, the dialectical relationship between the white John's still white body, "bathed in sunshine and blood," and Jones's "great black arm" suggests the paradigm of the victimized white male at the hands of the brutish, savage nature of the black male. In this image, Jones is materially decentered—he is represented only as a "great black arm,"—while the white Jones is depicted through the revised trope of the innocent depersonalized white male.

The "great black stump" that initially offers both a resting place and a site for the white John to ponder his options becomes at once both the "great black arm" that strikes him with "pent-up hatred," and the trope for Jones's eventual demise. After he walks back to the house, he tells his mother: "Mammy, I'm going away,—I'm going to be free" (153). Looking at the North Star, a trope within the nineteenth-century African American oral tradition that signifies freedom, he tells his mother that he is going north, a desire once shared by his racial double. As he seats himself on the same "great black stump" on which the white John pondered his imprisonment in the small town, he recalls images of innocence between himself and the "other John," how, as children, he and the dead boy had played together beneath the trees. Then, as he wonders what became of "the *other* boys at Johnstown" (153, my emphasis), he includes himself in the category of "other": "And Jones,—Jones? Why, *he* was Jones, and he wondered what they would all say when they knew, when they knew, in that great long dining-room with its hundreds of merry eyes" (153). Jones's disembodied discourse here suggest his alienation from himself as the black subject. This decentered language gives way to his personal tragedy that is completed with the sound of men on horses galloping nearer in search of him:

> he saw in front that haggard white-haired man, whose eyes flashed red with fury. Oh, how he pitied him,—pitied him,—and wondered if he had the coiling twisted rope. Then, as the storm burst round him, he rose slowly to his feet and turned his closed eyes toward the Sea.
> And the world whistled in his ears (154).

Jones's double tragedy echoes the blues refrain that structures the community's consciousness. Just as he initially attempts to deconstruct the representations of black males as commodified black bodies that serve the interests of the dominant hegemony, the refrain, "When John comes," offers the possibility to the community members to represent themselves as other than servants, the subservient racialized others, of whites. Jones's inability to represent himself through the duality of mind/spirit ends in the tragedy implicit within the tropes of the mind/body binary that privilege the black body. This is signified by the refrain that degenerates into legend and is unavailable to the community for constructing identity. His inability to claim "that form of negation which gives access to the recognition of difference" reduces him to a signifier of "race as anything other than its fixity as racism."[12]

In the closing song within this narrative, Du Bois disrupts the Romantic moment and frustrates closure with an intertextual play on the wedding march from Wagner's opera *Lohengrin*. Du Bois changes the song's original text from "treulich geführt, ziehet dahin" to "freudig geführt . . . ," or, in English, a change from "faithfully led, pass along to that place" to "joyfully led. . . ." It is as if gaiety and bliss must be denied; the South must lose two sons because the black John represents the South's most dangerous nightmare: the word made flesh as a "dangerous Nigger," as the embodiment

---

12. Bhabha, *Location of Culture*, 75.

of the negation of blackness fixed in the tropes of the black body. In other words, John represents the danger of literacy that stands at the center of racial discourse in the South. Before the black John "comes" in all of the senses the word implies, a violent and repressive social text exists that delimits black achievements and being. Hence, one may see the ending of this narrative as a closed cultural text in that there is no blues catharsis, no way out of the tragedy. Du Bois uses European high art to point out the moral and theological bankruptcy of the American South, a land that cannibalizes its sons.

The movement of descent in the blues structuring of Du Bois's text is mirrored in Jean Toomer's "Kabnis." The refrain "when John comes," which determines the community's discourse and Jones's representation, is much like that in "Kabnis," with the repeated phrase "I've got to get myself together"; "Come, Ralph, old man, pull yourself together" (85, 86, 87). This refrain is central to the representation of Kabnis, since he is depicted as a fragmented individual who initially struggles to give primacy to his mind and spirit to order the horrifying possibilities that living in Georgia offers. Terrified at night while in his cabin, "Ralph Kabnis, propped in his bed, tries to read. To read himself to sleep."[13] His attempt to privilege his mind and spirit over his body, however, is futile, since his material surroundings fortify his fears: His cabin room is "spaced fantastically," the oil lamp "burns unsteadily," the "hearth and chimney" are "whitewashed," a construct borrowed from biblical discourse that suggests its surface signifies one thing while its nature is quite another; the cracks between the boards in the walls are "black," permitting the "night winds" to whisper their blues-structured song:

> White-man's land.
> Niggers, sing.
> Burn, bear black children
> Till poor rivers bring
> Rest, and sweet glory
> In Camp Ground. (83)

The double-voiced discourse of the night wind's song indicates the representation of African Americans, including Kabnis, through the tropes of the dominant racial hegemony of the South. Lines 1, 3, and 5 voice the delimited nature of blacks as divided selves, black subjects, whose value is restricted to the market rate of their participation in the southern economy. Lines 2, 4, and 6 reflect the cultural response of the black subjects

13. Jean Toomer, *Cane* (1923; reprint, New York: Norton, 1988), 83. All citations refer to this edition.

in their efforts both to resist commodification through social labor and to structure communal discourse that embodies the community's logos. The former voice presents the black subjects at the whims of the whites who own the land; the latter offers the spiritual response of these black subjects to their otherized status.

This blueslike song structures the narrative's discourse. Kabnis, who is represented as a mulatto, has difficulty locating his physical body. His "thin hair . . . streaked on the pillow," "slim silk" mustache, "brown eyes," "lemon face," and thumb that attempts to "be trying to give squareness and projection" (83) to his chin, occupy the other end on the scale of color differentiation within the black race represented by Du Bois's "dark silhouettes" (143). They are equally problematic in that both lack material essence. When Kabnis speaks, he wonders if he is "the real Kabnis" or if he is a "dream": "And dreams are faces with large eyes and weak chins and broad brows that get smashed by the fists of squared faces" (83). After receiving a warning for him to leave town that is written on a paper wrapped around a stone and thrown through Fred Halsey's window, Kabnis becomes a "splotchy figure," a "scarecrow replica" of himself, and "awkwardly animate" (93). The imagery here reflects the relationship of blacks as dreams to the whites, the "squared faces," who smash the "soft" faces of dreams.

In language oppositional to the trope of dreams, Kabnis questions whether he has "come to the South to face it," if, in fact, he "could become the face of the South" (83–84). Continuing the blueslike structure of the night wind's song, Kabnis offers that if he can deconstruct the tropes of mind and body that have rendered him without a unified identity, his "lips would sing for it, my songs being the lips of its soul" (84). Much like John Jones, however, who rejects the tropes of the black body that suggest the African American is little more than the commodified black subject who asserts identity through the cultural texts of the gospel tradition, Kabnis rejects the soul as the core of black identity: "Soul. Soul hell. There ain't no such thing" (84). His attempt to privilege mind over spirit reflects his urge to break with the delimiting representations of blacks that rested at the center of nineteenth-century racist discourse.

While he differs with representations that sustain the relationships between blacks and whites, Kabnis finds no solace in his attempt to gain control over the chaos of racial harmony and his own mixed heritage: Unsettled by the night wind's song, he "slides down beneath the cover, seeking release" (83). The images of commodified black subjects saturate his consciousness: "Dust of slavefields, dried, scattered . . ." (84). Likewise, Kabnis inverts the tropes of barnyard animals, usually signifiers of harmony between human beings and nature, into hostile images. In a complex scene that combines images of both Kabnis's representation of the Georgian landscape as the other and the embodiment of southern romance, he engages in domestic battle with a hen who has invaded the privacy of his cabin, chases and catches the "she-bitch," and "with his fingers about her neck, he thrusts open the outside door and steps out into the serene loveliness of Georgian autumn moonlight" (84).

Although Kabnis succeeds in separating the chicken's head from her body, this oppositional discourse introduces revisions of tropes of judgment and apocalypse. Like the smoke of the city that "hangs wearily above the valley" (143) in Du Bois's narrative, "a band of pine-smoke, silvered gauze, drifts steadily" across the autumn landscape (84) in Toomer's narrative. Toomer inverts the half-moon, a familiar trope of unrequited love, to underscore Kabnis's alienation: "The half-moon is a white child that sleeps upon the tree-tops of the forest" (84).

This discourse structures the double-voiced narrative of the white winds, which croon,

> rock-a-by baby . .
> Black mother sways, holding a white child on her bosom.
> when the bough bends . .
> Her breath hums through pine-cones.
> cradle will fall . .
> Teat moon-children at your breasts,
> down will come baby . .
> Black mother. (84)

The blueslike structure represents discourse between the romanticism of the South in verses 1, 3, 5, and 7, and the commodification of the black mother as the black body whose value is restricted to her ability to nurture white children. In an attempt to impose order on the chaos he confronts, Kabnis represents himself as "Earth's child," and says "the earth my mother." Yet, his effort does not bring symbolic closure in his quest to confront the South as the other. He curses God as a "profligate red-nosed man about town" and constructs his own identity as a "bastard son" (85). The contrast between the discourse of the white winds' song and Kabnis's representation of the earth, specifically the land of the South as his mother, suggests that his construct of bastardy is not restricted to religion. Rather, it is a trope against the negation of his historical consciousness through European colonial and American racist discourse that casts a paradigm of the person of African descent as a cultural bastard. This trope embodies every speech that denotes Kabnis and his race as bastards, including the designation of Africa as the "dark continent" deprived of history and civilization that has its genesis in fifteenth- and sixteenth-century European discourse, and the generally held belief in America from the seventeenth through the late nineteenth centuries that people of African descent who were born in America had no history, culture, or traditions, and therefore, were the bastards of the American slave institution. This conception led many nineteenth-century historians, such as John Clarke Ridpath, to designate Africans and their descendants in America as "Hamites," the bastard race that had no cultural integrity in themselves, but rather pointed to the signifiers within American immigrant cultures for authentication.[14]

Kabnis's internalization of secular bastardy leads him to represent himself by negating Christianity, considering it a religious system that had failed to serve the interests of African Americans in their attempt to represent themselves through the tropes of sacred discourse. He constructs a binary between the "radiant beauty" (85) of the night, a trope within the African American tradition that signifies the relationship of blacks, slave and free, to the dominant hegemony represented by the daylight, and the "ugliness" of the moral injustices that God allows. In a poetic double-voiced monologue that signifies on the discourse of prayer, Kabnis says,

> "God Almighty, dear God, dear Jesus, do not torture me with beauty. Take it away. Give me an ugly world. Ha, ugly. Stinking like unwashed niggers. Dear Jesus, do not chain me to myself and set these hills and valleys, heaving with folk-songs, so close to me that I cannot reach them. There is radiant beauty in the night that touches and . . . tortures me. . . . What's beauty anyway but ugliness if it hurts you? God, he doesn't exist, but nevertheless He is ugly. Hence what comes from Him is ugly. Lynchers and business men, and that cockroach Hanby, especially." (85)

Kabnis's tendency to equate social injustice with God, especially Hanby, the principal of the school at which he teaches, leads him to say, "God and Hanby, they belong together. Two godam moral-spouters" (85). The window of Fred Halsey's home "looks out on a forlorn, box-like, whitewashed frame church. . . . Above its squat tower, a great spiral of buzzards reaches far into the heavens. An ironic comment upon the path that leads into the Christian land" (88). He describes Professor Layman as a "tall, heavy, loose-jointed Georgia Negro, by turns teacher and preacher" (88). During a conversation with Halsey and Layman, Kabnis rejects the spirituality of blacks by saying that rather than taking direct action against racism, blacks are a "preacher-ridden race. Pray and shout. Theyre in the preacher's hands. . . . And the preacher's hands are in the white man's pockets" (90). Black Christianity, for Kabnis, is little more than a commodified structure that serves the ends of both "whiteness" and "blackness."

14. Blacks as bastards of the West is a leitmotif in James Baldwin's *Go Tell It on the Mountain* (1952) and his classic essay "Stranger in the Village" (1955). On blacks as "Hamites," see John Clarke Ridpath, *Great Races of Mankind VI* (Cincinnati: Jones Brothers, 1893), 473–580.

The tension in Kabnis's discourse generates a blues refrain that structures his narrative. After pondering his relationship to the other—which he personifies here as beauty, ugliness, and God—he tells himself, "Come, Ralph, old man, pull yourself together" (85). After listening again to the night wind, and deconstructing his own discourse, Kabnis "totters as a man who would for the first time use artificial limbs. As a completely artificial man would" (85). He experiences difficulty locating the "large frame house, squatting on brick pillars, where the principal of the school, his wife, and the boarding girls sleep"; it "seems a curious shadow of his mind" (85). The only essences he can locate are "white minds, with indolent assumption," which "juggle justice and a nigger" (85–86). Toomer's linguistic play on "mind" here constructs an image that recalls the body/mind binary. While he attempts to privilege his mind as human agency over the primacy the South ascribes to his black body, he can only perceive as "real" white minds that maintain privileges by otherizing black subjects.

This blues refrain structures Kabnis's consciousness, since he can only "see" or locate images of the dominant southern hegemony—the land, Augusta—as dynamic, while he perceives the North, Washington, as dormant: "Washington sleeps," and New York is "a fiction" (86). Further, this blues structure is intensified by Kabnis's inability to buffer himself from his "mind" by sleeping, and his observation, albeit untested, that "Negroes within it [Georgia] are content. They farm. They sing. They love. They sleep" (86). Unable to go to sleep, Kabnis's "mind" again attempts to order chaos, but he finds that his efforts only regenerate the blues refrain. In the tormenting stillness, during which he imagines that he is in a place where "they burn and hang men" (85–86), and the appearance of ghosts, a trope against the construct of the black body, Kabnis tells himself, "Come, Ralph, pull yourself together" (86). The tropes of the night cause Kabnis to repeat the refrain three times in anticipation that the next day, Sunday, will come swiftly. In a final bid to escape his mind, Kabnis closes his eyes, slips under the sheets, and tells himself,

> "Think nothing . . a long time . . nothing . . nothing, nothing. Dont even think nothing. Blank. Not even blank. Count. No, musnt count Nothing . . blank . . nothing . . blank . . space without stars in it. No, nothing . . nothing . ." (87)

His attempt to deconstruct creation and his own mind by appropriating this nihilistic structure, thinking nothing, "space without stars in it," is undermined by the subtext of the night wind's foreboding blues song.

Fred Halsey's home is the logos for Kabnis's narrative. Halsey, a racially mixed African American, described as a "well-built, stocky fellow, hair cropped close" (88), fills his house with cultural artifacts that establish continuity between the African past, slavery, and the present status of black subjects. The family clock that does not run suggests these three eras are fused into one continual present distinguished by its ritualistic repetition on tropes that sustain the dominant racial hegemony. The portraits of Halsey's family lend insight into his racial heritage: His great-grandfather, "an English gentleman," has "black hair, thick and curly. The eyes are daring. The nose, sharp and regular." The mouth of his great-grandmother, who is of undeniable "Negro strain," "is seen to be wistfully twisted. The expression of her face seems to shift before one's gaze—now ugly, repulsive; now sad, and somehow beautiful in its pain." The portraits of the rest of his family show his father as "rich brown. The mother, practically white. Of the children, the girl, quite young, is like Fred; the two brothers, darker" (87–88). These images signify the cultural hybridism that mirrors Kabnis's initial self-representation. Kabnis's hybridism manifests itself in race and class structures. Just as he finds difficulty in locating his material essence in the geography of rural Georgia, he also feels the difference between himself and other blacks who are indigenous to the region.

Moreover, Halsey and Kabnis themselves represent the mind/body binary: Halsey embraces black subjecthood, working with his hands and rejecting higher education for blacks, while Kabnis assigns primacy to his mind and negates the tropes of the black body. During a discussion on lynching among himself, Layman, and Halsey, Kabnis attempts to establish a difference between the trio, a "gentleman—fellows, men like us three here—" (89), and the black other, by implying whites would not lynch anyone like them. Layman, the teacher-preacher who has traveled over most of Georgia, responds by collapsing Kabnis's construct in a blunt corrective to his conspiratorial misreading: "Nigger's a nigger down this way, Professor. An only two dividins: good and bad. An even they aint permanent categories. They sometimes mixes um up when it comes t lynchin. I've seen um do it" (89). Layman's discourse suggests that "blackness" in Georgia is a floating signifier, constructed by "whiteness" to represent black subjecthood.

While Kabnis embraces the duality of mind and body, he rejects the mind/spirit binary. When he hears a woman's voice swell "to shouting," in a "voice, high-pitched and hysterical," and "perfectly attuned to the nervous key of Kabnis" (his own voice) (92), Kabnis's "face gives way to an expression of mingled fear, contempt, and pity" (90). His rejection of the body/spirit binary is embodied in his rejection of the emotionalism, especially shouting, of the black church. He says "that stuff gets to me. . . . Couldnt stand the shouting, and thats a fact. We dont have that sort of thing up North. We do, but, that is, some one should see to it that they are stopped or put out when they get so bad the preacher has to stop his sermon for them" (91). Layman, offering a "logical" analysis that explains both the type of black who shouts and his or her reasons for demonstrating

such excessive emotionalism, responds to Kabnis's attempt to have shouting halted in the black church by saying that he agrees shouting should be
suppressed:

> "An its th worst ones in th community that comes in th church t shout. . . .
> You take a man what drinks, th biggest licker-head around will come int th
> church and yell th loudest. An th sister whats done wrong, an is always doin
> wrong, will sit down in th Amen corner an swing her arms an shout her head
> off. Seems as if they cant control themselves out in th world; they cant control
> themselves in church." (91)

Layman's discourse here suggests that he, like Kabnis, privileges the
mind over spirit, even though Layman is a preacher himself. After someone hurls a stone wrapped in paper through the window of Halsey's home,
with the inscription, " 'You northern nigger, it's time fer y t leave. Git along
now' " (92), Kabnis, consumed with fear, joins the others, remembers the
"words, and [begins] to shift them about in sentences" (93). Layman even
construes them grammatically. Yet, Layman insists that the black mind,
confined to the black space of subjecthood, lacks the social being to negate
the tropes of racist discourse. He says, "White folks know that niggers talk,
an they dont mind jes so long as nothing comes of it." (92). As he constructs
a narrative that horrifies Kabnis, Layman tells him about Mame Lamkins,
a black woman who was murdered in the street for trying to hide her husband from a white lynch mob. While in public, the mob kills her on the
street " 'and some white man seein th risin in her stomach as she lay there
soppy in her blood like any cow, took an ripped her belly open, an th kid
fell out. It was living; but a nigger baby aint supposed t live. So he jabbed
his knife in it an stuck it t a tree" (92).

Kabnis's construct of southern racial hierarchy is deconstructed when
he finds that the note attached to the stone was meant for Lewis, who
is described as a man who looks like Kabnis, and was thrown by black
folks who, Lewis says, "have grown uncomfortable at my being here."
(97). Kabnis initially feels a bond with Lewis, whom Halsey says rejects
black subjecthood and "ain't bowed t none of them. Nassur. T nairy a one
of them nairy an inch nairy a time. An only mixed when he was good an
ready." (98). Halsey further represents Kabnis as the racial double of Lewis;
he otherizes both Lewis and Kabnis by saying that Lewis ought to know
something about Kabnis, because "one queer bird ought t know another,
seems like t me" (110). Kabnis, the narrator reminds us, appears to Lewis
as "a promise of a soil-soaked beauty; uprooted, thinning out. Suspended
a few feet above the soil whose touch will resurrect him" (98). While Kabnis feels a strong impulse to reject Lewis, he notices that "His eyes call,
'Brother' " (98).

Kabnis's refusal to privilege the black spirit is tempered by the church choir's spiritual narrative:

> My Lord, what a mourning,
> My Lord, what a mourning,
> My Lord, what a mourning,
> When the stars begin to fall. (93)

This gospel song signifies the black subjects' attempt to construct identity through the tropes of spirituality rather than those of racist discourse.[15] But Kabnis, after the paper-wrapped stone is thrown through Halsey's window, is unable to appropriate these structures; he runs to his cabin and, at the sound of someone approaching, grabs a poker, then realizes that Halsey and Layman have followed him home. In an attempt to calm Kabnis's fears, Halsey tells him, "Nobody's after y, Kabnis, I'm tellin y. Put that thing down an get yourself together" (94). Kabnis is unable to construct identity through the tropes common to blacks indigenous to Georgia, and Halsey imposes order on the chaos in Kabnis's mind. Rather than engaging Kabnis in the process of getting himself together through spirituality, Halsey asserts a blues structure—he offers him a bottle of liquor.

The patrician Hanby represents Kabnis's desire to cast himself as an orator rather than as a preacher. Hanby is

> a well-dressed, smooth, rich, black-skinned Negro who thinks there is no one quite so suave and polished as himself. To members of his own race, he affects the manners of a wealthy white planter. Or, when he is up North, he lets it be known that his ideas are those of the best New England tradition. To white men he bows, without ever completely humbling himself. Tradesmen in the town tolerate him because he spends his money with them. He delivers his words with a full consciousness of his moral superiority. (95)

The images here of Hanby are oppositional to those constructed of the black subject. Instead of singing spirituals, working in the cane fields, and confining himself to black space, Hanby is well-dressed, "smooth," "rich," "bowing to white men but never completely humbling himself." Yet Hanby, the colored school's "humble president," collapses black identity into a paradigm of racial essentialism and asserts that "the progress of the Negro race is jeopardized whenever the personal habits and examples set by its guides and mentors fall below the acknowledged and hard-won standard of its average member" (95). Hanby's statement suggests that race leaders must deconstruct the tropes of black subjecthood through maintaining "personal habits and examples" that construct identity that

15. Du Bois's magisterial reading of the spirituals, including this one, serves as a useful intertext. See "The Sorrow Songs," in *The Souls of Black Folk*.

establishes difference from racial paradigms constructed by nineteenth-century racist discourse. Convinced that Kabnis has violated the "hard-won standards" by drinking liquor on school premises, Hanby demands Kabnis's resignation from the faculty.

While Halsey counters Hanby's insistence that Kabnis resign and leave the school premises with his own assertion that Kabnis is to work for him, Kabnis responds to both demands to gain control of his self-representation either as a worker in Halsey's shop or race leader as teacher by attempting to "rise and put both Halsey and Hanby in their places. He vaguely knows that he must do this, else the power of direction will completely slip from him to those outside. The conviction is just strong enough to torture him" (96).

Kabnis's recognition that he must control his own representation, expressed here through the directional metaphor *rise*, is further developed when he states that he must regain control of "the power of direction" or it will be relegated to "those outside." The internalizing of human agency here asserts the blues structure of the narrative; it leads Kabnis to resolve his attempt to regain control of his representation by working for Halsey in "an old building just off the main street of Sempter," characterized by little-used utilitarian objects that suggest the owner "has no worth-while job on foot" (99). While Halsey's workshop is the center of the narrative, "The Hole," the cellar that is both the home of "a very old man," Father John, and the seat of human agency for Halsey, serves as the logos in Kabnis's attempt to represent himself.

In "The Hole," Kabnis is initially depicted as a child in need of the custodial care of Halsey, as "awkward and ludicrous, like a schoolboy in his big brother's new overalls" (99–100). After botching the job of fixing Ramsey's, a white customer's, hatchet handle, he follows Halsey, Lewis and Layman, "hangdog-fashion" (102). Ramsey, depicted as "a shriveled, bony white man," tells Halsey, "still breaking in the new hand, eh, Halsey? Seems like a likely enough faller once he gets th hang of it" (102). Resisting Ramsey's attempt to represent him through the tropes of the black subject as laborer, Kabnis "burns red," "feels stifled" (102), and sees Ramsey as the embodiment of the entire white South that burdens his consciousness.

Influenced by liquor, Kabnis is depicted as "a ridiculous pathetic figure in his showy robe" (110). Cora and Stella, two black prostitutes whom Halsey defines through the tropes of slavery as a "common wenches" (110), embody subjecthood as the black erotic other that is constructed by the lust of white and black men. While Cora, at the urging of Halsey, sits Kabnis down in a chair, sits down in his lap, squeezes his head into her breasts, and "almost stifles him," Stella attempts to fulfill her femininity through mothering Kabnis; she would "like to take Kabnis to some distant pine grove and nurse and mother him" (112).

Stella's attempt to domesticate Kabnis by symbolically subsuming him within the tropes of black motherhood are set against Kabnis's desire to construct his identity by establishing difference from the paradigm of race leadership represented by black preachers. He represents himself as an orator, "born and bred in a family of orators," not preachers, whom he characterizes as "wind-busters" (111). In discourse that begins to shape his identity, Kabnis says that while Halsey is "all righ f chopping things from blocks of wood," he "was good at that th day I ducked th cradle. An since then, I've been shaping words after a design that branded here. . . . Been shaping words t fit my soul" (111). Kabnis's emphasis on expressing his soul through shaping words is significant. Not only does he assert his identity through the tropes of the black oral tradition, but his speech also otherizes Halsey. His words, which shape his soul, are sometimes "beautiful and golden an have a taste that makes them fine t roll over with y tongue" (111). Then, he tells Halsey that his tongue "ain't fit f nothin but t roll and lick hog-meat" (111). Kabnis's language here is interesting because he represents himself through the discourse of the dialogic system of African American folk culture rather than that of racial uplifting, but in doing so, "signifies" on Halsey with speech that both assumes antagonism and defers meaning.

Although Halsey counters Kabnis's verbal play by telling Stella to give him a shovel, the protagonist's newly constructed voice continues to assert his identity. Constructing a speakerly text, Kabnis asserts the priority of words that "feed" or structure his soul,

> Not beautiful words . . . Misshapen, split-gut, tortured, twisted words. Layman was feedin it back there that day you thought I ran out fearin things. White folks feed it cause their looks are words. Niggers, black niggers feed it cause theyre evil an their looks are words. Yallar niggers feed it. This whole damn bloated purple country feeds it cause its goin down t hell in a holy avalanche of words. (111)

Kabnis's belief that only his words, not those of the preachers, can feed his soul is partly the result of his desire to distinguish himself from lower-class blacks by insisting that his ancestors were southern blue-blooded, upper-class blacks who could have passed for whites, to which Lewis offers a corrective, "and black" (108). Seeking to collapse difference between blacks centered in color differentiation, Kabnis responds, "aint much difference between blue and black" (108).

Perhaps Kabnis's attempt to privilege words or mind over the tropes of the black body is best depicted in his confrontation with Father John, whom Kabnis calls Father Satan. Father John, who lives in the Halseys' cellar, and is described as both deaf and blind, gains voice in response to Kabnis's verbal attacks that characterize him as a "dead fish man, an black at that" (115) who died "way back there in th' sixties" (114). In response to Kabnis's discourse, in which he speaks of "sin" as a floating signifier, a spiritual error that is specific to the situation and audience, that points to "whats done against th soul" (116), Father John speaks through discourse that unites the tropes of slavery, Africa, and southern segregation. He fixes sin, through revising and repeating the discourse of slave narratives, in white misrepresentations of Christianity through misreading the Bible. He distinguishes between the true gospel of Jesus and "th sin th white folks 'mitted when they made th Bible lie" (117). Seemingly unaffected by Father John's deconstruction of his discourse, Kabnis responds by revising Father John's construct of sin: "So thats your sin. All these years t tell us that th white folks made th Bible lie. Well, I'll be damned" (117).

Just as Father John's voice establishes continuity between the tropes of black resistance to the dominant racial hegemony, Carrie K., "the pure, untouched Negro soul, throbbing with the promise of life and love, a kind of fertility symbol—the ideal lover and the potential earth mother,"[16] creates a spiritual bridge between Father John and Kabnis. Carrie, who attends to Father John's needs in "The Hole," a trope of black genocide during the Middle Passage, offers a resolution to Kabnis's hybridism. After voicing her criticism, within the dialogic system of the black religious community, of Kabnis's attempt to deconstruct Father John's discourse by saying, "Brother Ralph, is that your best Amen," she

> turns him to her and takes his hot cheeks in her firm cool hands. Her palms draw the fever out. With its passing, Kabnis crumples. He sinks to his knees before her, ashamed, exhausted. His eyes squeeze tight. Carrie presses his face tenderly against her. The suffocation of her fresh starched dress feels good to him. Carrie is about to lift her hands in prayer, when Halsey, at the head of the stairs, calls down. (117)

Carrie's impact on Kabnis suggests both faith healing and religious conversion. Toomer seems to offer a structure that may resolve Kabnis's problem of self-representation in Carrie and Lewis. Taken together, they combine the black soul buttressed by the strength of the black's ancient spirit drawn from the life force of the soil and history of the primal past, with "purpose guided by an adequate intelligence" (117) into the logos that can provide Kabnis with the moral center from which to construct identity from the perspective of the African American folk dialogic system. Even though this paradigm offers interesting possibilities, Toomer tempers the applicability of his model by insisting that Kabnis must reject both nineteenth-century black bourgeois ideologies and moral-religious cultural codes that

16. Frank Durham, *Studies in Cane* (Columbus: Charles E. Merrill, 1971), 112.

sustain "blackness" as the social construct of "whiteness." Carrie's attempt to heal Kabnis's soul is less an act of faith healing than the providing of a spiritual continuum that reconnects him to the black ancient spirit represented by Father John. Her aborted attempt to pray for him suggests that divine intervention is not necessary, since her hands "draw the fever out" (117) and heal his black body.

Although Kabnis sinks to his knees before Carrie and assumes the symbolic posture of repentance for sin and religious conversion, the tropes of salvation, specifically prayer, are supplanted by Halsey's blues discourse: "Well, well. What's up? Aint you ever comin? . . . Take you all mornin t sleep off a pint? Youre weakenin, man, youre weakenin. The axle and th beam's all ready waitin f y. Come on" (117). The tension between Halsey's blues and Carrie's salvific discourse suggest that Kabnis's self-representation exists between the two poles. After Halsey interrupts her prayer for Kabnis with the demand that the protagonist represent himself through the tropes of black labor, Carrie walks to Father John and "slips to her knees before him. Her lips murmur, 'Jesus, come' " (117). The dialectical relationship between Kabnis's ascending the steps from the cellar and Carrie's directional discourse that invokes Jesus as Savior to come down to "save" Kabnis signifies that his salvation is centered in a blues structure, his upward movement to participate in black labor. Carrie's aborted attempt to heal Kabnis's spirit denies him the possibility of liberation from fixity as a signifier of the tropes of the black body.

Just as Kabnis's dilemma of self-representation may be resolved through the structure represented by Carrie and Lewis, it may also be centered in the figures of Carrie and Father John. While Carrie and Lewis offer an alternative to the representation of Kabnis as the black subject commodified through the tropes of black labor, Carrie and Father John posit a resolution centered in the tropes of the black religious experience through salvific discourse that signifies against the delimited social construct of "blackness."

Toomer's narrative revises and repeats tropes of black subjecthood that are at the center of Du Bois's construct of double-consciousness. While Toomer locates the essence of African Americans by reestablishing a relationship between differing representations of black bodies, Du Bois identifies the black essence through the construct of racial doubling. Both Toomer and Du Bois, however, establish the black logos in the dialectical tension between blues and gospels. The blues offers the refrains—"When John comes" for Du Bois and "I've got to get myself together" for Toomer—that structure black discourse by signifying on the tragic nature of black subjecthood. The gospels, meanwhile, allow each author to revise the tropes of salvific discourse that signify against the sins of the dominant racial hegemony. Du Bois's "Of the Coming of John" and Toomer's "Kabnis" depict the dilemma of self-representation in that both John Jones and Ralph Kabnis attempt to construct identity through the tropes of nineteenth-century race leadership but find their efforts generate a disturbing conundrum: The blues refrain delimits their representation to the tropes of black subjecthood, the racialized other.

W. E. B. Du Bois and the Construction of Whiteness

Keith Byerman

W. E. B. Du Bois's construction of blackness through the trope of double-consciousness has been much commented on, especially in recent years. Its sources in nineteenth-century philosophy and psychology, its centrality to Du Bois's own thought in other areas, and its continuing relevance to African American experience have been the subject of analysis and debate.[1] But corollary to and inherent in this definition is another, that of whiteness. After all, the "twoness" he described resulted from white attitudes and behavior; those who looked on "in amused contempt and pity" were being characterized in such a phrase as much as those who were the object of their gaze. And while Du Bois's critics during his life certainly felt they knew his views on the subject of whiteness—he was either white-hating or white-loving—his texts of the early twentieth century in fact reveal considerable subtlety in his representations. This essay focuses on four "moments" of construction of whiteness: the "Forethought and "Afterthought" of *The Souls of Black Folk* (1903), the opening paragraphs of "Of Our Spiritual Strivings" (originally published in 1897), and the essay "The Souls of White Folk" (originally published in 1910). In each of these texts, Du Bois reverses the gaze of racial domination in order to make whites the object rather than the subject of attention. He uses devices of irony, parody, and sarcasm to reconfigure racial power, especially the power of self-definition stolen from blacks in the reality of double-consciousness.

The "Forethought" appears to follow the nineteenth-century genteel convention of apology and apologia for the writer's humble efforts:

1. See Arnold Rampersad, *The Art and Imagination of W. E. B. Du Bois* (Cambridge: Harvard University Press, 1976); Keith Byerman, *Seizing the World: History, Art, and Self in the Works of W. E. B. Du Bois* (Athens: University of Georgia Press, 1994); Eric Sundquist, *To Wake the Nations: Race in the Making of American Literature* (Cambridge: Harvard University Press, 1993); Gerald Early, ed., *Lure and Loathing: Essays on Race, Identity, and the Ambivalence of Assimilation* (New York: Allan Lane/Penguin, 1993); and Shamoon Zamir, *Dark Voices: W. E. B. Du Bois and American Thought, 1888–1903* (Chicago: University of Chicago Press, 1995).

> Herein lie buried many things which if read with patience may show the strange meaning of being black here in the dawning of the Twentieth Century. This meaning is not without interest to you, Gentle Reader; for the problem of the Twentieth Century is the problem of the color-line.
>
> I pray you, then, receive my little book in all charity, studying my words with me, forgiving mistake and foible for sake of the faith and passion that is in me, and seeking the grain of truth hidden there.
>
> I have sought here to sketch, in vague, uncertain outline, the spiritual world in which ten thousand thousand Americans live and strive.[2]

The passage is parodic as well as self-effacing. The deferential tone is contradicted by a text that provides a massive dose of the racial truth that whites have refused to acknowledge. "Gentle Readers" have to be coddled initially because, contrary to their self-image, they lack the moral and intellectual strength to face reality. What has been "buried" is the black experience whites have suppressed and ignored and which readers may continue to deny despite the author's best efforts. The meaning of that experience is "strange" not because blacks are truly alien, but because white prejudice has constructed them as the "other," lacking a common humanity. Moreover, this "little book" takes as its vast subject *the* problem of the twentieth century, which affects ten million African Americans, as well as, by implication, the rest of the nation. In addition, there is nothing "vague" or "uncertain" about the history and social reality detailed in the book. Such terms are relevant only to the extent that whites have refused to see the moral, social, and political contradictions that have been in front of them for centuries. Du Bois appeals to the forgiveness and toleration of his readers, who would expect such behavior from blacks, when the text that these words introduce clearly asserts the audience's responsibility and guilt for the conditions the book describes.

The "Forethought," then, is a signifying performance that reveals its black author as a literary ventriloquist who imitates the white audience's genteel rhetoric as a means of subverting its claims to be the nation and to define the nation as inherently good. He manipulates the language of the dominant culture in order to gain mastery over the cultural masters, thereby exposing their dangerous innocence and incompetence. When he invites them to "study" his words along with him, he is in fact inviting them into a discursive space foreign to them only because of their incompetence and self-deception.

"Of Our Spiritual Strivings" opens with an assault on those "Gentle Readers," specifically northern whites who consider themselves sympathetic to black "strivings." The narrator speaks in the first person about

---

2. W. E. B. Du Bois, *The Souls of Black Folk*, ed. Henry Louis Gates Jr. and Terri Hume Oliver (New York: Norton, 1999), 5. Subsequent references to this edition are cited parenthetically in the text.

being defined as a "problem" and about those responsible for such a designation. They are not violent southern racists, but northern liberals who see blacks not as persons but as a political difficulty:

> Between me and the other world there is ever an unasked question: unasked by some through feelings of delicacy; by others through the difficulty of rightly framing it. All, nevertheless, flutter round it. They approach me in a half-hesitant sort of way, eye me curiously or compassionately, and then, instead of saying directly, How does it feel to be a problem? They say, I know an excellent colored man in my town; or, I fought at Mechanicsville; or, Do not these Southern outrages make your blood boil? At these I smile, or am interested, or reduce the boiling to a simmer, as the occasion may require. To the real question, How does it feel to be a problem? I answer seldom a word. (9–10)

We need to appreciate the humor of this passage, as Du Bois offers us images of "fluttering" whites trying their best to find just the right way to talk to their "alien" guest, while he reduces the "boiling" to a simmer. He is the one who is gracious and tolerant in the face of their awkwardness and ineptitude. Unable to conceptualize him as a person of culture like themselves, they assume that the only thing he can possibly know about is race. This despite the fact that he is Harvard and Berlin educated, a world traveler who speaks to them in a clipped New England accent much like their own. Also, despite their "good breeding" and social etiquette, they focus in their comments on themselves, on their actions, acquaintances, or attitudes. In the process, at least some of them commit one of the great racial faux pas of the twentieth century: claiming connection to some "good" black person.

If we are to understand Du Bois's construction of whiteness as foolishness, we must comprehend the point of making sympathetic whites—those, in fact, most likely to buy and read his book—the initial target for attack. One answer is that they are the ones who control the national culture; as the political, economic, and cultural establishment, they have the patriarchal prerogative of defining and shaping not only black life but also the experiences of the entire South. If Du Bois is to achieve his purpose of making blacks a part of American culture, he must deconstruct and defamiliarize the assumptions of those who exercise cultural hegemony. He does this by offering his own version of white voices; by pointing out what whites *really* mean when they speak to him, he reverses the act of racial definition. In the age of Social Darwinism, the strenuous life, and robber barons, he depicts the "master" race as bumbling, sentimental, and incapable of facing the truth about themselves and about a so-called inferior race.

This language of subversion operates within the context of his recognition of the real power of whites, both northern and southern. To parody or satirize white behavior and language is not, of course, to deny their often overwhelming effects on black life. In fact, calling attention to whiteness in this manner is necessitated by Du Bois's awareness that there are few ways for the powerless to change circumstances unless those who dominate are willing to change. Only by making whites aware of their position as a racial group rather than as the norm against which blacks (and others) are negatively judged is it possible to reconfigure the social order.

His reframing of racial identity in this way, so that the anxiety of whites about their privilege is placed in the foreground, allows him to structure the notion of "problem" in a fundamentally different way. The effort to make him (and others like him) the problem exposes underlying white uncertainty about their own identity and status. If speaking to Du Bois causes anxiety and discomfort among people who otherwise move effectively through the world, then he may not be the problem at all. If they have to prove themselves to him, if they are limited in their understanding of him, if they can be so easily made the target of his humor, and, finally, if *the* problem of the coming century is a color line they created and maintain (as they do in the scenario he depicts), then *they* are the problem.

Du Bois follows this cultural critique with a brief personal narrative that demonstrates the impact of assumed white superiority. Because it is a story of childhood, it implicates the society as a whole, since it is adults who teach racial attitudes.

> In a wee wooden schoolhouse, something put it into the boys' and girls' heads to buy gorgeous visiting-cards—ten cents a package—and exchange. The exchange was merry, till one girl, a tall newcomer, refused my card,— refused it peremptorily, with a glance. Then it dawned on me with a certain suddenness that I was different from the others; or like, mayhap, in heart and life and longing, but shut out from their world by a vast veil. I had thereafter no desire to tear down that veil, to creep through; I held all beyond it in common contempt, and lived above it in a region of blue sky and great wandering shadows. That sky was bluest when I could beat my mates at examination-time, or beat them at a foot-race, or even beat their stringy heads. (10)

What is usually discussed in this story is the effect of the affront on Du Bois; it serves as his racial initiation and leads him to a position of antagonism and competition with his white schoolmates. He becomes the victim of the "white gaze" and thereby enters the realm of double-consciousness. But it is also important to understand what the narrative says to the white audience, who, after all, would instinctively identify with the girl and the other students, not with the author. It is worth noting that the girl is a newcomer and thus not necessarily familiar with local racial mores or with the community's view of "Willie" Du Bois. But despite her "alien" status, she claims white privilege; whether it is good social form or not, she has the right to reject his participation in the society and to do so without apology or explanation. She can define him as less than human with her "peremptory" glance and be confident that her behavior will be tolerated by other whites.

It is perhaps this toleration of racism that is the real though unnamed focus of the story. Du Bois does not record the responses of teachers or other students to this affront. Instead, he registers his changed relationship to them. His alienation from those with whom he had previously been identified (after all, he assumed his inclusion in the visiting-card ritual) suggests their violation of his trust. They deserve his abuse because they have implicitly taken the side of the white outsider against him. They have made him rather than her the problem. Symbolically, those childhood friends are his white audience; they have made blackness the problem by refusing to act against those who victimize blacks. And like that community, they have resisted the truth about themselves in such a way as to be surprised and offended that he (and blacks generally) might see them as opponents and even want, at times, "to beat their stringy heads." Thus, whiteness is characterized as a status of privilege that can both exempt itself from the moral and social loyalties of friendship and community and simultaneously remain innocent of such betrayal.

The "Afterthought" acknowledges white power while appealing for white self-recognition and criticism. Like the "Forethought," it does so through rhetorical devices, though they are different from the earlier ones:

> Hear my cry, O God the Reader; vouchsafe that this my book fall not still-born into the world-wilderness. Let there spring, Gentle One, from out its leaves vigor of thought and thoughtful deed to reap the harvest wonderful. Let the ears of a guilty people tingle with truth, and seventy millions sigh for the righteousness which exalteth nations, in this drear day when human brotherhood is mockery and a snare. Thus in Thy good time may infinite reason turn the tangle straight, and these crooked marks on a fragile leaf be not indeed
> THE END. (164)

Here the reader becomes a divinity with the power of life and death over this articulation of black experience. We do not find the same level of parody, even though the language is similarly genteel. Having made the effort to sensitize his readers to their blindness and lack of understanding and having explained to them in great detail the black experience that they have too long ignored, Du Bois must confront their authority over his word. Whiteness may well be a feeble, fluttering, inhumane condition, but it is still linked to an arrogant assumption of superiority and privilege. His commentary on Booker T. Washington, his delineation of the psychological effects of racism, his portrait of white insensitivity at his son's funeral may all say something true about American race relations, but his audience, because of their whiteness, can cause that truth to be "still-born."

But this recognition cannot be allowed to suggest submission to white power. The parenthetical comment intrudes into the text to rehumanize and criticize that same reader. Because whites unconsciously think of their color as sacred, they must be reminded of their guilt and of their misuse of their Godlike power. Instead of using it to create a higher order, they have made of human brotherhood a "mockery and a snare." This passage was written at a time of intense racial violence, including dozens of lynchings annually, of more restrictive segregation, of an intellectual community that takes for granted the scientific validity of white supremacy, of a compromised black leadership led by Washington, and of a recent war in part against peoples of color elsewhere in the world. As Du Bois wrote his "Afterword," whites were acting the part of imperious and imperial gods who assume the right of their race to define and control the rest of the nation and the world.

The point of the figuration of the reader as divine is not to validate such notions of white supremacy but rather to point to the power of the audience to change the world. The responsibility to do so is evident in the reference to guilt and in the call of the text, which waits to be answered through the deeds of the readers. Whiteness, which has been throughout these passages associated with a kind of willful innocence, a corrupt arrogance, and an imposition of responsibility onto its victims, still has the possibility of redemption through an engagement with the truth of Du Bois's book.

If whiteness is constructed in *The Souls of Black Folk* through a rhetoric of indirection and moral appeal that assumes a real if flawed white humanity, in "The Souls of White Folk" whiteness is constituted as the very being of the demonic. It can in fact be argued that the title is a bitter irony in that, unlike the profound souls of black folk, this essay suggests that whites have no souls at all. It opens with its own comic gesture through the "black gaze":

> I see these souls undressed and from the back and side. I see the working of their entrails. I know their thoughts and they know that I know. This knowledge makes them now embarrassed, now furious! They deny my right to live and be and call me misbirth! My word is to them mere bitterness and my soul, pessimism. And yet as they preach and strut and shout and threaten, crouching as they clutch at rags of facts and fancies to hide their nakedness, they go twisting, flying by my tired eyes and I see them ever stripped,—ugly, human.[3]

3. W. E. B. Du Bois, "The Souls of White Folk," in *Darkwater: Voices from within the Veil* (1920; reprint, New York: Schocken, 1969), 29.

The authority of blacks is precisely their position as servants, as subaltern. When you have seen the powerful in their nakedness, it is hard to take seriously their pretensions of grandeur and superiority. That whites know that blacks—the very ones placed in positions of service because they are assumed to be inferior—can thereby see white flaws and weaknesses, creates its own discomfort and rage. Imperial whiteness becomes a kind of silliness as it strives to maintain that its own bare skin is the grandest of clothing. The richness of the image is in Du Bois's recognition that the emblem of superiority, white skin, when understood as a simple physical reality, becomes associated with vulnerability and shame. Thus, whiteness is caught in its own paradox, its own double-consciousness: Because nakedness can be weakness, white skin must be mostly hidden if it is to symbolize power rather than absurdity. But to conceal it is to grant to the subaltern the power of a shaming gaze. To paraphrase Du Bois's most famous line: In this essay, the problem of the twentieth century is the problem of the white body.

"The Souls of White Folk" works from this starting point of the performance of whiteness as farce to more significant manifestations. In this context, it is useful to understand that this essay was originally published in 1910 but was modified with references to World War I for incorporation in *Darkwater* in 1920. Like recent social constructionists, Du Bois argues that race generally and whiteness specifically is a recent invention, a product of the nineteenth century, and thus not a permanent aspect of human reality.[4] What begins as absurdity in thinking and behaving turns to "tragedy" as belief in color superiority leads to paternalism toward one's so-called inferiors. The problem for this stage of whiteness is that the inferiors do not necessarily accept their assigned status; they refuse to be the necessary complement to white nobility.

This refusal to be enslaved and dominated in relationship to European and American civilization and religion leads to a new stage in the formulation of whiteness, one in which hatred and violence become necessary to the maintenance of domination. Whiteness becomes, Du Bois says, the only standard of morality; anything done in its name is acceptable, even if it violates all other principles of western civilization. This not only leads to assaults on whatever groups of nonwhites come within the sights of

4. On the idea of the social construction of race, see Michael Omi and Howard Winant, *Racial Formation in the United States, from the 1960s to the 1990s*, 2d ed. (New York: Routledge, 1994). On the concept of whiteness as racial construction, see Joe R. Feagin and Hernán Vera, *White Racism* (New York: Routledge, 1995); David Theo Goldberg, ed., *Anatomy of Racism* (Minneapolis: University of Minnesota Press, 1990); Mike Hill, ed., *Whiteness: A Critical Reader* (New York: New York University Press, 1997); and Richard Delgado and Jean Stefancic, eds., *Critical White Studies: Looking behind the Mirror* (Philadelphia: Temple University Press, 1997).

white nations or alliances, but also inevitably leads to the self-destruction of world war.

Whiteness for Du Bois comes to be associated with all possible evil and sinful qualities: demonic Christianity, greed, war, violent colonialism, theft, delusion, cruelty, exploitation, dishonesty. He sees America as the vanguard of human hatred:

> Up through the foam of green and weltering waters wells this great mass of hatred, in wilder, fiercer violence, until I look down and know that today to the millions of my people no misfortune could happen,—of death and pestilence, failure and defeat—that would not make the hearts of millions of their fellows beat with fierce, vindictive joy! Do you doubt it? Ask your own soul what it would say if the next census were to report that half of black America was dead and the other half dying. (33)

At the very moment that American newspapers were displaying sensational headlines about the atrocities committed by Turks and Germans, they maintained a strange silence about their own nation's racial violence, which amounts, in Du Bois's view, to a genocidal impulse. Their arguments for the superiority of the United States is subverted by the failure of democracy and equality in their midst. Given the commitment to white supremacy, only the disappearance of nonwhites can make that ideal nation possible. Thus, whiteness necessarily is equated to violence and inhumanity.

Du Bois works though all the elements of western civilization to demonstrate that each—religion, economics, government, art and philosophy, science—has been turned to the purposes of holocaust and self-aggrandizement. White Christianity, for example, "is a miserable failure." He asserts that the number of whites who actually practice "the democracy and unselfishness of Jesus Christ" is so small that it is ludicrous and would be an appropriate subject of satire if the effects were not so deadly. The belief in religious superiority helps to justify virtually any behavior in the European colonies and in the United States. Because God is on the side of whiteness, and because God is in fact an expression of whiteness, the rules of religious practice do not apply to the treatment of nonwhites. But the irony Du Bois develops in response to this claim is that Christianity, like all the world's major religions, is a product of the darker world that whites hate and would destroy. Jesus, Muhammad, Confucius, and Buddha all belong to "inferior" races. It is only historical chance that has made Europe the center of Christianity. Implicit in this recognition is an argument that whites, unable to generate a faith of their own, have had to expropriate one from their moral and cultural elders. Like the girl from his school days, they are outsiders who have claimed a privilege and possession that is not truly theirs. In this sense, it is not surprising that they have never gotten it right. And, again, the subaltern knows:

> These super-men and world-mastering demi-gods listened, however, to no low tongues of ours, even when we pointed silently to their feet of clay. Perhaps we, as folks of simpler soul and more primitive type, have been most struck in the welter of recent years by the utter failure of white religion. We have curled our lips in something like contempt as we have witnessed glib apology and weary explanation. . . . Nor would we be unfair in this criticism: We know that we, too, have failed, as you have, and have rejected many a Buddha, even as you have denied Christ; but we acknowledge our human frailty, while you, claiming super-humanity, scoff endlessly at our shortcomings. (35–36)

Du Bois struggles somewhat here to resist his own feelings of superiority. He parodies the discourse of white supremacy, but he admits to a contemptuous gaze in noting the reality of that discourse. He becomes playful in identifying with Buddhists, but he returns to the dehumanizing scoffing of whites. In this sense, whiteness is maddening; it keeps claiming, against all the evidence, a position above and in control of those who are its moral and cultural betters.

But whites are not to be understood as recalcitrant children, for their intelligence and power is too great for that. Whiteness is rather a kind of demon that has taken every useful thing, whether stolen or created, and turned it to the destruction of all human values. It has used science to create a technology of war greater than any previously imaginable. It has devised an economic system that values nothing but acquisition; a political system dependent on domination. The crucial example for Du Bois is Belgium, which was depicted in the American press as the poor victim of German brutality. Yet it was this same small nation that murdered twelve million people in the Congo as it committed all forms of savagery in order to make itself wealthy. All of this was done, of course, in the name of Christianity and civilization.

Whiteness has, in effect, constructed itself as the very opposite of what it claims as validation for its superiority. It violates all of its own principles and therefore cannot stand. World War I becomes for Du Bois the logical conclusion of the reality whiteness has made for itself. An identity constructed on domination and illusions of superiority must eventually produce self-destructive excess; because whiteness is a historically specific construction, each version of it eventually must come into conflict with others. Because its basis is greed and not genetics, white nations turn against each other once they begin to see the limits of exploitation of the nonwhite world. But Du Bois is careful to point out that the war is not an aberration:

"This is not Europe gone mad; this *is* Europe; this seeming Terrible is the real soul of white culture—back of all culture,—stripped and visible to-day" (39).

He returns us here to white nakedness, but now it is pure madness that is exposed. Europe (and America) is the madness. It is not really an embodiment at all; it is a force set loose in the world that ordinary human beings take on as their identity, their clothing, but which they cannot control. Whiteness is a destructive energy that compels ordinary people to assume attitudes and engage in behaviors that are counter to their and everyone else's humanity. The foolishness of white people is in believing that this force that they created is one that they can control and one that in fact is themselves. But it is a terrible foolishness, not simply (or primarily) because it does harm to them, but because it allows for the destruction, either in reality or fantasy, of the rest of humanity.

It is essential to keep in mind that Du Bois's ultimate concern is not the salvation of white souls, but the preservation of black (and other) bodies. He returns after his diatribe against Europe to his own nation, which he sees as moving in the same direction as Europe and possibly becoming the leader of the forces of white supremacy. As the nation reluctantly takes in those it had not previously defined as white, it grants them racial status by teaching them to hate its older, darker citizens. It replicates the European model by making hatred and violence the essence of whiteness. Thus, it, too, begins the cycle of self-destruction. Its claims to democracy and Christianity will continue to be empty as it recirculates the energies of racial madness.

In the end, as is often the case in Du Bois's work, he balances hope with defiance and anger. He positions himself as an observer above the storm that has been created by war, greed, and murder. He worries that his voice of reason cannot be heard amid the noise of destruction. Caught in his gaze is the "Soul of White Folk," a Prometheus bound by its own racial myth:

> I hear his mighty cry reverberating through the world, "I am white!" Well and good, O Prometheus, divine thief! Is not the world wide enough for two colors, for many little shinings of the sun? Why, then, devour your own vitals if I answer even as proudly, "I am black!" (52)

If whiteness is the binding force, then recognition of it as myth rather than reality will liberate not only whites, but also Du Bois, who will no longer have to take refuge from the racial storm in the tower, and by extension all people of color, who will no longer have to suffer from the effects of the illusion. If whiteness is merely a physical condition, then it can be accepted as one part of a spectrum of humanity.

But Du Bois does not seem quite satisfied with this pluralistic solution, and it is here that his anger seems to feed back into the "problem." If Prometheus is loosed from the bonds of whiteness, meaning that race is deconstructed, in what sense would whiteness continue to have meaning such that it would be necessary for Du Bois to proudly counterassert his blackness? In fact, he does not envision the white soul freed at all. At the beginning of the essay, he claimed to "see the working of their entrails," as well as their nakedness. At the end, he seems almost to taunt the white Prometheus, who will devour those very parts if black pride is proclaimed. Alongside the hope for a more humane world in which peoples of color and especially African Americans can take their rightful place, Du Bois would place the demand for justice, the punishment of whites for what they have done in the name of the evil force they created, took on as an identity, and turned upon their historical victims. It is this righteous indignation, this controlled anger, that compels Du Bois to challenge rather than implore his readers and to engage in frontal assault when he deems it appropriate. By 1920, then, whiteness for Du Bois is not simply a "social construction" to be discussed in the cool language of social science or in the genteel rhetoric of moral appeal; it is a demonic, horrific invention that its creators must be compelled to destroy.

The Intersecting Rhetorics of Art and Blackness in *The Souls of Black Folk*

Amy Helene Kirschke

W. E. B. Du Bois often spoke passionately about the veil that African Americans had to endure, shut out from the white world, always seeing themselves through the revelation of the other world. This double consciousness, the topic that is woven throughout *The Souls of Black Folk* (1903), also applies to the visual arts. Du Bois began to establish his commitment to the visual arts when he was writing and compiling *The Souls of Black Folk*, a commitment that he later carried out in his years as editor of the *Crisis*, the official organ of the NAACP. Although there are only a few specific references to the visual arts in *Souls*, Du Bois nevertheless believed in the significance of the visual arts as an important part of the development of a black aesthetic. The power of a visual artist to express the ideals of Du Bois is exemplified in the artistic contrast of the works of Henry O. Tanner, an African American artist active when *Souls* was written, and Aaron Douglas, the leading visual artist of the Harlem Renaissance, who worked diligently for Du Bois in the 1920s at the *Crisis*.

From his writing in *Souls*, it is evident that Du Bois understood that Americans saw high culture as a measure of their greatness and level of civilization. Yet the opportunities for African Americans to receive training or pursue a career in the arts were extremely limited, in fact almost nonexistent, when this book was published. The black artist could attempt to uplift himself in the eyes of white men, could serve his race by creating objects of beauty that would be worthy of great pride, but in order to do this, the artist would need proper training. (This dilemma was one that white artists in the United States faced as well but was a far more profound problem for African American artists.) Du Bois also referred to the confusion and doubt in the soul of the black artist, "for the beauty revealed to him was the soul-beauty of a race which his larger audience despised,

The author wishes to thank Thomas Schwartz and Beth Aplin Rollins for their helpful comments and criticisms of earlier drafts of this essay.

and he could not articulate the message of another people" (12). Art was an obvious way to express one's beliefs, to showcase the best of a race, and to encourage self-consciousness, self-realization, and self-respect (14). In Du Bois's eyes, the black artist would carry a burden, a great social responsibility. Later, during the Harlem Renaissance of the 1920s, Du Bois would more fully describe the great responsibility of the artist to support, propagate, and better his race, but in his early writings, he only alludes to this responsibility.

The black artist in America had few opportunities for formal training, so he often had to go abroad, especially to Paris, to be trained. Then, the harsh reality of the vast differences between Europe and America, and the opportunities not available to him upon his return, confronted him. Universities needed to provide black artists with the tools to express the essence of their race. As Du Bois noted, they played a pivotal role in "that fine adjustment between real life and the growing knowledge of life, an adjustment which forms the secret of civilization" (60). The black citizen, too, needed to receive that higher education, the end of which is culture (11). Du Bois emphasized the need of the individual, including the black artist, to realize more deeply than he did at present "the need of uplifting the masses of his people."[1] One way to do that was through thoughtful, dignified representations of African Americans. Du Bois did pay homage to the roots of Africa, most especially through music and through the church. But he would not recognize until much later the need to connect to African arts, a connection that one of his greatest protégés, Aaron Douglas, was able to make for him visually in the *Crisis*.

Du Bois noted in his *Conversation of Races* of 1897 that black people had "not as yet given to civilization the full spiritual message which they are capable of giving . . . for the development of Negro genius, of Negro literature and art, of Negro spirit, only Negroes bound and welded together, Negroes inspired by one vast ideal, can work out in its fullness the great message we have for humanity."[2] Du Bois looked for sources—including visual artists—of this spiritual oneness in *The Souls of Black Folk*, but he found few examples. Up until then, most black visual artists did not depict black subject matter in their work. They avoided it for many reasons, most importantly because white patrons either had no interest in or despised such subject matter. Black artists needed a sufficient audience of black middle-class patrons to support such endeavors, an audience that would not develop for some time.

Few black artists were known at the time Du Bois wrote *Souls*. Joshua

1. W. E. B. Du Bois, *The Souls of Black Folk,* ed. Henry Louis Gates and Terri Hume Oliver (New York: Norton, 1999), 6. Subsequent references will be to this edition.
2. W. E. B. Du Bois, "The Conservation of Races," in *The Souls of Black Folk,* ed. David W. Blight and Robert Gooding-Williams (Boston: Bedford, 1997), 232–33.

Johnson painted his early *Portrait of a Cleric*, a depiction of an African American minister in 1805–1810. Edmonia Lewis had sculpted her *Forever Free* in 1867, portraying two freed African American slaves. Edward Mitchell Bannister had painted his *Newspaper Boy* in 1869, which appears to be a portrait of a young African American boy. However, these were among the few pieces known to include African American subjects actually created by African Americans. Du Bois did mention Henry O. Tanner, who had created his black genre works before *Souls* was published. His works had received a great deal of attention in the press as soon as they were complete.

The great father figure of African American art, Tanner fit the Du Boisian ideal of an educated, directed member of the race. Henry Ossawa Tanner was born in 1859 in Pittsburgh, the son of Benjamin Tucker Tanner, a college-educated and a seminary-trained minister of the African Methodist Episcopal Church who eventually became a bishop in 1888. Tanner grew to understand both religious and racial issues through his father, who dealt with these topics in his writings. Tanner's mother was a former slave who also had a strong interest in education, which she helped instill in her seven children. Although Henry was the most famous of the children, all of them were well educated and professionally successful, including Tanner's sister Halle Tanner Dillon Johnson, a doctor who became the first woman and the first black licensed to practice medicine in Alabama. Tanner eventually received his training at the Pennsylvania Academy of the Fine Arts, under the famous American painter Thomas Eakins. Despite the excellent training he received at the academy, Tanner encountered racial prejudice and discrimination from his fellow students and eventually chose to leave in 1882. He moved to Atlanta, where he opened a small photography studio, utilizing techniques he had learned from Eakins. In 1891 Tanner escaped the racial hostility and limitations of America and sailed for Europe, settling in Paris. Here, he attended the Académie Julien, where he was able to receive first-rate direction from visiting instructors from the government-operated Ecole des Beaux-Arts, which could not admit foreign students. It was in this period that he painted his only works to include African American subjects, including two portraits he did of his mother and father in 1897. These African American subjects meet Du Bois's expectations for showing the spirit, dignity, and grace of his people. While few in number, they are some of his most famous works.

Tanner did not shun his race in his works. As the son of an African Methodist Episcopal bishop and a devout Christian himself, he felt called to share God's message through his art, a goal that would also meet with Du Bois's assertion of the devoutness of the black race, outlined in his chapter 10, "Of the Faith of the Fathers." Tanner could carry out the words of the preacher, whom Du Bois called "the most unique personality developed by the Negro on American soil" (120). Du Bois considered the Negro church the "social centre of Negro life in the United States, and the most characteristic expression of African character" (121). As a gifted artist as well as a devout Christian, Tanner was in the unique position to spread God's word to both black and white audiences. Tanner had been shut out of the white art world by the "vast veil" to which Du Bois so often referred. His response to artistic apartheid was to live in Paris, where he could paint freely as a black painter and welcome and help guide other black artists when they came to study abroad.

Tanner's early paintings in Paris included genre scenes from African American life. Tanner took on the responsibility of showing his race in ordinary situations, lifting the veil, not allowing the viewer to see those depicted in his works as anything else but average people going about their daily lives, with a message in tow. This was truly groundbreaking work. Tanner was familiar to earlier artists such as Lewis and Bannister but knew that he was forging a new path with his black genre scenes.

Tanner painted his *Banjo Lesson* in 1893, most likely executed in Philadelphia during a brief return to the U.S., where he stated in his own words, using the third-person:

> Since his return from Europe he has painted mostly Negro subjects, he feels drawn to such subjects on account of the newness of the field and because of a desire to represent the serious, and pathetic side of life among them, and it is his thought that other things being equal, he who has most sympathy with his subject will obtain the best results. To his mind many of the artists who have represented Negro life have only seen the comic, the ludicrous side of it, and have lacked sympathy with and appreciation for the warm big heart that dwells within such a rough exterior.[3]

In August 1893 Tanner underscored this point in a paper he delivered, "The American Negro in Art," before the World's Congress on Africa, held in Chicago at the same time as the World's Columbian Exposition.[4] Tanner was willing to accept the burden of being a spokesperson for his race via his portrayals of black life and his religious paintings. The plight of the poor, the mission that Du Bois spoke of in the first chapter in *The Souls of Black Folk*, "Of Our Spiritual Strivings," is evident in Tanner's works. First working from a study photograph, Tanner developed the composition for the *Banjo Lesson,* featuring an older black man with gray hair seated in a chair, guiding a black youngster as he plays the banjo. The picture also emphasizes uniquely American music, here black American music, which Du Bois considered to be one of the greatest gifts of black America, as he makes

3. Dewey F. Mosby, *Henry Ossawa Tanner* (Philadelphia: Philadelphia Museum of Art, 1991), 116.
4. Ibid., 116.

1. Henry Ossawa Tanner (1859–1937), *The Banjo Lesson*, oil on canvas, 49" × 35 ½".
Collection of Hampton University Museum, Hampton, Virginia.

evident in his fourteenth chapter, "The Sorrow Songs." Tanner paints his piece in characteristic Impressionist style, no doubt a style he developed both with Eakins and during his first brief stay in Paris, where Impressionism still thrived. The interior is simple, the lighting is soft, the two figures are closely engaged in their task, both figures with their hands on the banjo, in deep concentration. It is a straightforward, dignified, loving scene, and no white audience could disdain such a work. The critics immediately noted the skill of the work, and the fact that it was greatly admired and surrounded frequently by a large crowd of spectators. One white critic particularly admired Tanner's work but was unable to ignore Tanner's race when he described the two figures by saying "old Uncle Ned, bald and venerable, has a bare-footed little darkey of seven or eight years between his knees." The same critic conceded, however, that "The heads are especially well drawn, that of the child being a study Mr. Tanner may well be proud of, and the faces are informed with intelligence and expression."[5]

Why would Tanner have taken up African American subjects in his brief stay in Philadelphia in 1893–1894? Dewey Mosby has summed up the work of several scholars on Tanner, suggesting that his participation in the Chicago congress forced him to "reacquaint himself with American prejudices, and inspired him to take up the black cause in art." Tanner, Mosby continues, also might have turned to African American subjects in response to a challenge, actual or implied, from his father "to demonstrate that he could make positive statements about his race from the canvas just as effectively as his father could form the pulpit." While the subject of the banjo player is not unusual, Tanner shows his figures with sympathy and in a scene of musical education, departing from other artists' "ludicrous" or "comic" depictions of black Americans. Tanner may also have chosen a cliché to show that he could reinterpret the scene with compassion and dignity.[6]

Tanner's second known genre scene of black life was painted sometime in 1894, *The Thankful Poor.* Such a subject was commonplace in European painting, but Tanner replaced Dutch or French peasants with two African Americans. Again, an elderly man and young boy make up the composition, this time seated across a table, bowing their heads in thankful prayer for the meager meal they are about to share. The window on the left provides the sole source of light, illuminating the face of the young boy and obscuring the features of the elderly man on the left, presenting him in silhouette. The figures again are depicted with great skill and respect; they are dignified and devout. Tanner's artistic skill is combined with his father's messages in this work. The dignified depiction of an elderly man

5. Ibid., 118.
6. Ibid., 120.

and boy praying before their humble meal transcends any other image of black Americans in American art.[7]

Tanner's final work of this period, which focuses on an African American figure, *The Young Sabot Maker,* was completed in 1895 after a series of sketches fine-tuned the composition. This work again turned to the serious side of African American life. The final version of the work shows a young boy—who in earlier studies did not appear to be black, but is now clearly a young man of African American heritage—in deep concentration while his white mentor observes approvingly as he earnestly carves the wooden shoes. The work is again in the style of the Impressionists, this time with a slightly tighter brush stroke. It was exhibited in Paris, although it was not singled out for special praise.

Finally, Tanner would abandon his African American genre scenes and turn back to religious painting. He returned to Paris for the opportunities the capital of the art world would allow him. He had a greater social freedom there as well as more opportunities to exhibit and sell his works. His abandonment of this subject matter was not from a lack of interest in the subject or his race; he continued to assist black artists who came to Paris. Rather, Tanner, the bishop's son caught in what Du Bois called "the contradiction of double aims" (11), believed that the greatest way he could serve his race and, more importantly, God, was to illuminate God's words in his works.

Tanner felt the commitment to guide other African American artists, many of whom would seek him out for advice and direction in Paris. He spoke of meeting an African American in Paris, shortly before his death in 1937. He recognized that the young man probably had not heard of him but also noted that it was not all for himself that he had tried in the measure of his ability to make a success of his life. Tanner's great success was providing a role model for other black artists of his time, and those of succeeding generations. It was not only his black genre paintings that would provide inspiration but also his religious works that would show that he was able to combat the racial "veil" and become a leader of his race through his art. Upon seeing his religious painting *Christ and Nicodemus* (1899), Aaron Douglas would cite Tanner as the reason he was inspired to become an artist.

Tanner was a player in the social revolution of which Du Bois spoke in *The Souls of Black Folk* (25–29). In "The Negro in Literature and Art," published in 1913, Du Bois praised Tanner as one of those black artists who had earned distinction in something other than literature: "One need only mention Henry O. Tanner whose pictures hang in the great galleries of the world, including the Luxembourg. There are a score of other less known

7. Ibid.

painters including Bannister, Harper, Scott and Brown." In 1921 Du Bois referred to Tanner in "The Contribution of the Negro to American Life and Culture," where he stated: "The American Negro has his painters like Tanner, known throughout the world, and sculptors like Edmonia Lewis once widely known, but now forgotten."[8]

After the publication of *The Souls of Black Folk,* Du Bois continued to write and reflect on the significance of the visual arts for African American culture in the pages of the *Crisis.* In "Criteria of Negro Art," Du Bois asserted the obligation of the black artist, to which he first alluded in *The Souls of Black Folk:*

> Thus it is the bounden duty of black America to begin this great work of the creation of beauty, of the preservation of beauty, of the realization of beauty, and we must use in this work all the methods that men have used before. And what have been the tools of the artist in times gone by? First of all, he has used the truth . . . again artists have used goodness . . . justice, honor and right . . . as the one true method of gaining sympathy and human interest.[9]

In *Souls,* Du Bois already felt that art needed to have a message, that African Americans, including artists, had a new self-respect, a new power, and a social responsibility. In 1921 he wrote in "Negro Art" that:

> Negro Art is today plowing a difficult row, chiefly because we shrink at the portrayal of the truth about ourselves. We are so used to seeing the truth distorted to our despite, that whenever we are portrayed on canvas, in story or on the stage, as simply human with human frailties, we rebel. We want everything that is said about us to tell of the best and highest and noblest in us. We insist that our Art and Propaganda be one.
> This is wrong and in the end it is harmful.[10]

Only five years later, feeling that much more radical action was necessary for change to occur, Du Bois altered his position dramatically and articulated these issues in his "Criteria of Negro Art" in the *Crisis.* Du Bois now stated that art should serve a purpose, the purpose of propaganda, which he had previously criticized:

> Thus all art is propaganda and ever must be, despite the wailing of the purists. I stand in utter shamelessness and say that whatever art I have for writing has been used always for propaganda for gaining the right of black folk to love and enjoy. I do not care a damn for any art that is not used for

8. Du Bois, "The Negro in Literature and Art," *Annals of the American Academy of Political and Social Science* 49 (September 1913): 235; Du Bois, "The Contribution of the Negro to American Life and Culture," *Pacific Review* 2 (June 1921): 130.

9. Du Bois, "Criteria of Negro Art," *Crisis* 32 (October 1926): 296–97.

10. Du Bois, "Negro Art," *Crisis* 22 (June 1921): 55.

propaganda. But I do care when propaganda is confined to one side while the other is stripped and silent.[11]

Du Bois refers in *Souls* to the need for African Americans to have a voice, including through the ballot. He also states that "Negro blood has a message for the world. . . . He simply wishes to make it possible for a man to be both a Negro and an American, without being cursed and spit upon by his fellows, without having the doors of Opportunity closed roughly in his face" (11). Scholars have interpreted this change as consistent with the era's emerging Marxist aesthetics, anticipating the black arts movement of the 1960s in its recognition of the ideological nature of art.[12] In *Souls*, Du Bois planted the seed that a black aesthetic cannot just be theoretical, it must also be practical and grounded in the experience of the community. He challenged black artists to transform images and to question the ethics of a community that excludes them from almost any affirmative representation in life and in art. This was a message that an artist could convey, and by 1926 Du Bois had developed it fully from the seed he planted in *The Souls of Black Folk* at the dawn of the century. And it was a message coming from a man who had seen the great European masterpieces, was very moved by them, and well understood the power of art.

In *Dusk of Dawn*, published in 1940, Du Bois noted the commitment he had to the visual arts in his own magazine as early as 1910. He stated that he encouraged the graphic arts not only by magazine covers with "Negro themes and faces" but in portrayals of the faces and features of "colored folk." He noted how rare that was in 1910, as "colored papers carried few or no illustrations; the white papers none. In many great periodicals, it was the standing rule that no Negro portrait was to appear."[13] Du Bois also attempted to bring positive visual imagery to African American children in 1921 in *The Brownie's Book,* which gave him great satisfaction but which he admitted did not pay for itself. In "Negro Writers," Du Bois again made reference to his commitment to visual arts in the *Crisis* in 1920: "Since its founding, *The Crisis* has been eager to discover ability among Negroes, especially in literature and art."[14]

11. Du Bois, "Criteria of Negro Art," 296–97.

12. Keith E. Byerman, *Seizing the Word: History, Art, and Self in the Works of W. E. B. Du Bois* (Athens: University of Georgia Press, 1994), 101; see also Addison Gayle, ed., *The Black Aesthetic* (Garden City, N.Y.: Doubleday, 1971). While Du Bois argued for an "activist and political" role for cultural expression, Locke argued that art and literature should strive for excellence and eschew specifically political aims. See Alain Locke, "Art or Propaganda," in *The Critical Temper of Alain Locke: A Selection of His Essays on Art and Culture,* ed. Jeffrey C. Stewart (New York: Garland, 1983).

13. W. E. B. Du Bois, *Dusk of Dawn: An Essay toward an Autobiography of a Race Concept* (1940; reprint, New York: Schocken Books, 1968), 271.

14. Du Bois, "Negro Writers," *Crisis* 19 (April 1920): 298–99. For a discussion of the role magazines such as *Crisis* and *Opportunity* played in the making of an African Amer-

In the last two chapters in *The Souls of Black Folk*, "Of the Coming of John" and "The Sorrow Songs," Du Bois asserted his belief that art expresses social, political, and historical realities. For Du Bois, both the making and the evaluation of art carried ideological weight. The protoganist in the "Of the Coming of John" becomes educated, cultured, and as a member of the Talented Tenth, comes home to educate his own people, only to be frustrated by black provincialism and white resistance to black advancement. The message of John's hopeless situation is one of self-sacrifice. This story shows Du Bois's unfailing efforts towards racial equality and a sense of despair as well in the face of the realities of white America. In "The Sorrow Songs," Du Bois celebrates the authentic "master songs," those that retain the authenticity of the slave experience, turning to true black expressions, the spirituals, as spiritually based art that transcends history. So, too, he looks for an authentic voice in art, one that expresses African American history and rich cultural tradition.

Du Bois understood the importance of African culture, making reference to it in *The Souls of Black Folk* and then referring to it later in several writings. For example, in "The Answer of Africa," he writes: "The sense of beauty is the last and best gift of Africa to the world and the true essence of the black man's soul. African art is the offspring of the African climate and the Negro soul . . . the primitive art of Africa is one of the greatest expressions of the human soul in all time . . . 'that black men invented art as they invented fire.' " In 1916 he wrote in "The Drama among Black Folk" that "The Negro is essentially dramatic. His greatest gift to the world has been and will be a gift of art, of appreciation and realization of beauty."[15] In short, Du Bois challenges the black artist to join him in a bold reconceptualization of beauty.

Du Bois tries to bring us to recognize the suffering of African Americans and their art in *The Souls of Black Folk*. Du Bois expresses the tragedy of the "twoness" of black life and the refusal of whites to see the Negro as a partner in creating the nation's culture, and their continuing denial of their ties to black folk.[16] Du Bois sought to realize the goals he set forth in *Souls* by sponsoring and encouraging black artists. His most successful protégé was Aaron Douglas, a former high school teacher from Kansas City, who would become the leading visual artist of the Harlem Renaissance. After having seen a cover of the magazine *Survey Graphic*, which was graced by

---

ican intellectual tradition, see Abby Arthur Johnson and Ronald Maberry Johnson, *Propaganda and Aesthetics: The Literary Politics of Afro-American Magazines in the Twentieth Century* (Amherst: University of Massachusetts Press, 1979).

15. Du Bois, "The Answer of Africa," in Maurice Maeterlinck, Dhan Gopal Mukerji, et al., *What Is Civilization?* (New York: Duffield, 1926), 46; Du Bois, "The Drama among Black Folk," *Crisis* 12 (August 1916): 169.

16. See *Souls*, ed. Blight and Gooding-Williams, 11.

a Winold Reiss portrait of actor Roland Hayes, Douglas decided to join the black artists he read about by traveling to Harlem. Almost immediately after he arrived, the twenty-six-year-old Douglas was introduced to Du Bois. Du Bois recognized Douglas's talent immediately and hired him to provide illustrations for the covers, stories, and poems of the *Crisis*. In *Dusk of Dawn*, Du Bois stated he had sought dignified depictions of blacks to grace his magazine. By 1925 he was determined to make visual arts, the one neglected element of the Harlem Renaissance, a vehicle to express the ideals of the movement. Douglas was the perfect artist to carry this message to Du Bois's readers. He was young, extremely talented, and able to execute his pieces rapidly under quick deadlines.

Du Bois hoped that Douglas would be the one artist in the pages of the *Crisis* who could create art with an authentic black voice. He helped Douglas by purchasing many of his pieces and encouraging him to include African influences in his work. Most importantly, he offered Douglas a job in the mail room of the *Crisis*, where he could make ends meet by working there in the mornings and studying art and painting in the afternoons and evenings. Douglas had mixed feelings about Du Bois, yet he realized that he could help open many doors ahead. He was pleased when Du Bois took a genuine interest in his career. "Dr. Du Bois' little curt smile and stiff handshake have turned to an ear to ear grin and warm and sincere grip. I admit my confusion. . . ."[17]

The rival *Opportunity* magazine, the journal of the Urban League, also regularly purchased Douglas's drawings. The competition for Douglas's work led Du Bois to try to tie the artist more closely to the *Crisis* by listing him as the magazine's art editor in March 1927. While Douglas was grateful for Du Bois's vote of confidence, he resigned the post four months later in order to turn fully to his own work. Douglas remained close to Du Bois even after his resignation, however, accepting criticism from him and responding to suggestions of political angles Douglas could develop in his work. One of Douglas's earlier pieces, the *Poster of Krigwa Players Little Negro Theatre of Harlem*, appeared in the May 1926 issue of the *Crisis;* it was an artistic showstopper. Douglas's poster was not attached to any particular play, but served rather to advertise Du Bois's theater project as a whole. This illustration is heavily influenced by Egyptian and African imagery.

It is in solid black and white, very boldly executed, almost resembling a woodblock print. The poster shows a single figure, sitting in a cross-legged position, with his or her face turned to the side in profile. The figure is very angular, a primarily rectilinear form, with exaggerated thick lips, the

---

17. Douglas to Alta Sawyer, n.d., box 1, folder 8, Douglas Papers, Schomburg Center for Research in Black Culture, New York Public Library.

2. Aaron Douglas. *Krigwa Players Little Negro Theatre of Harlem. Crisis*, May 1926. Copyright *The Crisis*.

appearance of tribal makeup in geometric form, an Afro hair style and a large hoop earring dangling from the only visible ear. Stylized plants and flowers, resembling both African motifs and Art Deco patterning, surround the figure, as does a palm tree. The figure's left hand holds an African mask or ancestral head. Above the figure the influence of Egypt is everywhere, with pyramids on the left, a sun form above, and a sphinx on the right. Wave patterns form the bottom third of the composition, perhaps representing the Nile. The obvious inspiration is Africa, an Africa that proudly included Egyptian civilization. Du Bois wanted Douglas to remind the *Crisis* audience of their African ancestry and to inspire in them an interest in their common heritage. Egypt was the common vocabulary to achieve this goal.

Du Bois's interest in African-influenced art inspired Douglas. Douglas produced one of his most notable *Crisis* covers in September 1927, entitled *The Burden of Black Womanhood*. This composition includes the figure of a woman in a long Egyptian-influenced garment, with a side view of hips and frontal body silhouette, holding up a round shape, the world. She looks up, with face in profile and the same slit eyes that resemble African Dan masks of the Ivory Coast, a style frequently employed by Douglas and which he later discussed:

> The only thing that I did that was not specifically taken from the Egyptians was an eye. I made an eye that I followed throughout instead of . . . getting behind perspective, let's say. So you saw it in three dimension. I avoided the three dimension and that's another thing that made it sort of unique artistically. It took so quickly. The artistic people understood that you never presented a thing with volume and depth. It was always flat. They reduced everything to a flat and treated it in that way.[18]

A cityscape is included below, which resembles Art Deco drawings of skyscrapers with the billowing smoke of industry behind it. One simple cabin—possibly representing the woman's humble beginnings—is on the far right. On the left, we see three pyramids and a palm tree, perhaps indicating her ancestral origins. Papyrus blossoms in outline, with a Deco handling, are scattered in the composition.[19]

In his work, Douglas also echoed Du Bois's insistence on political art, or art as propaganda, and his involvement in pan-Africanism. Some of his most interesting illustrations were executed for Paul Morand's 1929

18. Aaron Douglas interview with L. M. Collins, July 16, 1971, Black Oral Histories, Fisk University Special Collections, Nashville, Tennessee.

19. The skyscrapers, showing modern city life, resemble those found in architectural drawings of the 1920s, such as Alfred J. Tulk's designs for a repoussé plaque for the executive offices in the Chanin Building, in Alastair Duncan, *American Art Deco* (New York, 1986), 11.

3. Aaron Douglas. *The Burden of Black Womanhood. Crisis*, September 1927. Copyright *The Crisis*.

4. Aaron Douglas. *Africa*, copyright 1929, renewed © 1957 by The Viking Press, Inc., Illustrations, from Paul Morand, *Black Magic*, trans. Hamish Miles. Used by permission of Viking Penguin, a division of Penguin Putnam Inc.

book, *Black Magic*. The third part of the book, "Africa," begins with a chapter entitled "Good-bye, New York!" chronicling a cruise from New York to Africa. Douglas depicts Africa by showing two people in profile, with slanted eyes of a Dan mask, looking up towards an idol influenced by Egyptian and Dan Ivory Coast art. This idol, resembling a Fang male reliquary guardian, is similar to idols that appear in several Douglas compositions depicting Africa. Douglas learned of this art by viewing the substantial African art collection at the Barnes Foundation, from art books, and from the photographs in the *New Negro* featuring African art. In the background two seated figures, seemingly nudes, also look up at the idol, which is surrounded by light concentric circles, as are the heads of the two front-profiled viewers. Tropical palms frame the top of the composition. Douglas seems to be contrasting peoples of different African origins, thus expressing pan-Africanism. The two front figures are contemporary, sophisticated figures indicated by the women's modern hairstyle and earrings; perhaps they are black visitors from New York in search of their heritage. The figures in the background seem to be native to the area. The two cultures come together, with common roots, as they observe the idol in the center of the composition.

Douglas was able to carry out Du Bois's desire for a dignified art that represented the best of African American life, touched by the influences of African art. He recognized the unique beauty of his black subjects and was able to depict them with the authenticity Du Bois had championed since writing *Souls*. Douglas wrote of a new beauty: "We are possessed, you know, with the idea that it is necessary to be white, to be beautiful. Nine times out of ten it is just the reverse. It takes lots of training or a tremendous effort to down the idea that thin lips and straight nose is the apogee of beauty. But once free you can look back with a sigh of relief and wonder how anyone could be so deluded."[20]

Douglas was able to develop his own unique style, combining African art—both West African and Egyptian—Cubism, and Art Deco design in his own personal style. Douglas encouraged other artists of the Harlem Renaissance, as they did him, to forge a new black aesthetic. He wrote to Langston Hughes in 1925:

> Your problem, Langston, my problem, no our problem is to conceive, develop, establish an art era. Not white art painted black. . . . Let's bare our arms and plunge them deep through laughter, through pain, through sorrow, through hope, through disappointment, into the very depths of the souls of our people and drag forth material crude, rough, neglected. Then let's sing it, dance it, write it, paint it. Let's do the impossible. Let's create something

20. Douglas to Alta Sawyer, 1925, box 1, folder 1, Douglas Papers, Schomburg Center for Research in Black Culture, New York Public Library.

transcendentally material, mystically objective. Earthy. Spiritually earthy. Dynamic.[21]

The message that Du Bois knew that "Negro blood" had for the world could be taught through many art forms, including through the visual arts. For Du Bois, both Henry O. Tanner and Aaron Douglas provided the ideal artistic vehicles to illustrate graphically his message of power, self-consciousness, self-respect, and self-realization. Tanner used genre scenes from everyday black life and religious scenes to illustrate these points. Douglas used the imagery of Africa to bring the proud heritage of the African American to the forefront of American culture. Despite being ignored by a white audience, both artists felt great social responsibility and were willing to assume the burden that Du Bois referred to in *Souls*, to forge ahead even when shut out from the artistic world by "a vast veil." They illuminated the issues of race, and they uplifted the masses of their people.

21. Douglas to Langston Hughes, December 21, 1925, James Weldon Johnson Memorial Collection of Negro Arts and Letters, Beinecke Rare Book and Manuscript Library, Yale University.

"Looking at One's Self through the Eyes of Others"

W. E. B. Du Bois's Photographs
for the 1900 Paris Exposition

Shawn Michelle Smith

In *The Souls of Black Folk*, W. E. B. Du Bois describes "double-consciousness" as the "sense of always *looking at one's self through the eyes of others*," and thereby draws upon a *visual* paradigm to articulate "the strange meaning of being black" in the Jim Crow United States.[1] For Du Bois, African American subjectivity is mediated by a "white supremacist gaze,"[2] and it is therefore divided by contending images of blackness—those produced by a dominant white culture, and those maintained by African American individuals, within African American communities. It is the negotiation of these violently disparate images of blackness that produces the "twoness" of Du Bois's double consciousness, the psychological and social burden of attempting to assuage "two souls, two thoughts, two unreconciled strivings; two warring ideals" (11).

This essay was first published in *African American Review* 34:4 (2000): 581–99, and I am grateful for permission to reprint it here. I am indebted to Laura Wexler for encouraging me to pursue this argument, and to Joe Masco for his careful critiques of several versions of this essay. I am also very grateful for the generous support I have received to continue my ongoing research on these images from an External Research Fellowship at the Center for the Humanities at Oregon State University, an Irene Diamond Foundation Fellowship at the Schomburg Center for Research in Black Culture, and a Visiting Research Fellowship from the Obert C. and Grace A. Tanner Humanities Center at the University of Utah.
    1. W. E. B. Du Bois, *The Souls of Black Folk*, ed. Henry Louis Gates Jr. and Terri Hume Oliver (New York: Norton, 1999), 11, 5, emphasis added. Subsequent references to this edition will be cited parenthetically.
    2. bell hooks, "In Our Glory: Photography and Black Life," in *Picturing Us: African American Identity in Photography*, ed. Deborah Willis (New York: New Press, 1994) 42–53, 50.

Recognizing the visual paradigms that inform Du Bois's conception of double consciousness can help us to understand a remarkable collection of photographs Du Bois assembled for the American Negro Exhibit at the Paris Exposition of 1900.[3] These largely unknown images appear at first enigmatic, but when read against the turn-of-the-century "race" archives they originally engaged, we can see how the photographs emblematize the complicated visual dynamics of double consciousness. Du Bois's "American Negro" photographs disrupt the images of African Americans produced "through the eyes of others" by simultaneously reproducing and supplanting those images with a different vision of the "American Negro." Specifically, Du Bois's photographs contest the discourses and images of an imagined "negro criminality" that were evoked to legitimize the crime of lynching in turn-of-the-century U.S. culture. With this analysis I aim not only to restore a key text to the visual archives of U.S. race relations, but also to underscore the importance of W. E. B. Du Bois's work as a *visual* theorist of "race."

Du Bois's "American Negro" photographs include 363 images of African Americans made by unidentified photographers. Du Bois organized the photographs into four volumes and presented them in three separate albums, entitled *Types of American Negroes, Georgia, U.S.A.* (volumes 1–3) and *Negro Life in Georgia, U.S.A.*[4] The albums constituted one of three displays Du Bois supervised for the American Negro Exhibit, including a series of charts and graphs documenting the social and economic progress of African Americans since the Civil War, and a three-volume set containing the complete legal history of African Americans in Georgia.[5] These displays joined other exhibits celebrating work in African American education and

3. Throughout this essay I occasionally refer to the images Du Bois collected for the American Negro Exhibit at the 1900 Paris Exposition as "Du Bois's photographs." I would like to clarify that Du Bois himself probably did not make any of the photographs assessed here. The photographers who made these images are not cited; however, I have identified Thomas Askew, an African American photographer in Atlanta, as a producer of many of the photographs. And yet, while Du Bois may not have actually taken the photographs he collected, it is his name that is embossed on the album spines, and as archivist and presenter of the images, Du Bois played a central role in shaping their meaning.

4. The American Negro Exhibit at the 1900 Paris Exposition was a relatively new kind of African American forum, inaugurated most conspicuously in 1895 with the Negro Building at the Cotton States International Exposition in Atlanta, Georgia. While Du Bois's participation in the 1900 Paris Exposition was not nearly so prominent as that of Booker T. Washington's at the 1895 Atlanta Exposition, it marked a parallel attempt by Du Bois to represent and to shape the history of African American social advancement, and race relations, at a moment when Washington and Du Bois were becoming increasingly ideologically polarized.

5. These materials are housed in the Prints and Photographs Division of the Library of Congress. See also Shawn Michelle Smith, "Photographing the 'American Negro': Nation, Race, and Photography at the Paris Exposition of 1900," in *With Other Eyes:*

African American literary production, which together were organized under the direction of Thomas J. Calloway for the exposition.[6] The American Negro Exhibit was housed in the Palace of Social Economy, and it won a 1900 Paris Exposition grand prize.

The photograph albums that Du Bois assembled for the American Negro Exhibit contain a variety of images, but by far the most numerous and notable are the hundreds of paired portraits that almost fill volumes one and two. In examining these portraits, I would like to suggest that Du Bois was not simply offering up images of African Americans for perusal, but was critically engaging viewers in the visual and psychological dynamics of "race" at the turn of the century. That very year Du Bois would declare, "The problem of the Twentieth Century is the problem of the color line,"[7] and with his "American Negro" photographs for the 1900 Paris Exposition, Du Bois asked viewers to consider their places in relation to that color line.

Du Bois's "American Negro" portraits are disturbing, even shocking, in the way they mirror turn-of-the-century criminal mugshots. Indeed, the images appear uncannily doubled, connoting both middle-class portraits and criminal mugshots simultaneously. Drawing upon Henry Louis Gates Jr.'s theory of "signifyin(g)" in order to tease out the *doubled* signifying registers the photographs evoke,[8] I would like to suggest that by replicating the formal characteristics of both the middle-class portrait and the criminal mugshot, Du Bois's "American Negro" photographs subvert the visual registers and cultural discourses that consolidated white middle-class privilege against an image of "negro criminality" at the turn of the century. Interrogating both middle-class identity and whiteness, Du Bois's images signify across the multivalent boundaries that divide the "normal" from the "deviant," challenging not only the images of African Americans produced "through the eyes of others," but also the discursive binaries of privilege that maintain those images. Through a process of visual doubling, Du Bois's "American Negro" portraits engender a disruptive critical commentary that troubles the visual and discursive foundations of white middle-class dominance by destabilizing their oppositional paradigms.

Looking at Race and Gender in Visual Culture, ed. Lisa Brown (Minneapolis: University of Minnesota Press, 1999), 157–86.

6. W. E. B. Du Bois, "The American Negro at Paris," *The American Monthly Review of Reviews* 22, no. 5 (November 1900): 575–77.

7. Du Bois first made this declaration at the Pan-African Association Conference in London in July 1900. He would later repeat this now-famous statement in *The Souls of Black Folk* (5, 17, 33). See Manning Marable, "The Pan-Africanism of W. E. B. Du Bois," in *W. E. B. Du Bois on Race and Culture,* ed. Bernard W. Bell, Emily R. Grosholz, and James B. Stewart (New York: Routledge, 1996), 193–218, 197; and Arnold Rampersad, *The Art and Imagination of W. E. B. Du Bois* (New York: Schocken, 1990), 64.

8. Henry Louis Gates Jr., *The Signifying Monkey: A Theory of Afro-American Literary Criticism* (New York: Oxford University Press, 1988).

Repetition with a Difference

In an essay entitled "In Our Glory: Photography and Black Life," bell hooks states: "The camera was the central instrument by which blacks could disprove representations of us created by white folks."[9] It is in this resistant spirit that I think one should read the photographs W. E. B. Du Bois collected for display at the Paris Exposition of 1900. The portraits Du Bois arranged in *Types of American Negroes, Georgia, U.S.A.* work against dominant, white-supremacist images of African Americans perpetuated both discursively and in visual media at the turn of the century. Certainly the images differ dramatically from the racist caricatures of Sambo, Zip Coon, and Jim Crow, stereotypes that fueled white fantasies of natural racial superiority. As Du Bois himself said of the Paris Exposition photographs, they "hardly square with conventional American ideas."[10] More importantly, however, the photographs problematize the images of "negro criminality" that worked to consolidate a vision of white middle-class privilege at the turn of the century.

Du Bois was well aware that challenging the discourses and images of "negro criminality" was a particularly important political necessity for African Americans. Increasingly over the course of the late nineteenth century, white Americans evoked the imagined "new negro crime" of raping white women in order to legitimize violence upon African American bodies.[11] White lynch mobs called forth an image of the black male rapist in order to justify the torture and mutilation of black men. As Ida B. Wells observed in the 1890s, lynching served as a form of economic terrorism, as a racialized class warfare translated into the terms of sexual purity and transgression.[12] Many white supremacists argued that African American criminal behavior had increased dramatically during the postbellum era, and suggested that newly emancipated blacks were reverting to their "natural" state of inferiority without the guidance of their former masters. In "The Negro Problem and the New Negro Crime," one writer for *Harper's Weekly* contended that "such outrages are sporadic indications of a lapse

9. hooks, "In Our Glory," 48.

10. Du Bois, "American Negro at Paris," 577.

11. "The Negro Problem and the New Negro Crime," *Harper's Weekly* 47 (June 20, 1903): 1050–51; "Some Fresh Suggestions about the New Negro Crime," *Harper's Weekly* 48 (January 23, 1904): 120–21. See also the following letters to the editor: George B. Winton, "The Negro Criminal," *Harper's Weekly* 47 (August 29, 1903): 1414; and Mrs. W. H. Felton, "From a Southern Woman," *Harper's Weekly* 47 (November 14, 1903): 1830.

12. Ida B. Wells, *Crusade for Justice: The Autobiography of Ida B. Wells,* ed. Alfreda M. Duster (Chicago: University of Chicago Press, 1970); Ida B. Wells, *Southern Horrors: Lynch Law in All Its Phases* (Salem, N.H.: Ayer Company Publishers, 1892); Ida B. Wells, *Selected Works of Ida B. Wells-Barnett,* ed. Trudier Harris (New York: Oxford University Press, 1991).

of the Southern negro into a state of barbarism or savagery, in which the gratification of the brutish instincts is no longer subjected to the restraints of civilization."[13] A *Harper's* correspondent concurred: "In slavery negroes learned how to obey, and obedience means self-control." Lamenting the demise of "discipline" under slavery, the same writer proposed that "a substitute must be found" to ensure the "mental and moral discipline" of the African American.[14] In this way, some white Americans fabricated discourses of "negro criminality" to evoke the imagined inherent inferiority of African Americans and to justify increasing social surveillance, segregation, and violence.

Du Bois explicitly challenged dominant and extreme white perceptions of "negro criminality," particularly the tenets that "the negro element is the most criminal in our population," and that "the negro is much more criminal as a free man than he was as a slave," in his edited volume *Notes on Negro Crime, Particularly in Georgia*.[15] In this text, Du Bois argues that slavery was not a check on inherent criminal tendencies; it was instead an institution that encouraged criminal behavior. In discussing the "faults of negroes" in the "causes of negro crime," such as "loose ideas of property" and "sexual looseness," Du Bois quotes Sidney Olivier, who states: " 'All these faults are real and important causes of Negro crime. They are not racial traits but due to perfectly evident historic causes: slavery could not survive as an institution and teach thrift; and its great evil in the United States was its low sexual morals; emancipation meant for the Negroes poverty and a great stress of life due to sudden change. These and other considerations explain Negro crime.' "[16] In delineating the "faults of the whites" in producing "negro criminality," Du Bois notes "a double standard of justice in the courts," "enforcing a caste system in such a way as to humiliate Negroes and kill their self-respect," and "peonage and debt-slavery."[17] In *Notes on Negro Crime*, Du Bois demonstrates how discourses of innate "negro criminality" directed public attention away from the material circumstances of extreme poverty and racism under which many "free" African Americans struggled to survive by sharecropping in the post-Reconstruction South.

Du Bois, like Ida B. Wells, knew that many whites viewed African American economic success as a threat to white cultural dominance, as a privilege "stolen" from white possessors. Indeed, many whites linked an imagined

13. "Negro Problem," 1050.
14. Winton, "Negro Criminal," 1414.
15. *Notes on Negro Crime, Particularly in Georgia* (A Social Study Made under the Direction of Atlanta University by the Ninth Atlanta Conference), Atlanta University Publications, no. 9, ed. W. E. Burghardt Du Bois (Atlanta: Atlanta University Press, 1904): 9.
16. According to Du Bois's citation, Olivier made these comments first in the *British Friend*, December 1904.
17. *Notes on Negro Crime*, 55–57.

"negro criminality" to "talk of social equality."[18] Du Bois examines this position in *The Souls of Black Folk,* in a chapter entitled "The Coming of John."
In his fictional depiction of an encounter between a white judge and an educated African American teacher in the postbellum South, Du Bois demonstrates how white anxiety over social and economic equality with African
Americans was intertwined with white violence upon the black body in
turn-of-the-century U.S. culture. Du Bois's white judge proclaims:

> Now I like the colored people, and sympathize with all their reasonable as-
> pirations; but you and I both know, John, that in this country the Negro must
> remain subordinate, and can never expect to be the equal of white men. In
> their place, your people can be honest and respectful; and God knows, I'll
> do what I can to help them. But when they want to reverse nature, and rule
> white men, and marry white women, and sit in my parlor, then, by God! we'll
> hold them under if we have to lynch every Nigger in the land. (150–51)

The immediacy with which Du Bois's white judge moves from an imagined social equality to the desire to lynch is both terrifying and telling. In
Du Bois's depiction, the middle-class African American man is, in and of
himself, a source of white rage. Further, Du Bois's story marks the dependence of white conceptions of African American "honesty" on a system
of racial subordination. In Du Bois's rendition of the African American
image produced "through the eyes of [white] others," African Americans
"can be honest" only when they remain "in their [subordinate] place," a
position well outside the bounds of the white middle-class parlor. Du Bois
knew that examples of African American economic success circulated under white eyes waiting to proclaim "usurper," "liar," "thief." For many
whites, the image of the successful African American was necessarily also
an image of one who had stolen cultural privilege from its "rightful" owners. In other words, when projected through the eyes of white others, the
image of the African American middle-class individual often transmuted
into the mugshot of an African American criminal. It is precisely this transformation of the black image in the eyes of white beholders (a transformation from middle-class portrait into criminal mugshot), that Du Bois's
"American Negro" portraits unmask.

In Du Bois's albums, the first images displayed (which frame a reading
of later images) replicate with striking precision the formal style of the

18. In "Some Fresh Suggestions," a *Harper's Weekly* editor links "the new negro
crime" to "the talk of social equality that inflames the negro, unregulated and undis-
ciplined." This same writer also links the disfranchisement of African Americans in
Mississippi to the eradication of "the new negro crime" in that state. Many whites
upheld Mississippi as a case study that demonstrated the imagined link between social
equality and negro criminality. It is plain how such arguments fueled movements to
disfranchise African American voters (121). See also "Negro Problem," 1050.

criminal mugshot. An adaptation of Henry Louis Gates Jr.'s theory of "sig-nifyin(g)" to the domain of visual texts suggests that Du Bois's portraits "signify on" the formal visual codes of criminological photography. While Gates defines *signifyin(g)* as an African American manipulation of signs that applies primarily to verbal and musical texts, I propose that one can also use this theoretical tool in reading visual media.[19] Certainly one can identify a wide store of "received" images in U.S. culture, and one might also delineate a set of tropes or styles specific to different kinds of visual signification.[20] While the assumed link between photographic signifier (the photograph) and photographic signified (the subject represented) may prove more tenacious than the visually arbitrary linguistic signifier, it is still possible to repeat visual codes, "with a difference,"[21] and thereby trouble the assumed naturalness of photographic representation. Indeed, to men-tion one well-known example, the artist Cindy Sherman has reproduced iconic images from Hollywood films in order to show how meaning can be manipulated by repeating images within different interpretive frames. Sherman's "stills" problematize Hollywood's gendered visual strategies by over-naturalizing them, thereby destabilizing the normative power of the images she imitates. Also, her repetitions work not only to undermine representational strategies, but also to disrupt the position of passive ob-servers; her images critique dominant visual codes and engender critical observers.[22] It is this doubly critical strategy, of denaturalizing both images and viewing positions, that signifying on dominant representations can effect.

In Gates's terms, Du Bois's photographs repeat the visual tropes of the criminal mugshot "with a difference," directing reading of the images by "indirection," and thereby inverting the dominant signification of these particular photographic signs.[23] Du Bois's initial portraits show expression-less subjects photographed from the shoulders up, both head on and in right-angle profile, replicating uncannily the full face and profile headshots

19. Gates, *Signifying Monkey,* 69. Coco Fusco also utilizes Gates's theory of signifying in her analysis of Lorna Simpson's photographic art. See Coco Fusco, in *"*Uncanny Dis-sonance: The Work of Lorna Simpson,*" English Is Broken Here: Notes on Cultural Fusion in the Americas* (New York: New Press, 1995), 97–102, especially 100.

20. Sander L. Gilman offers a fascinating comparative analysis of this kind in "Black Bodies, White Bodies: Toward an Iconography of Female Sexuality in Late Nineteenth-Century Art, Medicine, and Literature," in *"Race," Writing, and Difference,* ed. Henry Louis Gates Jr. (Chicago: University of Chicago Press, 1986) 223–61.

21. Gates, *Signifying Monkey,* 51.

22. For a recent analysis of Cindy Sherman's *Untitled Film Stills,* see Kaja Silverman, *The Threshold of the Visible World* (New York: Routledge, 1996), 207–27.

23. Gates's definition of *signifying/signifyin(g)* is much more complicated, and much more encompassing, than I have described it here. Repetition with a difference and direction by indirection are simply two of the important ways that signifying works, according to Gates. See Gates, *Signifying Monkey,* especially 51, 63–68, 74–79, 81, 85–86.

of the prison record. Further, Du Bois's photographs depict subjects posed against a plain gray background, devoid of props and frills, and reminiscent of the institutionalized walls against which legal offenders are posed. In short, the images in Du Bois's albums repeat the formal signifiers of the criminal mugshots institutionalized in U.S. prisons and police archives in the late nineteenth century.

In replicating the formal attributes of the criminal mugshot, Du Bois was signifying on a pervasive cultural icon. "Rogues' galleries," showcasing criminal mugshots for public perusal grew alongside middle-class portrait galleries from the very inception of photography. As early as 1859, the *American Journal of Photography* ran an article that proclaimed: " 'As soon as a rascal becomes dangerous to the public, he is taken to the Rogues' Gallery, and is compelled to leave his likeness there, and from that time on he may be known to any one.' "[24] Popular criminal archives encouraged middle-class citizens to survey the populus for social deviants and criminal intruders, those who might attempt to steal the property upon which middle-class cultural privilege largely rested. Specifically, such archives trained middle-class individuals to scrutinize the bodies of their acquaintances for telltale markers that would reveal them to be criminals in disguise. In his published rogues' gallery of 1886, *Professional Criminals of America*, Thomas Byrnes, the New York City chief police detective, proposes: " 'There is not a portrait here but has some marked characteristic by which you can identify the man who sat for it. That is what has to be studied in the Rogues' Gallery—detail.' "[25] The scrutiny of physical detail encouraged by rogues' galleries promulgated the myth of a successful surveillant society in turn-of-the-century U.S. culture.

The desire to look for outward signs of hidden criminality resonated powerfully with white attempts to delineate the mythological "signs of blackness" by which anxious whites hoped to identify racial passers, and thereby to reinforce a belief in the exclusive bounds of white privilege. Indeed, the systems of surveillance established by popular rogues' galleries in order to stop what was deemed "criminal passing" coincided with nearly hysterical discourses of racial passing in the United States at the turn of the century. In a culture characterized both by a legacy of forced racial mixing and by heightened racial segregation, many whites viewed racial passing as a threat to their cultural privilege. The laws that equated "one drop" of "African blood" with blackness encouraged those who imagined themselves to be white to scrutinize other white bodies for the imagined

24. Quoted in Alan Trachtenberg, "Illustrious Americans," in *Reading American Photographs: Images as History, Mathew Brady to Walker Evans* (New York: Hill and Wang, 1989), 21–70, 28–29.

25. Thomas Byrnes, *Professional Criminals of America* (1886; reprint, New York: Chelsea House Publishers, 1969), 53.

signs of hidden blackness. If discovered passing (wittingly or unwittingly), a white person legally defined as African American could instantly fall not only beyond the pale of society, but also into the terrain of ("negro") criminality, as one who defied the jurisdiction of "whites only."

By playing on the formal characteristics of the criminal mugshot, Du Bois's photographs signify on the surveillance under which African Americans lived in turn-of-the-century U.S. culture. More importantly, Du Bois's images work to trouble the power of that surveillance. Du Bois's photographs begin to disrupt the authority of white observers by collapsing the distance between viewers and objects under view that is held generally to empower observers. Specifically, Du Bois's photographs trouble that distance through a process of doubling. The photographs replicate a misrepresentation "with a difference," in much the same way that Henry Louis Gates Jr., following Bahktin, uses the notion of the "double-voiced" word to exemplify one mode of signifying.[26] The first few images in the albums present portraits of African Americans *as* mugshots; indeed, the images appear to be doubled, signifying simultaneously as middle-class portraits and as criminal mugshots. The careful grooming of the subjects suggests a premeditated desire to be photographed typical of the middle-class portrait, while the visual patterns of close-cropped, expressionless frontal and profile poses replicate the tropes of the criminal mugshot. Through one lens, the images portray middle-class subjects, while through another they portray criminal offenders.

Du Bois's initial images suggest that for some white viewers the portrait of an African American is ideologically equivalent to the mugshot of a criminal. Making explicit the discursive assumptions that situate African Americans beyond the pale of white society, and behind a "veil" where they are invisible to white eyes blinded by racist stereotypes, these portraits-as-mugshots make explicit the "shadow meanings" of white-supremacist images of African Americans.[27] However, after this introduction, inaugurated by images that repeat so closely the formal style of criminal mugshots, Du Bois's albums gradually come to resemble middle-class family albums. As viewers continue to progress through the albums, they find subjects posed increasingly in three-quarter turn, rather than in right-angle profile. Gradually more and more of the body is represented, and subjects are supported by the stuffed chairs, patterned carpets, books, lamps, and lace draperies that signify middle-class parlors. Thus, as one moves through Du Bois's albums, one finds that the stark mugshot gradually fades into the middle-class portrait.

In situating these visual poles of identity in such close proximity, Du

26. Gates, *Signifying Monkey*, 50–51.
27. For an analysis of verbal shadow meanings, see ibid., 46.

Bois's albums expose the dependence of middle-class identity on the coun-terimage of a criminal other. Indeed, Du Bois's photographs are unsettling because they signify at the limits of middle-class photographic portraiture. The images inhabit the very boundary that separates authorized identities from those the state deems in need of careful surveillance and discipline. As Allan Sekula has argued in "The Body and the Archive," the photo-graphic portrait became the site of middle-class self-recognition precisely as the rogues' gallery came to signify the boundary of respectable middle-class inclusion in the late nineteenth century. In many ways, the rogues' gallery functioned as a public counterexample to the middle-class portrait gallery; analogously, the criminal body served as a point of distinction against which middle-class citizens could identify themselves. According to Sekula, "To the extent that bourgeois order depends upon the system-atic defense of social relations based on private property, to the extent that the legal basis of the self lies in the model of property rights, in what has been termed 'possessive individualism,' every proper portrait has its lurk-ing, objectifying inverse in the files of the police."[28] Du Bois's photographic portraits signify across the binary that stabilizes white middle-class iden-tity, resembling in formal pose the mugshot, while also reproducing the accoutrements of the middle-class portrait.

Du Bois's photographs highlight the disturbing resemblance that links the middle-class photographic portrait to the criminal mugshot, and the middle-class citizen to the criminal body. The images draw out the cor-respondence Thomas Byrnes suggests in his description of the rogues' gallery. Through the voice of a fictional detective, Byrnes states, " 'Look through the pictures in the Rogues' Gallery and see how many rascals you find there who resemble the best people in the country. Why, you can find some of them, I dare say, sufficiently like personal acquaintances to admit of mistaking one for the other.' " Linking the criminal's middle-class appearance to a middle-class lifestyle, Byrnes declares: "Remember that nearly all the great criminals of the country are men who lead double lives. Strange as it may appear, it is the fact that some of the most unscrupulous rascals who ever cracked a safe or turned out a counterfeit were at home model husbands and fathers."[29] The imagined "double lives" of criminals passing for middle-class citizens generated an anxiety that rattled the op-positional paradigm upon which middle-class identity was established, and encouraged the surveillance discussed above. Du Bois's doubled por-traits similarly shake the assumptions upon which middle-class identity is founded by blurring the distinctions between middle-class and crimi-nal. As we have seen, Du Bois's photographs point toward the "doubled

28. Allan Sekula, "The Body and the Archive," *October* 39 (winter 1986): 3–64, 7.
29. Byrnes, *Professional Criminals*, 55, 54.

meanings" the African American portrait may have held for white viewers trained to distrust middle-class African Americans as usurpers of cultural privilege (that is, as ipso facto criminals). Further, Du Bois's images pose a critical cultural position, a place from which African Americans can gaze back at white beholders. As bell hooks reminds us in "Representations of Whiteness in the Black Imagination," despite the historical prohibition against the black gaze, especially during slavery, African Americans have observed white people with "a critical, 'ethnographic' gaze."[30] Indeed, the eyes that look back at viewers from the frontal portraits in Du Bois's albums may witness the doubled lives of some of their viewers, namely of those who passed both as white middle-class citizens and as racial terrorists at the turn of the century.

While Du Bois's photographs disrupt the binary dividing criminal from middle-class individual, they also challenge the dualism that maintains a stable white center in relation to a black margin in turn-of-the-century U.S. culture. If the middle classes consolidated their cultural legitimacy against the "othered" images of criminals who questioned their property rights, the *white* middle classes consolidated their cultural privilege not only in relation to legal offenders, but also in relation to racial others.[31] In these overlapping paradigms, an image of "negro criminality" provided a boundary that contained the cultural legitimacy of the white middle classes. Once again, it is precisely that doubled boundary that Du Bois's photographs contest.

Reflecting on Whiteness

As Du Bois aesthetically unifies the two opposing positions of "criminal" and middle-class subject in his albums, he also closes the divide that separates images of "whiteness" from images of "blackness." Du Bois's portraits signify on the rogues' gallery to connote the proximity between authorized middle-class selves and criminal others, and some of the images also reference a visual proximity between racially authorized "white" viewers and "black" objects under view. Du Bois's portraits of white-looking biracial individuals contest a racial taxonomy of identifiable (because visible) difference, and in so doing the images highlight a closeness that questions the imagined, autonomous superiority of the white viewer.

30. bell hooks, "Representations of Whiteness in the Black Imagination," in *Black Looks: Race and Representation* (Boston: South End Press, 1992), 165–78, 167.

31. In his important analysis of "The Jazz Singer," Michael Rogin demonstrates how ethnic white identities were Americanized, and "whitened," through white/black conflict; see Michael Rogin, "Blackface, White Noise: The Jewish Jazz Singer Finds His Voice," *Critical Inquiry* 18, no. 3 (spring 1992): 417–53, 420.

Du Bois's images of a young, blond, very pale African American girl challenge white supremacists' investment in separating the races by signaling an undeniable history of physical union between them. In Du Bois's visual archive, these images create a space "for an exploration and expression of what was increasingly socially proscribed" at the turn of the century, namely social and sexual contact between the races.[32] As Robert J. C. Young has argued in *Colonial Desire: Hybridity in Theory, Culture, and Race,* "The ideology of race . . . from the 1840s onwards necessarily worked according to a doubled logic, according to which it both enforced and policed the differences between the whites and the non-whites, but at the same time focused fetishistically upon the product of the contacts between them."[33] White hysteria over the "threat" of racial passing both spurred an increased fervor in racial surveillance at the turn of the century, and marked the extent to which a long history of forced racial mixing during slavery had blurred the color line of privilege in a postslavery world.[34]

By the turn of the century, several states had laws that deemed one thirty-second African or African American ancestry the key that distinguished "black" from "white," a distinction so narrow as to make explicit the invisibility of "blackness" and "whiteness" as racial categories. As Mary Ann Doane has argued, the individual of mixed ancestry, "whose looks and ontology do not coincide, poses a threat to . . . the very idea of racial categorization." According to Doane, the physical appearance of the person of mixed ancestry "always signifies a potential confusion of racial categories and the epistemological impotency of vision."[35] Individuals of mixed racial

32. Hazel V. Carby, *Reconstructing Womanhood: The Emergence of the Afro-American Woman Novelist* (New York: Oxford University Press, 1987), 89.

33. Robert J. C. Young, *Colonial Desire: Hybridity in Theory, Culture, and Race* (New York: Routledge, 1995), 180–81.

34. On the institutionalized rape of enslaved African American women in the antebellum South, and the representations of white and black womanhood that ideologically supported that rape, see Bettina Aptheker, *Woman's Legacy: Essays on Race, Sex, and Class in American History* (Amherst: University of Massachusetts Press, 1982); Nancie Caraway, *Segregated Sisterhood: Racism and the Politics of American Feminism* (Knoxville: University of Tennessee Press, 1991); Carby, *Reconstructing Womanhood,* especially 20–61; Angela Y. Davis, *Women, Race, and Class* (New York: Vintage Books, 1983); Paula Giddings, *When and Where I Enter: The Impact of Black Women on Race and Sex in America* (New York: William Morrow, 1984); and bell hooks, *Ain't I a Woman: Black Women and Feminism* (Boston: South End Press, 1981.

35. Mary Ann Doane, "Dark Continents: Epistemologies of Racial and Sexual Difference in Psychoanalysis and the Cinema," in *Femmes Fatales: Feminism, Film Theory, Psychoanalysis* (New York: Routledge, 1991), 209–248, 235, 234. Susan Gillman provides an important analysis of the "predicament" for white supremacists in her essay " 'Sure Identifiers': Race, Science, and the Law in Twain's *Pudd'nhead Wilson," South Atlantic Quarterly* 87, no. 2 (spring 1988): 195–218, 205. According to Barbara J. Fields, "The very diversity and arbitrariness of the physical rules governing racial classification prove that the physical emblems which symbolize race are not the foundation upon which race arises as a category of social thought" ("Ideology and Race in American History,"

ancestry challenge visual codes of racial distinction, showing a racial tax-onomy founded in visual paradigms of recognition to be a fiction, albeit a powerful one.

As Du Bois's images of white-looking African Americans trouble the veracity of nineteenth-century scientific racial taxonomies, they also prob-lematize nineteenth-century literary representations of biracial men and women. Du Bois's photographs of biracial individuals "hardly square" with the conventional literary figure of "the tragic mulatto." As Hortense J. Spillers has argued, "Mulatto-ness, is not, fortunately, a figure of self-referentiality." The term *mulatto* signifies "the *appropriation* of the interra-cial child by genocidal forces of dominance," and the power of this mis-representation lies in its ability to steal the "dynamic principle of living" from the historical subject it objectifies. In other words, the term derives its force from its capacity to objectify and to reify an historical agent. As an image produced "through the eyes of others," the "mulatto" masks the presence of biracial men and women. As Spillers has argued, "The 'mulatto/a,' just as the 'nigger,' tells us little or nothing about the subject buried beneath them, but quite a great deal more concerning the psychic and cultural reflexes that invent and invoke them." As the term *mulatto* "originates etymologically in notions of 'sterile mule,'" it bears the traces of mid-nineteenth-century scientific theories of racial difference that claimed to identify not only distinct racial types, but also unique racial *species*.[36] Despite the overwhelming evidence that individuals of mixed ancestry were not sterile, and thus not hybrids (the products of interspecies repro-duction), the mythology of the "tragic mulatto" (who dies and does not reproduce) kept alive culturally a notion of absolute biological differences between the races.[37]

Du Bois's "American Negro" portraits engage and disturb the "psychic and cultural reflexes" that fabricate the myth of the mulatto as an object in a racist taxonomy. If "the mulatto" is a racist myth, a misrepresenta-tion that objectifies and freezes the potential force of historical actors, then the photograph of an individual of mixed racial ancestry drives a wedge into the equation that collapses a biracial individual under the sign of "the mulatto." In this case, the tenacity of the photograph's representation, its

in *Region, Race, and Reconstruction,* ed. J. Morgan Kousser and James M. McPherson [New York: Oxford University Press, 1982], 143–77, 151).

36. Hortense J. Spillers, "Notes on an Alternative Model—Neither/Nor," in *The Dif-ference Within: Feminism and Critical Theory,* ed. Elizabeth Meese and Alice Parker (Phila-delphia: John Benjamin, 1989), 165–87, 166–67. See also Young, *Colonial Desire,* especially 122–27.

37. I am adapting Robert J. C. Young's insights about the power of the cultural con-struction of "race" to my understanding of the literary figure of the tragic mulatto. Ac-cording to Young, "The different Victorian scientific accounts of race each in their turn quickly became deeply problematic; but what was much more consistent, more pow-erful and long-lived, was the cultural construction of race" (*Colonial Desire,* 93–94).

claim on the real, works toward a potentially radical end. If the photograph carries a trace of the historical subject it objectifies, then a photograph can depict "the mulatta *type*," only after first acknowledging the presence of an individual. Here, then, I am interested in the ways in which Du Bois's portraits of a white-looking girl of biracial ancestry signify on the racist figure of "the mulatto."

If one imagines a turn-of-the-century European or Euro-American viewer engaged in looking at the photograph of a blond girl in Du Bois's albums, one might read this scene as a confrontation between an image of a biracial child and one who participates in maintaining the image of the mythological mulatto. As a historical subject with eyes that look back at viewers, the young girl refuses the objectifying category of "the mulatto." But what does the image of this girl make possible? According to literary scholar Ann duCille, the image of a biracial individual could enable an author "to insinuate into the consciousness of white readers the humanity of a people they otherwise constructed as subhuman—beyond the pale of white comprehension."[38] In thinking about Europeans and Euro-Americans perusing Du Bois's visual archive at the 1900 Paris Exposition, one might imagine the possibility of a kind of racial identification as those viewers turned to face the images of white-looking African Americans in a "Negro" archive. If we suppose a positive, if only momentary, identification between viewer and viewed in this case, an identification bridged by visual signs of similarity, then such images would serve not only to humanize African Americans in the eyes of white viewers, but also to suggest that self and other were very much the same.

While one can imagine this moment as one of psychological recognition, in order for the legally defined white viewer to identify with the image of a white-looking African American, to see a unified image of self in this photograph of the purported other, the viewer would have to suture over a long history of both visible and repressed violence. At the turn of the century, a superficial identification between blond Euro-American and African American subjects (on the basis of common hair color or skin tone) would have been enabled primarily by the history of violence and rape perpetuated in slavery. In this sense, then, Du Bois's photographs of a biracial child signal both white violence upon African American bodies, and white desire for the black body. Indeed, as Robert J. C. Young describes it, colonial desire is constructed precisely around the dynamic of the colonist's simultaneous repulsion from and attraction to the other.[39]

This white desire for the black body, coupled with the brutal enactment

---

38. Ann duCille, *The Coupling Convention: Sex, Text, and Tradition in Black Women's Fiction* (New York: Oxford University Press, 1993), 7–8.

39. Young, *Colonial Desire*, 106–9, 149–52.

of white power on that body in slavery, finds a direct corollary in turn-of-the-century lynchings. The shadow lurking behind a possible moment of visual identification between individuals divided by the color line is the image of white subjectivity foregrounded against a black corpse in the photographs of lynchings. In order to sustain an identification with African Americans, the authorized white viewer would have to confront the legacy of the utter racial divide engendered by the "new white crime" of lynching.

The photographs of lynched bodies that circulated at the turn of the century signified at the limits of white images of black otherness. As records of the lawless brutality of white supremacists, they registered a different kind of power than the mugshots procured in the police station. If the mugshot signaled a form of dispersed, institutionalized power that was implicitly white in a culture of white privilege, the photograph of a lynched black body signaled the embodied nature of white power. By juxtaposing the photographic mugshot to the terrifying photographs of lynchings that circulated in the same years, one finds two different manifestations of white power functioning simultaneously. Lynching represents an embodiment of power similar to the sixteenth- and seventeenth-century spectacles of ritualized torture that Michel Foucault describes in *Discipline and Punish.* Such scenes of torture made manifest the unquestioned authority of a monarch over his subjects, the physical power of the state as personified by one ruler. The mugshot corresponds to a later formation of power that emerged in the nineteenth century, the state of surveillance, in which power is increasingly diffused, disembodied, and located in the minds of subjects who discipline themselves according to an institutionalized image of normalcy.[40] In the coterminous juxtaposition of photographs of lynching and criminal mugshots at the turn of the century, one sees that, while the vehicle of power, the body that aligns itself with and enforces the bounds of normalcy and deviance, is absent from the photographic mugshot, those bodies that are the vehicles of a devastating physical power are represented over and over again with the victims of their wrath in the photographs of lynchings. In the images that display burned and mutilated black bodies set off by crowds of curious—even smiling—white spectators, one sees white supremacists attempting to locate power emphatically within the bounds of white bodies.[41] Following the artist Pat Ward Williams, one must ask:

40. Michel Foucault, *Discipline and Punish: The Birth of the Prison,* trans. Alan Sheridan (New York: Vintage, 1979).
41. For a reading of the convergence of "specular" and "panoptic" power in both antebellum slavery and postbellum lynching, see Robyn Wiegman, *American Anatomies: Theorizing Race and Gender* (Durham: Duke University Press, 1995), 35–42. One refinement I would make in Wiegman's fascinating analysis is simply to note that in most of the photographs of lynch mobs and their victims, white spectators are, remarkably, not veiled or masked. Thus, I would suggest that it was not only a "homogenized, known-

How can such images exist?[42] Or, to state the question differently: How do the photographs of lynchers, unmasked, facing the camera, and smiling, escape the rogues' gallery? Such images show the extent to which power is equated with white bodies that brutalize the bodies of others. The photographs of lynchers and of lynching demonstrate with grave clarity that the power of whiteness was not only invisible and dispersed, but also particular and embodied, in turn-of-the-century U.S. culture.

Photographs of lynchings circulated widely, reinforcing the association of whiteness with terror in African American minds. These images served, perhaps, as the "substitute" for slavery that white supremacists, like the *Harper's* correspondent cited earlier, hoped would ensure the "discipline" of African Americans in postslavery America. As Elizabeth Alexander argues, "There are countless stories of violence made spectacular in order to let black people know who was in control." Explaining further the psychological effects of these spectacles of white violence upon the black body, Alexander states: "Black men are contained when these images are made public, at the very same time that black viewers are taking in evidence that provides grounds for collective identification with trauma." This collective identification, felt and known in the body, can then become, according to Alexander, a "catalyst for action." Witnessing the scenes of violence depicted in photographs can enable a first step toward African American resistance. According to Christian Walker, reclaiming "a collective historical identity" is "the first line of defense against a legacy of cultural annihilation," and such reclamation was to become foundational in the multifaceted antilynching campaigns of the NAACP.[43]

---

but-never-individuated" form of white power that lynching reproduced, but also an explicitly embodied form of white power that marked white men and women as the particular bearers of an otherwise diffuse power (*American Anatomies*, 39).

42. See Pat Ward Williams's 1987 art piece *Accused/Blowtorch/Padlock*, in Lucy R. Lippard's *Mixed Blessings: New Art in a Multicultural America* (New York: Pantheon, 1990), 37. See also Elizabeth Alexander, "'Can You Be BLACK and Look at This?': Reading the Rodney King Video(s)," in *Black Male: Representations of Masculinity in Contemporary American Art*, ed. Thelma Golden (New York: Whitney Museum of American Art, 1994), 90–110.

43. Alexander, "'Can You Be BLACK and Look at This?'" 105–6; Christian Walker, "Gazing Colored: A Family Album," in *Picturing Us: African American Identity in Photography*, ed. Deborah Willis (New York: New Press, 1994), 64–70, 69. For an analysis of "the representation of whiteness as terrifying," see hooks, "Representations of Whiteness," 169. For a history of the NAACP's antilynching campaigns, see Robert L. Zangrando, *The NAACP Crusade against Lynching, 1909–1950* (Philadelphia: Temple University Press, 1980). The Library of Congress Prints and Photographs Division has an extensive, horrifying archive of photographs of lynchings collected by the NAACP (NAACP Collection of Photographs on Lynchings, LOT 10647). *Crisis*, the official magazine of the NAACP, published photographs of lynching as part of its campaign against racial terrorism and murder. For an example, see "Holmes on Lynching," *Crisis* 3, no. 3 (January 1912): 109–12.

How do such photographs function for white viewers? Whiteness is also consolidated around these images of violence, but for whites such images enable a very different kind of racial identification. On the surface these images encourage white viewers to reject the trauma of experienced physical violence and to identify with the perpetrators of that violence. On another level, the images make absolutely apparent the fact that, as Eric Lott suggests, whiteness is a split identity formulated on the violent repression of the other.[44]

If whiteness and blackness are so violently distinguished in turn-of-the-century lynching photographs, how can we understand the possibility that white American viewers may have recognized themselves in the white-looking "other" of Du Bois's "American Negro" albums? The European or Euro-American viewer who assumes herself to be white would experience a psychological rift in such an identification, perhaps becoming momentarily conscious of the violent split that establishes white identity. In order to sustain a unified image of the visual signs that constitute superficial whiteness, the white viewer could not help but see self in other. But in this identification is also the unraveling of whiteness as a boundary between self and other, for the image of this white-looking girl is in an archive of "Negroes." Indeed, Du Bois's albums make whiteness just one point in an archive of blackness, and specifically they show whiteness to be the repressed point in an archive of blackness. In what one might call the larger archive of "race," whiteness is the position repressed so thoroughly that it has reproduced itself everywhere. As Richard Dyer suggests, because of its very pervasiveness, whiteness becomes an invisible racial sign; it is the (repressed) norm of unseen seeing. This perhaps explains how white people in lynching photographs can be so prominently displayed, and yet remain "unseen" by legal authorities. Expanding on Dyer's thesis, Isaac Julien and Kobena Mercer have argued that "Whiteness has secured universal consent to its hegemony as the 'norm' by masking its coercive force with the invisibility that marks off the Other (the pathologised, the disempowered, the dehumanized) as all too visible—*'colored.' "*[45] But if the blackness produced "through the eyes of [white] others" as dehumanized spectacle is

44. Eric Lott, "Love and Theft: The Racial Unconscious of Blackface Minstrelsy," *Representations* 39 (summer 1992): 23–50, 36–37. Michael Rogin also examines the split racial self in his analysis of *The Jazz Singer*. According to Rogin, in *The Jazz Singer*, "the interracial double is not the exotic other but the split self, the white in blackface" ("Blackface, White Noise," 419).

45. Richard Dyer, "White," *Screen* 29, no. 4 (autumn 1988): 44–64, especially 44–47; Isaac Julian and Kobena Mercer, "Introduction: De Margin and De Centre," *Screen* 29, no. 4 (autumn 1988) ("The Last 'Special Issue' on Race?"): 2–10, 6. For a discussion of how "repression" works to proliferate discourses around the objects or acts it would supposedly deny, see Michel Foucault, *The History of Sexuality*, vol. 1, trans. Robert Hurley (New York: Vintage, 1978, 1980).

itself an image of whiteness, revealing more about those who produce the image than about those purportedly represented by its sign, then the self-identified white viewer must see in the dismembering of the African American body the structures of white identity. For some at least, this recognition would produce a psychological rift, a split subjectivity imploding with the violent impact of sameness.

Du Bois's images of a white-looking biracial girl demonstrate the arbitrary nature of visual racial classification. But this is not to suggest that Du Bois aimed to erase racial differences or to discount racial identities, for as he explicitly states in *The Souls of Black Folk*, "He would not bleach his Negro soul in a flood of white Americanism, for he knows that Negro blood has a message for the world" (11). Rather, Du Bois's photographs challenge a visual, and biological, paradigm of white supremacist racial differentiation. The violence that engenders the image of whiteness threatens always to tear it apart, so that white subjectivity remains always on the verge of fragmentation. This instability can, of course, function powerfully to perpetuate and to reinforce the image of (a volatile, vulnerable) whiteness in need of ever-more-aggressive consolidation. An imagined white wholeness can be recuperated quickly, out of its own fragments, by cultural privilege and the capacity to do violence. The dominant culture does not force the white viewer into an identification with otherness; indeed, the culture at large works against such recognition. Yet an image of "whiteness" that is also an image of "blackness" could effect a flash of recognition, in which white viewers might glimpse the phantasmal nature of "white wholeness," in which they might see the workings of whiteness. W. E. B. Du Bois's photographs of African Americans for the 1900 Paris Exposition pursue these ends, denaturalizing the assumed privilege of whiteness, and suggesting that the violent division (between "black" and "white") upon which the myth of white wholeness is founded is itself the most entrenched of color lines.

A Note on Contemporary Viewers

The very fact that images of imagined black criminality continue to function so powerfully in the United States today, becoming all-consuming points of media fascination for white viewers, indicates that Du Bois's photographs presented almost a century ago did not radically shift the privilege of the normative "white supremacist gaze." However, the images did open an important space for African American resistance to racist stereotypes, a space for contestation and for self-representation. As bell hooks has argued, "Photography has been, and is, central to that aspect of decolonization that calls us back to the past and offers a way to reclaim and renew life-affirming bonds. Using these images, we connect ourselves to a recuperative, redemptive memory that enables us to construct radical identities, images of ourselves that transcend the limits of the colonizing eye."[46] By reclaiming the importance of Du Bois's "American Negro" photographs, this essay aims to expand an archive of antiracist representations and thereby to reinforce an early foundation for the work of contemporary cultural critics.

Du Bois's photographs asked African American and white American viewers to interrogate the images of African Americans produced "through the eyes of [white] others," and to question the foundations of white privilege. Whether or not Du Bois's first viewers engaged his images at this level, witnessing the critique of whiteness embedded in his signifying practices, is now, perhaps, beside the point. Given the state of contemporary visual culture, it is time, once again, for viewers to confront Du Bois's images, and to do so by reading them self-consciously, with what Kaja Silverman has called a "productive look." In *The Threshold of the Visible World,* Silverman defines the "productive look" as a means of looking that is not completely predetermined by cultural paradigms or even by material objects under view. For Silverman, the "productive look" is a transformative look, a means of seeing beyond the "screen" of cultural programming. Accordingly, Silverman asserts that

> Productive looking necessarily requires a constant conscious reworking of the terms under which we unconsciously look at the objects that people our visual landscape. It necessitates the struggle, first, to recognize our involuntary acts of incorporation and repudiation, and our implicit affirmation of the dominant elements of the screen, and, then, to see again, differently. However, productive looking necessarily entails, as well, the opening up of the unconscious to otherness.[47]

An opening up of the unconscious to otherness would necessitate a profound disorientation for white viewers whose image of white wholeness is founded upon the repression of violent othering practices. Nevertheless, it is precisely this kind of interrogation of the psychological and cultural structures that enable the continuation of white dominance that needs to be undertaken if we are to continue Du Bois's project of pushing subjectivity past the color line.

46. hooks, "In Our Glory," 53.
47. Silverman, *Threshold of the Visible World,* 180–93; quote on 184.

1. From *Types of American Negroes, Georgia, U.S.A.*, compiled by W. E. B. Du Bois, 1900. Reproduced from the Daniel Murray Collection of the Library of Congress.

2. From *Types of American Negroes, Georgia, U.S.A.*, compiled by W. E. B. Du Bois, 1900. Reproduced from the Daniel Murray Collection of the Library of Congress.

3. From the photogravure, Alphonse Bertillon, *Identification Anthropométrique, Instructions Signalétiques,* new edition (Melun, France: Imprimerie Administrative, 1893). Reproduced from Manuscripts, Archives, and Special Collections, Washington State University.

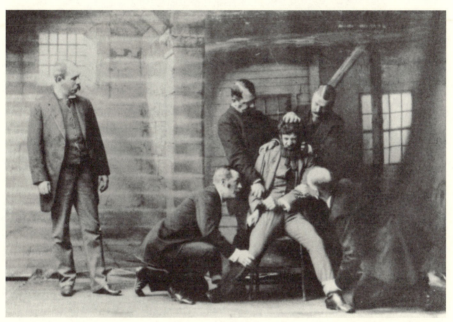

4. Thomas Byrnes, *Professional Criminals of America* (New York: Cassell, 1886).

5. From *Types of American Negroes, Georgia, U.S.A.*, compiled by W. E. B. Du Bois, 1900. Reproduced from the Daniel Murray Collection of the Library of Congress.

6. From *Types of American Negroes, Georgia, U.S.A.*, compiled by W. E. B. Du Bois, 1900. Reproduced from the Daniel Murray Collection of the Library of Congress.

7. From *Types of American Negroes, Georgia, U.S.A.*, compiled by W. E. B. Du Bois, 1900. Reproduced from the Daniel Murray Collection of the Library of Congress.

8. From *Types of American Negroes, Georgia, U.S.A.*, compiled by W. E. B. Du Bois, 1900. Reproduced from the Daniel Murray Collection of the Library of Congress.

9. Thomas Byrnes, *Professional Criminals of America* (New York: Cassell, 1886).

10. From *Types of American Negroes, Georgia, U.S.A.*, compiled by W. E. B. Du Bois, 1900. Reproduced from the Daniel Murray Collection of the Library of Congress.

Constructing a Psychological Perspective

The Observer and the Observed
in *The Souls of Black Folk*

Shanette M. Harris

The autobiographical style that W. E. B. Du Bois adapts in *The Souls of Black Folk* (1903) suggests that the perceptions and experiences of an individual can provide insight into the mind-set of a people. He becomes the filtering agent through which whites could learn what it means to be black. He discusses issues to encourage sociobehavioral change within the African American community and to develop European American empathy toward African Americans. Yet his own understanding of and empathy toward "black folk" was rather limited because of his few experiences with other African Americans. Du Bois's monoracial worldview emphasized social status and ethnicity until college attendance. It is this early orientation that subsequently contributed to an interpretive framework for his behavior and that of African Americans. Although he is credited with the application of scientific methodologies to understand the circumstances and life conditions of African Americans, principles of objectivity and impartiality are ignored in *Souls*. Given his strong allegiance to science, why is this particular publication so personalized and value laden? Is it possible that the observation and discussion of African Americans—the observed—made it impossible to avoid observation and discussion of the self? And if so, what impact did the personal attributes of Du Bois—the observer—have on his interpretations and perceptions of the African American experience? Finally, how were the multiple perspectives or voices, or "souls," characteristic of the African American community merged into a single perspective, in *Souls*?

The fourteen essays presented in *The Souls of Black Folk* consist of observations, opinions, and perceptions that represent a subjective rather than scientific worldview. Each essay reflects the degree to which Du Bois internalized aspects of culture both internal and external to the "veil," shaped by psychological defenses, beliefs, values, and internal strivings. *The Souls of Black Folk* is, in part, a looking glass that allows us to glimpse the inner life and spirit of an observer through recorded perspectives of those he observed. Thus, *Souls* actually mirrors the developmental progression of the soul of W. E. B. Du Bois. In many ways, Du Bois's willingness to share himself in such an intricate and intimate manner might be considered one of his most significant accomplishments. Observations outlined and discussed in *Souls* gave impetus to theories and assumptions that currently underlie "Black" or "African American Psychology" and premises that set the stage for today's focus on and concern with "multiculturalism." Prior to this work, the depth of the black psyche was largely unknown and unexplored, often assumed by European Americans to be nonexistent. The absence of knowledge of the inner life of African Americans made it so much easier for European Americans to oppress and dehumanize what was historically considered as an object and viewed as inhuman or at best, subhuman. In *Souls*, Du Bois's plea and presentation provide both Europeans and African Americans a concrete image of "Negro" culture and worldview that was previously invisible. Here the artifacts, values, beliefs, and customs of a displaced African people are described and clarified alongside the discussion of the spirit and thought of the individual. But what does psychology, particularly modern psychology, offer to our understanding of the relationship between this observer and those he observed? Can information about this relationship assist with present and future maladaptive conditions in the African American community? Given the precarious status of the African American community for the new millennium, it is important that visionaries bring fresh outlooks to existing viewpoints. This paper will examine *The Souls of Black Folk* through the lens of psychology with the aim to bring enlightenment for the twenty-first century from this slender volume of essays written by one of the greatest twentieth-century visionaries. What does a psychological reading of Du Bois's influential text tell us about ourselves as we enter the twenty-first century?

The Role of Psychology in Understanding *The Souls*

The Souls of Black Folk has most often been described and studied as a significant literary work. Du Bois uses the definite article before the word *souls* and thus makes "The Souls" convey a *black* essence, the intrinsic or indispensable properties that characterize or identify something, meaning the most important ingredient, the crucial element, or the oneness, that is characteristic of psychological study. However, he uses the plural, *souls*, to alert the reader to the "group" or collective of members. Moreover, his use of the word *soul* directs the reader to the inner, internal, and subjective as contrasted with the outer, external, and objective, regardless of whether he is referring to the individual or group. The intricacy of the reciprocal and bidirectional relationship between the inner world of the African American individual and the culture of the historically subjugated and oppressed group is brought to awareness through multiple and interwoven meanings.

Despite obvious intrapsychic themes in *The Souls of Black Folk*, this book is usually conceptualized as separate and distinct from Du Bois rather than as a map of the early phase of his life's mission to integrate or heal conscious and unconscious divisions. David Levering Lewis has referred to this period as Du Bois's "ego's learning decade, the ten or more years when the life and destiny of Africans in America merged inseparably with his own."[1] *Souls* is also frequently depicted as an objective product or outcome separate from the qualities of the author. I propose that this collection of essays is actually a reflection of the values and beliefs of Du Bois, couched in subjectively chronicled impressions and reactions to personal experiences and sociohistorical events. Literary critics' neglect of psychosocial and emotional issues presented in these essays, however, has prevented recognition that diverse interventions across multiple levels are necessary for successful problem resolution as we enter the new century.[2]

Unlike other disciplines, psychology can clarify many aspects of the relationship between the African American individual and racial or ethnic group membership. Themes and observations documented in *The Souls of Black Folk* can also contribute significantly to psychological information as regards the role of social factors in the development of the self and the interrelationship between this inner essence and the collective in which it is embedded. Given the potential for mutual influence between psychology and this publication, how is it that literary critics have, for the most part, ignored psychology as an explanatory model for the themes introduced by Du Bois?

1. David Levering Lewis, *W. E. B. Du Bois: Biography of a Race: 1868–1919* (New York: Henry Holt, 1993), 81.

2. Allison Davis, *Leadership, Love, and Aggression* (New York: Harcourt Brace Jovanovich, 1983), 3–243; and Arnold Rampersad, "Biography and Afro-American Culture," in *Afro-American Literary Study in the 1990s*, ed. Houston A. Baker Jr. and Patricia Redmond (Chicago: University of Chicago Press, 1989), are two notable exceptions to African American critics who avoid using psychological theory to understand African American leaders. Davis used modified psychoanalytic assumptions to examine leadership motivation and styles of leadership for four African American male leaders (Frederick Douglas, W. E. B. Du Bois, Richard Wright, and Martin Luther King Jr.). Rampersad encourages greater use of psychological paradigms to provide interpretive approaches for works of literature.

The omission of psychological analysis seems to relate to the influence of several factors, including Du Bois's educational training, interpretations of his writings, stylistic features of the book, critics' reluctance to consider qualities of the author, and a rather pervasive and deeply ingrained stigma held toward psychology by African Americans. The first fundamental barrier is that *Souls* has largely been examined from a sociopolitical perspective that is concerned with study of the group rather than the individual. The association between *Souls* and sociology stems from Du Bois's educational training and research interests in the African American collective. Even his emphasis on duality reflected in the usage of constructs such as "double duties," "double-consciousness," "twoness," "second sight," and "double life" has generally been considered from this orientation. During the 1960s, with its heavy emphasis on "black is beautiful," critics tended to rely on social and political paradigms that led to a mass publication of articles in which themes of duality were equated with oscillation between integrationist-assimilationist and nationalist-separatist ideologies. However, Du Bois studied psychology, philosophy, and history in the absence of university offerings in sociology. His repeated reference to duality and use of the concept "double-consciousness" also makes it difficult to imagine why psychological theory has been ignored as a framework from which to critique his book. Du Bois's relationship with William James, who coined the term *double consciousness*, itself provides a rationale for psychological inquiry. His admission that "I was repeatedly a guest in the house of William James" and his assertion that "of all teachers, [James] was my closest friend" support the influence of psychological assumptions on some of Du Bois's thinking.[3] The strong relation between philosophy and psychology, Du Bois's educational experiences with George Santayana, a Harvard university philosopher, and his familiarity with German writings (such as Hegel's *Phenomenology*) and concepts (such as "unhappy consciousness") also substantiate the impact of psychology on *Souls*.

When *The Souls of Black Folk* was published, the African American collective faced serious social obstacles (such as poverty, unemployment, and second-class citizenship), which had a significant impact on the use of sociopolitical rather than psychological theory. The urgency for strategies that addressed social ills encouraged theorists to focus on interpretations for the African American aggregate. A *zeitgeist* (spirit of the times) that called for eradication of sociopolitical problems also made it easier to uncover sociological and political messages in passages than psychological or individualistic themes. The use of a nontechnical and romantic writing style, characterized by unscientific, broadly defined, and ambiguous terms

3. Philip S. Foner, ed., *W. E. B. Du Bois Speaks: Speeches and Addresses, 1920–1963* (New York: Pathfinder, 1991), 29.

and concepts, also produced vague or imprecise meanings. This ambiguity concealed themes of a psychological nature and made it easy to distort or attribute multiple interpretations to the author's points of view.

The relative absence of psychological critiques of *Souls* appears partly attributable to discomfort with intrapsychic examinations of African American leaders in general, and W. E. B. Du Bois in particular. The infrequency with which psychology is applied to African American leaders gives the impression that individuals who advance to a certain status within the community are somehow exempt from emotional and behavioral scrutiny. The rapid erection of defenses in response to the psychological examination of certain topics and individuals also suggests that critical observation and open discussion introduce threats to the community. Yet the abuse perpetrated by European American society caused a state of psychological despair and anguish within many group members that produced a desperate need for vindication in the form of empowerment. This need for a hero or group member who could vindicate the group by confronting the European racist system on European American terms led critics to turn away from any psychological analysis of Du Bois. For the African American intelligentsia, he represented a larger-than-life symbol of power and courage to a community of members who felt powerless to challenge stereotypical images and biases designed to dehumanize. Du Bois's persistent and fierce exposure and deconstruction of European American exploitative sociopolitical tactics served to bolster group esteem and pride. As a result, few writers have attempted to understand the intricate relations that exist between Du Bois as writer/observer and the psychological dimension of *The Souls of Black Folk*.[4]

In the minds of many, close and critical inspection dishonors and devalues the contributions and talents of African American leaders. Any analysis of the relationships among leaders' beliefs or values and objectives and initiatives for the African American group is somehow interpreted as improper and even cruel. Many writers who would like to utilize theories of psychology to look "beyond the veil" are deterred because of fear that others will misconstrue psychological interpretations as disrespectful. In *Dark Voices: W. E. B. Du Bois and American Thought, 1888–1903*, Shamoon Zamir illustrates the reaction to writers who dare to search beyond the product and actually gaze at the author. A single, powerful sentence in the concluding lines of the introduction almost acts as a warning to those who would rely on a psychological framework. His statement that "The discussion here tries above all to respect the quality of Du Bois's response

---

4. Harold Cruse, in *The Crisis of the Negro Intellectual: A Historical Analysis of the Failure of Black Leadership* (New York: Morrow, 1967), 331–33, intricately examines the perspectives of Du Bois and other black leaders and their implications for social change among black Americans.

and to read the inventiveness of his response politically and culturally, not as an Oedipal anxiety of influence" draws parallels between "respect" and the political/cultural, and "disrespect" and psychological inquiry.[5] Fortunately, the silent consensus to eschew psychological theory in critiquing the work of Du Bois has not gone unnoticed.

In "Biography and Afro-American Culture," Arnold Rampersad, for example, proposes that the application of psychological theory as a model for literary criticism is a rarity because "so entrenched is the opposition to such work." The resistance to psychological scrutiny of African American leaders exists for a variety of reasons. A central factor relates to the historical and current scarcity of African American psychologists. The conspicuous absence of African Americans in this profession contributes to the perception that psychology is irrelevant and ill-suited to the African American experience. Applied and theoretical outcomes are influenced by the number of psychologists who understand the culture and value structure of a population of people. The underrepresentation of psychologists trained from an Afrocentric orientation affects the types of questions asked, the manner in which they are asked, and the interpretation and application of the knowledge obtained. A scarcity of culturally competent and committed professionals also increases the probability of the omission or distortion of community values, beliefs and dynamics.[6]

The historical misapplication of psychological principles and methodologies to promote racist ideologies has exaggerated the biases against psychology. Critics' lack of familiarity with psychological theories (other than Freudian theory, which ignores variation in family forms) and the impact of sociocultural influences help to perpetuate the myth that psychology is inappropriate for Americans of African descent. The skepticism that has arisen from the racist practices of some psychologists and the inappropriate generalization of irrelevant theories has fueled a sense of mistrust in the African American community. The pervasiveness of this mistrust and the public's lack of knowledge about the discipline have indirectly restricted paradigms from which writers can draw to lend clarity to their work.

However, psychology is a broad discipline that is composed of numerous explanatory models from traditional and recent theorists of different cultures and backgrounds. Members of the African American community can no longer afford to ignore the value of psychological knowledge for the resolution of problems that are rooted in psychoemotional issues and conflicts

5. Shamoon Zamir, *Dark Voices: W. E. B. Du Bois and American Thought, 1888–1903* (Chicago: University of Chicago Press, 1995), 19.

6. Rampersad, "Biography and Afro-American Culture," 201. Robert V. Guthrie, *Even the Rat Was White: A Historical View of Psychology,* 2d ed. (Boston: Allyn and Bacon, 1998), xi–54, discusses the scarcity of minority psychology professors and examines the relationship between anthropology and psychology that may influence these numbers.

such as substance abuse and dependence, interpersonal violence, relationship dysfunctions, AIDS, and poverty. Although Sigmund Freud, Abraham Maslow, Carl Rogers, and other renowned psychologists probably did not consider race and ethnicity during the conceptualization of their theoretical models, many traditional and more recent theoretical paradigms have the potential to assist with the delineation and improvement of the "Negro problem." Yet, any remedies based on images and presentations of African Americans discussed in *Souls* requires some analysis of the author/observer.

Applying an Adlerian Perspective to *The Souls of Black Folk*

Most critics who have used psychological theory to discuss African American leaders have employed some derivative of Freudian theory. For example, Allison Davis, in *Leadership, Love, and Aggression*, attempted to make sense of the lives of Du Bois and other black leaders such as Frederick Douglass, Richard Wright, and Martin Luther King Jr. by turning to "drives" and ways of handling aggression for explanatory purposes. However, his heavy-handed application of Freud's position on the role of the unconscious and strong emphasis on biological or instinctual forces seems more suited for understanding abnormal behavior or psychopathology than normal behavior. In particular, this model fails to consider social and cultural determinants of behavior that play such an important part in the well-being of African Americans. Moreover, several psychoanalytic theorists have presented formulations that might hold greater relevance than Freudian theory for the lives of African Americans in general and W. E. B. Du Bois as a member of this group. As a result, any theoretical model that examines *Souls* and Du Bois must consider the social and environmental factors that shaped his life and, indirectly, his product. Alfred Adler, a socially oriented psychiatrist who studied with Freud but rejected many of his assumptions, offers a perspective that includes environmental and social factors within the family. Adler emphasized the unique individuality of each personality and focused on consciousness and self-determination by emphasizing thoughts, feelings, attitudes, convictions, and beliefs and how they affect behavior.[7] Central to this theory is the subjective reality or manner in which people perceive and give meaning to their worlds.

7. T. W. Allen, "The Individual Psychology of Alfred Adler: An Item of History and a Promise of Revolution," *The Counseling Psychologist* 3 (1971): 3–24; H. L. Ansbacher and R. R. Ansbacher, eds., *The Individual Psychology of Alfred Adler* (New York: Harper and Row/Torchbooks, 1964); G. J. Manaster and R. J. Corsini, *Individual Psychology: Theory and Practice* (Itasca, Ill.: F. E. Peacock, 1982); H. Orgler, *Alfred Adler: The Man and His Work* (New York: Capricorn Books, 1963).

His system emphasizes the effects that social determinants, goal direction, and purposefulness have on behavior. The individual is not examined in isolation from a social network but is seen as an important part of a social system. The relationship of the self to other people and the self in relation to future objectives are stressed equally. A dominant theoretical tenet of importance to *Souls* and Du Bois is the concept of "social interest," which holds that success and happiness relate to how we share with and express concern about the well-being of others. Individuals have a need to be of value to others because it is only within the group that personal aspirations and potentials can be realized. In short, Adler makes a person's psychological health synonymous with a high level of social interest.

Adler also postulated that all humans are born with "organ inferiorities," or develop subjectively perceived psychological or social deficiencies that activate feelings of inferiority and provide impetus for perfection. *In Black Skin, White Masks* (1967), Frantz Fanon relied on Adler's later theories, using concepts such as inferiority, superiority, dominance, and social interest. However, Fanon viewed Adler's rigid and personalistic emphasis as inadequate to account for feelings of inferiority that emerged from a historical context rather than organic or familial dysfunction. According to this theorist, strivings of self largely account for observable behaviors, and feelings of inferiority stimulate a need or desire to strive for superiority. Although all express this dynamic force in different ways, to strive for superiority is normal and innate and motivates the individual throughout life. Striving for superiority involves trying to move beyond one's present state of being to live a more perfect life and is the primary motive of the personality and a natural reaction to feelings of inferiority. However, to strive for superiority does not necessarily mean that positions of leadership, prominence, status, or distinction will actually be attained. The goal is set to compensate for deficit feelings, and the behavior enacted to meet this objective may or may not be set in a direction opposite to feelings of inferiority. For example, feelings of inferiority about the body do not necessarily imply that the individual will strive to become an outstanding bodybuilder or fashion model. The goal is developed within the mind of an individual who creates a life pattern according to the fulfillment of his or her ideal, and a style of life is then chosen to achieve superiority based on types of feelings of inferiority. This lifestyle is influenced by family qualities such as climate or atmosphere and family composition. However, early experiences influence the future by way of interpretations of childhood events rather than the actual events themselves. We recall with razor sharpness those defining moments when we were reminded of our "differences" or "otherness" from the mainstream or the group. Although each person is born with this innate motive for success, some external circumstance or experience must activate the desire to strive.

W. E. B. Du Bois, a multiracial child of late-nineteenth-century America, was reared with few multiracial or African American models whom he respected in puritanical New England culture and was introduced early to the need to strive for superiority. In the collection's first essay, "Of Our Spiritual Strivings," Du Bois describes the external experience and its context that were powerful enough to make obvious emotions that were previously inaccessible to him. Du Bois recalls the moment that the impact of his physical self on the social environment was made salient and transformed him into a marginal figure in the supposedly safe harbor of the classroom. In this instance, however, "the other's" perspective of him was made clear, undeniably signifying his difference:

> I remember well when the shadow swept across me. I was a little thing, away up in the hills of New England, where the dark Housatonic winds between Hoosac and Taghkanic to the sea. In a wee wooden schoolhouse, something put it into the boys' and girls' heads to buy gorgeous visiting-cards—ten cents a package—and exchange. The exchange was merry, till one girl, a tall newcomer, refused my card,—refused it peremptorily, with a glance. Then it dawned upon me with a certain suddenness that I was different from the others; or like, mayhap, in heart and life and longing, but shut out from their world by a vast veil.[8]

Although Du Bois was aware of difference in race between himself and European American students and similarity between himself and the small number of Negro or African American students, prior to this interaction race had been of little consequence. This incident of social rejection produced great discomfort because the severity was of a magnitude to dismantle a denial system that previously offered protection from the harsh reality of racial overtones in New England. This experience initiated the development of a race schema into which prior race-related episodes (that once were readily attributed to other factors) were integrated, and forced Du Bois to acknowledge temporarily that racial background was more salient than academic performance. Interestingly, he equated this burgeoning racial awareness or consciousness with a "veil" because the insight that emerged from this awareness exposed the meaning of skin color differences.

A theme of duality emerges throughout the book that begins with a reinterpretation and application of the biblical usage of *veil*. Within the Bible this word takes on two meanings. In one instance it refers to ignorance, blindness, and hard-heartedness that prevented the Jews from understanding the scriptures, the spiritual meaning of the law, and from seeing that

---

8. W. E. B. Du Bois, *The Souls of Black Folk*, ed. Henry Louis Gates Jr. and Terri Hume Oliver (New York: Norton, 1999), 10. Further references to this work will be cited parenthetically in the text.

Christ was the law for righteousness. In the second context, the veil of the temple was that which separated the Holy Place from the Holy of Holies. Only the high priest could cross the separation on the Day of Atonement. The veil was stripped away only at crucifixion to indicate that all individuals could freely go to God. Du Bois applies both meanings to the racial differences in inequality and oppression suffered by African Americans at the hands of European Americans. First, he views the harsh plight and life circumstances of the African American group (including him) as outcomes of the ignorance, blindness, and spiritual bankruptcy of European Americans. This veil makes them unable to see African Americans as humans who deserve recognition and treatment in ways they would naturally expect and prefer for themselves. Because African Americans are not impaired spiritually as are their European American counterparts, they possess a greater sensitivity that allows them to see race and social matters in a more humanistic manner, with a kind of sixth sense. Thus, the veil accounts for racial group differences in values, perceptions, and social standards of living. Similar to the second biblical meaning, his other usage of the term focuses on legal and social boundaries that prevent interracial interaction—a disadvantage that produces a sense of separation or isolation. Interestingly, it is this usage of the term that seems more descriptive of the inner world of Du Bois than the community of which he writes. Here, he almost equates European American society with the "Holy of Holies" and possibly sees himself as one African American who should be allowed to pass through into this most sacred place as only the high priest could do on the Day of Atonement. The realization that skin of a certain color could "shut out" access to the European American world and its inhabitants produced psychological conflict for Du Bois. Despite his knowledge of race and how such differences were perceived, rejection because of race or skin color was incongruent with childhood socialization messages of education and unlimited achievement, individual determination, and control of one's destiny. Du Bois's inability to relinquish the irrationality of how racial group similarities in the inner or spiritual were so easily dismissed because of visible differences resulted in cognitions and affects that could be considered today as psychologically traumatic. Although this experience might not have elicited feelings of rage or pain in another male of the same race or ethnicity, Du Bois was already consumed with feelings of shame because of social status and family composition differences between himself and his European American peers.

Early in his development, Du Bois was also thrust into the role of caretaker with the expectation and understanding that he would successfully perform adult tasks to care for his mother. The emotional energy necessary to fulfill such demands, in all likelihood, also required the suppression, denial, or avoidance of feelings that might have been contrary to this family role. His mother made the young Du Bois aware that he carried the other family members' hopes, dreams, and desires of success. This position of hero took away from Du Bois childhood's sense of frivolity and freedom from worry and replaced them with a need for seriousness, independence, and persistence. His experience of rejection produced a shift in his consciousness and gave access to previously unavailable feelings that had been pushed aside and denied entry into his immediate awareness. His intense response to rejection evolved from feelings of anger, powerlessness, and sadness associated with physical and emotional abandonment from his father and, at best, the emotional unavailability of his mother. To experience rejection in the only environment perceived as personally rewarding (in terms of respect and admiration) exposed information that already existed at an intuitive level—primarily that he was somehow "less than" his classmates and powerless in a world that gave power to whiteness. This injury to his sense of self in the absence of other sources from which to draw self-worth and support could only evoke feelings of rage, followed with what seems to be resignation from feelings of helplessness and despair. In spite of his "otherness" or inferior social position, the young Du Bois determined to win some prizes: "That sky was bluest when I could beat my mates at examination-time, or beat them at a foot-race, or even beat their stringy heads. Alas, with the years all this fine contempt began to fade; for the worlds I longed for, and all their dazzling opportunities, were theirs, not mine" (10). Whereas most African Americans during this time period would have considered the possibility of rejection before offering their calling card, Du Bois's surprise and righteous indignation suggest that he had not given consideration to societal norms that prohibited such interracial behavior (particularly between males and females). As a result, anger and vengeance in the form of competitiveness quickly followed his disappointment and disillusionment. His pontification on the best path to take to strive for superiority and simultaneously overcome feelings of inferiority aroused by social rejection makes obvious his original inner struggle: "But they should not keep these prizes, I said; some, all, I would wrest from them. Just how I would do it I could never decide: by reading law, by healing the sick, by telling the wonderful tales that swam in my head,—some way" (10).

In Adler's words, Du Bois chose to strive for superiority and eradicate feelings of inferiority by seeking to obtain European "prizes." He rationalized that the attainment of these prizes would bestow upon him an equal or higher status than that of members of the European American racial group. Interestingly, he associates these "prizes" with professions or career choices, suggesting to the reader that he believed that only through the pursuit of specifically designated professions would he alleviate feelings of perceived weakness, insecurity, or inferiority. His decision to connect prizes with careers was directly related to subjective estimations and evaluations of his personal strengths and weaknesses. His natural talent in academics propelled him toward higher education and matters of the intellect and his physical stature pushed him away from nonacademic occupations. Indicative of his striving for superiority was the goal not to attend any college but to attend Harvard University—one of the most notable and elite institutions of European American higher education, during a time when only a minority of European Americans pursued higher education. This decision lends support to the hypothesis that Du Bois selected a lifestyle that could demonstrate and validate his superiority and also prove that he was not inferior to European Americans. Based on this worldview, educational attainment would make him more acceptable to Euro-Americans because shared appreciation and demonstrated excellence in certain cognitive and intellectual matters would allow them to see that his interior or "soul" was just like theirs. Underlying this logic was the assumption that European American oppression of African Americans evolved from the rational belief that African Americans were socially and intellectually inferior. This focus on the intellectual at the expense of the emotional resulted in blindness to the irrational nature of racism and the difficulty, if not impossibility, of eradicating irrationality with rationality.

Based on this understanding of race disparity and racial oppression, Du Bois naturally concluded that equitable treatment would be obtained if human equity between the races could be demonstrated; consequently, he willingly offered himself as a research subject in this experiment of truth. His childhood position as responsible one or family hero made it easy to transfer these role qualities to accept responsibility for the resolution of "the Negro problem" (16). However, he also expected that educational attainment and acceptance of this role would lead to a position of advantage among his same-race peers. The status of intellectual was somehow expected to elevate him above the realm of ordinary oppressed person (admitting him to the realm of the bluest of skies reserved for Euro-Americans only) and indirectly make him less Negro or African American than other race group members. Despite these rationalizations, however, Du Bois was quite aware that European American society would not willingly share "these prizes," and that regardless of intellectual talent, he would have to "wrest" them from them.

Synchronistically, the life plan or "striving" that evolved from Du Bois's early response to rejection from a European American female classmate initiated his first and well-known problem conceptualization and intervention for African Americans. Together, his physical and cognitive attributes (height, skin color, intelligence), social status (lower working class), family dynamics (absent father, dependent mother), and geographical background (predominantly white New England) interacted to promote and emphasize intellectual and academic achievement for the advancement of all African Americans. Du Bois accentuates this strong, positive regard for education of the Negro masses in the second essay, "Of the Dawn of Freedom." In the midst of heavy criticism levied against efforts of the Freedmen's Bureau, he applauds the educational pursuits of northern schoolteachers: "and, best of all, it inaugurated the crusade of the New England schoolma'am" (24).

The strong relation between intellectual prowess and superiority, coupled with the pervasive sentiment during that historical period that African Americans were deemed subhuman and incapable of abstract reasoning, influenced Du Bois's decision to associate the intellectual and academic with superiority. To compete and win in an arena designated by European Americans as evidence of superior talent and ability provided the opportunity to match, if not surpass, the European American standard. However, being both African American and an intellectual or scholar must have been an interesting position during this time. The scientific community's discussion of the relationship between race and intellectual or cognitive ability and general consensus that African Americans or Negroes occupied lower socioeconomic rungs of society because of biological or genetic inferiority introduced a conflict, whether conscious or unconscious, for all African Americans. However, the dilemma was significantly complicated for those who believed that educational and intellectual achievements were paths to equitable and fair treatment.

Although Du Bois was certainly knowledgeable of writings and empirical, pseudoscientific experiments that produced rationales for the assumed "inherent inferiority" of African Americans, this body of "inferiority" research and its assumptions are never mentioned in *The Souls of Black Folk*. Du Bois, however, deftly refutes the impact of this false logic, and its underlying assumptions are indirectly challenged in each essay, as is evident in the range and choice of subject matter: history, sociology, elegy, threnody, short story.[9]

Du Bois responds to the pseudoscientific thinking that has been used to justify the "inherent inferiority" of black people in the moving short story/essay, "Of the Coming of John." The protagonist goes to pieces under the weight of isolation, alienation, estrangement, and despair. Here, the reader can easily empathize with the emotional experience of Du Bois as he projects his inner conflicts related to racial group membership, organized religion, interracial interactions, and advanced education onto a young African American male who leaves a small southern town to attain

9. Arnold Rampersad, in *The Art and Imagination of W. E. B. Du Bois* (Cambridge: Harvard University Press, 1976), 69, offers critical comments on the spiritual insights in Du Bois's writings.

a higher level of education in the American North. The white and black Johns leave with the support, hope, and admiration of their respective communities; the black John returns much later to experience the impact of cognitive and social changes in his life. Personal changes brought about by varied cognitive and social dimensions of the educational process set him apart from members of his race and set him at odds with members of the European American community. In this short story, educational achievement is analogous to sight or vision for the individual who was previously blind but content. Prior to immersion into educational matters, the black John was oblivious to the barriers that impinged upon his life: racism from European Americans and adherence to nonprogressive religious doctrine by African Americans. The dissatisfaction with and rejection of a narrow interpretation of the Bible that places one in a theological straitjacket show similarities between the value structure of Du Bois and John and imply that the fury felt by John emanated from the emotional life of Du Bois. This rage is focused in dual directions in symbolism indicative of self-hate and hatred of the other—suicide and homicide. Yet the reader is left to consider whether this essay simply speaks to suicide and homicide as ways to cope with racism or if this tragedy is symbolic of something more.

The brutal and distressful ending of this story portrays a strategy for coping with feelings of alienation and separation from both the European and African American bloodlines that predominantly formed Du Bois's ethnic heritage. The state described by Du Bois and referred to as "double-consciousness" (11) involves the awareness of the self as belonging to two cultures and has been described as "a dual pattern of identification and a divided loyalty . . . [promoting] an ambivalent attitude." Theorists have referred to the psychological discomfort that evolves from relationships with two or more cultures as "marginal."[10] However, individuals who live in two or more cultures because of heritage or birth and socialization differences do not inevitably have to experience pain. For example, others suggest that "marginality" is only problematic and confusing if the individual internalizes the conflict between the two or more cultures of relevance.[11] The suicide and homicide in "Of the Coming of John" represent death to both ethnic and cultural aspects of Du Bois because of the recognition that assimilation was impossible. Conflict between the races that prohibited assimilation is shown in the European American male's assault on John's sister. This interracial assault was not selected by chance but chosen to

10. E. V. Stonequist, "The Problem of Marginal Man," *American Journal of Sociology* 7 (1935): 96; see also R. E. Park, "Human Migration and the Marginal Man," *American Journal of Sociology* 5 (1928): 881–93.
11. See M. M. Goldberg, "A Qualification of the Marginal Man Theory," *American Sociological Review* 6 (1941): 52–68; and A. W. Green, "A Re-examination of the Marginal Man Concept," *Social Forces* 26 (1947): 167–71.

provide a picture of racial tensions and relations, specifically between a black female and white male, that prevented assimilation and racial harmony. This image brings slavery to the forefront and draws a connection between Du Bois's relationship to other African Americans with use of the word "sister," which conveys a sense of family and unity. The decision to give the same name to both male characters and the parallel presentation of their similar and dissimilar experiences support an interpretation that accounts for the duality that is so characteristic of *Souls* and of Du Bois. The white John provides insight into the thoughts and behaviors and privileges of an educated European American male as compared and contrasted with those of the black John as an educated African American male. Ironically, both perspectives exist within the inner life of Du Bois, but without some form of assimilation, the only resolution is death to both because one does not and cannot exist without the other. The intricacy of the relationship between the two Johns makes the whole much more than the sum of its parts.

Legal and social prohibitions during the turn of the century made it impossible for Du Bois to integrate the internal division that was consistent with the outward separation of the African American and European American cultures. In contrast to the more recent move toward pluralism and multiculturalism in American culture that encourages some degree of assimilation or requires acculturation, neither was an alternative for Du Bois. He wanted to be absorbed into European American culture because of its dominance and because his socialization and educational experiences taught him to view this culture as highly desirable. However, Du Bois experienced isolation and alienation because he was never accepted and never saw himself as acceptable within this culture. Yet he was unaware of these feelings because he engaged in the ego-defense mechanism of projection. Throughout *Souls*, Du Bois attributes his attitudes, desires, and impulses that are unacceptable to conscious awareness to others. It is the reliance on projection as a defense that leads him to use the construct "double-consciousness" that he generalizes to all African American people. He also attributes unacceptable thoughts about African Americans and himself to European Americans that would cause great pain if allowed access to his awareness. For example, Du Bois wrestles with concern about or fear of his own inferiority in the essay "Of the Training of Black Men" by raising the possibility that African American men may be incompetent:

> And last of all there trickles down that third and darker thought,—the thought of the things themselves, the confused half-conscious mutter of men who are black and whitened, crying "Liberty, Freedom, Opportunity— vouchsafe to us, O boastful World, the chance of living men!" To be sure, behind the thought lurks the afterthought,—suppose, after all, the World is right and we are less than men? Suppose this mad impulse within is all wrong, some mock mirage from the untrue? (63)

Several psychological studies also show that the greatest incidence of negative symptoms, such as poor emotional states, low self-esteem, and poor social relationships, occur in individuals who desire to identify with a particular group but encounter barriers to assimilation. Thus Du Bois was placed in a position that almost forced him to claim his blackness but reject his whiteness because of the absence of any observable fusion between the groups. These conditions presented little hope for a holistic or integrated self, which, in turn, caused the stress and anxiety that eventually resulted in the self-destructiveness seen in "Of the Coming of John."

Issues of Identity and Achievement: Differentiating between Self and Group

Other essays in *The Souls of Black Folk* also convey information about experiences and situations that influenced the development of an identity or subjective self of the author and members of the community about which he wrote. In addition to acculturation and assimilation, reciprocal and bidirectional interactions between internal processes and external events are described that involve socioeconomic status and racial identification—issues that all minority populations must resolve in relation to a powerful and dominant other population. However, Du Bois's description of a group experience or process is actually an explication of his individual transformation. Some of the concerns identified within the African American community and recommendations offered for their resolution evolved from his racial identity status and life plan chosen to achieve superiority during this developmental phase. However, Du Bois failed to recognize the dynamic and mutual influence among his insecurities, fears, conflicts, and strivings; thus, he often proposed what might have been appropriate and even necessary life objectives for himself as aims for *all* African Americans. Inadequate direction and guidance in sociopolitical and economic areas in the face of community suffering led critics to interpret essays in *Souls* in a way that centralized concerns of the African American group but shifted the individual to the periphery. This substitution of self for group resulted in the espousal and interpretation of personal aims as appropriate and desired strivings for the collective. Failure to differentiate between self and group silenced the diversity that existed in African American culture and contributed to an initial set of time-limited and subgroup-specific solutions.

Although it appears that Du Bois formulated and enacted his lifestyle independent of the African American group, Adlerian theory suggests that the goal to strive for superiority is inexorably interconnected with social group membership. If, however, Du Bois's response to assuage feelings of inferiority and enhance feelings of superiority through education had been successful, it is unlikely that *Souls* would have been written. But his personal goals and academic accomplishments were insufficient to alter feelings of inferiority. The intricate link between himself as an "individual" and himself as "a member of an oppressed racial group" made the relation between inferiority and need or desire for superiority significantly complex. Individual strivings and achievements alone could not satisfy his quest for superiority. To truly experience superiority was only possible if the race to which he was socially assigned also achieved this distinction. Thus, the interrelatedness of the individual and social group made the personal alleviation of shame and humiliation and establishment of power and respect contingent upon eradication of the perception of inferiority for those racially similar to him. Unfortunately, the fulfillment of this ideal required that other racial group members also adopt a similar life goal and pattern.

Adler posits that striving for superiority is a natural response to human dependencies and weakness that become evident during childhood. However, his theory also allows for psychopathological strivings referred to as behaviors that are executed to overcompensate for perceived deficiencies—in other words, striving is normal but overcompensation is abnormal. The repeated acquisition of education represented tangible and observable evidence of Du Bois's intellectual superiority and ritualistically presented self-justification of his competence. This compulsion to demonstrate his worth as a human via his intellectual validation by European academicians eventually promoted an inner war and set the stage for the making of an inferiority complex. Self-disparagement based on evaluations as seen through the eyes of European Americans and self-aggrandizement because of more education than other African Americans exacerbated his inner turmoil.

A life plan to force European Americans to see that African Americans were not inherently inferior shaped Du Bois's interpersonal and social relations. A great deal of this life stage was geared toward impressing and seeking the approval of European Americans. His beliefs and convictions about educational achievement interacted with his need for superiority and produced a dogmatic, perfectionistic, and critical way of relating to himself and others. Beliefs that superiority was synonymous with academic achievement and that competencies considered unacceptable to European Americans were indicative of inferiority often placed him in a position to move against or away from others in his social environment.

Du Bois's inability to differentiate between "self" and "group" because of an inferiority complex gave rise to the need for others to adopt his lifestyle. This overriding need that set him at odds with others was especially problematic in his pattern of reaction to black leaders. Although an argument could be made that value or political differences about race relations were central to these conflicts, a psychological interpretation suggests that other factors deserve consideration.[12] If Du Bois had reserved his rejecting manner for a single leader, it would make sense to simply attribute this approach to an idiosyncratic or stylistic tendency; however, he behaved in a similar way toward Booker T. Washington and Marcus Garvey. His basic pattern of reaction generally began with a written or verbal endorsement of a leader's plan. These expressions of praise and support were then followed with discussions that compared and contrasted the aims and objectives of his plan with those of the leaders. However, what began as a complimentary and supportive evaluation or critique turned into hostile criticism and personal attack.

His lack of positive relationships with adult male models during childhood and adolescence made it easy to misinterpret the actions of African American leaders. An absence of childhood and adolescent socialization experiences with African American male peers also prevented the formation of alliances with leaders because of unfamiliarity with cultural practices and norms that would have extinguished uncertainty and discomfort. Few occasions to witness others show respect to elders or community leaders in positions of power (other than those of European status) also evoked stereotypical evaluations about which man was worthy to lead the race. These circumstances combined to make it difficult for Du Bois to know if, when, and how to relate respectfully to male leaders of the same race.[13]

His reactions were also shaped by the inability to see Washington and Garvey as individuals and the inclination to see them as symbolic representations of other men in his life who were associated with pain and frustration. Inconsistencies between his usual social manner and behaviors displayed toward these leaders support this hypothesis. For instance, Du Bois's preference for emotional restraint and New England formality contrasted sharply with his almost uncivil and public attack on Washington. His demonstration of blatant disregard for the impact of political divisiveness conflicted greatly with his verbalized concern for the well-being of African Americans and undercut his expressed hope to become their leader. Such discourteous and antagonistic behavior was especially inappropriate in the context of his unfamiliarity with the southern Negro community, absence of interpersonal knowledge about Washington, and failure to extend an invitation to either leader before criticism.

12. Davis, *Leadership, Love, and Aggression*, 117–20. Davis discusses Du Bois's ambivalence about race and implies that internalized racism influenced his reactions to other African American leaders.

13. Rampersad, *Art and Imagination*, and Lewis, *Biography of a Race*, present detailed biographical information of relevance to Du Bois's interpersonal relations and attitudes.

The social status of and potential for advancement of Washington and Garvey among African Americans presented a threat to Du Bois's desire for superiority. The willingness of thousands of African Americans to follow Garvey and Washington aroused childhood feelings of helplessness and competitiveness in Du Bois. The realization that these men were considered "the Negro leaders" evoked the inferiority complex that was often concealed with narcissism and arrogance. The swiftness with which he offended and took offense to these leaders was prompted by anger and the belief that these men were less worthy and capable than he of holding a station of prominence. Unfortunately, unresolved emotional conflicts because of deficits in self-esteem and self-confidence undermined his stated desire to fight the cause of the "Negro."

Du Bois's perception of and response to Alexander Crummell substantiates further the psychoemotional threat posed by Garvey and Washington. In the essay "Of Alexander Crummell," it is obvious that Du Bois admires and respects this man and that the strength of his affinity for him was as intense as his feelings of hostility for Garvey and Washington. At first glance, his description of Crummell seems antithetical to the presence of unresolved problems with African American men. However, closer attention to the qualities he associates with this admired person shows that Du Bois was quite able to express affiliative statements because Crummell represented little if any threat to his need for dominance and superiority. Crummell was a relatively mild-mannered, humble, and rather obscure man invested with great social interest for African Americans. Whether these characteristics accurately depict the personhood of Crummell is questionable. It seems more likely that Du Bois projected his conflicted feelings about African American men on Crummell, Garvey, and Washington. His way of handling anxiety associated with men of his race did not allow him to hold an objective perspective of any of these men. Unresolved feelings almost forced him to project his inner split or division outward: forming the "good daddy," and "bad daddy" images incorporated internally during childhood to cope with the father he never knew. The passive, nonthreatening, self-sacrificing, giving, and noncompetitive male forms the "good daddy," whereas the active, assertive, and politically and socially interactive male becomes the "bad daddy," thus eliciting competition, producing threat, and requiring censure.

If we employ Adlerian theory, feelings of rage, shame, and humiliation that easily gave way to hostility and animosity toward African American males in positions of power could have stemmed from his birth-order position; Du Bois was second to an older brother. Adler suggests that the second born, having an older brother (who may have contributed to his economic well-being), works diligently to establish a personal identity that is easily differentiated from this brother. Du Bois's responses to Garvey and Washington clearly give witness to a need to clarify differences between their views and his own, as if to carve out a separate identity.[14]

Paternal neglect and abandonment and the lack of a bond with a same-race male authority figure might also have contributed to his rapid and uncensored reaction to male leaders.[15] Sadly, three important male figures in his early life were psychologically, if not physically, unavailable by his fifth birthday. To grow up without a father would make it difficult as an adult to perceive other males in authority as anything but threatening and intrusive, especially when his childhood family role was free from this type of boundary. The anger and criticism held over from the past because he was denied the safety, security, and a carefree childhood that a father could offer was also easily generalized to other males. Finally, Du Bois may have responded to these men as if they were African American representations of him. Any stereotypes or feelings of inferiority were directed at these objects as a way to rid the self of psychological anguish. The force of these unresolved feelings made it easy to project unkind motives and attributes onto other African American men in roles of perceived dominance.

Du Bois's contempt was further fueled by actual differences between his objectives for the race and those of the other two leaders. Whereas Du Bois desperately depended on educational competence to command racial respect and equality with European Americans, Washington believed in the achievement of racial parity through skills development that he believed would lead to the acquisition of wealth and capital. Unlike Du Bois, but similar to Washington, Garvey agreed with principles of group independence and self-sufficiency but also held that African Americans should fight for equality in Africa rather than America. These practical and sociopolitical differences contributed to Du Bois's perception that his outline of Washington's plan described in the essay "Of Mr. Booker T. Washington and Others" encouraged European Americans to see African Americans as inferior. Ironically, it was Du Bois's attacks on Washington and Garvey that suggest a need for attention, low self-esteem, and feelings of inadequacy. Basically, Du Bois's opposition was intertwined with the hidden belief that Washington and Garvey held places or positions that he, Du Bois, rightfully deserved. His obsession with these leaders and compulsive need to discredit and remove them indicate the intensity of his pathological anger and hostility. At first glance, his reactions seem consistent with adjectives used by some who have described him as conceited, overpowering, and

14. See W. E. B. Du Bois, *Black Titan: W. E. B. Du Bois; an Anthology by editors of Freedomways*, ed. John Henrik Clarke (Boston: Beacon Press, 1970).

15. See Davis, *Leadership, Love, and Aggression*, 105–52, for information about Du Bois's relationships with powerful European American males.

spoiled.[16] A closer examination reveals a wounded man full of hurt and humiliation who eventually turned his anger into motivation that fueled much of his achievement. However, over time, this same impelling force was channeled inappropriately toward himself and others. His emphasis on education as sole means to attain "respect" and cynical dismissal of economic achievement as an alternative way of eliminating oppression mediated his construction of experiences for years to come.

Resolving the Negro Problem, or the Du Boisian Conflict? The Influence of Racial Identity Attitudes

Souls offers information about the intrapsychic worldview that influenced the relationship between Du Bois's identity and the lifestyle he selected to strive for superiority and eradicate inferiority. His psychological response to identity progression and resolution during the early period of his life was intricately tied to a desire for his own and the "Negro" identity that he presented as the wish "to make it possible for a man to be both a Negro and an American, without being cursed and spit upon by his fellows, without having the doors of Opportunity closed roughly in his face" (11).

This wish shows the difference between European and African Americans in their move to establish an identity, namely that identity development for African Americans is significantly more complex because of the racism that must be confronted. The tendency to be defined as "a problem" and to be "shut out from their world by a vast veil" (10) requires an integration of multiple internal selves that exist because of the internalization of a racially divided external environment. As Du Bois suggests, the external world thrusts onto African Americans an identity crisis that produces an inner conflict within *some* group members. The conflict centers on separation between nationality and race and gives the "sense of always looking at one's self through the eyes of others, of measuring ones' soul by the type of a world that looks on in amused contempt and pity. One ever feels his two-ness,—an American, a Negro; two souls, two thoughts, two unreconciled strivings; two warring ideals in one dark body, whose dogged strength alone keeps it from being torn asunder" (11).

As a result of the legacy of African people in America and Africa, black

---

16. See Lewis, *Biography of a Race;* and the following works by Manning Marable: *W. E. B. Du Bois: Black Radical Democrat* (Boston: Twayne Publishers, 1986); *Beyond Black and White: Transforming African American Politics* (New York: Verso, 1995); *Black Leadership* (New York: Columbia University Press, 1998); and *Dispatches from the Ivory Tower: Intellectuals Confront the African American Experience* (New York: Columbia University Press, 2000).

skin becomes a sign and symbol of inferiority and blacks are forced to identify with Africa. However, blackness is at odds with acceptance of self as
American and identification with that which is American is, in part, also
a rejection of that which is traditionally African or black. This conflict can
cause great psychic pain and produce damaging behavioral outcomes. Psychologically, blacks are working at cross-purposes, and, according to Du
Bois, "Such a double life, with double thoughts, double duties, and double
social classes, must give rise to double words and double ideals, and tempt
the mind to pretense or revolt, to hypocrisy or to radicalism" (127).

He also charged that "This waste of double aims, this seeking to satisfy
two unreconciled ideals, has wrought sad havoc with the courage and faith
and deeds of ten thousand thousand people,—has sent them often wooing
false gods and invoking false means of salvation, and at times even seemed
about to make them ashamed of themselves" (12).

Interestingly, Du Bois makes these proclamations as if his experiences
were the same for other African Americans. His perspectives, based on
European American ideals, and his personal shame and sense of racial
marginality prevented him from recognizing the diversity that characterized the African American population. As is frequently the case with theorists today, Du Bois mistakenly assumed that categories such as Negro
or African American provide information about the spiritual or psychoemotional essence of a person. Irrespective of the observers' racial group
membership or the person under observation, it is the self-selected identity that is likely to be more predictive of behaviors, attitudes, and values than racial categorization. As a result of this faulty assumption, Du
Bois generalized from his own soul to *The Souls of Black Folk*. This generalization is unfortunate because the issue of identity development must
have been compounded for Du Bois. Compared to most southern same-
race group members, Du Bois lacked significant and meaningful exposure
to African American models and cultural norms, although biologically related to both racial groups within a classist environment. Consistent with
these factors, David Levering Lewis suggests that Du Bois's emphasis on
double consciousness emerged from his biraciality and observations and
experiences with two social classes.[17] However, I propose that his "double-
consciousness" did not arise from biraciality or dual biological or genetic
heritage per se, but his desire for assimilation. This desire produced a sense
of marginality and racial identity development issues for a "marginal" man
in an environment that devalued blackness. Regardless of social status, ethnicity, or geographical background, Americans of African descent must resolve identity issues related to race. The development of an inferiority complex in Du Bois stemmed from his racial identity, attitudes, feelings, and

17. Lewis, *Biography of a Race*.

behaviors; he responded to his alleged inferiority based solely on race by overcompensating in matters of intellectual achievement. Unfortunately, Adlerian theory does not offer concepts or premises to account adequately for racial identity. However, several models have been presented and discussed that describe psychological efforts to minimize the impact of deracination perpetuated by European American society.

Applying Racial Identity Theory

Many of the themes and messages found in *The Souls of Black Folk* share commonalities with characteristics of various stages of racial identity development models. Most of these models involve four or five stages through which African American individuals are assumed to progress as a function of life events and situations that promote movement from one level to the next in the process of becoming black. The most widely examined model of identity development, put forth by William Cross and developed further by Janet Helms, consists of five stages or levels, including the Pre-encounter level, Encounter level, Immersion-Emersion level, Internalization level, and Internalization-Commitment level.[18]

The Pre-encounter level of identity is characterized by a worldview that is basically European or white in nature. A person in this stage tends to behave and think in ways that devalue blackness associated with anti-black and pro-white attitudes. The Encounter level occurs in relation to experiences that interfere with or disrupt the values and beliefs consistent with a Pre-encounter standard. Personal or social events, situations, or experiences that challenge the Pre-encounter assumptive world promote attitudinal changes that correspond more closely to a pro-black or anti-white frame of reference. The Immersion-Emersion level is characterized by behavioral efforts to become more aware and knowledgeable of black culture, history, and heritage. The person increases involvement in understanding his most recent race-related experiences and moves away from Pre-encounter perspectives in psychological and behavioral ways. The Internalization level is associated with psychological health and is characterized by inner tranquillity, nondefensiveness, and more tolerance and openness to people irrespective of race or ethnicity. At this level, emphasis is placed on interpersonal and social harmony across groups, although "black" remains

---

18. See William E. Cross Jr., "The Negro to Black Conversion Experience," *Black World* 20 (1971): 13–27; William E. Cross Jr., "The Psychology of Nigrescence: Revising the Cross Model," in *Handbook of Multicultural Counseling,* ed. Joseph G. Ponterotto, J. Manuel Casas, Lisa A. Suzuki, and Charlene M. Alexander (Thousand Oaks, Calif.: Sage, 1995); and Janet E. Helms, *Black and White Racial Identity* (Westport, Conn.: Greenwood Press, 1990).

the normative or reference group. Finally, the Internalization-Commitment level is similar to Internalization, and the only difference seems to relate to the focus and emphasis on interest and commitment to actions. At this point, individuals are engaged in behaviors that indicate their devotion to the purpose of harmony.

Du Bois certainly saw the world in many ways across his lifespan but his predominant worldview during the first phase of his adult life seemed consistent with beliefs, behaviors, and emotions characteristic of the first, Pre-encounter level of identity development. Socialization experiences that encouraged separation from other African Americans and an individualistic rather than collectivist orientation to others partly accounted for the many years it took for Du Bois to move beyond this level of racial identity. He was reared in New England, a region with a small African American population; he encountered few blatant forms of racism, although social status and ethnic intolerance and prejudice were obvious; his assimilation caused him to use a similar cultural angle to interpret behavior as did European Americans. Despite the early experience of a white classmate's rejection, until very late in his life, Du Bois's emotions, attitudes, and behaviors seemed to closely match the following description of the Pre-encounter status offered by William Cross, Thomas Parham, and Janet Helms:

> At the core of Pre-encounter is an aggressive assimilation-integration agenda. An individual in Pre-encounter is simultaneously searching for a secure place in the socioeconomic mainstream and attempting to flee from the implications of being a "Negro." A Negro in Pre-encounter is depicted as a deracinated person who views Black as an obstacle, problem, or stigma rather than a symbol of culture, tradition, or struggle. A Negro in this stage is preoccupied with thoughts of how to overcome his stigma, or how he or she can assist Whites in discovering that he or she is "just another human being" who wants to assimilate.[19]

Much of Du Bois's anguish and internal strife evolved from attempting to avoid the social and cultural consequences of being black or "Negro." During adolescence and early adulthood, he seemed to perceive blackness as cumbersome and negative; the perception of blackness as a burden produced self-consciousness and embarrassment. This perception motivated his selection of a lifestyle that would relieve feelings of shame, humiliation, and embarrassment associated with blackness in post-slavery America. Consistent with a Pre-encounter belief system, his greatest desire was to somehow demonstrate to the European American others that he was just like them, and, therefore, deserved to be treated like them.

19. William E. Cross Jr., Thomas A. Parham, and Janet E. Helms, "The Stages of Black Identity Development: Nigrescence Models," in *Black Psychology,* 3d ed., ed. R. L. Jones (Los Angeles: Cobb and Henry, 1991), 322.

His method to achieve this outcome was to attain education. Based on his worldview, an immersion in the assumptions, premises, and theories of European culture would remove social inequities. It was largely the European educational system that placed European culture at the center of the world that constructed his European American orientation. Du Bois also sought a niche in society that was free from talk about race and free from separatism but instead focused on integration. In many ways, he hoped to slip out of the darkness of the veil and into the oblivion of mainstream society. A description of his feelings during training in Germany acknowledges his relief from racially related matters and satisfaction with the chance to interact without racial hindrances. Unlike individuals with Pre-encounter racial attitudes, however, Du Bois did not display greater concern for individual success and achievement and the success of individuals within the group than the group in its entirety. Yet similar to characteristics of the Pre-encounter stage, his strategy for the well-being of "the Negro" benefited only an insignificant percentage of the collective (ten percent).

Interestingly, Du Bois writes about African Americans as if he were an objective and impartial observer. He disperses this type of distance throughout the majority of *Souls* in a way that separates him from those he writes about. Rhetorically, he conveys this distance in *The Souls of Black Folk* by writing mostly about blacks in the third person. This manner of positioning is seen in his description of his childhood views of African Americans when he says: "there were a few new colored people, 'contrabands,' who came to town. One family particularly I liked, they were so jolly and darkly handsome."[20]

The need to erect invisible barriers between himself and "contrabands" is indicative of the distance maintained between Du Bois and other African Americans. Intragroup and intergroup elitism sanctioned and promoted as a part of his early socialization gave rise to the prejudice he sometimes displayed toward his own. Although Du Bois vehemently objected to the notion that blacks were inferior, he held the belief that some people were "naturally" superior. The essay "Of the Wings of Atalanta" speaks to his beliefs that individuals did not have the same passion or ability and that some were suited to become scholars or thinkers and others for crafts or industrial work. Based on these assumptions, Du Bois developed and promoted his well-known social mobility plan for the African American community (the "talented tenth"). Du Bois's deep admiration and respect for Crummell is also supportive of Pre-encounter racial attitudes. Crummell

20. See also W. E. B. Du Bois, *Dusk of Dawn: An Essay toward an Autobiography of a Race Concept* (New York: Schocken Books, 1968); and *W. E. B. Du Bois Writings: The Suppression of the African Slave-Trade/The Souls of Black Folk/Dusk of Dawn/Essays and Articles*, ed. Nathan Huggins (New York: Library of America, 1986), 561.

and Du Bois shared many values and beliefs about "blackness." Similar to Du Bois, Crummell was intent on showing the intellectual prowess of "the Negro." At the same time, he contrasted the majestic wonder of the English language spoken by Europeans over African languages and viewed them as less complex in structure and form, less unappealing in sound and enunciation, and insufficient in worthy ideas.[21] Like Du Bois, Crummell also believed that assimilation and acculturation into European American culture represented the only route for African Americans to acquire social equality and intellectual empowerment. Du Bois's idealization of European American culture and belief that African Americans somehow needed European cultural traditions (implying African Americans did not have a culture) supports a worldview consistent with a Pre-encounter status of racial identity: "I tried to take culture out into the colored community of Boston; I visited, joined clubs, lectured, and once actually gave the *Birds of Aristophanes* in a colored church on Thanksgiving night."[22]

His emotional and behavioral distance from those he observed seemed guided by various rationalizations. This is quite evident in his belief that ignorance alone was the cause of race prejudice and that intellectual exchange between racial groups would lead to less oppression because of more European American race empathy—in the form of education—for African Americans. In "Of the Training of Black Men," Du Bois, however, makes it clear that the education of African Americans in "taste and culture" can remedy prejudice and that the economic and career preparation tasks of traditional black educational institutions are inadequate. Thus, Du Bois's life objective, to win the prizes of European Americans, was promoted as the "panacea" for the African American group. However, education and college training did not protect Du Bois from the harsh realities of racism. It could be argued that advanced education and intellectual accomplishments made it more difficult to deny the psychological impact of a racist environment, which is a leitmotif in "Of the Coming of John."

Interestingly, Du Bois moved to identify with African Americans or the collective in the concluding paragraphs of "The Sorrow Songs," in his journey toward wholeness. Unlike the issues and concerns that led him to maintain a sense of separateness and emotional aloofness, he moves in this chapter rather quickly and forcefully to claim identification, as, for example, when he presents the "strengths" of the race in his rousing conclusion:

21. Henry Louis Gates Jr., "Canon-Formation, Literary History, and the Afro-American Tradition: From the Seen to the Told," in *Afro-American Literary Study in the 1990s*, ed. Houston A. Baker Jr. and Patricia Redmond (Chicago: University of Chicago Press, 1989), 14–39.
22. See also *Dusk of Dawn*, in *W. E. B. Du Bois Writings*, ed. Huggins, 579.

> Your country? How came it yours? Before the Pilgrims landed we were here. Here we have brought our three gifts and mingled them with yours: a gift of story and song—soft, stirring melody in an ill-harmonized and un-melodious land; the gift of sweat and brawn to beat back the wilderness, conquer the soil, and lay the foundations of this vast economic empire two hundred years earlier than your weak hands could have done it; the third, a gift of the Spirit. (162)

These gifts of singing, physicality, and matters of the spirit seem rather stereotypical and quite similar to those that researchers have found for more than a hundred years as qualities consistently cited by European Americans as characteristics of African Americans. But from another perspective, Du Bois's fascination with and attraction to African American singing originated while he was young in New England, as did his understanding of the physical demands of slavery. Although he uses "we" and "our" to refer to the three assets of the African American group, he worked diligently for the early part of his life to avoid association with these same attributes. In some instances within *Souls*, it seems as if his statements and strivings were made to take him as far from these "gifts" as possible. Thus, an analysis of his vow in the first essay to wrest away the prizes of the European Americans using some intellectual means sheds more light on his reference in this final essay to "our three gifts." Du Bois gives no indication throughout any of the essays that he views physical abilities in a positive way. In fact he clearly and repeatedly acknowledges the value and greater importance of intellectual than physical tasks and endeavors (especially in his rejection of Washington's approach). Although his views of singing and music are less clear, his beliefs about and perceptions of the African American church seem inconsistent with his favorable portrayal of spirituality.

Implications of the Observer and the Observed for the New World Order

This analysis concentrated on the explicit and implicit content in *The Souls of Black Folk*. The content depicts a series of developmental experiences of a man who espoused assimilation and coped with European American oppression by competition and intellectualism. Together, the themes of these essays offer fertile ground for an analysis of psychological issues specific to the African American community that deserve confrontation for full participation in the new world order. Various assumptions, themes, and positions posited by Du Bois must be reconsidered in light of changes that have occurred within and external to the African American group.

Despite the generally accepted and unquestioned tradition of using the slave narrative and black autobiography as a foundation for the African American literary tradition, the voice of one individual should not be mistaken or misinterpreted as the *current* multiplicity of voices within the African American community. I propose that the slave narrative tradition provided a valuable and worthy orientation to understanding literary works prior to *Souls*. However, the publication of Du Bois's book introduced the start of a paradigmatic shift for the African American experience that opened the door to nontraditional models of literary interpretation. In many ways, the book opposes assumptions of the slave narrative (for example, deemphasis on bodily based experiences of slavery, separation of body and self, emphasis on social uplift) and by doing so, it validates the evolution of a novel worldview. This view maintains a connection to slave narrative in the African American experience by continuing with aspects of this perspective but relying significantly less on the form and structure of slave themes than was traditional. The emphasis in *Souls* ever so gently but forcefully moved African Americans to a state of psychological readiness for sociopolitical change that would take years to emerge in America. The willingness to confront slavery and evaluate the postbellum status of African Americans against a backdrop of a discussion of spirit and spiritualism, in a symbolic movement toward intercultural and interracial equality, created a space for the acknowledgment and examination of the inner African American. Here, Du Bois also joins or reconnects the previously separate "Negro" to both Africa and America and gives meaning to the word *race* that is almost synonymous with the meaning of *culture*. This presentation of a continuum that ranged from Africa to America along which African Americans could establish multiple identities—including racial identity, social class, cultural values, and ethnicity—and a disassociation of the Africa American body from spirit or soul, engendered the need for a psychology of African Americans. Du Bois's identification and acknowledgment of cultural "gifts" served to enhance self-efficacy and give life to this new African American sense of self. The subjective nature of the work also shows how Du Bois attempted to forge a bicultural identity in a racially hostile environment as he moved from denial and unawareness of the significance of race to greater awareness, albeit accompanied with emotional experiences of pain, shame, and anger. Just as Du Bois had to face and work to resolve the impact of race in his life, each African American eventually confronts this issue in the development of an identity. However, the experience of Du Bois cannot be generalized to the development and implementation of interventions for future race group members. The effectiveness or success of orchestrated change must include within-group variation because personal attributes and qualities influence the readiness for and reactions to various community-based efforts. Varied responses, worldviews, and experiences characteristic of the modern

African American collective must be considered in order to initiate, implement, and maintain psychosocial and economic change. Thus, the resulting outcome of applying a psychological narrative analysis to *Souls* might be expected to yield a different interpretation for the future than what might emerge from the application of a slave-narrative tradition. In a way that differs from the sense of human solidarity and views of progress and advancement in the slave narratives, I suggest that what is good for the goose is not necessarily good or even appropriate for the gander.

Strategies developed with elite or advantaged socioeconomic status African American group members that previously had social change possibilities may be ineffective today. The once-held notion that economically and educationally privileged African Americans can enhance the well-being of other group members is based on the assumption that positive working alliances exist between subgroups of this population. However, many African Americans have little contact with members of socioeconomic levels different from their own. This lack of interaction frequently translates into an inability of social classes to empathize with or take the perspective of the other, which, in turn, limits intergroup understanding and thus prevents modifying specific conditions that affect all group members. An approach to problem resolution that relies on a social status hierarchy also silences those who most need to speak and inflates the self-worth of those who have received the greatest materialistic benefit from European society. Unlike the strategy proposed by Du Bois, any intervention designed to address social problems must consider diversity as regards gender, stage of racial identity, sexual orientation, social class, geographical locale, and ethnic heritage. These and other personal qualities interact to influence interpretations of the world, and the effectiveness of change agents depends on knowledge of these characteristics. For instance, Du Bois referred to "double-consciousness" and used the notion of duality throughout many of his essays; however, gender remained constant as seen in his consistent reference to men.

Throughout *Souls,* women are rather invisible. In the few instances that this "other" gender is mentioned, Du Bois remains loyal to the patriarchal standards of European cultural traditions, despite his call for greater inclusiveness. African American women and females are constructed as passive, dependent, and in need of a caretaker. His fleeting references to females seem to follow a pattern that demanded release of African America male manhood from European American men so that they could enact a similar role with African American women as did European men with their own. Surprisingly, Du Bois's childhood images of his own mother had little impact on his adult perception of intragroup variation among women and their rightful receipt of equality as American citizens. Even his speech to a group in support of suffrage that spoke to the disenfranchisement of

Negroes and the disenfranchisement of women ignored the juxtaposition of womanhood and blackness. In his words, as stated in *Dusk of Dawn*, "I should have probably been an unquestioning worshiper at the shrine of the social order and economic development into which I was born." When he discusses women—for example, the pathetic figure of Josie in "Of the Meaning of Progress" and his wife in "Of the Passing of the First-Born"— he discusses them in the context of the inability of black men to protect and defend the sanctity of black womanhood.[23] However, females currently make up the largest percentage of the African American collective, represent a greater number of household heads, and live longer than do men. Any plan for the future that would ignore this population would surely fail before its inception. What has been referred to as "double-consciousness" might then require reinterpretation from a gendered perspective to consider "triple or multiple levels of consciousness."[24] In general, the diversity within the African American community indicates that opportunities, ideas, and strategies require the involvement of diverse individuals to truly reflect the rainbow representation of gender, status, region, and other relevant qualities.[25]

Second, efforts to improve the condition of the collective need to concentrate on qualities, beliefs, and values of individuals who identify with the classification of African Americans based on an African and African American worldview. Attempts to resolve problems and advance a population must be based on the underlying orientation and perspectives particular to that people. To judge a group according to the norms and standards of another can only result in conflict and confusion because of the implied message that one is more adequate or appropriate than another. Such is the dissonance that Du Bois experienced for the greater part of his life, an internal

---

23. *W. E. B. Du Bois Writings*, 573. Hazel V. Carby, *Race Men* (Cambridge: Harvard University Press, 1998), 5, mentions the marginality of African American women in relation to the emphasis on masculinity as regards the black intellectual.

24. Darlene Clark Hine, " 'In the Kingdom of Culture': Black Women and the Intersection of Race, Gender, and Class," in *Lure and Loathing: Essays on Race, Identity, and the Ambivalence of Assimilation*, ed. Gerald Early (New York: Allen Lane/Penguin Press, 1993), 337–51, provides a discussion of the complex interactions among gender, race, and class that have led to multifaceted identities among African American women as adaptive responses to varied oppressive experiences and events and comments on the rather patriarchal stance held by Du Bois. Nellie Y. McKay, "The Souls of Black Women Folk in the Writings of W. E. B. Du Bois," in *Reading Black, Reading Feminist: A Critical Anthology*, ed. Henry Louis Gates Jr. (New York: Penguin Books, 1990), 236, praises Du Bois for recognizing black women in *The Souls of Black Folk* during a period when other black male writers treated black women of relevance to them and the black community as invisible. See also Davis, *Leadership, Love, and Aggression*, 116–17, for a discussion of Du Bois's hostile attitudes shown toward women.

25. Patricia Hill Collins, *Black Feminist Thought: Knowledge, Consciousness, and the Politics of Empowerment* (New York: Routledge and Kegan Paul, 1991).

anguish that emerged from the role of spectator as compared to participant in his life. Specifically, Du Bois made major decisions for himself and the African American community based on European Americans' evaluations of him and his racial group. This perspective led him to promote European traditions, values, and customs as mechanisms for group well-being and satisfaction. However, the objective for African American growth and advancement is not necessarily consistent with the beliefs, perspectives, and behaviors of European Americans. Efforts and attempts to follow the European lifestyle are partly responsible for a great deal of the current social and economic concerns of African Americans. Only African Americans can serve as a mirror for other African American group members. Even African descendants who arrive in America from the black world, including Africa and the West Indies, have values and beliefs that distinguish them from Africans of North American slavery and free Negro heritage. The application of evaluative criteria that fails to include culturally relevant and appropriate components to assess the efforts, products, and outcomes of the African American community can interfere with the acquisition of accurate information and thus prevent the eradication of social and economic problems.

The individual, family, or community must determine the standards of improvement and goal attainment. For example, in the essay "Of the Meaning of Progress," Du Bois introduces the issue of the assessment of progress for rural, southern African Americans who lack access to the knowledge and resources of middle-class European Americans. This essay makes clear the need for different definitions or evaluative standards of "progress" for a population long denied the rights of a European American comparison group. Most empiricists would prefer a quantitative indicator of change, success, or progress, but the magnitude of the socioeconomic gap between the European and African American communities requires the use of a qualitative means of assessment. Only the perceptions of those who saw themselves as part of a community can be used to ascertain factors and expectations that influence whether and to what extent progress occurs at different points in time. Subjective meanings of progress and change can better highlight the conditions and needs of impoverished communities than the theories and projections of those looking from the outside inward. The generalization of norms that are based on expected change for other ethnic or race populations hold much less meaning than do norms created and enacted by the community members themselves. For example, the use of European criteria, such as materialism, denies the cultural values of those who emphasize other indicators, such as interpersonal relations and spirituality, as evidence of growth and change.

Finally, the dramatic depiction of the role and power of education to lead to the production of a second inner self, challenges African Americans to consider more appropriate ways to alleviate the psychosocial turmoil experienced by the African American intellectual than those depicted by Du Bois. The avoidance-avoidance conflict experienced by John Jones resulted from the internalization of a monocultural education that shaped his identity and values and made it difficult for him to see the world from a perspective other than that taught during his training. Today, educational programs and various forms of media that place European American culture at the head of the world indirectly produce and maintain the "double-consciousness" experienced by Du Bois. Research that shows African American college students report greater peer difficulties than other students when they incorporate academic interests into their lifestyles demands that community members of all social levels integrate an Afrocentric perspective throughout all stages of life. However, the integration of information about one's history and culture is not for competition but to reduce the sense of inferiority that drives some to embrace other cultures but feel ashamed of their own.

A psychological approach to *Souls* lends understanding to the way that individuals in the African American collective think, behave, and feel, in order to promote what is observed as group behavior or cultural norms. This perspective sheds light on the way those cultural norms and standards are transmitted and how these standards are transmitted intergenerationally. A framework that allows for examination of the thoughts and attitudes of specific group members also introduces information about the impact of these cognitions on individuals' relations with the group or collective. Likewise, this framework guides our conceptualization of how the larger group influences the behavior of individuals. Thus, the individual or subjective worldview of a single member exerts an effect on the smallest unit, such as the family, that influences the extended family, which in turn impacts the community and society. The role of the individual is extremely clear in the impact of Du Bois's personal strivings, objectives, attitudes, and accomplishments on his perceptions of the African American race/cultural group that have long since shaped the views of others and the behaviors of those within and external to the group. Information from this perspective can offer a lens from which to examine and modify maladaptive behaviors of individuals that can have devastating effects on the group. The psychological model also generates hypotheses about relations between the individual and the group that can help us to differentiate between group and individual standards, a difference often overlooked when discussing African Americans.

Souls provides a window into the spirit and mind of W. E. B. Du Bois but serves as a guide for the future of African Americans. Many of the concerns and issues perceived by the author continue to affect the lives of African Americans, although their presentation and complexity have grown. However, this collection of essays reminds us that we can give more attention to the multiplicity of voices by formulating hypotheses about the group as we obtain a basis for understanding from the subjective reality of the individual. Psychology and the many areas included within this discipline can assist African Americans as the new millennium ushers in lessons learned from the past and the opportunity to begin once again.

W. E. B. Du Bois and *The Souls of Black Folk*

Generating an Expressive Repertoire for African American Communication

Carolyn Calloway-Thomas and Thurmon Garner

Introduction

In his canonical work *The Souls of Black Folk* (1903), W. E. B. Du Bois writes, "It is a peculiar sensation, this double-consciousness, this sense of always looking at one's self through the eyes of others, of measuring one's soul by the tape of a world that looks on in amused contempt and pity."[1] The statement was pure Du Bois, but he was to go much further in that work in staking intellectual claims to guide our understanding of African Americans' response to forced exile in the New World. He recognized that the experiences of blacks have been forged out of servitude and oppression. It is, for example, a fact that Negro spirituals, the "sorrow songs," as Du Bois poetically refers to them, were a response to the pain and anguish of slavery. He not only makes a trenchant observation on their lyrical and expressive qualities, but also makes foundational comments on how the power of the black church was used to frame the histories and experiences of black folk.[2]

A careful review of the literature on Du Bois shows that his insights have had incalculable influences on the way in which we interpret black expressive culture.[3] One of the most marked characteristics of Du Bois is the ease

1. W. E. B. Du Bois, *The Souls of Black Folk*, ed. Henry Louis Gates Jr. and Terri Hume Oliver (New York: Norton, 1999), 11. All further references to this edition will be included in the text.

2. See also Lawrence Levine, *Black Culture and Black Consciousness: Afro-American Folk Thought from Slavery to Freedom* (New York: Oxford University Press, 1977).

3. For an excellent account of *The Souls of Black Folk*, see Paul Gilroy, *The Black Atlantic: Modernity and Double Consciousness* (Cambridge: Harvard University Press, 1993), 111–45; see also Arnold Rampersad, *The Art and Imagination of W. E. B. Du Bois* (New York:

with which he treats themes of liberation, political reaction, the terrors of slavery, and the impact of all these upon the consciousness of black people. No other aspect of Du Bois's work carries as much intellectual explanation and strength for understanding black expressive culture as his conception of double-consciousness. He readily understood that black creative expression was generated as the result of an intersection among slavery, its aftermath, and the possibilities of freedom.

We believe scholars know a great deal about *what* Du Bois was saying, but it is now time to examine the "how." How did slavery and freedom shape the content of black communicative behavior? And how did that content, in turn, give rise to rhetorical strategies that blacks used to "talk" their way from slavery to freedom? Of course we are mindful that other forms of protest, such as slave insurrections, boycotts, and the Underground Railroad, also helped blacks to secure their freedom. We want to focus, however, on the process and evolution of black experiences that gave rise to their expressive qualities as articulated in *The Souls of Black Folk.*

Our basic argument is that Du Bois's *Souls* advances the claim that black communicative modes were generated from African Americans' experiences of and responses to their inhumane conditions in the New World, in their roles as slaves and free persons. We understand the complexity of the term *communication* and the tensions generated by the racial term *black.* By "black communicative modes," we mean the shared, discursive system and repertoire of black expressive behaviors that call attention to the individual and/or the group, including language both verbal and nonverbal, rhetorical strategies, songs, sermons, arguments, and appeals. It is through these and other traditional forms of communication that African American culture is constituted. Of course, this particular insight is not new; what is appealing, however, is the fact that Du Bois lays out rather convincingly a generative but rhetorical core for how blacks responded to their New World situation. Long before the groundbreaking work of the past half century, Du Bois made the blueprint for understanding black expressive behavior.[4]

———
Schocken, 1990); and Cornel West, *The American Evasion of Philosophy: A Genealogy of Racism* (Madison: University of Wisconsin Press, 1989).

4. See Molefi Asante, *The Afrocentric Idea* (Philadelphia: Temple University Press, 1987); Henry Louis Gates Jr., *The Signifying Monkey: A Theory of Afro-American Literary Criticism* (New York: Oxford University Press, 1988); Calvin M. Logue and Thurmon Garner, "Shift in Rhetorical Status of Blacks after Freedom," *The Southern Speech Communication Journal* 54 (fall 1988): 1–39; Melbourne Cummings and Jack L. Daniel, "African American Linkages to Africa through Oral Discourse," in *Handbook on Communications and Development in Africa and the African Diaspora,* ed. Melbourne S. Cummings, Lyndrey A. Niles, and Orlando L. Taylor (Needham Heights, Mass.: Ginn Press, 1992), 17–24; Carolyn Calloway-Thomas and John Louis Lucaites, eds., *Martin Luther King Jr. and the Sermonic Power of Public Discourse* (Tuscaloosa: University of Alabama Press,

While other scholars certainly have recognized Du Bois's work, only a few have emphasized the association between slavery and black folks' ability, as Paul Gilroy put it, "to mediate the enduring effects of slavery's terror."[5] Few, however, have examined the sociohistorical relationship between blacks' experiences in slavery and how those experiences generated black communicative strategies, based on Du Bois's own presentation of these modes of interpretation and analysis. The roots of these expressive activities are located in the paradoxical mode of the black self: the state of double-consciousness.

To explain how Du Bois accounted for the social construction of black Americans' expressive repertoire of communication, we must first delineate Du Bois's notion of the meshing of slavery and an African worldview. Next, we must explain the rhetorical posturing and strategies often used by black Americans, which Du Bois finds are fundamental to understanding the evolution of black communicative behaviors. This leads to an explanation of Du Bois's insights into the effects of social order on communicative interaction between blacks and whites.

Slavery, Africa, and the African Worldview

Du Bois reminds us, "We [must] remember that the social history of the Negro did not start in America" (123). Though the captains of the ships on which Africans sailed forbade them to transport artifacts such as drums, gourds, pottery, wood carvings, sculpture, and pestles for pounding yams, Africans nevertheless carried their culture to the New World in their persons. History has shown that black oral expressive culture has had a profound effect on the New World. What is particularly significant about Du Bois, however, is his ability to identify the concepts, phenomena, and techniques that came to be part of African American communication tradition during two of the most critical historical phases of black culture: slavery and post-Reconstruction. His observations would be expanded by succeeding generations of students of black communication.[6] Thus it is useful to focus on the major phases of slavery that Du Bois mapped out to develop his understanding of the roots of black expressive communication behavior.

Du Bois painstakingly notes the social transitions that occurred in black culture after the Africans' arrival in North America. With keen observa-

1993); Geneva Smitherman and Jack L. Daniel, "How I Got Over: Communication Dynamics in the Black Community," *Quarterly Journal of Speech* 62 (February 1976): 26–39; and Deborah Atwater and Molefi Asante, "The Rhetorical Condition as Symbolic Structure," *Communication Quarterly* 34 (spring 1986): 170–77.

5. Gilroy, *Black Atlantic*, 120.

6. See Melville J. Herskovits, *The Myth of the Negro Past* (New York: Harper, 1941).

tional skills, he comments on the first changes that occurred in blacks' efforts to adapt to the New World, most fundamentally the fact that the "plantation organization replaced the clan and tribe, and the white master replaced the chief with far greater and more despotic powers." This "terrific social revolution," as Du Bois calls these drastic changes, includes the disappearance of African kinship ties, the elimination of polygamous life, and the powerful influence of the African priest (123).[7] The consequences of these life changes forged in the transplanted Africans' a new paradigm, and it is Du Bois's theoretical underpinnings that continue to serve as a guide for an understanding of communication as an activity of and from black culture. Still, we would be remiss if we did not mention that *Souls* is set in African customs.

In *Soul Force: African Heritage in Afro-American Religion,* Leonard E. Barrett describes the traditional African worldview as "the vision of a cosmic harmony in which there exists a vital participation between animate [God, man] and inanimate things."[8] The African worldview consists of: (1) the supreme being and lesser deities, (2) the ancestors, (3) the belief in spirits and power, (4) the belief in sacrifice, (5) the belief in magic, good and evil, and (6) African wisdom in proverbs and folklore. This view suggests that African people see a vital relationship of being between each individual and his descendants, his family, his brothers and sisters in the clan, his antecedents, and also his God, "the ultimate source of being."[9]

We would be hard-pressed to demonstrate that Du Bois actually used the terms *African worldview.* Yet, one cannot read *The Souls of Black Folk* without seeing the sketches of such a view throughout the work, albeit a suppressed one. In chapter 1, "Of Our Spiritual Strivings," Du Bois outlines the great spiritual quest of slaves, and in chapter 14 he explores the messages in religious songs. But in chapter 10, "Of the Faith of the Fathers," Du Bois identifies the basic framework of the traditional African worldview. Understandably, his vision of an African worldview is based on a religion that has its roots in Africa. More importantly, his articulation and structuring of the framework serves as the sine qua non of black communication and sets the tone and direction, Africa to the present, for others to follow.[10] It is to this framework and the relationship between it and black forms of communication that we now turn.

The influence of religion was for Du Bois vital to understanding the development of African American culture. Du Bois notes that "three things

7. Leonard E. Barrett, *Soul Force: African Heritage in Afro-American Religion* (Garden City, N.Y.: Anchor Press, 1974), 17–31.

8. Ibid., 17.

9. Ibid., 17–31; quote on 17.

10. For an analysis of the traditional African worldview, see John S. Mbiti, *African Religions and Philosophy* (New York: Doubleday, 1970).

characterized" the religious life of the slave up to the Emancipation: "the Preacher, the Music and the Frenzy" or the shout (120). The preacher, "the most unique personality developed by the Negro," was "a leader", "an orator," "an intriguer," and "an idealist," which, when combined with his "adroitness," "earnestness," and "tact," gave him preeminence over slaves. The "Priest or Medicine-Man" was the "chief remaining institution" (123) that slaves relied on during their transition from African freedom to American slavery and it was from the priest or medicine man that the preacher evolved. Second, Du Bois finds that the "Music of Negro religion" "sprung from the African forests," "still remains the most original and beautiful expression of human life and longing yet born on American soil" and "became the one true expression of a people's sorrow, despair, and hope" (120). Third, Du Bois found that the "Frenzy or 'Shout' " that seized a worshiper when the "Spirit of the Lord passed by" was of major importance in understanding the religion of slaves (120). The "Shout" was a visible manifestation of the God, and without it "there could be no true communion with the Invisible" (121).

Du Bois observes that after Emancipation the black church became "the social centre of Negro life in the United States, and "the most characteristic expression of African character" (121). The church predates the black home, and therefore it has had a profound impact on how blacks interact with the outside world, in religion, economics, and politics as well as the multiple modes of communication interaction.[11] One way or another the slaves complemented and extended the communal ways of participating and belonging that the priestly Old World African community had bestowed upon them. Christianity played a crucial role in altering the life experiences of black Americans in the New World, rendering the relationship among the individual and the Invisible of less importance. Therefore, despite their debased condition something else was needed: a system of communicating signs and symbols in order to make the African American's world meaningful.

The intersection of African religion and Christianity would alter the source of life and meaning for black Americans. Slavery transformed the role of a greater God and the communion with Spirit, and it had weakened African religion, creating new and different means by which blacks communicated with each other and how they interacted with white Americans. The modes of communicating with the master in the New World had their roots in the paradoxical nature of the relationship among Christianity, what the slaves could do with it, and how they adapted to this new religious form, both linguistically and behaviorally.

---

11. Kwame Anthony Appiah, *In My Father's House: Africa in the Philosophy of Culture* (New York: Oxford University Press, 1992), 81.

More importantly for our purposes, the African worldview helps to explain the interactive nature of black communication with its back-and-forth movement between speaker and listener, in both sacred and secular realms. For example, expressive responses in traditional black churches, such as "Preach, Reverend," "Amen," and "My Lord," are manifestations of a synthetic African worldview. In addition, expressive responses in the secular world, such as "tell the truth," "all right," and "go, girl," also attest to the mutual compatibility between speaker and listener. By mutual compatibility, we mean the dynamic, collective participation between speakers and listeners in communication interactions. The antiphonal call-response is an example of mutual compatibility.

This compatibility, however, has another overarching purpose: It fosters a concern for coherence and communal values among African people. In *Language, Communication, and Rhetoric in Black America*, Arthur L. Smith (Molefi Asante) notes, for instance, that in traditional African societies, "the stability of the community is essential, and public speaking, when used in connection with conflict solution, must be directed toward maintaining community harmony."[12]

While it is true that Mbiti, Barrett, Smitherman, and Daniel also support this view as the undergirding framework for African American communication, not all scholars support the notion of an all-encompassing African worldview. Kwame Anthony Appiah, for example, denies "a metaphysical and mythic unity to African conceptions." This debate, however, need not concern us here. The point, in relation to our purposes, is that Du Bois, a serious student of black history and culture, while describing what he considered to be "midnight orgies and mystic conjurations," and other rituals among the African slaves, provided an intellectual foundation for understanding the genesis of African American communication (125).[13]

When the slaves came to the New World, they brought with them "the humanist foundations of communalism" with their concomitant virtues of "fellow-feeling, solidarity and selflessness."[14] In the midst of these moral precepts were also, according to Du Bois, the African virtues of courtesy, strength, and an "appreciation of the beautiful" (125). Du Bois saw these African values as evolutionary conduits for the development of patterns of black communication. For example, he argues that the manner in which slavery and Christianity were rendered and played out in the conscious-

12. Arthur L. Smith, ed., *Language, Communication, and Rhetoric in Black America* (New York: Harper and Row, 1972), 369.

13. Appiah, *In My Father's House*, 81; see also Smith, *Language, Communication, and Rhetoric*, 369.

14. Segun Gbadegesin, *African Philosophy: Traditional Yoruba Philosophy and Contemporary Realities* (New York: Peter Lang, 1991), 61, 65.

ness of African Americans reconceptualized the way that blacks related to their social world.

In particular, Du Bois claimed, "The long system of repression and degradation of the Negro tended to emphasize the elements in his character which made him a valuable chattel: courtesy became humility, moral strength degenerated into submission, and the exquisite native appreciation of the beautiful became an infinite capacity for dumb suffering" (125). This is a significant point. Through Du Bois's celebrated attempt to explain the constituent ideals of blacks, we can see how the abyss of slavery altered black modes of communication, especially if the language of courtesy is understood as a language of humility or the signs of respect become signs of deceit. Invariably, the "elements" in blacks' character came to be defined as the very opposite of the communicative impulses that came out of Africa. More than anything, the idea that African forms of communication, particularly the nature of orality, were insufficient and unnecessary in antebellum America, is one of the products of slavery in a world turned upside down.

Du Bois's codified thoughts about "the long system of repression and degradation of the Negro" have profound implications for our understanding (or misunderstanding) of black linguistic communication. Indeed, his astute observations have generated several important questions about how one makes sense of what we call black communication. For example, has a heavier communication burden been placed on the shoulders of African Americans than on whites? To what extent do blacks' assertiveness and aggressiveness become internalized by European Americans as confrontation, anger, hostility, and violence? Are black expressions of confidence and cockiness, say, in becoming a successful entrepreneur, viewed in the same manner as similar black expressions in the entertainment and athletic arenas? And where and how do blacks channel their aggression and suppressed energies in a society that has altered what blacks hold to be sacred?

In any case, Du Bois outlines with considerable emphasis how the slaves took their "what-they-did-know" cognitive, affective, and behavioral repertoire and turned it into "what-they-had-to-know-and-do" communication repertoire. This shift consisted of yoking African values and the characteristics of the African priest or medicine man: "the healer of the sick, the interpreter of the Unknown, the comforter of the sorrowing, the supernatural avenger of wrong, and the one who rudely but picturesquely expressed the longing, disappointment, and resentment of a stolen and oppressed people" (123). According to Du Bois, these traits would later, as we shall see, evolve into characteristics of the "Negro Preacher."

In his analysis of black expressive culture, Du Bois defines the Negro as a "religious animal—a being of that deep emotional nature which turns instinctively toward the supernatural." According to Du Bois, there is an ontological reason for this emotional stance: the African American is "endowed with a rich tropical imagination and a keen, delicate appreciation of Nature; the transplanted African lived in a world animated with gods and devils, elves and witches; full of strange influences,—of Good to be implored, of Evil to be propitiated" (124).

What Du Bois somewhat sensationally characterizes as "heathenism," "exorcism and witchcraft," and the "mysterious Obi worship with its barbarous rites, spells and blood-sacrifice" (125), is nothing more than a truncated version of the traditional African worldview as explicated by John Mbiti, Leonard E. Barrett, and Geneva Smitherman and Jack Daniel.

It is significant that these social and communal functions of the priest or medicine man played a generative role in creating the personality of the Negro preacher. In Du Bois's view, as the shaman's role as spiritual guide, diviner, and healer diminished in form and scope, a new occupation arose on the plantation, that of the Negro preacher. Du Bois is particularly insightful here regarding the metamorphosis of the African priest into the Negro preacher. Du Bois suggests that the priest became in the United States the "bard, physician, judge, and priest, within the narrow limits allowed by the slave system" (123).

It was in this search for a solution to his New World oppressive environment that the black preacher began to discover that he could maintain vestiges of his ancestral skills, not because of, but in spite of, his plight. Note that Du Bois words this as "the narrow limits allowed by the slave system." Undoubtedly, he is referring to the constraints that were placed on the slaves' and the priests' ability to carry on their African "client/practitioner relationship" that manifested a "common cultural substructure."[15] Therefore, instead of openly propitiating their African gods and stirring their herbal concoctions in earthen jars, the slaves adapted to their New World status through a change not only in the name of their functionary, the black preacher, but also through a change in what this new communication form would dictate.

In this way, slavery began to erode sacred African communal values. But it was harmful in other ways, too. The temporal longevity of slavery produced its compelling sociological consequences, for much emerged directly from it—quite simply, it ultimately created a debasing form of communication.

What Thomas S. Kuhn writes in *The Structure of Scientific Revolutions* can also be said of the slaves who came to the New World: "The child who transfers the word 'mama' from all humans to all females and then to his

15. Barrett, *Soul-Force*, 27.

mother is not just learning what 'mama' means or who his mother is. Simultaneously he is learning some of the differences between males and females as well as something about the ways in which all but one female will behave toward him."[16] Clearly the slaves observed that their New World status demanded of them a rearranging of the furniture of their minds, because of the brutal assault of slavery and colonialism upon them.

Du Bois asserts that the rearrangement has not been a one-way street, however, but that blacks have had a profound impact upon American society, albeit unacknowledged at the time. He notes, for example, that blacks had used their minds in a way that led to three basic gifts, "a gift of story and song—soft, stirring melody in an ill-harmonized and unmelodious land; the gift of sweat and brawn to beat back the wilderness, conquer the soil, and lay the foundations of this vast economic empire . . . the third, a gift of the Spirit" (162). In each of these, Du Bois draws a parallel among three dominant capacities of blacks to create, build, and inspire, corresponding to artistic, economic/physical, and emotional domains. Using a creative canvas, Du Bois argues convincingly that Africans brought meaning to America in the form of storytelling and songs, which are genetically related to communication because the two artistic forms give order and elegance to human experience.

Rhetorical Responses

The abyss of slavery, with its two-toned obligations, one to the master and one to the African American, produced more than anguish; it gave rise to the socially constructed "wrenching of the soul." Beyond this point, Du Bois argues, emerged "double thoughts, double duties, and double social classes," which paved the way for later communication developments—witness the effects of split consciousness on the rhetorical strategies that marked changes in the intellectual attitudes of African Americans, one giving rise to "pretence or revolt," and the other giving rise to "hypocrisy or radicalism" (127). These changes in black thought and consciousness were, we claim, precursors of linguistic changes in terms of the strategies that Booker T. Washington elevated during the 1890s and well into the 1900s.[17]

In Du Bois's linguistic construction, *pretense*, united with *hypocrisy* and *revolt*, joins the word *radicalism* to set the rhetorical direction that blacks took in their response to oppression and their movement toward freedom (33). In Du Bois's view, these rhetorical strategies had distinct geographical

16. Thomas S. Kuhn, *The Structure of Scientific Revolutions* (Chicago: University of Chicago Press, 1962), 128.

17. See, for example, Louis Harlan, *Booker T. Washington: The Making of a Black Leader, 1856–1901* (New York: Oxford University Press, 1972).

parallels; they formed two movements: one in the North, led by black abolitionists, and one in the South, composed of southern slaves and their descendants. Frederick Douglass, Henry Highland Garnet, Sojourner Truth, Charles and Sarah Remond, and a cadre of other speakers and journalists, forged, according to Du Bois, the revolt mode or the radical expressive mode, while many blacks in the South, with avenues of expression closed to them, resorted to linguistic patterns of "deception and flattery" (128).

The northern, abolitionist mode of revolt and radicalism has been well-documented.[18] But the southern pattern deserves more attention. There, Booker T. Washington, a chief practitioner of "deception and flattery" (to Du Bois's way of thinking), with his striking personality, emerged from a confluence of politics, economic conditions, the Ku Klux Klan, personal biography, and local circumstances. Washington found that he could exhibit control over his own world, and the world of many African Americans, by simply taking the mode of "politeness" and "deception and flattery" to its logical, instrumental conclusion, the very linguistic behavior that slavery and its sociological and cultural legacy had spun. Washington used the language of submission rather than the language of revolt. This, after all, had long been the favorite mode of the master in forging an organic relationship between master and slave. Employing this mode, of course, became problematic, and Du Bois ultimately clashed with Washington over its practice.[19]

Indeed, Du Bois's astute observations about Washington's linguistic modes demonstrate the complexities and subtleties of black communication. Different communication styles clearly have implications for how blacks use speech daily, as well as in the political arena. For example, paradoxically, while Du Bois casts much intellectual light on the sociocultural forces in America that led to blacks' employment of "deception and flattery" as a survival strategy, he also attacks Washington for drawing upon a communication heritage that is rooted in indirection rather than direction and confrontation. Du Bois's strategies were concretized in the National Association for the Advancement of Colored People (NAACP), which he cofounded.

Also intertwined in Du Bois's comments about Washington is the question of whether Du Bois's disagreement with Washington was as much over strategy and tactics as it was over language and rhetoric. The answer is probably both. What Du Bois recognized but perhaps failed to appreci-

---

18. See John W. Blassingame, *The Slave Community*, rev. ed. (New York: Oxford University Press, 1979).

19. See Kenneth Burke, *A Grammar of Motives and a Rhetoric of Motives* (Cleveland: Meridian Books, 1962); and Hugh Dalziel Duncan, *Communication and Social Order* (New Brunswick, N.J.: Transaction Publishers, 1989). See also Peter Paris, *Black Leaders in Conflict* (New York: Pilgrim Press, 1978).

ate was the full range and rhetorical sophistication of Washington's communicative strategies. At the center of the controversy are differing views about the language or forms of communication that blacks should use; such differences persist to this day (in the recent debate about Ebonics, for example). The fight often is about performance of the language, standardized versus African American pronunciation, as well as about what strategies are necessary to blacks' struggle for freedom. By extension, the debate between Du Bois and Washington also has significant pedagogical implications for the study of African American literature. For example, if individuals do not understand the signifying aspects of black communication, they will probably miss the voice or point of view of Zora Neale Hurston's *Their Eyes Were Watching God* (1937) or *The Sanctified Church* (1983).[20]

In any case, although in chapter 3 of *Souls*, "Of Mr. Booker T. Washington and Others," Du Bois directs much of his criticism toward Washington, it is clear that there are also implicit references to Washington throughout the book, most especially in Du Bois's comments about the evolution of black expressive thought. Du Bois argues, however, that black rhetorical modes find their most striking evolution in the relationship between Christianity and its practices. In particular, Du Bois demonstrates convincingly how circumstances conspired to produce a vindictive style of worship among African Americans. He writes that because "the public conscience is ever more deaf to his righteous appeal," and because "all the reactionary forces of prejudice, greed, and revenge are daily gaining new strength and fresh allies, the Negro faces no enviable dilemma" (127). Although the quotation plainly refers to the post-Reconstruction period, there is a historically preslave dimension to the comment as well.

Du Bois also highlights the Jim Crow period of American history for its conspicuous production of demeaning black thought and expression. During this era, Du Bois maintains that the black person's religion, "instead of a worship, is a complaint and a curse, a wail rather than a hope, a sneer rather than a faith" (127). Thus, Du Bois leaves us in no doubt that blacks' degrading circumstances removed from them their very reason for being in church or practicing Christianity: to serve Christ. Instead, repetitive complaints, wailing, and sneers were the inevitable communicative outcomes of the perverted civic system.

Throughout the South, especially during the Jim Crow period, it was not unusual for blacks to speak in "whispers" or "hushes." In fact, this linguistic perversion sustained itself beyond the 1970s. One of the authors, for example, remembers during her youth that some southern blacks had become so accustomed to the "complaint" mode of adjustment that they

---

20. For a discussion of black talk, see Geneva Smitherman, *Talkin and Testifyin* (Boston: Houghton Mifflin, 1977), 35–72.

spoke in "whispers," in church and elsewhere, about their abject condition. Even when whites were absent, blacks were surely mindful of the power of words to travel beyond their original domain of utterance.[21]

Our point is that in *Souls* Du Bois is careful to show how external and internal exploitation and coercion combined to make "complaining" part of blacks' communicative repertoire. Some scholars and critics would like to push this connection even further to claim that vestiges of those socio-cultural happenings have had an electrifying effect on the communicative consciousness of the masses of blacks up to this very day.[22] For example, Jesse Jackson's penchant for excoriating against the evils of racism appear as if he is constantly sniveling and complaining, rather than explaining the obstacles in the way of black progress. We must be careful, however, not to generalize too much. Nevertheless, Du Bois caught splendidly the inherent limits of a "complaint" mode of African American communication.

More importantly, Du Bois identifies two additional, albeit related, communicative and "hardly reconcilable streams of thought and ethical strivings" that he believes blacks chose in response to their social, political, and economic condition. One mode of thought was "in anarchy," and the other "in hypocrisy" (127). The mode of thought related to "hypocrisy" led to traitorous and cowardly behavior. If it is indeed true that our language and thoughts canalize our behavior, then Du Bois saw this connection in a powerful way. "Anarchy," Du Bois claims, fosters "ideals remote, whimsical, perhaps impossible of realization" (127).

Having explained the origins of that mode of talk, Du Bois next turned to the geography that fostered one mode over the other. Again, the northern mode was conceptually, historically, and sociologically significant; we see once again that the North "tended toward radicalism," and "the South toward hypocritical compromise" (128). The emotional tenor of Du Bois's construction is indeed critically relevant, given the feud that occurred between Du Bois and Washington, fueled in part by Washington's communicative style of accommodation to southern whites. Du Bois opposed modes of flattery and encouraged direct, assertive responses to the social plight of African Americans.

Du Bois's analysis of these rhetorical strategies, however, reaches back to the Abolition movement of the 1830s through the 1850s; in fact, he identi-

---

21. The practice of speaking in "whispers" was more prevalent in the South than in the North. Vestiges of this activity are gradually disappearing throughout the South, however.

22. See, for example, Patrick J. Buchanan, *The Death of the West: How Dying Populations and Immigrant Invasions Imperil Our Country and Civilization* (New York: Thomas Dunne Books, 2002); Thomas Sowell, *Race and Economics* (New York: D. McKay, 1975); Thomas Sowell, *The Economics and Politics of Race: An International Perspective* (New York: W. Morrow, 1983); and Roger Kimball, *Tenured Radicals: How Politics Has Corrupted Our Higher Education* (New York: Harper and Row, 1990), 27–28.

fies three constituent responses that blacks had used up to Reconstruction in their battle for freedom and equality: "physical defence," "political defence," and "the defence of deception and flattery, of cajoling and lying" (128).

How did the constituent responses extend from blacks' reactions to their capture in Africa to post-Reconstruction? As Du Bois saw it, the first response, the physical mode, had its roots in particular forms of resistance that blacks used during the Middle Passage. This mode has always figured most prominently at the outset of black experience in the New World. Du Bois identifies Denmark Vesey and Nat Turner not only as representatives of this form of resistance, but also as reminders of "the present hopelessness of physical defence" (128). In other words, Du Bois clearly recognized that although a physical response to danger and harm is natural, blacks' best chances for reform lay in marshaling evidence and arguments. Later, Dr. Martin Luther King Jr. would make similar claims in response to Malcolm X's and the Black Panthers' sneering comments about King's rhetorical mode during the Civil Rights Movement, especially the March on Washington in 1963.[23]

The second constituent response, political defense, became less powerful during the period of Booker T. Washington because southern whites during the 1880s and 1890s systematically denied blacks opportunities to present, in court and elsewhere, legal arguments that relied upon propositional content, such as linear, analytical presentations to white audiences. In the North, radicalism found its most intense expression among free blacks during slavery primarily because, as Du Bois put it, "The free Negro leader early arose and his chief characteristic was intense earnestness and deep feeling on the slavery question. Freedom became to him a real thing and not a dream. His religion became darker and more intense, and into his ethics crept a note of revenge, into his songs a day of reckoning close at hand" (126).

The notion of blacks seeking not submission but freedom is parallel to Orlando Patterson's conception of the role that free women played in denouncing slavery in Western culture. Patterson observes that when the "average woman of sixth- and even fifth-century Greece" paused to think of her condition vis-à-vis the slaves, "her musings must have run along the lines of 'There but for the grace of the gods go I.' By empathizing with the slave end of the master-slave relation, then, women became more con-

23. See Calloway-Thomas and Lucaites, *Martin Luther King Jr.*; Celeste Michelle Condit and John Louis Lucaites, *Crafting Equality: America's Anglo-African Word* (Chicago: University of Chicago Press, 1993); David Howard-Pitney, *The Afro-American Jeremiad: Appeals for Justice in America* (Philadelphia: Temple University Press, 1990); and Taylor Branch, *Parting the Waters: America in the King Years, 1954–1963* (New York: Simon and Schuster, 1988).

scious of freedom by the ever-present experience of powerlessness, natal alienation, and dishonor, the three basic elements of all slavery seen from the viewpoint of the slave; of the three, the most important was the simple horror of powerlessness."[24]

There is a demonstrably analogous relationship between Du Bois's conception of the free blacks' role in creating strategies for liberation and Patterson's astute comment about Greek women. Because free blacks could taste some measure of freedom and because they also recognized their own "iron cages" of powerlessness, there was in their bosom a yearning to be free, beyond nominalism. They began to valorize personal liberty, which created a strong social link to southern slaves. Ronald Takaki aptly reminds us that even though free blacks composed "two percent of the northern and thirty-three percent of the southern population, they were peripheral to industrial production in the North and essential to agricultural production in the South. Still, everywhere, whites 'branded' blacks as 'children' and 'savages.'" Takaki further mentions that "Racism was both virulent and violent in the states above the Mason and Dixon Line during the years before the Civil War."[25]

Recognizing their precarious and much-excluded status, free blacks never lost sight of their condition, and they began to appreciate all the more the possibility for significant change. This is why they created a vigorous protest, planned the way to freedom during the Abolition movement, smuggled messages in bales of cotton to their brothers and sisters in the South, and held meetings and conventions to plan for the emancipation of all blacks. For many southern blacks, protest took the form of the Underground Railroad. In 1843, for example, Henry Highland Garnet, a free black Presbyterian minister, sent a pointed message in his "Address to the Slaves of the United States of America" speech at a Negro Convention in Buffalo, New York. He exhorted the slaves to "use every means" necessary to garner their freedom one hundred years before Malcolm X made a similar cry a household phrase during the 1960s.[26]

The central role that free blacks played emanated from their ability to formulate arguments and bend ideals toward liberty. Du Bois aptly points out that as a result of the abolition movement, " 'The Coming of the Lord' swept this side of Death, and came to be a thing to be hoped for in this day" (126). In doing so, free blacks transferred messages from the internal, private realm to the external, public realm. This explains one major reason

24. Orlando Patterson, *Freedom* vol. 1, *Freedom in the Making of Western Culture* (New York: Basic Books, 1991), 78.
25. Ronald Takaki, *Iron Cages: Race and Culture in Nineteenth-Century America*, rev. ed. (New York: Oxford University Press, 2000), 110.
26. Philip S. Foner, *The Voice of Black America*, vol. 1 (New York: Capricorn Books, 1975), 201.

why black expression took the route that it did. For example, free blacks' arguments, according to Du Bois, began to reflect a "hoped for in this day" ideal rather than an "other-worldly" ideal. This helps to explain why black rhetoric during the abolition period uniformly yielded to what James L. Golden and Richard D. Reike classify as the "rhetoric of assimilation," a strategy that was and is almost entirely fused with hope.[27]

Even when black abolitionists employ the most angry, intense, and emo-tionally piercing rhetoric in the introduction and body of a public speech, in the conclusion they nearly always return to the motif of hope. To illus-trate, Frederick Douglass, in his "What to the Slave Is the Fourth of July?" oration, vigorously castigates America for its hypocrisy. Despite his strong claim that "America is false to the past, false to the present, and solemnly binds herself to be false to the future," in the conclusion, Douglass offers words of hope and faith in the belief that things will ultimately change for the better: "Allow me to say, in conclusion, notwithstanding the dark pic-ture I have this day presented, of the state of the nation, I do not despair of this country." One can also see this leitmotif in similar speeches by Charles Remond, Robert Brown Elliott, Martin Luther King Jr., and others.[28]

Additionally, it is important that when these hoped-for things became a possibility of reality, northern blacks began to claim their place within the civic culture. They seriously promoted an "irrepressible discussion" and made "the desire for freedom" their "one ideal of life" (126). Making free-dom their life's ideal led the free blacks to develop a freedom-conscious movement in the South, albeit through various clandestine modes, includ-ing smuggling, the Underground Railroad, and the drinking gourds that they and other friendly and good-spirited souls left outside their homes to announce pathways to freedom for the black slaves. The impassioned de-fenses of freedom given by the escaped slaves Harriet Tubman, Henry Bibb, Henry "Box" Brown, William and Ellen Craft, and a host of other black abo-litionists is striking testament to these rhetorical activities and behaviors.[29] Through their rhetorical strategies, free blacks also offered solidarity with the black masses. This was a brilliant strategy that infused not only their talk, but their songs as well.

Du Bois contends that the rhetorical efforts of free blacks emboldened the slaves to sing "O Freedom, O Freedom, O Freedom over me! / Before

27. James L. Golden and Richard D. Rieke, *The Rhetoric of Black Americans* (Columbus: Charles E. Merrill, 1971), 51.

28. Frederick Douglass, "What to the Slave Is the Fourth of July? An Address Deliv-ered in Rochester, New York, on 5 July 1852," in *Narrative of the Life of Frederick Douglass, an American Slave, Written by Himself,* ed. William L. Andrews and William S. McFeely (New York: Norton, 1997), 137, 150; see also Foner, *Voice of Black America.*

29. See Benjamin Quarles, *Black Abolitionists* (New York: Oxford University Press, 1975); and Henry Bibb, *Narrative of the Life and Adventures of Henry Bibb, an American Slave* (1849; reprint, Madison: University of Wisconsin Press, 2001).

I'll be a slave / I'll be buried in my grave, / And go home to my Lord / And be free" (126). In a sense, the song became an anthem for the black abolitionist movement in the same way that "We Shall Overcome" became the anthem for the Civil Rights Movement of the 1960s.

Therefore, as a result of free blacks' striking communicative modes of encouraging their southern slave sisters and brothers to participate in their own liberation efforts, black slaves ceased to take enslavement for granted. And in the process, as Du Bois claims, "For fifty years Negro religion thus transformed itself and identified itself with the dream of Abolition, until that which was a radical fad in the white North and an anarchistic plot in the white South had become a religion to the black world" (126). This religion, in turn, became a mode of transcendence, and when the Thirteenth Amendment was passed on December 18, 1865, blacks concretely, not figuratively, proclaimed Emancipation "a literal Coming of the Lord" (126).

A point to stress here is one emphasized in 1987 by Asante, in *The Afrocentric Idea*, that "A protest speaker . . . originates the protest universe of discourse from the unique cultural conditions accompanying the state of oppression or denial that gives birth to the protest in the first place."[30] Du Bois argues the same in *The Souls of Black Folk*. By pointing out this connection, we do not intend to deflect from Asante's and other communication scholars' findings, but rather to underscore Du Bois's seminal contribution to our understanding of how the birth pangs of freedom led to a rhetoric of resistance.

Strategic Interactions

While physical resistance and political defense were strategic responses used by blacks to secure freedom and equality, Du Bois recognized the strategic importance of indirect communicative behavior. Du Bois considered the third constituent response, "deception and flattery," as the most potent response that blacks mustered in the 1880s and 1890s. Washington was the chief promoter of this style of communication, and by the 1870s and 1880s northern whites had exploited the idea of sectional reconciliation, thus choosing the economic route to the restoration of the South at the expense of the lives of many southern blacks.[31]

Du Bois unequivocally understood the role of the social order in generating linguistic intercourse. He understood "the rhetoric of ruling: com-

30. Asante, *Afrocentric Idea*, 110–11.
31. See Irwin Unger, *These United States: The Questions of Our Past* (Englewood Cliffs, N.J.: Prentice-Hall, 1995), 424–40; and John Hope Franklin and Alfred A. Moss Jr., *From Slavery to Freedom: A History of African Americans* 7th ed. (New York: Alfred A. Knopf, 1994).

munication and authority," and also how this rhetoric changed blacks' vocabularies.[32] In *Souls*, Du Bois writes of the Jim Crow era: "To-day the young Negro of the South who would succeed cannot be frank and outspoken, honest and self-assertive, but rather he is daily tempted to be silent and wary, politic and sly; he must flatter and be pleasant, endure petty insults with a smile, shut his eyes to wrong; in too many cases he sees positive personal advantage in deception and lying" (128). Implicitly, Du Bois warns of how certain generative modes of talk would become a vital part of black consciousness. Not only did this mode produce the speech of accommodation, as practiced by Washington and many southern blacks, but in the process it also undoubtedly gave rise to veiled modes of talk, which characterized black talk at least until the early 1990s.[33]

Although Du Bois is cautious to note that the majority of black Americans eschewed the old Washington mode of accommodation, it is apparent that he saw other grand distinctions between the two groups. One example of this divided perception appears in his opening comment in chapter 10 of *Souls*, concerning his instant comparison of the black style of worship with styles of worship in Berkshire. "To be sure," Du Bois notes, "we in Berkshire were not perhaps as stiff and formal as they in Suffolk of olden time; yet we were very quiet and subdued" (119). While one might consider this comment a recognition of class tensions, we appreciate it for the historical value it adds to our understanding of the variety of linguistic strategies used by African Americans and the conflict caused by the duality of language use even today.

Of course, it can be argued that Du Bois was merely applying interpretation and analysis to what he saw. Note, though, that in *Souls*, Du Bois comments further not only on the differences between the two dominant communicative modes but also on "the air of intense excitement that possessed that mass of black folk" (120). Similar comments are found throughout *Souls*. Sprinkled throughout the book are descriptions such as "black American peasant" (used several times, in fact) and "black sturdy, uncouth country folk, good-natured and simple, talkative to a degree . . ." (77, 98). From the comments that Du Bois makes about these two groups, we can glean a fair amount of information about his views of the black masses and their concomitant communication patterns. What we should always bear in mind, however, is that geography and status were decisive determinants of the conception of communication that Du Bois held. Above all, we should bear in mind that Du Bois drew from the wisdom of black culture to formulate his theories about black communication.

32. Unger, *These United States*, 452; Duncan, *Communication and Social Order*, 213.
33. Geneva Smitherman, *Black Talk: Words and Phrases from the Hood to the Amen Corner* (Boston: Houghton Mifflin, 1994).

Conclusion

The Souls of Black Folk is certainly a remarkable book about the lives of African Americans, regardless of one's theoretical view. We examined it from the perspective of communication scholarship and found that it lays a broad foundation or outline for African American communication. Du Bois recognized long before 1903 that servitude had an impact on the worldview of the African American slave, that changes in black thought resulted in shifting rhetorical strategies necessary to fight slavery, and that bondage transformed the ethos of black folk, especially in the strategic responses that they made to their sociocultural environment, whether in religion or music.

There is much more for the serious student of African American culture to explore in *Souls*. Each chapter illuminates ideas to be followed: race relations, black ethos, African American struggle individually and collectively, black anger, white anger, and prejudice, to name a few. We suggest that *Souls* should be reread, not only for its views on double-consciousness as a political concept, but for the fruitful ways in which Du Bois explores the areas of black discourse. Du Bois reveals many permutations about the nature of multiple audiences, intrapersonal communication, and narrative as a genre. Above all, his work is a testament to the elegance and strength of African American communication.

The "Musical" Souls of Black Folk

Can a Double Consciousness Be Heard?

Christopher A. Brooks

Our song, our toil, our cheer, and warning have been given to this nation in blood-brotherhood. Are not these gifts worth the giving? Is not this work and striving? Would America have been America without her Negro people?

—W. E. B. Du Bois

I

At the core of *The Souls of Black Folk* is the issue of Du Bois's use of African American spirituals. Was he attempting to communicate some secret message by using them as a musical epigraph at the beginning of each chapter? Was it a statement of race pride, or was there some other intent? Meanwhile, the most memorable concept of the book is Du Bois's celebrated "double-consciousness" theory, which has generated considerable scholarly interpretation and speculation. If we explore the theory from a musical perspective—along the way considering the impact of the spirituals in their historical context and their influences on Du Bois—a "musical" double consciousness can be discerned.

Much remains unclear regarding the origins of the genre that would come to be called "spirituals." It attracted considerable commentary, interpretation, and debate from many quarters during the latter half of the nineteenth century, and this attention continued into the twentieth century. The growing interest in "folk" genres, where a specific author or composer of a musical work could not be identified, made spirituals ripe for the speculative treatment they received. Although many of these speculations remain unconfirmed, there are certain things we know. The genre was a cultural outgrowth of African enslavement in America and Protestant Christianity. We are also not aware of a similar genre developing on the African continent, nor anywhere else in the African Diaspora (where enslavement was practiced). So to that degree the spirituals appear to be uniquely American. Even if we accept that premise, we must still ask, What is a spiritual?

In addition to being the decade of Du Bois's birth, the 1860s also appeared to have the earliest consistent printed references to an African American religious musical tradition.[1] With the elusive author C. W. D.'s "Contraband Singing" in the September 7, 1861, issue of *Dwight's Journal of Music,* written recognition of what would come to be called "spirituals" had begun.[2] This work was followed by several articles, expository essays, and commentaries. Of these works, "Negro Spirituals," by Thomas Wentworth Higginson, deserves mention because it was published in an 1867 issue of the *Atlantic Monthly* and as such had a wider readership.[3] It contained thirty-six religious songs. Higginson, a military major in charge of African American soldiers in Charleston, South Carolina, subsequently produced other works referring to spirituals. A later collection of African American religious music attracted greater attention; the well-known *Slave Songs of the United States,* edited by William Allen, Charles P. Ware, and Lucy McKim Garrison, appeared in 1867. The compilers had come from an abolitionist tradition and drew on a combination of songs that they had collected from African Americans in different parts of the country with material gleaned from other sources and collectors. The 136 songs were loosely divided according to the region of the country where they were heard along with whatever background could be gathered as to the song's origin.

The compilers (specifically William Allen) took pains in an extensive preface to explain the challenges involved in transcribing and annotating the music. Among other things, Allen described the inability of Western musical notation to faithfully communicate the unique African American vocality. He also said that even though each song had been assigned a

1. Eileen Southern indicates that printed references to an African American religious musical tradition began to appear in the early nineteenth century, although the term *spiritual* was not used. See her *Music of Black Americans: A History,* 3d ed. (New York: W. W. Norton, 1997).

2. This article may have been preceded in 1861 by a relatively obscure collection entitled *"The Songs of the 'Contraband,' 'O Let my people go.' " Words and Music obtained through the Rev. L. C. Lockwood, Chaplain of the "Contraband" at Fort Monroe,* by L. C. Lockwood. It is not known when the word *spiritual* was first used in print, and this has contributed to the difficulty of defining it. *Sorrow song,* used by Du Bois in *The Souls of Black Folk,* was one of many names that the genre would acquire.

3. Bruce Jackson, *The Negro and His Folklore in Nineteenth-Century Periodicals* (Austin: University of Texas Press, 1977), 82. See also Southern, *Music of Black Americans;* and Dena J. Epstein, *Sinful Tunes and Spirituals: Black Folk Music to the Civil War* (Urbana: University of Illinois Press, 1977).

specific geographical location, variants of the same song could be heard in other parts of the country. Despite these difficulties, the resulting collection was the most comprehensive effort up to that date to document an African American religious musical tradition. As such, it received considerable critical attention and praise, but at least one unsigned review of the collection, published the year after its appearance, took a negative view:

> . . . Have not all the colored musicians we have known been of mixed blood? Is it not the musical genius of the white man grafted upon the African's love of music? Frank Johnson is well remembered by all middle-aged Philadelphians. Thirty years ago, his band, and at the Springs, was the best to be had. But Frank, like the famous Bogle . . . , was a mulatto. . . . We think it can be proved that the negro requires the mixture of white blood to develop in him the musical qualities which, if they exist at all in his native state, are, at least, dormant.[4]

Between the 1870s and the early twentieth century, essays, articles (containing spirituals), collections, and similar works with African American religious songs appeared in increasing numbers. In the 1870s, there was *Hampton and Its Students*, with fifty plantation songs arranged by Thomas Fenner (1874); J. B. T. Marsh's *The Story of the Jubilee Singers; with their Songs* (1877); and Theodore Seward's *Jubilee Songs, as Sung by the Jubilee Singers of Fisk University* (1872).[5] In the 1880s, there was Z. A. Coleman's *The Jubilee Singers* (1883); Helen Ludlow's *Tuskegee Normal and Industrial School, for training colored teachers, at Tuskegee, Alabama: Its story and its songs* (which included eighteen songs arranged by R. H. Hamilton in 1887); James C. Macy's *Jubilee and Plantation Songs*;[6] and J. J. Sawyer's *Jubilee Songs and Plantation Melodies* (1884). In the 1890s there was the well-known William Barton collection, *Old Plantation Hymns*, a collection of hitherto unpublished melodies of slave and the freedman, with historical and descriptive notes (1899), and the overly sentimental Marion Haskell article in *Century Magazine*, "Negro 'Spirituals,' " which appeared in the same year.

The early twentieth century saw no let-up in the appearance of such collections. Although Jeanette Robinson Murphy's *Southern Thoughts for Northern Thinkers* did not appear until 1904, she had delivered lectures and published some of the songs in *Southern Thoughts* as early as 1898 in a

4. Review of *Slave Songs* in "Literature of the Day: Slaves of the United States" *Lippincott's Magazine*, March 1868, 341–43.

5. In 1877, Fenner would edit the songs in *Hampton and Its Students* and publish them separately as *Cabin and Plantation Songs as Sung by the Students;* this would be enlarged again in 1901 (with other compilers and editors) as *Cabin and Plantation Songs as Sung by the Hampton Students*. In 1884, Seward and George White enlarged the collection in a new edition entitled *Jubilee Songs, as Sung by the Jubilee Singers*.

6. This work was described as a combination of favorites from the Hampton and Fisk collections with some additions.

Century Magazine article, "Gawd bless dem Yankee!"[7] There was also M. L. Mitchell's *Songs of the Confederacy and Plantation Songs* (1901) and Frederick J. Work's *New Jubilee Songs, as sung by the Fisk Singers of Fisk University* (1902). If the enumeration of such collections, essays, and articles was extended to the 1920s, the list would grow dramatically. For the present purpose, it is sufficient to consider only those collections and essays that appeared before the first printing of *The Souls of Black Folk* in 1903, which Du Bois might have had access to and which most likely influenced him. This body of black music had a shaping influence on Du Bois, evidenced by his reference to attending the small black church in his hometown, his three years at Fisk, his two summers working in east Tennessee, and in all likelihood during his Boston years. Of course, his coming into contact with European high culture at Harvard and in Germany forced him to come to grips with the spirituals and what it meant to be black in America.

Attention was being drawn to spirituals not only in collections, essays, books, and articles, but through live performances as well. By the 1870s concerts of spirituals had become a fund-raising vehicle for struggling African American colleges, most notably Calhoun, Fisk, Hampton, and (to a lesser extent) Tuskegee. Several of these groups made highly successful overseas tours in what Laubenstein has called the *Ausbreitung* (spreading) of African American music around the European continent.[8]

With the frequency and popularity of these overseas tours by the 1890s, European (and American) audiences were exposed to a kind of African American musical talent different from that featured in minstrel shows. When Bohemian composer Antonín Dvořák recognized the uniqueness of the genre and encouraged his students, such as Harry T. Burleigh and Will Marion Cook, to compose and arrange more spirituals, it was little more than icing on the cake.[9] Dvořák made his progressive comments during his tenure as the director of the National Conservatory of Music in New York between 1891 and 1894 and in a 1895 article in *Harper's Magazine* entitled "Music in America."[10]

A dissenting view of the genius of the African American spiritual came from Dvořák's fellow European, Richard Wallaschek, in the work *Primitive Music*, where he asserts:

> There still remains to be mentioned one race which is spread over all America and whose musical powers have attracted the attention of many

7. Newman Ivey White, *American Negro Folk-Songs* (Cambridge: Harvard University Press, 1928), 476.

8. Paul Fritz Laubenstein, "Race Values in Aframerican Music," *The Musical Quarterly* 6, no. 3 (July 1930): 378.

9. White, *American Negro Folk-Songs*, 476.

10. Dvořák, "Music in America," *Harper's New Monthly Magazine*, February 1895, 428–34.

Europeans—the negro race. . . . I think I may say that, speaking generally, these negro-songs are very much overrated, and that as a rule they are mere imitations of European compositions which the negroes have picked up and served up again with slight variations. Moreover, it is a remarkable fact that one author has frequently copied his praise of negro-songs from another, and determined from it the great capabilities of the blacks, when a closer examination would have revealed the fact they were not musical songs at all but merely simple poems. . . . I cannot think that these and the rest of songs [in the Allen, Ware, and Garrison collection] deserve the praise given by the editors, for they are unmistakably "arranged"—not to say ignorantly borrowed—from the national songs of all nations.[11]

In "A White Origin for the Black Spiritual," Dena J. Epstein critiqued Wallaschek's statements as ill-informed (even for that time period) because he was basing his remarks on the very conventional musical transcription that Allen, Ware, and Garrison had already acknowledged as "a faint shadow of the original."[12]

II

Clearly, then, spirituals were viewed as an important genre by the time of the appearance of *The Souls of Black Folk;* this leads to the next questions: Why was this genre important? Was it the only African American genre worthy of serious interest? Despite the critical attention they received, spirituals were not the most popular African-derived musical tradition at that time. Instead, ragtime, or syncopated piano music, was more popular by far. This genre also had a long history, which dated back to the end of the Civil War.[13] Ragtime is characterized by a syncopated melody, played by the right hand, and an "oompah" bass pattern played by the left hand. Ragtime piano music hit its peak of popularity between the 1890s and the end of the World War I era, and it had a much wider following than the spirituals. Like the spirituals, it quickly spread (if not dramatically) outside the African American community.[14] Also like spirituals, ragtime garnered the attention of the mainstream public as well as the composers of European classical music, several of whom were inspired by it. Claude Debussy, Igor

11. Richard Wallaschek, *Primitive Music* (1893; reprint, New York: Da Capo Press, 1970), 60–61.

12. Dena J. Epstein, "A White Origin for the Black Spiritual? An Invalid Theory and How It Grew," *American Music* (summer 1983): 53–59; William Francis Allen, Charles Pickard Ware, and Lucy McKim Garrison, *Slave Songs of the United States* (New York: Peter Smith, 1867), iv–vi.

13. Southern, *Music of Black Americans*, 313–14.

14. A number of ragtime music composers, such as Scott Joplin, were able to secure copyrights for their music and sell it as sheet music.

Stravinsky, Paul Hindemith, and other composers employed the characteristic syncopated melodies and bass patterns of ragtime in their works.

While ragtime music had a large audience, it also had questionable as-
sociations with racism. This was especially true for that segment of the
African American community that was concerned with presenting the
most positive image of the race (such as Du Bois and Booker T. Washington). The musical legacy of blackface minstrelsy and its musical successor,
the "coon song," out of which ragtime music grew, clearly had negative
connotations, which progressive leaders at the time wanted to avoid. In
his preface to the Afro-British composer Samuel Coleridge-Taylor's 1904
publication, *Twenty-Four Negro Melodies*, Booker T. Washington echoes this
sentiment:

> It is especially gratifying that at this time, when interest in the plantation
> songs seems to be dying out with the generation that gave them birth, when
> the Negro song is in too many minds associated with "rag" music and the
> more reprehensible "coon" song, that the most cultivated musician of his
> race, a man of the highest aesthetic ideals, should seek to give permanence
> to the folk-songs of his people by giving them a new interpretation and an
> added dignity.[15]

There was no question that the spirituals yielded far greater political and
psychological advantages than any musical tradition that African Americans had produced up to that point. The spirituals and the "tragic figure"
(the enslaved black man and woman) who produced such a music despite
the circumstance ennobled slavery in the eyes of sympathetic white song
collectors and compilers and made spirituals more socially palatable for
turn-of-the-century black leaders.

To those African Americans concerned with political, economic, and social uplift, the romanticized tragic figure (a kind of "noble savage," to bor-
row Rousseau's term) who had little control over his circumstances was
certainly easier to identify and reckon with than the alternative image (the
stereotypical African savage).[16] The ultimate damage of musical and theatrical minstrelsy and its caricatures was to foster an image of the African
continent and its inhabitants from which many African Americans wanted
to distance themselves. This helped to create an estrangement between
Africans on the continent and many of their turn-of-the-century, socially
mobile New World peers. Washington intimates as much in his preface to

15. Booker T. Washington, preface to *Twenty-Four Negro Melodies,* by Samuel
Coleridge-Taylor (Boston: O. Ditson, 1905), viii.
16. For a review of images of blacks at the turn of the century, see Sterling A. Brown,
Negro Poetry and Drama and *The Negro in American Fiction* (1937; reprint, New York:
Atheneum, 1969).

Twenty-Four Melodies: "Mr. Coleridge-Taylor is himself an inspiration to the Negro, since he himself, the child of an African father, is an embodiment of what are the possibilities of the Negro under favorable environment."[17]

Washington put his finger on the choice of socially constructed images the New Negro for the New Century had to confront. There was the tragic slave who, out of his long suffering, dejection, and hope for a better life in the afterworld, produced the spirituals. Alternately, there was the savage African who, by the turn of the century, was perceived by most Americans (both black and white, as a result of blackface minstrelsy) as wallowing in uncivilized conditions on the African continent.[18] The choice was clear: enter W. E. B. Du Bois and his use of spirituals in *The Souls of Black Folk*. With the publication of the book, Du Bois joined the battle for the representation of African Americans.

With all the collections, essays, articles, and commentary (not to mention his own exposure to the genre from his days at Fisk) that were in print before *The Souls of Black Folk*, it is plausible to argue that Du Bois saw greater value in embracing spirituals "as of me and mine . . ." than in not doing so. Du Bois saw the spirituals as a form of art that was a counterpoint to the debasement of black expression in theatrical minstrelsy and its caricatures. Twenty years later, he asserted in the pages of the *Pittsburgh Courier* (1923) that "all art is propaganda and must be, despite the wailing of purists." These words resonate clearly throughout the pages of *The Souls of Black Folk* as Du Bois joins the battle over art, aesthetics, and representation. Because of the extensive number of spiritual collections and commentaries as well as Du Bois's borrowed knowledge of them, I would differ with David Levering Lewis's statement regarding the importance of Du Bois's groundbreaking insight into the genre: "What he wrote has for the most part stood the test of scholarship, primarily, no doubt, because academic appreciation of the spirituals was for a long time indebted to his pioneering excursion into the sociology of this music."[19]

17. Washington, preface to *Twenty-Four Negro Melodies*, ix.

18. Eric Lott, *Love and Theft: Blackface Minstrelsy and the American Working Class* (New York: Oxford University Press, 1993); Kevin K. Gaines, *Uplifting the Race: Black Leadership, Politics, and Culture in the Twentieth Century* (Chapel Hill: University of North Carolina Press, 1996). Washington describes how certain spirituals communicated information about escape attempts, among other usages. There was a powerful minstrel caricature, Rastus, who represented the failed attempt of Western civilization to tame the continental African. Rastus, on a moment's notice, could turn violent. He was also excited to be around chicken coops, where his only desire was to steal chickens. Better-known caricatures were "Jim Crow" and "Zip Coon."

19. W. E. B. Du Bois, *The Souls of Black Folk*, ed. Henry Louis Gates Jr. and Terri Hume Oliver (New York: Norton, 1999), 155 (citations to this edition will hereafter appear parenthetically in the text); Du Bois's *Pittsburgh Courier* quote in Herbert Aptheker, *An-*

The evidence suggests that Du Bois was following the collective interest of compilers of spirituals (in the tradition of Allen, Ware, and Garrison) and commentators (in the tradition of Washington among many others) in the trend to elevate the genre. This tradition had been established well before the appearance of *Souls*, perhaps because of the popularity of the genre or for political reasons. In *To Wake the Nations*, Eric J. Sundquist makes it abundantly clear that Du Bois (given his privileged, if not elitist, background vis-à-vis the masses of African Americans) had little in common with the producers of the spirituals or their experience.[20] This statement is not intended to diminish the significance of Du Bois's use of spirituals in *The Souls of Black Folk*, because it was creative at the very least.

Certainly, any discussion of the musical usage in *The Souls of Black Folk* must take into consideration chapter 5 in Sundquist's *To Wake the Nations*. That chapter, "Swing Low: *The Souls of Black Folk*," is the most comprehensive discussion to date of how Du Bois infused the spirituals into the fabric of *The Souls of Black Folk*. Sundquist examines the texts of the songs and the significance of their usage in *The Souls of Black Folk*, and he speculates on the theory and function of the songs in African American culture as Du Bois constructs it.[21] While I regard Sundquist's discussion as required reading for an overall understanding of *The Souls of Black Folk*, there are areas where we have interpretational differences. Before examining those areas, however, an explanation of how Du Bois used the spirituals in *The Souls of Black Folk* is necessary.

Before starting each chapter of *Souls*, Du Bois presents some musical epigraph, poem, or verse at the top. Just under it are a few bars of a spiritual. The brief musical notation appears without the text of the spiritual and does not always start from the beginning of the song. For example, chapter 1, "Of Our Spiritual Strivings," has the first three bars of music of the spiritual, "Nobody Knows the Trouble I've Seen." Similarly, chapter 2 has as its musical epigraph "My Lord, What a Mourning!" Du Bois's double entendre suggests both the time of day (morning) and the bemoaning of a sad occasion (mourning). Chapter 3 uses "A Great Camp Meeting," but that musical phrase comes from a passage within the spiritual, not from the beginning. Sundquist expertly traces Du Bois's musical borrowings to two major collections of spirituals, *Hampton and Its Students* and *The Story of the Jubilee Singers*. This, of course, is further evidence of Du Bois's knowledge of the spiritual's significance as a genre and use of these two collections.

notated Bibliography of the Published Writings of W. E. B. Du Bois (Millwood, N.Y.: Kraus-Thomas Organization, 1973), 993; David Levering Lewis, *W. E. B. Du Bois: Biography of a Race, 1868–1919* (New York: Henry Holt, 1993), 286.

20. Eric J. Sundquist, *To Wake the Nations: Race in the Making of American Culture* (Cambridge: Harvard University Press, 1993), 460–61.

21. Ibid., 467.

In chapter 14 of *Souls*, "The Sorrow Songs," Du Bois attempts an explanation of his use of the songs at the beginning of each chapter; however, I agree with Sundquist that Du Bois's explanations are not always clear. For example, Du Bois does not offer any explanation of his selection of the song "A Great Camp Meeting" at the beginning of the chapter where he comments on Booker T. Washington among others. Sundquist suggests that the specific passage from "A Great Camp Meeting" that Du Bois uses for that chapter, "Gwine to mourn an' nebber tire . . . ," is a subtle repudiation, if not a ridicule, of Washington's accommodationist views. If that is the case, Du Bois does not draw attention to it, as he does in his use, for example, of "Nobody Knows the Trouble I've Seen" at the beginning of chapter 1.

Sundquist and I have minor differences concerning two points: why Du Bois does not use the texts of spirituals, and his "radical positioning" of the spirituals in *The Souls of Black Folk*. To the latter issue, Sundquist argues that Du Bois's embrace of spirituals was to symbolically "usurp" the genre from his more celebrated rival, Booker T. Washington, whose southern roots, background, upbringing, and sensibilities gave him a greater claim to the genre. Washington had, after all, discussed the importance and impact of the genre in his autobiography, *Up from Slavery* (1901), long before the appearance of *The Souls of Black Folk*. However, given Du Bois's own Western classical music leanings (as we will consider in greater detail), and recalling Washington's advice in the preface of *Twenty-Four Negro Melodies* that the songs be given a "new" and "dignified" interpretation (that is, treatment as a true classical art music), Du Bois's and Washington's positions on the importance of African American spirituals seem closer than they are separate. As to the issue of the absent texts in *The Souls of Black Folk*, a more detailed explanation is necessary.

Sundquist argues that Du Bois did not use the texts of the spirituals because the inclusion of the black dialect (especially juxtaposed to the lofty European prose or verse) would have lowered the genre's overall status. This would have subsequently caused them to be dismissed by white as well as educated black readers. Sundquist offers this explanation because of Du Bois's own privileged background and educational achievements. There may be some merit in that explanation; however, my view is based on Du Bois's statement in *The Souls of Black Folk:* "In these songs, I have said, the slave spoke to the world. Such a message is naturally veiled and half articulate. Words and music have lost each other and new and cant phrases of a dimly understood theology have displaced the older sentiment" (159). Du Bois's use of the spiritual without the words, therefore, seems linked to his well-known "veil" theory, according to which only part of the message is communicated. Or to put it metaphorically, only part of the soul is revealed.

Du Bois's unique use of musical epigraphs as a form of coded language raises other questions. Does the presence of the music without the text (and thus the use of an African American dialect that would unmistakably identify it) dilute the overall message? Can a song without words be a spiritual? Several of the collectors (such as Allen, in the preface to *Slave Songs*) had, after all, mentioned the inability of Western musical notation to capture, in transcription, the melodies of many songs, much less the stylized African vocalities such as falsetto, moans, screams, raspy voice, and yodels. These musical notations, therefore, represent a "faint shadow of the original."[22] So there is at least some reason to view the transcriptions (as presented by Du Bois at the beginning of each chapter in *Souls*) as a musical compromise of the original source, and the absence of the text could be a further dilution. Du Bois would undoubtedly counter such an argument. Even though the Western notated or arranged versions may differ from the original spirituals, the essence, or soul (as represented by the music even without the text), is maintained.

Such a position is further supported by arguing that, during African enslavement in this country, the so-called "alert" songs were an effective means of communication. Ostensibly religious, these songs secretly communicated an encoded message, about some coming event, such as an escape attempt, a secret meeting, or some other clandestine communiqué. Examples of alert songs are "Swing Low, Sweet Chariot," "Wade in the Water," "Moses," and "Sheep, Sheep, Don't You Know the Road." These songs were effective in their purposes though they did not always have the benefit of words.[23] Sometimes the melody alone (as in a hum or a whistle) would have to suffice in certain instances. So Du Bois's use of the musical epigraphs could have been operating at an even deeper level. Literally, from his standpoint, they sounded some "echo of haunting melody from the only American music which welled up from black souls in the dark past" (8). Thus, as we can see, there are several interpretations of what Du Bois was attempting in *The Souls of Black Folk* by using the musical epigraphs before each chapter.

III

If we accept comments offered by David Levering Lewis, this discussion can proceed in an entirely different direction. In *W. E. B. Du Bois: The Biography of a Race*, Lewis argues that Du Bois juxtaposed the lofty European

22. Allen, Ware, and Garrison, preface to *Slave Songs*, iv–vii.
23. John Lovell Jr., in his book *Black Song: The Forge and the Flame, the Story of How the Afro-American Spiritual Was Hammered Out* (New York: Paragon House, 1986), searches spirituals for their hidden meaning.

and American verse of Browning, Byron, Lowell, and Schiller (in untranslated German, no less!), among others, to the African American spiritual in *Souls* to raise the musical genre to the level of high European prose.[24] This also seems to indirectly support Sundquist's explanation for Du Bois's unwillingness to use the spiritual's text in the musical epigraph because the language had the potential to undermine the position that he was trying to achieve for the spirituals in the work. This points to Du Bois's conflict with his personal "two-ness," "two souls," "two thoughts," "two unreconciled strivings," "two warring ideals." Specifically, Du Bois embraced both Western art music and the African American spiritual, and this raises other questions. Was a double musical consciousness manifesting itself at the time that Du Bois wrote *The Souls of Black Folk*? And if so, did it continue beyond the book's appearance?

At the heart of the double musical consciousness argument is Du Bois's fascination with European culture, his Harvard and Berlin education, his New England birth, and his deep love of Western art music. Lewis and Sundquist are in resolute agreement concerning Du Bois's affinity with those things European. Dating from his days at Fisk in the mid-1880s, Du Bois leaves a record of his musical interests and exposure. Yet in a November 1887 editorial for the *Fisk Herald*, Du Bois refers to African American music as "the strangest, sweetest" in the world and called for African Americans to "build up an American school of music which shall rival the grandest schools of the past." Just a few months later, in an April 1888 editorial, he remarks, "our race, but a quarter of a century removed from slavery, can master the greatest musical compositions." Du Bois made this statement in regard to a performance of Felix Mendelssohn's oratorio *Elijah* done by Fisk's Mozart Society, of which Du Bois was an ardent member.[25]

Du Bois's double musical interest followed him after his graduation from Fisk in 1888. For a brief period he served as business manager of the Fisk Glee Club Quartet (forerunner of the Jubilee Singers) before he was admitted to Harvard. He attempted to join the Harvard Glee Club, where they most likely sang Western music (certainly not African American spirituals), but he was rejected. Du Bois had every reason to expect to be accepted into the organization. He had, after all, a refined Western music background and aesthetic, he was a New Englander, and perhaps most important, he had a fine singing voice. But he was also a black man attempting to penetrate an all-white music club in the 1890s. He subsequently (or perhaps simultaneously) elevated the African American spiritual to the same status

24. Lewis, *Biography of a Race*, 278.
25. Du Bois quoted in Aptheker, *Annotated Bibliography*, 6, 7; see also Lewis, *Biography of a Race*, 74; and Nathan Huggins's notes in W. E. B. Du Bois, *The Souls of Black Folk* (New York: Vintage Books, 1990), 195.

of Western art music. Symbolically, the groundwork for his double consciousness theory seems to have been laid.

It was while Du Bois was at Harvard that he seems to have come in contact with the double consciousness theory formally. Although the term had been in use from the early nineteenth century, Du Bois's professor and mentor William James had just published a book, *Principles of Psychology* (1890), in which he examines the concept from a psychological perspective. In addition to the medical/psychological use of the term, there was also a more ethereal, Romantic concept of *Sturm und Drang* associated with the term. Translating as "storm and stress," and representative of the conflict between such opposing ideas as godly and ungodly, man and nature, or other dualities, this notion is examined in Emerson's 1843 published lecture "The Transcendentalist."[26]

When Du Bois went to Germany in the 1890s, he attended operas, symphony concerts, and recitals. This also appears to be his earliest exposure to the operas of Richard Wagner, which seem to have fascinated him well into the twentieth century. Several of the characters in Wagner's operas deal with *Sturm und Drang* dualities, which Du Bois may have viewed as some manifestation of double consciousness. For example, while in Eisenach, Lewis tells us, Du Bois mastered the libretto of Wagner's opera *Tannhäuser.* This opera, which Du Bois heard performed on several occasions, is full of the Romantic era's conflicts: "two-ness," "two souls," "two thoughts," "two unreconciled strivings," "two warring ideals in one dark body."[27]

Tannhäuser is a medieval knight and minstrel who wanders into the fabled and forbidden land (known as the Venusberg) of Venus, the goddess of physical pleasure and sexual indulgence. He becomes the consort of Venus herself. After some years of this sensual indulgence, Tannhäuser feels guilt about his actions and wants to return to his former life as a knight and seek penance. He begs his leave of Venus, who pleads with him to stay. He ultimately calls on the name of the Virgin Mary and Venusberg disappears. His return is heralded by his fellow knights, but most especially by the ruling landgrave's niece, Elizabeth, whose devotion to him has been steadfast.

The return of Tannhäuser to the Wartburg castle (actually not far from Eisenach) occasions a celebration, which features a song contest. When it is his time to perform, Tannhäuser sings a song hailing Venus and the joys of physical pleasure and thus unwittingly reveals his whereabouts for the past several years. The assembled knights are so horrified by his ungodly behavior that they demand his life on the spot. He is only saved by Elizabeth, who literally shields him from any harm. The landgrave agrees to

---

26. Dickson D. Bruce Jr., "W. E. B. Du Bois and the Idea of Double Consciousness," *American Literature* 64, no. 2 (June 1992): 282, 303, 306; Lewis, *Biography of a Race,* 282.
    27. Lewis, *Biography of a Race,* 129.

spare his life provided he joins some pilgrims en route to Rome. He is ordered to seek forgiveness from the Pope himself for his iniquity.

After some time Tannhäuser returns from his pilgrimage dejected. He narrates his journey to Rome to one of his fellow knights. The Pope was so outraged by his life in Venusberg that Tannhäuser could no more expect redemption for his sins than the papal staff could grow flowers! With this final condemnation, Tannhäuser calls out to Venus to take him back, and she readily appears to accept him. He is stopped only when he is told that Elizabeth has given her life praying for his salvation. Venus disappears as Elizabeth's body is brought from the Wartburg castle. Seeing her remains, Tannhäuser falls dead. Just then, some of the pilgrims return from Rome with the papal staff, which has miraculously grown flowers, symbolizing Tannhäuser's salvation.

At the core of this opera is the struggle of sensuality (as seen in the lustful world of Venus) and spirituality (as represented by Elizabeth). Tannhäuser's irreconcilable conflict in the opera is, in many ways, the quintessence of the double consciousness concept, albeit in a fantasy world. His death brings the ultimate resolution of the conflict between sensuality and spirituality. These two ideas compete throughout, and the character of Tannhäuser is the embodiment of the double consciousness that influenced Du Bois in the 1890s. Similar dualities can be seen in other Wagner operas such as *Tristan und Isolde,* where the main characters must hide their love after drinking a love potion. In contrast to standard connotations in literature and drama, night comes to signify good, when Tristan and Isolde are free to meet and express their love, and day signifies evil, when they must hide it. Although Sundquist makes clear that Du Bois's fascination with Wagner did not reach its maturity until the 1920s, it is clearly manifested in *The Souls of Black Folk* at the beginning of the new century.

In chapter 13, "Of the Coming of John," Du Bois allows the reader some insight into his Wagnerian fascination. The fictitious black John in the chapter is transformed by the music of Wagner's *Lohengrin* (another opera Du Bois was particularly fond of) which he hears at a concert. For his white counterpart, John, who is also in attendance, it is just another concert. Once undergoing the musical transformation, the black John himself becomes a classic study in Du Bois's double consciousness. After receiving a northern education, like Tannhäuser he returns to his rural southern town feeling out of place, unable to relate to, and clearly out of touch with, the people of his own hometown, as seen in his remarks in the church: "To-day . . . the world cares little whether a man be Baptist or Methodist, or indeed a churchman at all, so long as he is good and true. What difference does it make whether a man be baptized in river or wash-bowl, or not at all? Let's leave all that littleness, and look higher" (149).

Like Tannhäuser's bursting into song about the pleasures of Venusberg, his comments are received by the congregation with scorn, to the black John's surprise. He also makes obvious faux pas, such as going to the front door of the judge's house as opposed to the customary back entrance, among other mistakes. In other words, the black John is clearly experiencing a double consciousness, being out of touch in one world and not accepted by the other. At the close of the chapter, having killed the white John (who returned to the same town under very different circumstances) to protect his sister from an assault, the black John reflects on the musically transformative melody of the well-known "Bridal March" from *Lohengrin,* "Freudig geführt, ziehet dahin" (Joyfully guided, come to this place).[28] Du Bois does not translate, paraphrase, or summarize the German text. His decision not to translate the text gives greater strength to John's musical transformation (his alienation from his black southern roots) and the reality of the double consciousness that he experiences in the face of his inevitable lynching. All of this must have been present in Du Bois's mind as we see in the skillful weaving of *Lohengrin* into this chapter of *Souls.*

When we consider Du Bois's continuing interest in Wagner and opera, the parallels with his plot and that of *Lohengrin,* and the fact that he used the double consciousness of Wagner's opera to add dimension to the story of the black John, the argument presented here is very plausible.[29] At the very least, this view offers us an interesting, if not unique, perspective of Du Bois's double consciousness theory.

Du Bois may have had the final laugh after all. *The Souls of Black Folk* may have been a masterful exercise in his ability to be ambiguous and allow his readers to draw from it what they wanted. After considering revisions to respond to criticisms of the work, Du Bois declined and decided to "leave the book as first printed, as a monument to what I thought and felt in 1903."[30]

Indeed, while many praised Du Bois's work as ground-breaking, one major African American scholar, E. Franklin Frazier, drew a very different picture of *Souls* and an even dimmer picture of the double consciousness theory:

> But Du Bois, aristocrat in bearing and in sympathies, was in fact a cultural hybrid or what sociologists have termed a "marginal man." . . . In *The Souls of Black Folk* we have a classic statement of the "marginal man" with his double consciousness: on the one hand highly sensitive to every slight concerning

28. Sundquist, *To Wake the Nations,* 522. Although this is the opening line of the bridal chorus from *Lohengrin,* Du Bois uses "freudig geführt" (joyfully guided), while Wagner's version is "treulich geführt" (faithfully guided).

29. In two October 1936 editorials in the *Pittsburgh Courier,* Du Bois expresses his interest in Wagner. In the second of the editorials, "Opera and the Negro Problem," Du Bois's references several Wagner operas for a modern-day interpretation and relates them to social experiences of African Americans.

30. Huggins, notes to *Souls* (Vintage edition), 219.

the Negro, and feeling on the other hand little kinship with or real sympathy for the great mass of crude uncouth black peasants with whom he was identified. For, in spite of the way in which Du Bois has written concerning the masses, he has no real sympathetic understanding of them. *The Souls of Black Folk* is a masterly portrayal of Du Bois' soul and not a real picture of the black masses.[31]

Aside from calling Du Bois a "cultural hybrid," Frazier castigates him for his attacks on the likes of Booker T. Washington, who, according to Frazier, was in far greater contact with the black masses than Du Bois ever was. He further suggests that Du Bois's "mulatto characteristics" afforded him greater access and opportunity to the white world, which resulted in his cultural hybridism. So the relevance of the double consciousness is yet to be resolved.

By the early 1950s, *The Souls of Black Folk* had gone through over thirty reprintings. The debate continues over the validity of his double consciousness theory, but as for the idea of a musical double consciousness, Du Bois gives his readers all the evidence they need for such a case.

A study of Du Bois's life makes clear that he moved with apparent ease through two worlds—black and white—and had a musical affinity for several traditions. While Du Bois's musical diversity is not hard to understand, his interest in politicizing the spiritual as others had and incorporating it in such a scholarly way in *Souls* at the turn of the twentieth century was unique and innovative. It is from his other pronouncements, musical exposure, and sensibilities that the double musical consciousness theory gains its credibility. It is entirely plausible that given Du Bois's background, he could have rejected the spiritual altogether, as many African Americans of his social class and background did. It is clear, however, that the "musical" souls of "black folks" at the turn of the century was far too diverse for any one person to be the definitive spokesperson. We can look at Du Bois's effort as a statement that has withstood the passage of a century.

31. E. Franklin Frazier, "The Du Bois Program in the Present Crisis," *Race* (winter 1935–1936): 11–12.

The Wings of Atalanta

Classical Influences in *The Souls of Black Folk*

Carrie Cowherd

W. E. B. Du Bois learned Latin and Greek in high school and continued his study at Fisk University. At Harvard he considered majoring in philosophy. His first employment after Harvard was as the chair of classics at Wilberforce University.[1] Although Greek and Latin languages and literatures were not among his primary interests, the body of his work reveals that his training and reading in classics contributed to the totality of his thinking and to who he was.

The Souls of Black Folk has much to offer the reader who notices classical references, both direct and indirect. These fall into three broad categories: (1) casual, incidental use of Latin or Latinate phrases, Roman historical references, and Greek and Roman philosophy, myth, and religion; (2) direct references that are more or less important to the structure of the chapters; and (3) underlying attitudes, associated with Cicero, Socrates, and Plato, that are expressed in varying ways throughout *The Souls of Black Folk*, including as a second leitmotif after that of the Veil, and that operate as a kind of ring composition for the entire text. Ultimately, because the underlying attitudes help to determine other choices, the three categories are interrelated.

Du Bois uses several Latin expressions; however, these expressions are all more a part of the scholarly language of Du Bois's time than they are derived from classical Latin literature.[2] In fact, the more striking aspects of his vocabulary might not be noticed if one were not on the lookout; an example is the word *riddle*, among those words to which Arnold Rampersad

---

1. See *The Autobiography of W. E. B. Du Bois: A Soliloquy on Viewing My Life from the Last Decade of Its First Century*, ed. Herbert Aptheker (New York: International Publishers, 1968), 101, 112–13, 183–87.

2. Latin expressions used are *toto caelo* (28), *trivium* and *quadrivium* (58), *tertium quid* (62, 106), *a priori* (68), *ipso facto* (113), and *dum vivimus, vivamus* (129).

calls attention in *The Art and Imagination of W. E. B. Du Bois*. As we shall see later in reference to other topics, Du Bois starts his thinking with the literal, but he makes it his own; the riddle of the Sphinx from the Oedipus story is his starting point, but Du Bois is not particularly interested in the actual riddle, "It is two-footed and four-footed and three-footed upon the earth and has one voice." Rather, he is interested in the idea of the riddle or even the answer to the riddle, and in the Sphinx. Sometimes the Sphinx is the Greek monster; sometimes it is the monumental sculpture at Giza; sometimes it is neither, as in the Du Bois poem cited by Rampersad, "The Riddle of the Sphinx."[3] From *The Souls of Black Folk:*

> The riddle of existence is the college curriculum that was laid before the Pharaohs, that was taught in the groves by Plato. (58)[4]
> . . . .
> [N]o secure civilization can be built in the South with the Negro as an igno-rant, turbulent proletariat. . . . [T]hey will not cease to think, will not cease attempting to read the riddle of the world. (71)
> . . . .
> You will not wonder at [Alexander Crummell's] weird pilgrimage,—you who in the swift whirl of living, amid its cold paradox and marvellous vision, have fronted life and asked its riddle face to face. And if you find that riddle hard to read, remember that yonder black boy finds it just a little harder. (141)
> . . . .
> So wofully unorganized is sociological knowledge that the meaning of prog-ress, the meaning of "swift" and "slow" in human doing, and the limits of human perfectability, are veiled, unanswered sphinxes on the shores of sci-ence. (162)

The riddle of existence, the riddle of the world, and the riddle of life are not the riddle of the Sphinx—even "The Riddle of the Sphinx" is not—although the *answer* to Oedipus's riddle may be the riddle of Du Bois: What is man?

Ironically, the "riddle of existence" from "Of the Wings of Atalanta" ad-dresses some of the issues raised by the "riddle of the world" from "Of the Training of Black Men." A direct connection is made in the phrase, "strange to relate," which translates the Latin, *mirabile dictu*. "What place in the fu-ture development of the South ought the Negro college and college-bred man to occupy?" (71). The voices that hail the renaissance of university education for the white South are, "strange to relate, largely silent or an-tagonistic to the higher education of the Negro. Strange to relate! for this is

3. Arnold Rampersad, *The Art and Imagination of W. E. B. Du Bois* (1976; reprint, New York: Schocken, 1990), 67; for the poem, see W. E. B. Du Bois, *Darkwater: Voices from within the Veil* (1920; reprint, New York: Schocken, 1969), 53–55.
4. W. E. B. Du Bois, *The Souls of Black Folk*, ed. Henry Louis Gates Jr. and Terri Hume Oliver (New York: Norton, 1999). All references in this essay are to this edition and are cited parenthetically.

certain, no secure civilization can be built . . ." (71). It is fair to say that the only purpose of "strange to relate" is to evoke Vergil's *Aeneid*, from which it comes. The only other evocation of the *Aeneid* occurs in "Of the Wings of Atalanta," in the same paragraph as the "riddle of existence." Du Bois describes Atlanta University and its students:

> In the morning, when the sun is golden, the clang of the day-bell brings the hurry and laughter of three hundred young hearts from hall and street, and from the busy city below,—children all dark and heavy-haired,—to join their clear young voices in the music of the morning sacrifice. In a half-dozen class-rooms they gather then,—here to follow the love-song of Dido, here to listen to the tale of Troy divine; there to wander among the stars, there to wander among men and nations,—and elsewhere other well-worn ways of knowing this queer world. Nothing new, no time-saving devices,—simply old time-glorified methods of delving for Truth, and searching out the hidden beauties of life, and learning the good of living. The riddle of existence is the college curriculum that was laid before the Pharaohs, that was taught in the groves by Plato, that formed the *trivium* and *quadrivium*, and is to-day laid before the freedmen's sons by Atlanta University. And this course of study will not change; its methods will grow more deft and effectual, its content richer by toil of scholar and sight of seer; but the true college will ever have one goal,—not to earn meat, but to know the end and aim of that life which meat nourishes. (58–59)

The "love-song of Dido" is the fourth book of the *Aeneid;* the "tale of Troy divine" is the second. This passage is important on several counts.

Rather than list all of the other scattered references and individual words, I call the reader's attention to one: *paradox*. As it happens, the word *paradox* is quoted above with the riddle of the life of Alexander Crummell. What is striking is that Du Bois uses the word at least once in each of the first ten chapters and in chapter 12; the position of Booker T. Washington entails a triple paradox. In the previously written material and the new, the paradox remains. A simple interpretation of Du Bois's fondness for the word is that it well described the confrontation of black reality with American ideals.

Du Bois separated his earlier article, "The Negro as He Really Is," into chapter 7, "Of the Black Belt," and chapter 8, "Of the Quest of the Golden Fleece."[5] Almost all of chapter 7 is new material, but Du Bois reestablishes the severed connection to chapter 8 and foreshadows his use of the myth of Jason and the Golden Fleece through his reaction to coming upon a deserted village in Dougherty County: "I could imagine the place under some

5. For convenience in identifying the eight original "fugitive pieces," see David Levering Lewis, *W. E. B. Du Bois: Biography of a Race, 1868–1919* (New York: Henry Holt, 1993), 641–42 n. 31. "Of the Wings of Atalanta" was Du Bois's presidential address to the ANA; see Alfred A. Moss, *The American Negro Academy: Voice of the Talented Tenth* (Baton Rouge: Louisiana State University Press, 1981), 63.

weird spell, and was half-minded to search out the princess" (80). The premier princess with spells is Medea, the daughter of Aeetes, king of Colchis, a city at the eastern end of the Black Sea. Jason obtained the fleece with Medea's aid, and it is to Medea that the "witchery" of the first paragraph of chapter 8 refers.

> Have you ever seen a cotton-field white with the harvest,—its golden fleece hovering above the black earth like a silvery cloud edged with dark green, its bold white signals waving like the foam of billows from Carolina to Texas across that Black and human Sea? I have sometimes half suspected that here the winged ram Chrysomallus left that Fleece after which Jason and his Argonauts went vaguely wandering into the shadowy East three thousand years ago; and certainly one might frame a pretty and not far-fetched analogy of witchery and dragon's teeth, and blood and armed men, between the ancient and modern Quest of the Golden Fleece in the Black Sea. (89)

I would suggest that the inspiration for this use of the myth of Jason and Medea comes not only from the fleecy appearance of cotton in the fields but also from the pun suggested by thinking of the "Black Belt" alternatively as a sea of black folk, a "Black and human Sea." Since the fleece of the cotton is golden only in the wealth it provides, the effort of establishing the color and connection is apparent in the labored first sentence. Du Bois does add to the myth by naming the previously unnamed ram; the name "Chrysomallus" represents the Greek *chrusomallos*, "golden-fleeced," found in Apollodorus 1.9.1 in his narration of the escape of Phrixus and Helle from Boeotia. The ram carried Phrixus through the sky on its back to Colchis; hence it is called winged. And, of course, the "pretty and not far-fetched analogy" became Du Bois's novel *The Quest of the Silver Fleece* (1911).

The only other classical allusions in chapters 7 and 8 are historical. Less important is the comparison of the "unwritten law . . . that the character of all Negroes unknown to the mass of the community must be vouched for by some white man" to the Roman patron/client system (98–99). More important, given the countless references to and interpretations of the phrase by critics, is the designation of Dougherty County as the "Egypt of the Confederacy" (81–83). While I would not deny the resonance of Egypt as the place of bondage of the Israelites, the literal meaning of the metonym is that Dougherty County was a major source of food for the Confederacy. Like Sicily before it, Egypt has been commonly called the "granary of Rome." After the suicide of Cleopatra VII in 30 B.C., Egypt became a Roman province and control passed to Octavian, who would soon afterward be named Augustus. The importance of the grain supply from Egypt to Rome can be seen in Suetonius's chapter on Augustus and in Josephus's *Jewish War* (2.385). That the equation "Dougherty County, the Egypt of the Confederacy" is meant to suggest "Egypt, the granary of Rome" is made clear in the second of the three uses: "This was indeed the Egypt of the Confederacy,—the rich granary whence potatoes and corn and cotton poured out to the famished and ragged Confederate troops" (83).

The most sustained use of classics is found in chapter 5, "Of the Wings of Atalanta." As is often the case, Du Bois's words are densely packed and have several layers of meaning. He plays on the resemblance between the names of the city, Atlanta, and the huntress, Atalanta. The first references, however, are to Lachesis and Mercury. The Fates, *Moirai* in Greek, are also called the Spinners, *Klothes* (*Odyssey* 7.197), and are imagined as three in number with Clotho (I Spin) spinning out the thread of a person's life, Lachesis (Distributor of Lots) deciding the length and quality, and Atropos (The Inflexible) cutting it. Atlanta as the "Queen of the cotton kingdom" spun and wove the thread and sold fabrics and "stretched long iron ways to greet the busy Mercury in his coming" (55). Mercury appears here in his role as god of travelers, merchants, and trade.

The story of Atalanta serves as an allegory for the dangers of lust and greed and is the connecting thread through the chapter. Because of Rampersad's casual suggestion that " 'The Quest of the Golden Fleece' sends him back to his Bulfinch" (77), it is important to note that the details that Du Bois offers indicate that his source was not Bulfinch or another popularizer but Ovid himself, in *Metamorphoses* 10.560–704, and perhaps also Hesiod, in fragment 14 of the *Catalogues of Women*. The particular details of interest are "winged maiden," "dull Boeotia," "swarthy Atalanta, tall and wild," "wily Hippomenes laid three apples of gold in the way," and the end, "the blazing passion of their love profaned the sanctuary of Love, and they were cursed" (55). "Winged" is represented in Ovid, 10.587, *passu volat alite virgo*, "the maiden flies with winged stride." In the myths, there is confusion over her parentage. Bulfinch does not name her father; Ovid names her father, Schoeneus, through the patronymic. Schoeneus was a king in Boeotia and Boeotia was proverbial in antiquity for the stupidity of its people, hence "dull Boeotia." Du Bois calls Atalanta "swarthy," and this is taken up as "black young Atalanta" (57). The mythical Atalanta could easily have been dark, as dark at least as men who spent time outside, since she lived in the woods and ran, half-clothed, against her suitors. In ancient art, Greek women were rendered in white while the men were shown as dark because, ideally, women were secluded at home while the men spent their time outside. Nevertheless, Ovid explicitly describes Atalanta as ivory-colored, *eburnea*, and then as having a girlish whiteness, *candore* (10.592, 594). Atalanta's wildness comes both because she was untamed by marriage and in anticipation of her being turned into a lioness, part of the race of wild animals, *genus . . . ferarum* (10.705), the point of Ovid's story and the curse in that of Du Bois. On the other hand, Hippomenes' wiliness is perhaps derived from the fragment of Hesiod, where he is so described;

Hesiod also suggests that the apples are thrown (not laid) in the way, but as they ran, not before the race. Ovid specifies that Hippomenes threw the apples off course, the last one far into the side of a field. That the apples are laid in the way is important to Du Bois's manipulation of the story.

For the literal-minded among us, the greatest change made by Du Bois is that Atalanta and Hippomenes profaned the sanctuary of Love. In Ovid, Love—that is, Venus—makes them violate not her own temple but a temple of Cybele because Hippomenes had forgotten to thank Venus for giving him the golden apples. But the sanctuary of Love is more to Du Bois's purposes and relates to the general discussion of the pursuit of wealth rather than ideals.

> How fleet must Atalanta be if she will not be tempted by gold to profane the Sanctuary!
> The Sanctuary of our fathers has, to be sure, few Gods,—some sneer, "all too few." There is the thrifty Mercury of New England, Pluto of the North, and Ceres of the West; and there, too, is the half-forgotten Apollo of the South, under whose ægis the maiden ran,—and as she ran she forgot him, even as there in Boeotia Venus was forgot. (56)

Mercury had a broad sphere of influence, but the association with New England requires Mercury, the god of trade and merchants. Although Pluto is the Roman god of the underworld, in that capacity he has no more relevance for the North than for any other area of the country. Du Bois here refers to the Greek source of the Roman name, *ploutos* (wealth). Wealth is the god of the North. Ceres is particularly the goddess of grain, and so appropriate to the West, especially the West of Kansas and the other Great Plains states.

Like Mercury, Apollo oversees several areas. He is god of prophecy, and it is to this function that at least one level of meaning of the clause "under whose ægis the maiden ran" refers. In response to an inquiry about a husband, the god Apollo had told Atalanta to avoid marriage (*Metamorphoses* 10.564–66). Frightened, she raced to preserve her virginity; suitors who could not catch her were killed. In yielding to the desire for Hippomenes' golden apples, Atalanta forgot Apollo's warning, even as Hippomenes forgot to acknowledge that Venus, Love, was responsible for his victory. Because Apollo had the epithet Phoebus, "Bright," he was sometimes identified with the Sun, properly Helius. Atlanta is called "Gateway to the Land of the Sun" and so this perhaps is a connection for Apollo with the South, but the key to the interpretation lies in the term "half-forgotten." Atalanta is at once herself and Atlanta, and Hippomenes is both himself and the Atlanta merchant. Atlanta "forgot the old ideal of the Southern gentleman,—that new world heir of the grace and courtliness of patrician, knight, and noble; forgot his honor with his foibles, his kindliness with his carelessness, and stooped to apples of gold,—to men busier and sharper, thriftier and more unscrupulous" (56). What is half-forgotten is culture, and Apollo as god of the lyre and leader of the Muses is the god of culture. Du Bois himself makes this association more clearly: "The need of the South is knowledge and culture,—not in dainty limited quantity, as before the war, but in broad busy abundance in the world of work; and until she has this, not all the Apples of Hesperides, be they golden and bejewelled, can save her from the curse of the Boeotian lovers" (60). The Hesperides are the daughters of Evening; the tree they guarded was given to Juno as a wedding present by Earth; securing apples from this tree was one of the final Labors of Hercules. These are the ultimate golden apples, far surpassing those Venus happened to have with her when Hippomenes appealed to her.

Before she forgot, the goal of Atalanta's racing was the preservation of her virginity.

> Work and wealth are the mighty levers to lift this new land; thrift and toil and saving are the highways to new hopes and new possibilities; and yet the warning is needed lest the wily Hippomenes tempt Atalanta to thinking that golden apples are the goal of racing, and not mere incidents by the way. (56)
>
> . . . .
>
> The Wings of Atalanta are the coming universities of the South. They alone can bear the maiden past the temptation of the golden fruit. They will not guide her flying feet away from the cotton and gold; for—ah, thoughtful Hippomenes!—do not the apples lie in the very Way of Life? But they will guide her over and beyond them, and leave her kneeling in the Sanctuary of Truth and Freedom and broad Humanity, virgin and undefiled. (60)

Not for nothing is Hippomenes called wily, are the apples *laid* in the way. The goal of virginity has become purity, which has itself become the ideal, which, though one, manifests itself as Truth, Beauty, and Goodness (57, 58); Justice, Righteousness, and Wisdom (57); or here Truth, Freedom, and Humanity, "virgin and undefiled" (60). These ideals are the true goals of the race spurred by Apollo, whose most prestigious sanctuary was at Delphi, on the side of the mountain Parnassus, watered or sweetened by the Castalian Spring, sacred to the Muses and a source of poetic inspiration.

Because Du Bois identifies the goal of Atalanta's race, virginity, with what sound like versions of Platonic ideals or of the virtues, it is legitimate to put emphasis on the placement of Parnassus between the "groves" of Plato and Academus (58–59). The "groves of Academe" are familiar to us. The phrase refers first to the location of Plato's school and then to the school itself. Plato and Apollo converge at Socrates, particularly as Plato has Socrates explain his life's work in the *Apology*. Socrates began engaging his fellow citizens in conversation, questioning them, because his friend

Chaerophon had asked at Delphi whether anyone was wiser than Socrates, and the Pythia had responded that no one was wiser. After cross-examining those with a reputation for wisdom and representatives from various vocations, Socrates concluded that he was wiser than they because he knew that he didn't know (21a–22e).

Two passages from the *Apology* may suffice to show its influence in *The Souls of Black Folk*. Before Socrates is convicted, he suggests that some would be willing to let him go if he promised to give up philosophy.

> I would say to you, "Athenian men, I salute you and love you, but I will obey the god rather than you, and as long as I breathe and can, I will not stop doing philosophy and encouraging you and declaring to whomever of you I happen upon, saying the very sorts of things I am accustomed to say, 'Excellent of men, being an Athenian, a citizen of the greatest and most highly esteemed city for wisdom and strength, aren't you ashamed when you pay attention to wealth, how you will have as much as possible, and to reputation and to honor, but you do not pay attention to good sense and truth and the soul, how it will be as good as possible, nor do you care?' " (29d–e)[6]

After Socrates is condemned, he has to propose a suitable punishment. In much the same context, he suggests that some suppose that he could go into exile and keep quiet:

> Perhaps someone would say, "Socrates, aren't you able to live, going away from us, being silent and keeping quiet?" Indeed this is the most difficult thing of all to persuade some of you. For if I say that this is to disobey the god and on account of this it is impossible to keep quiet, you will not believe me on the ground that I am being ironic; and if I say again that this happens to be the greatest good for a person, every day to speak about virtue and the other things concerning which you hear me conversing and examining myself and others, and that the unexamined life is not worth living for a person, you will believe me still less when I say these things. (37e–38a)

The two significant lessons from Plato's *Apology* are the necessity for self-examination and self-knowledge and the superiority of the pursuit of virtue, wisdom, and excellence of the soul over the pursuit of wealth, reputation, and honor. Chapter 5, "Of the Wings of Atalanta," and Socrates are, therefore, to be read back against chapter 3, "Of Mr. Booker T. Washington and Others," and perhaps these passages can constitute part of the answer to Du Bois's wondering what Socrates would say to Washington (35). But the contrast that Socrates sets forth recurs elsewhere and particularly as the goal of the true college being "not to earn meat, but to know the end and aim of that life which meat nourishes" (59) and as the function of the university being "not simply to teach bread-winning . . . above all, to be the

6. Translations mine.

organ of that fine adjustment between real life and the growing knowledge of life, an adjustment which forms the secret of civilization" (60).

The influence of Socrates and Plato can be seen also in Du Bois's "rule of inequality":

> that of the million black youth, some were fitted to know and some to dig; that some had the talent and capacity of university men, and some the talent and capacity of blacksmiths; and that true training meant neither that all should be college men nor all artisans, but that the one should be made a missionary of culture to an untaught people, and the other a free workman among serfs. And to seek to make the blacksmith a scholar is almost as silly as the more modern scheme of making the scholar a blacksmith; almost, but not quite. (59–60)
>
> . . . .
>
> [H]ow foolish to ask what is the best education for one or seven or sixty million souls! shall we teach them trades, or train them in liberal arts? Neither and both: teach the workers to work and the thinkers to think. . . . And the final product of our training must be neither a psychologist nor a brickmason, but a man. And to make men, we must have ideals, broad, pure, and inspiring ends of living,—not sordid money-getting, not apples of gold. The worker must work for the glory of his handiwork, not simply for pay; the thinker must think for truth, not for fame. And all this is gained only by human strife and longing; by ceaseless training and education; by founding Right on righteousness and Truth on the unhampered search for Truth; by founding the common school on the university, and the industrial school on the common school; and weaving thus a system, not a distortion, and bringing a birth, not an abortion. (61)

These two quotations remind us of passages in the *Republic*, especially in book 4, in which Plato divides the soul into a rational part, a spirited part, and an appetitive part, with each individual ruled by one of these parts over the others. Each individual then should follow that occupation which relates to the dominant part of his soul, to his nature. On the other hand, since all three parts coexist, in the individual and in the state the rational part should be in control. Du Bois argues for the possibility for those who are ruled by reason to have access to training and education. The "missionary to an untaught people" corresponds to the prisoner who left the Cave and returned in the Allegory of *Republic* 7. The image of weaving brings us back to Lachesis, "spinner of web and woof for the world," and the reference to birth and abortion may well stem from Socrates' calling himself a midwife.[7]

7. Shamoon Zamir, in developing the comparison of the end of "The Sorrow Songs" with the Allegory of the Cave shows, rather, that there is little similarity; see Zamir, *Dark Voices: W. E. B. Du Bois and American Thought, 1888–1903* (Chicago: University of Chicago Press, 1995), 178–90. See also his chapter included in the Norton Critical Edition of *The Souls of Black Folk*, 352–55. For Socrates as midwife, see Plato, *Theaetetus* 149a–151d.

In the collection *Against Racism*, Herbert Aptheker includes Du Bois's application to Harvard, with a listing of the courses taken at Fisk.[8] Among these is the *Phaedo* of Plato, which purports to represent the last day of Socrates' life, the time between when he was released from his shackles and when he drank the poison and died. Through these hours Socrates tries to console his friends by persuading them of the immortality of the soul. Of particular importance for Plato's setting and for *The Souls of Black Folk* is the coincidence of the Orphic doctrine that the body *(soma)* is the tomb *(sema)* of the soul, generally referred to as *soma sema,* and the physical reality of the imprisonment of Socrates. In the *Phaedo,* the body is the prison rather than the tomb of the soul; death is a separation of the soul from the body (62b). If one has lived as a philosopher, despising the body and striving to know truth, goodness, justice, and beauty through reason, at death the soul is freed from the body as from shackles (67d) and can commune with the gods and contemplate the forms themselves.

Du Bois's connection to the Orphic doctrine *soma sema* and the *Phaedo* is made indirectly in "Of Our Spiritual Strivings" through the "shades of the prison-house" (10). The phrase comes from the fifth stanza of Wordsworth's "Ode: Intimations of Immortality from Recollections of Early Childhood."[9]

> Our birth is but a sleep and a forgetting;
> The soul that rises with us, our life's star,
>   Hath had elsewhere its setting,
>   And cometh from afar:
>   Not in entire forgetfulness,
>   And not in utter nakedness,
> But trailing clouds of glory do we come
>   From God, who is our home:
> Heaven lies about us in our infancy!
> Shades of the prison-house begin to close
>   Upon the growing boy,
> But he beholds the light, and whence it flows
>   He sees it in his joy;
> The youth, who daily farther from the east
>   Must travel, still is Nature's priest,
>   And by the vision splendid
>   Is on his way attended;
> At length the man perceives it die away
> And fade into the light of common day.

8. W. E. B. Du Bois, *Against Racism: Unpublished Essays, Papers, Addresses, 1887–1961,* ed. Herbert Aptheker (Amherst: University of Massachusetts Press, 1985), 4–13.

9. The epistrophic "for there had passed a glory from the earth" (137, 138) also comes from this poem (line 18).

Wordsworth here refers vaguely to the Platonic proof of the immortality of the soul through the argument from recollection found in the *Phaedo* and elsewhere, to the Myth of Er from the *Republic,* and to the *soma sema* doctrine. It can be demonstrated from other writings that Du Bois had Plato in mind. Du Bois accepts the doctrine but distinguishes the prisons:

> The shades of the prison-house closed round about us all: walls strait and stubborn to the whitest, but relentlessly narrow, tall, and unscalable to sons of night who must plod darkly on in resignation, or beat unavailing palms against the stone, or steadily, half hopelessly, watch the streak of blue above. (10)

Although the body is the prison of the soul for everyone, the black body is a worse prison for the souls of black folk.

That this version of the *soma sema* doctrine was an integral part of Du Bois's thinking can be seen in "The Evolution of Negro Leadership" and its rewritten version, "Of Mr. Booker T. Washington and Others," where he refers obliquely to black people as an "imprisoned group" (37) even though nothing he says before suggests "imprisoned." Similarly, where Du Bois uses the metaphor of the Veil in *The Souls of Black Folk* in chapters previously published, he also used it in the earlier articles; that is, while the "Veil" serves to unify *The Souls of Black Folk,* it preexisted as part of Du Bois's thinking about race. The metaphor of the Veil is so joined with the *soma sema* doctrine that black people are imprisoned or prisoned by the Veil, by the blackness of their bodies; and like "the prison-house," the Veil casts a shadow.

> [T]he one panacea of Education leaps to the lips of all . . . such training as will give us poise to encourage the prejudices that bulwark society, and to stamp out those that in sheer barbarity deafen us to the wail of prisoned souls within the Veil, and the mounting fury of shackled men. (64)
>
> . . . .
>
> Surely there shall yet dawn some mighty morning to lift the Veil and set the prisoned free. Not for me,—I shall die in my bonds,—but for fresh young souls who have not known the night and waken to the morning. (133)
>
> . . . .
>
> If somewhere in this whirl and chaos of things there dwells Eternal Good, pitiful yet masterful, then anon in His good time America shall rend the Veil and the prisoned shall go free. (163)

The souls of black people will be released from their prisons, not at death, but when America becomes "another word for Opportunity to *all* her sons" (94).

The "Eternal Good," quoted above, is "the good itself," one of the forms or ideals of Plato, the end of life. In the *Phaedo,* the most frequent combination of ideals is the just, the beautiful, and the good; but the combinations vary. Du Bois is particularly fond of "Truth, Beauty, and Goodness" (57, 58), "the good, the beautiful, and the true" (106), although he seems to vary with "the good and noble and true" (117) ("noble" and "beautiful" translate the same word, *kalon*).

Throughout *The Souls of Black Folk*, Du Bois shows his acceptance of the Delphic maxim, *gnothi sauton*, "know yourself," especially associated with Socrates and assumed in *Apology* 38a, quoted above, "the unexamined life is not worth living." The journey to "book-learning" "gave leisure for reflection and self-examination . . . he must be himself and not another" (14). In chapter 4, Du Bois says he grew to love Josie's family "for their knowledge of their own ignorance" (47). In chapter 6, from a discussion of the functions of the Negro college, "there must come a loftier respect for the sovereign human soul that seeks to know itself and the world about it" (73). The eulogy in chapter 12, "Of Alexander Crummell," is "the history of a human heart,—the tale of a black boy who many long years ago began to struggle with life that he might know the world and know himself" (134).

Du Bois's most intriguing classical reference is to Cicero's *Pro Archia* in chapter 4, "Of the Meaning of Progress":

> At times the school would dwindle away, and I would start out. . . . When the Lawrences stopped, I knew that the doubts of the old folks about book-learning had conquered again, and so, toiling up the hill, and getting as far into the cabin as possible, I put Cicero "pro Archia Poeta" into the simplest English with local applications, and usually convinced them—for a week or so. (49)

This is all Du Bois says explicitly about the *Pro Archia*, but the speech was important to him. Not only was this passage included in the *Autobiography*, published in 1968, as part of chapter 8, "I Go South," but also he reports in an article from the June 1928 *Crisis*, "So the Girl Marries," that he tried to use "pro Archia Poeta" to persuade his daughter to go to college. Orations of Cicero, including the *Pro Archia* and half of the *Pro Marcello*, are among the Latin works listed as studied at Fisk. *Diuturni silenti*, the first two words of the *Pro Marcello*, appear as the title of the scolding commencement address that Du Bois gave at Fisk in 1924, when his daughter graduated.[10] Although Du Bois does not spell out the significance of the *Pro Archia* for the Lawrences, his daughter, or himself, one may, nevertheless, conjecture.

In his defense of the Greek poet Archias, Cicero easily disposes of the charge that Archias was not a Roman citizen and was, therefore, subject

10. See Du Bois, *Autobiography*, 118; Du Bois, "So the Girl Marries" (1928), in *W. E. B. Du Bois: A Reader*, ed. David Levering Lewis (New York: Henry Holt, 1995), 129; and Du Bois, *Against Racism*, 6.

to expulsion from Rome. Arguing that if Archias were not a citizen, the Romans should make him one, Cicero devotes most of his speech to the value of literature and of poets. It is rash to select passages that might have made the greatest impact on Du Bois, but certainly 6.12 through 7.17 must have been prominent. This section asserts that literature refreshes the spirit and provides examples of right action and excellence. Time devoted to studies is better spent than time devoted to personal business, sport, resting, parties, or other pleasures. Many with innate virtues have succeeded without literary training; however, such training added to outstanding natural talent produces something distinguished and singular. N. H. Watts's translation of *Pro Archia* 7.16 is particularly revealing:

> But let us for the moment waive these solid advantages; let us assume that entertainment is the sole end of reading; even so, I think you would hold that no mental employment is so *broadening to the sympathies* or so enlightening to the understanding. Other pursuits belong not to all times, all ages, all conditions; but this gives stimulus to our youth and diversion to our old age; this adds a charm to success, and offers a haven of consolation to failure. In the home it delights, in the world it hampers not. Through the night-watches, on all our journeying, and in our hours of country ease, it is our unfailing companion.[11]

The words translated above as "broadening to the sympathies" and "enlightening to the understanding" are *humanissimam*, "most human, most proper to men; most cultured, most refined," and *liberalissimam*, "most befitting a free man." It is by the sheerest coincidence (or an undiscovered common source) that Du Bois likewise has "broad sympathy" as part of the object of education. This view is distilled in the first paragraph of "The Talented Tenth," the famous essay in the 1903 book, *The Negro Problem:*

> The Negro race, like all races, is going to be saved by its exceptional men. The problem of education, then, among Negroes must first of all deal with the Talented Tenth; it is the problem of developing the Best of this race that they may guide the Mass away from the contamination and death of the Worst, in their own and other races. Now the training of men is a difficult and intricate task. Its technique is a matter for educational experts, but its object is for the vision of seers. If we make money the object of man-training, we shall develop money-makers but not necessarily men; if we make technical skill the object of education, we may possess artisans but not, in nature, men. Men we shall have only as we make manhood the object of the work of the schools—intelligence, *broad sympathy*, knowledge of the world that was and is, and the relation of men to it—this is the curriculum of that Higher Education which must underlie true life. On this foundation we may build bread

11. See N. H. Watts, *Cicero*, vol. 11, Loeb Classical Library (Cambridge: Harvard University Press, 1923), 25.

winning, skill of hand and quickness of brain, with never a fear lest the child and man mistake the means of living for the object of life.[12]

Given a fuller appreciation of Du Bois's views, we must construe "men" and even "manhood" to include women, as we must in the translation of *liberalissimam* and *humanissimam*.

Much of "The Talented Tenth" is found also in chapter 6, "Of the Training of Black Men." The sentiments that can be expressed under the term "broad sympathy," and that I relate to the *Pro Archia*, can be found particularly in chapter 1, "Of Our Spiritual Strivings"; chapter 5, "Of the Wings of Atalanta"; chapter 6, "Of the Training of Black Men"; and chapter 9, "Of the Sons of Master and Man," where Du Bois uses both "deep sympathy" (110) and "broad-minded sympathy" (116). These reiterations of support for liberal education for black folk reinforce his criticisms of Washington in chapter 3.

Taken altogether, the references to classics in *The Souls of Black Folk* suggest that Plato and Cicero were significant influences on Du Bois's thinking. Such Socratic dicta as "Virtue is knowledge" and "No one does wrong willingly" find expression in his appeals to the better classes of whites. The display of his genius and training show his determination to "be himself and not another." He concurs with Cicero that literature produces men, the most fully realized human beings. He does not, however, box up these ideas as "academic knowledge," but in the manner of Cicero and Socrates he applies them to the real problems of the United States, the Negro problem, the problem of the color line. The "Wings of Atalanta," set directly in the middle of the world "without the Veil," overarches the whole: the students at Atlanta University studying Vergil and Plato, coworkers in the kingdom of culture, free.

12. The emphases in the *Pro Archia* and "The Talented Tenth" are added. I must thank my Howard University colleague Dr. Eleanor Traylor, chair of English, for impressing this paragraph upon my consciousness. It provides the thematic and theoretical basis for our two-semester sequence "Introduction to Humanities."

W. E. B. Du Bois and the Invention of the Sublime in *The Souls of Black Folk*

Dolan Hubbard

The Music of Negro religion is that plaintive rhythmic melody, with its touching minor cadences, which, despite caricature and defilement, still remains the most original and beautiful expression of human life and longing yet born on American soil.

—W. E. B. Du Bois

Background Considerations on the Sublime

I approach this critique of the sublime in the firm belief that it is important to attend to both aesthetic and cultural questions as we examine the issue of representation, especially as it relates to the African presence in the modern Western world. Admittedly, it is difficult to cover the whole of this topic, especially within the pages of a single essay. However, this essay can serve as a reevaluation of a term—the *sublime*—that an Anglo-European intellectual cartel has reserved for themselves and that apparently resides only in the ether of their imaginations. Though discussions of the sublime are by nature rife with subjective evaluation, W. E. B. Du Bois recognized that such discussions, nevertheless, are laden with objective implication. The underlying significance is that this notion creates a linkage of knowledge with power, as we see in the dislocating effects of knowledge without power for black and colored people.[1] In *The Souls of Black Folk* (1903), Du Bois challenges this aesthetic doctrine.

My project is guided by three interrelated questions. First, how do post-Enlightenment ideas of the sublime shape our notion of humanity in the modern Western world? Second, why does Du Bois feel compelled to invent the sublime? Du Bois deconstructs the European notion of the sublime and constructs a black sublime. He locates this sublime in the religiosity

1. Edward W. Said, *Orientalism* (New York: Vintage, 1979), 5–14.

of black people. Hence, Du Bois drenches the term *souls* in the corporate history of black America. Third, how does Du Bois's engagement with the sublime relate to his grand project for the redemption of Africa? His goal is to reconnect people of African descent culturally by centering Africa as the source of black discourse. Until he recovers the sublime, Du Bois's grand project of the redemption of Africa is moot.[2]

The primary intellectual orientation Du Bois espouses in *The Souls of Black Folk* has been one of hermeneutics as a general theory of cultural formation and interpretation. He applies these methodological meanings to theoretical studies of black life and culture; central to these studies is religion, for religion is inseparable from aesthetics, the sublime, and identity formation. Through his interrogation of the sublime, Du Bois thus calls into question the philosophical foundation of the modern Western world, to the degree that this foundation excludes people of color. Though the sublime tinges all areas of discourse, many scholars fail to establish its connections with black American religious discourse and its engagement with the Eurocentric construction of the sublime. In his unceasing determination to recover the sublime and place Africans at the center of the Atlantic formation, Du Bois gave black artists, writers, and intellectuals an accessible history, which they used to discuss their comparative black identities.[3]

By the time "the sublime" entered the discourse of modernity through the works of John Locke, Edmund Burke (in his 1756 *Essay on the Sublime and Beautiful*), Henry Home (in his 1762 *Elements of Criticism*), Samuel Johnson (in his 1755 *The Dictionary of the English Language*), and Immanuel Kant, the image of the African in the Western mind was already deformed. The cultural script of the West had reduced blacks to contextual invisibility and darkness. They were judged by a standard of beauty that did not even recognize their humanity. They were prisoners of a philosophy of negation that betrayed the original liberating impulse of the Enlightenment. Trapped in a prison house of language, blacks seemed—like Ralph Ellison's nameless protagonist surrounded by mirrors of hard, distorted glass—unable to see their own beauty. Deprived of agency, they struggled to come to grips with their "otherness."[4] This "otherness" arose from the creation of the sublime, a cultural trope generated during the European Enlightenment that privileged the expected fair-skinned physical appear-

2. For a discussion of Du Bois's goal of making history "talk," see my essay "Riddle Me This: Du Bois, the Sphinx, and the Crisis of Identity," in *W. E. B. Du Bois and Race: Essays Celebrating the Centennial Publication of* The Souls of Black Folk, ed. Chester J. Fontenot Jr., 26–44 (Macon, Ga.: Mercer University Press, 2001).

3. This section is informed by the observation of Charles H. Long, letter to the author, April 4, 1997.

4. As Charles H. Long notes, the African's otherness is rooted in the very term *civilization;* see "Primitive/Civilized: The Locus of a Problem," in Long's *Significations: Signs, Symbols, and Images in the Interpretation of Religion* (Philadelphia: Fortress, 1986), 79–95.

ance of Europeans over the anticipated dark-skinned and broad, elongated features of Africans.

Nature and Significance of the Sublime

Derived from Latin, the term *sublime* means "(on) high, lofty, elevated."[5] It is most closely identified with the author commonly known as Longinus and his work *On the Sublime* (written approximately A.D. 80). In the two thousand years since then, Longinus was perhaps most influential during the eighteenth century. At that time, there appeared not only the first modern treatises on aesthetics, such as Edmund Burke's *Essay on the Sublime and Beautiful* and Henry Home's *Elements of Criticism*, but also Kant's *Observations on the Feeling of the Beautiful and Sublime* (1764) and the *Critique of Judgment* (1790), the latter of which was his mature statement on aesthetics.[6]

Rhys Roberts, in *Longinus on the Sublime* (1899), gives a concise summary of the five sources of the sublime: "The first and most important of these is grandeur of thought—the power of forming great conceptions. This power is founded on nobility of character. Elevated thoughts are also, we are told, the result of the imitation of great models, of imaginative power, and of the choice and grouping of the most striking circumstances." Other distinguishing marks of sublimity include "vehement and inspired passion," elevated figures of speech, noble phrasing of diction, and elevation in the arrangement of words.[7] Collectively, these distinguishing marks of sublimity make for greatness of spirit in literature. In the modern world, cultural sophisticates have tended to "embrace *excellence of expression* as another rendering for what has been called sublimity."[8]

Sublime, then, refers to an aesthetic value in which the primary factor is the presence or suggestion of transcendent vastness or greatness, as of power, of heroism, or of extent in space or time. The sublime differs from greatness or grandeur in that these are, as such, capable of being completely grasped or measured. By contrast, the sublime, while in one respect apprehended and grasped as a whole, is felt as transcending our normal standards of measurement or achievement, especially with regard to the terrors of nature held in check by myth and magic. The "sublime" itself is

5. *Princeton Encyclopedia of Poetry and Poetics*, ed. Alex Preminger (Princeton: Princeton University Press, 1974), 819.

6. Allan H. Gilbert, *Literary Criticism: Plato to Dryden* (Detroit: Wayne State University Press, 1962), 144; see also Eva Schaper, "Taste, Sublimity, and Genius: The Aesthetics of Nature and Art," in *The Cambridge Companion to Kant*, ed. Paul Guyer (Cambridge: Cambridge University Press, 1992).

7. Longinus, *On the Sublime*, trans. W. Rhys Roberts (Cambridge: Cambridge University Press, 1935; reprint, New York: AMS Press, 1979).

8. Gilbert, *Literary Criticism*, 145–46.

the "totally" other, the presence of the totally different and untouchable, and, as such, the impenetrable mystery *(mysterium tremendum):* While in the midst of being overwhelmed, one experiences a certain pleasure. This overwhelming and awe-inspiring other is given the name of "the sublime." The experience of the sublime—not the sublime itself—could possibly be analyzed in Kantian terms. From Kant's perspective, this pleasure results from an awareness that we have powers of reason that are not dependent on sensation, but that legislate our senses. The sublime thus displays both the limitations of sense experience (and hence our feeling of displeasure) and the power of our own mind (and hence the feeling of pleasure).[9]

However, the emerging concept of the sublime was fraught with paradox. On the one hand, Europe of the Enlightenment was able to grasp its own concrete place within an overall rational scheme. Most of the giants of European thought were preoccupied with logic, scientific language, and empirical fact, with trying, in other words, to resolve the tension between reason and freedom.[10] They broke the back of the sacred imagination, ushering in the dethroning of God as the absolute other, and paving the way for man in secular society; they offered up vigorous autocritiques; and they brought about the collapse of ancient culture and shattered the edifice of idealization. On the other hand, in a dialectical twist, they conceived of the African as nothing more than a child of nature—not emancipated from myth and magic. Thus, if the African is said to lack "powers of reason," then he or she cannot have an experience of the sublime. This assertion, supported by an insistent emphasis on a cognitive and technological superiority, went beyond solving the above aesthetic problem. It also settled an economic issue: Once the African was considered beyond the pale of humanity, a creature of lower intelligence, Europeans could justify African enslavement on a large scale.

One of the ironies of history is that the entry of the sublime into English discourse in the eighteenth century coincided with the modern slave trade and mercantile imperialism to create an exalted self at the expense of the "other."[11] The aesthetic die was being cast; excellence of expression was

9. I draw on the following works in my observation on the sublime: Hazard Adams, ed., *Critical Theory since Plato,* rev. ed. (Fort Worth, Tex.: Harcourt Brace Jovanovich College Publishers, 1992); Cain Hope Felder, *The Original African Heritage Study Bible* (Nashville: James C. Winston, 1993); Simon Blackburn, *The Oxford Dictionary of Philosophy* (Oxford: Oxford University Press, 1994), 774; Anthony J. Cascardi, "Immanuel Kant," in *The Johns Hopkins Guide to Literary Theory and Criticism,* ed. Michael Groden and Martin Kreiswirth (Baltimore: Johns Hopkins University Press, 1994), 438–40; Robert Gooding-Williams, "Du Bois's Counter-Sublime," *Massachusetts Review* 35, no. 2 (summer 1994), 202–24; and *The Internet Encyclopedia of Philosophy,* 1997, http://www.utm.edu/research/lev/s/sublime.htm.

10. Charles Altieri, "G. W. F. Hegel," in *Johns Hopkins Guide to Literary Theory and Criticism,* 369–70.

11. Long, *Significations,* 80–81.

reserved for Europeans only. The English gentleman, for instance, was defined as an aristocrat and a sophisticate, a man of discriminating taste and
refinement, read against a backdrop of leisure and luxury. Consequently,
"the sublime" became an expression of the national character. Thus, as it
became the tool of New World philosophers, its creators were obligated to
describe how that character changed but did not disappear.

On How Post-Enlightenment Ideas of the Sublime Shape Our Notion of Humanity in the Modern Western World

On the whole, the emergence of the concept of the sublime coincided
with a number of telling philosophical developments. In "A Genealogy of
Modern Racism," Cornel West provides us with a trenchant observation on
how an exclusionary aesthetic colors modern Western discourse. He illuminates the metaphors, notions, categories, and norms that "shape the predominant conceptions of truth and knowledge in the modern West," radi-
ating outward from three major historical processes: "the scientific revolution, the Cartesian transformation of philosophy, and the classical revival."
The scientific breakthroughs were pre-Enlightenment, most of which took
place during the seventeenth century and marked the end of the era of
"pagan Christianity." The scientific revolution emphasized two fundamental ideas: *observation* and *evidence*, establishing the primacy of scientific
authority over orthodox religion. Science's major proponents were two
philosophers, Francis Bacon (1561–1626) and René Descartes (1596–1650).
Bacon promoted the "philosophical importance of the inductive method as
a means of arriving at general laws to facilitate human mastery." Descartes
is a pivotal figure because his thought provided "the controlling notions of
modern discourse: *the primacy of the subject and the preeminence of representation.*" Widely regarded as the founder of modern philosophy, Descartes,
according to West, "associated the scientific aim of predicting and explaining the world with the philosophical aim of picturing and representing the
world." Philosophically, Descartes crystallized the move from subject to
object, from the veil of ideas to the external world, and from certainty to
doubt. These intellectual moves were "motivated primarily by an attempt
to provide a theoretical basis for the legitimacy of modern science."[12]

12. Cornel West, "A Genealogy of Modern Racism," in *Prophesy and Deliverance! An
Afro-American Revolutionary Christianity* (Philadelphia: Westminster Press, 1982), 50, 51;
I draw freely on the observations of Cornel West in this section, for the sublime is im-
plicit in his discussion. See also Frank M. Snowden, *Blacks in Antiquity: Ethiopians in
the Greco-Roman Experience* (Cambridge: Harvard University Press, 1970); and Henry
Louis Gates Jr., "Critical Remarks," in *Anatomy of Racism*, ed. David Theo Goldberg
(Minneapolis: University of Minnesota Press, 1990).

The last major historical process that circumscribed and determined the metaphors, notions, categories, and norms of modern discourse was the classical revival, as a way of responding to religious dogmatism. The thrust and development of the Enlightenment were basically a revolt against absolute political and religious authority, and hence the Enlightenment was a culture-intrinsic movement. Its primary (or "thetical") thrust was a critique and a movement from theology and dogma as the major and absolutely certain premise in the syllogism of knowledge toward a liberation of the imagination. This liberation was achieved differently by the empiricists (Hobbes, Locke, Hume) and by the intellectualists (Descartes, Leibniz, Kant, Hegel). The result was a slow freeing of the search for truth from dogmatic assertions leading to the establishment of a realm of "free" research. (However fertile this critical engagement may have been in establishing its own prejudices, it must be said that the intellectual discourse spawned in the Enlightenment was accompanied by continuous autocritiques of the emerging information society.) With the exception of Kant, the rest of the Renaissance and Enlightenment thinkers and scholars generally were not professors at any of the established universities. The first university to establish "freedom of learning" and "freedom of teaching" was the University of Berlin, under Humboldt, around 1812. The "free" researchers' concomitant move stimulated by the Enlightenment was against absolute monarchies and power prerogatives. The Enlightenment revolt against the authority of the church and the search for models of unrestrained criticism led to a highly charged recovery of classical antiquity and, especially, to a new appreciation and appropriation of the artistic and cultural heritage of ancient Greece.[13]

The classical revival stands as first among equals in the Trinitarian structure of modern discourse, for it uses aesthetics to consolidate the findings of modern science—rooted in observing, comparing, measuring, and ordering the physical characteristics of human bodies. The European intellectual community looked to a supposedly pristine Greece for its aesthetic models. Greek ocular metaphors and classical ideals of beauty, proportion, and moderation formed the building blocks of modern discourse, privileging "the epistemological model of intellect (formerly Plato's and Aristotle's Nous, now Descartes's Inner Eye)" and giving rise to "a conception of truth and knowledge governed by an ideal value-free subject engaged in observing, comparing, ordering, and measuring in order to arrive at evidence sufficient to make valid inferences, confirm speculative hypotheses, deduce error-proof conclusions, and verify true representations of reality."[14]

13. West, "Genealogy of Modern Racism," 53. I am indebted to my colleague at Morgan State University Otto Begus, professor and chair of the Department of Philosophy and Religious Studies, for his insights on the sublime.
14. West, "Genealogy of Modern Racism," 48, 53.

The dialectical underside of the Enlightenment was the establishment of scientific methodologies (or simply the scientific episteme) as the only garden where truth was grown and cultivated, reducing the human being itself to but an object. Out of this trend come the new "scientific" concepts of race, of measurabilities, of qualitative differences—from Galton and Spencer to Hitler and to Hernstein. And, in line with traditional humanism's faith in progress, are, of course, the value judgments of "lower" and "higher," of "beautiful" and "ugly," and so on. Another stratum of this "underside" of the sublime was the individualization of property rights and commercial activity—the origins of capitalism. The intellectual ordering that accompanied capitalism placed the African at the center of the circle of commerce, thus making the continent the international postal card for chattel slavery. Ancient African civilization was devalued; Europe turned its gaze toward Greece for cultural legitimacy.[15]

The end result of the recovery of classical antiquity in the modern West produced what Cornel West and others call a "normative gaze," namely an ideal from which to order and compare observations that gave rise to the idea of white supremacy. Natural history, with its reliance on *classificatory* categories to impose some degree of order or representational schema on a broad field of characteristics, took the lead in promoting this "normative gaze" from the supposedly value-free position of the disinterested observer. One sees the *authoritative power* inherent in the network of significations associated with this "normative gaze" in the *Natural System* (1735), the first authoritative racial division of humankind, written by the most preeminent naturalist of the eighteenth century, Carolus Linnaeus. For example, compare Linnaeus's description of the European with that of the African:

> European: White, Sanguine, Brawny. Hair abundantly flowing. Eyes blue. Gentle, acute, inventive. Covered with close vestments. Governed by customs.
> African: Black, Phlegmatic, Relaxed. Hair black, frizzled. Skin silky. Nose flat. Lips tumid. Women's bosom a matter of modesty. Breasts give milk abundantly. Crafty, indolent. Negligent. Anoints himself with grease. Governed by caprice.[16]

15. For an illuminating discussion of the devaluation of Africa in the modern Western imagination, see Cheikah Anta Diop, *Civilization or Barbarism: An Authentic Anthropology*, trans. Yaa-Lengi Meema Ngemi (1981; reprint, New York: Lawrence Hill, 1991); Cheikah Anta Diop, *Precolonial Black Africa*, trans. Harold Salemson (New York: Lawrence Hill, 1987); Ali A. Mazrui, *The Africans: A Triple Heritage* (Boston: Little, Brown, 1986); Chancellor Williams, *The Destruction of Black Civilization* (Chicago: Third World Press, 1987); Molefi Asante, *The Afrocentric Idea* (Philadelphia: Temple University Press, 1987); and Martin Bernal, *Black Athena: The Afroasiatic Roots of Classical Civilization* (New Brunswick, N.J.: Rutgers University Press, 1987).

16. Quoted in Wihthrop D. Jordan, *White over Black: American Attitudes toward the Negro, 1550–1812* (Chapel Hill: University of North Carolina Press, 1968), 220–21.

We can discern in Linnaeus's "normative gaze" an implicit hierarchy by means of personal preference, with Europe at the top and Africa at the bottom, as well as an aesthetic labiectomy or the intellectual equivalent of excising Europe from almost any vestige of a connection to Africa, the "dark" continent. The canon of beauty adhered to a European standard. In short, the African that was created through the "normative gaze" of the European was created as a problem. Speaking for his age, Linnaeus, with the catalogs of scientific observation to support him, confidently asserted that Africans are not a true representation of the Divine. The norms, as supported by the authority of science, were consciously projected and promoted by many influential Enlightenment writers, artists, and scholars. West reminds us that Montesquieu and Voltaire of the French Enlightenment, Hume and Jefferson of the Scottish and the American Enlightenment, and Kant of the German Enlightenment "not merely held racist views; they also uncritically—during this age of criticism—believed that the *authority* for these views rested in the domain of naturalists, anthropologists, physiognomists, and phrenologists."[17]

The sublime is the gossamer thread of the imagination. It functions as a metasymbolic narrative that informs a people's relation to the Divine. The severing of this umbilical cord of a culture leads to epistemic violence, for the people lose their aesthetic mooring. The rise of the modern Western world gave birth to this phenomenon of epistemic violence on a global scale when Europeans defined themselves as superior to the black world, imposing a racial hierarchy. The interpretive stance of the new generation of Western philosophers shook the aesthetic foundation of the black and colored world, and it still reverberates to this day. The epistemic violence done to African religions in the New World produces a sublime deficiency or holocaust of the imagination, on the part of the oppressed. In spite of the oppressor's "all-pervading desire to inculcate disdain for everything black,"[18] Du Bois reminds us that the community of the oppressed strives mightily to resist definitional negation.

The Kantian Sublime

The modern philosopher that is most closely aligned with the sublime is Immanuel Kant (1724–1804). This German idealist philosopher argued that reason is the means by which the phenomena of experience are translated into understanding. In his *Critique of Judgment*, Kant distinguishes between the aesthetic (sublime), moral (social), and scientific (cognitive) faculties

17. West, "Genealogy of Modern Racism," 61.
18. W. E. B. Du Bois, *The Souls of Black Folk*, ed. Henry Louis Gates Jr. and Terri Hume Oliver (New York: Norton, 1999), 15. Subsequent references to this edition will be cited parenthetically in the text.

of human understanding and intellect. In Kant's epistemology, human beings possess all three faculties and cast structures that exalt one over the other. For example, the scientist privileges the scientific; the philosopher, the moral; and the creative intellect, the aesthetic or sublime. The aesthetic or sublime, for instance, sees the material object in terms of its internal beauty, that is to say, the way the various parts interplay to construct the whole. The object, then, has no other purpose than to please the aesthetic sensibilities of the beholder. Its value lies not in its relationship to the external world or its utilitarian use in the culture, but in its existence as a thing of aesthetic contemplation, which the creative individual considers the highest form of intellectual activity. The Eurocentric concept of aestheticism or sublimity is largely grounded in Kant's construct.

Kant's philosophy served as the intellectual boilerplate for the New Critical aesthetic that would have a profound effect on the hermeneutics of civilization, the semantic domain, the underlying conception of human nature, and the objectification of the African. Aesthetics is that branch of philosophy that deals with the nature and expression of beauty, but in Kantian philosophy, aesthetics is the branch of metaphysics concerned with the laws of perception, which was congealed into a law of moral absolutism or ethnic purity by the apologists of mercantile imperialism. In his introduction to *Observations on the Feeling of the Beautiful and Sublime*, Goldthwait details Kant's contribution to aesthetics. Goldthwait's observations bear quoting at length:

> [Kant asserted that] even aesthetic experience depended upon the functioning of two of the intellectual faculties, the imagination and the understanding. Its distinguishing characteristic was that aesthetic pleasure is *disinterested*, not a satisfaction depending on the actual existence of the pleasant object, as, for example, when the satisfaction of one's hunger depends upon the actual eating of the food in which one takes delight. Furthermore, since aesthetic satisfaction depends on the harmony of two of the intellectual faculties, one of which is free in its function, then the judgment of the *beauty* of an object is subjective; whereas judgments of its color and shape and other such attributes are objective. This subjectivity was the dominant feature of the Critical aesthetic, and for Kant to have grounded it in reason and intellect was immediately recognized as the most remarkable feature of a remarkable new philosophy of beauty.[19]

This new philosophy of beauty or concept of aestheticism helped define the values of the modern Western world. In the Kantian worldview, the philosopher became the gatekeeper of taste, or aesthetic standards. Our mode of valuation of the sublime and the beautiful is informed by taste,

19. John T. Goldthwait, introduction to Immanuel Kant, *Observations on the Feeling of the Beautiful and Sublime*, trans. John T. Goldthwait (Berkeley: University of California Press, 1960), 4–5.

the fulcrum of the imagination. Taste is the ability to respond with immediate pleasure and unclouded vision to beauty in nature and in art, and, further, to "communicate the pleasure to others who are capable of sharing it."[20] Armed with the sublime, which had become more proprietary (read: Eurocentric) in the post-Enlightenment, and with the mercantilist imperative at their backs, the New World philosophers possessed the philosophical Rosetta stone that provided them with the key to the decipherment of the hieroglyphics of modernity (black bodies in white social space). Distance informed difference and visible differences implied underlying differences.[21]

When we unpack the term *sublime*, we see that its tenor became more proprietary in the Enlightenment as Europe became more self-conscious and invented the word *civilization*. As Charles H. Long reminds us in *Significations: Signs, Symbols, and Images in the Interpretation of Religion*, the word *civilization*, which first appeared in Western languages in the late eighteenth century, is "a *totalizing* symbol that includes the meaning and definition of primitive." *Civilization* not only carries within its "definitional framework the will to power," but this framework is also dictated "by a prior history that shaped how the modern Western world shaped the 'other.' " Long challenges us to widen our critical lens and see Kant's *disinterested* discussion of aesthetic appreciation, indeed aesthetic judgments, as part of a network of significations used by the modern Western world "to form a basis for the symbolic and mythological languages used to describe and interpret the new worlds discovered by the Europeans since the fifteenth century."[22] Gradually, "the sublime and beautiful" became a proxy for the term *civilization*.

Straddling two worlds, the New World philosophers tapped into the linguistic fissure caused by the importation of alien worlds and words to tease order out of disorder, namely *the anxiety over the influence of blackness*. These New World philosophers practiced a semantic lawlessness while insisting on a fixed position for black people. This lawlessness formed the genesis of the West's crisis of representation.[23] In his introduction to his *Philosophy of History*, Hegel dismisses all of Africa as the "dark continent" that has contributed nothing to the development of Western civilization because

---

20. Schaper, "Taste, Sublimity, and Genius," 372.
21. John Hope Franklin, *Color and Race* (Boston: Houghton Mifflin, 1968), 116.
22. Long, *Significations*, 80, 82 (my emphasis).
23. For a discussion of this semantic lawlessness, see Michael North, *The Dialect of Modernism: Race, Language, and Twentieth-Century Literature* (New York: Oxford University Press, 1994). In his work on value theory, Alain Locke helped to unveil "the crisis of consciousness" that lay athwart the Western mindset; see Abiola Irele, *The African Experience in Literature and Ideology* (Bloomington: Indiana University Press, 1990), 1; and Alain Locke, "Values and Imperatives," in *American Philosophy Today and Tomorrow*, ed. Sidney Hook and Horace Kallen (New York: Lee Furman, 1935).

the people are pagans, have no culture or traditions, and have produced nothing of cultural value. His position is grounded in his construct in his text, *Phenomenology of Mind*, that privileges those things that he asserts in *Philosophy of History* that Africans supposedly lack. Hegel's cultural bias authenticates the same discourse of whiteness that "otherized" people of African descent and, like Kant's, provides the intellectual justification for the colonization of Africa and for the modern enslavement of Africans.

Kant, whose views were based heavily on David Hume's infamous footnote to his essay, "Of National Characteristics," held that "the negroes of Africa have by nature no feeling that rises above the trifling." In his *Observations on the Feeling of the Beautiful and Sublime*, Kant noted:

> Mr. Hume challenges anyone to cite a simple example in which a negro has shown talents, and asserts that among the hundreds of thousands of blacks who are transported elsewhere from their countries, although many of them have even been set free, still not a single one was ever found who presented anything great in art or science or any other praiseworthy quality, even though among the whites some continually rise aloft from the lowest rabble, and through superior gifts earn respect in the world. So fundamental is the difference between the two races of man, and it appears to be as great in regard to mental capacities as in color.[24]

Kant and the other European philosophers restrict beauty to Europeans. The Enlightenment opens up two problematic constructs. Private space is reserved for bourgeois white men and public space is set aside for women and blacks. These philosophers also apply the construct for blacks later to delimit the roles of women when the Industrial Revolution freed them from genderized social space. The Victorians, for example, attribute to women the emotions and childlike behavior and dependency and attribute the intellect to men.[25]

The Romantics are the metaphor for the Europeans' projection of their fears and imagined visions first onto nature (what Kant calls the "the terrifying sublime") and second onto the "other." If nature provided the gateway from abstraction to verisimilitude, then black people provided the step away from "conventional verisimilitude into abstraction," as is evident in the work of the Romantics who "popularized" these constructs

24. Kant, *Observations on the Feeling of the Beautiful and Sublime*, 110–11. See also Richard H. Popkin, "Hume's Racism," *The Philosophical Forum* 9, nos. 2–3 (1978): 213–18.

25. Dolores Hayden details white women's struggle to break out of the domestic sphere in nineteenth-century America. Three works that challenge the image of the woman as helpless and dependent (and signify on this sexist and racist construct) on men are Charlotte Perkins Gilman's "The Yellow Wallpaper" (1892), Kate Chopin's *The Awakening* (1899), and Zora Neale Hurston's *Their Eyes Were Watching God* (1937). See Dolores Hayden, *The Grand Domestic Revolution: A History of Feminist Designs for American Homes, Neighborhoods, and Cities* (Cambridge: MIT Press, 1981).

(such as the woman exhibiting childlike behavior and the African as exotic other) among an emerging middle-class reading public.[26] When the European confronted the African on the textual meeting ground of nature and race, the European was primed to yield to this projection. Translated, the Western construction of the sublime often projects an eroticized African or black object who lives in a zone of indeterminacy. This construction carries with it the license to create and to destroy. The African's otherness is rooted in the very term *civilization* itself.[27] Civilized compared to what? The sublime as description of an indulgent horror of the enormity of nature was congruent with the European fantasy of Africa as a wild, unfathomable, unnatural place, as typified in Conrad's *Heart of Darkness* (1899).

The Souls of Black Folk

In *The Souls of Black Folk* (1903), W. E. B. Du Bois seeks to reverse the deformation brought about as a result of African enslavement in the New World. He prompts a radical reassessment of the American history that predates the publication of *The Souls of Black Folk*. In addition, Du Bois adds his voice to the literary-philosophical debate over aesthetic judgment, the nature of modernity, the ideals of freedom, the culture of the Enlightenment, and their relationship to the New World. For Du Bois, the issue at stake, then, is a major one for the proponents of civilization who consign blacks to a position of textual invisibility. They must come to grips with the metaphors by which they live (civilization, conquest, domination), as hermeneutics must survive "the radical destruction of its unquestioned totalizing and bifurcating tendencies." In a central way, this is one of the bases of Du Bois's interjecting himself into a global conversation that renders black people invisible.[28]

At the time Du Bois was writing, the whole notion of black culture was at its height, as white America became aware of black peoples' contribution to the Republic. Blacks were migrating from the American South to the North and to the West. These migrants were in conflict with white Americans. Du Bois elevates what Africa has to offer, and he presents black religion as the locus of creativity and vitality, with the "sorrow songs" or spirituals as the acme of black creation in the New World. With their understated elegance, the sorrow songs are Du Bois's metaphor for human creativity. Du Bois sees

26. North, *Dialect of Modernism*, 61. The story of this emerging middle class is captivatingly told in G. Kitson Clark's *The Making of Victorian England* (New York: Atheneum, 1979).

27. Long, *Significations*, 80, 82.

28. Satya P. Mohanty, "History at the Edge of Discourse: Marxism, Culture, and Interpretation," *Diacritics* (fall 1982): 34.

the grandeur of the human community in this body of music, which he considers the gold standard in New World black cultural production. Though they are a product of and response to the modern African slave trade, the teleology of the sorrow songs points towards something that transcends the individual. As Du Bois reminds us, the sorrow songs reflect a belief that there is in human existence something eternal and immutable: "Through all the sorrow of the Sorrow Songs there breathes a hope—a faith in the ultimate justice of things" (162).[29]

In broad theoretical brush strokes, Du Bois addressed the issue of religion through aesthetics and the strategies black people developed in order to deal with their "otherness," or the disconnectedness in their lives as they struggled to make themselves whole and to see the face the larger community denied them—their own. This struggle is aesthetically and ethically obscured and confused by the actuality of the language and rhetoric of the real relationships among the democratic liberalizing powers of modernity and the simultaneous invention of modern imperial colonialism, slavery, and racism. Du Bois gets at the submerged religion in *The Souls of Black Folk* through his constant reference to "life behind the Veil," "double-consciousness," and the rhetoric of black invisibility. Black invisibility is based on a discourse of difference—one that projects European standards as the norm. The "slash" itself (civilized/barbarian, religion/superstition, me/other, black/white, straight/gay) is implicated and enveloped in the sublime, if by "sublime" we mean one's ability to think lofty thoughts and render aesthetic judgements. The West defines itself against that which is not pure, or free of sediment (dregs, deposit, settlings, residue, grounds). The West promotes a rhetoric of negation. Accordingly, the black or colonial subject is constructed as the antithesis of the sublime: unworthy, uncivilized, and undesirable. Africans in the modern Western world have been excluded from the category human, judged by Europeans as incapable of reason and of nobility of expression. Hence, New World Africans were reduced to speaking in what Fanon, in *Black Skin, White Masks*, calls a "divine gurgling."[30]

29. Commentators on the sorrow songs include John Lovell Jr., *Black Song: The Forge and the Flame, the Story of How the Afro-American Spiritual Was Hammered Out* (1972; reprint, New York: Paragon House, 1986); Howard Thurman, *Deep River* and *The Negro Spiritual Speaks of Life and Death* (Richmond, Ind.: Friends United Press, 1975); Eileen Southern, *Music of Black Americans: A History*, 3d ed. (New York: Norton, 1997); James A. Cone, *The Spirituals and the Blues* (New York: Seabury Press, 1972); Wyatt T. Walker, *"Somebody's Calling My Name": Black Sacred Music and Social Change* (Valley Forge, Pa.: Judson Press, 1979); John Michael Spencer, *Blues and Evil* (Knoxville: University of Tennessee Press, 1993); Dena J. Epstein, *Sinful Tunes and Spirituals: Black Folk Music to the Civil War* (Urbana: University of Illinois Press, 1977); and Eric J. Sundquist, *To Wake the Nations: Race in the Making of American Literature* (Cambridge: Harvard University Press, 1993).

30. Franz Fanon, *Black Skin, White Masks*, trans. Charles Lam Markmann (New York: Grove Press, 1967), 20.

Blacks were conceived of as workers ("drawers of water and hewers of wood") and not poets and artists. Falling beyond the pale of the human race, they are therefore incapable of being composers; so wrote Thomas Jefferson in 1787: "Religion, indeed, has produced a Phillis Wheatley; but it could not produce a poet. The compositions published under her name are below the dignity of criticism."[31] In "Of the Training of Black Men," Du Bois observes that many whites held the "sincere and passionate belief that somewhere between men and cattle, God created a *tertium quid,* and called it a Negro,—a clownish, simple creature . . . straitly foreordained to walk within the Veil" (62).

Blacks, therefore, are not a satisfactory representation of the Divine. It is a representation that allows us to see God in ourself and our own inadequacy when measured against the Divine. If the sublime, as an aesthetic code, allows us to present what is, strictly speaking, unpresentable (the Divine), then the presentable (black and colored people when compared to whites) do not point toward the unpresentable and cannot confirm that it exists. The European construction of the beautiful and sublime negates blacks. They occupy a fixed position; they labor under the sign "nigger."[32] They struggle to move from a condition of inarticulateness to a threshold where they can approach total presence (or what Du Bois refers to as "true self-consciousness"). How can they be associated with the limitless magnitude of the universe or the limitless power of the Divine? Psychologically, it is like squeezing a square peg into a round hole. Deprived of agency, blacks struggle to become human. Reserving agency for themselves, whites struggle to become God.

Du Bois and the Invention of the Sublime

For Du Bois, the sublime must be invented because blacks (Africans) were excluded from the category of "human." *Invent* carries two principal meanings: 1) to conceive of or devise first; to originate (as poet or maker) and 2) to fabricate, make up—as, for example, to distort African history and give it back to blacks so they cannot recognize themselves as actors in history. The black in the West is an invention in the second sense, a purposeful misreading of history. The West invests much intellectual capital in keeping New World Africans from seeing themselves as agents in history, thus depriving them of agency. Du Bois plunges into the abyss to reclaim a discredited history and make it visible to his people: "The shadow of a mighty Negro past flits through the tale of Ethiopia the Shadowy and of Egypt the Sphinx" (11). Ethiopia and Egypt are metonymns for a displaced

31. Thomas Jefferson, *Notes on the State of Virginia* (1787), 135.
32. Houston A. Baker Jr., *Blues, Ideology, and Afro-American Literature* (Chicago: University of Chicago Press, 1984).

African history. The end point of this displacement, this theft of history, is to define blacks as Calibans or the "zero image," the antithesis of the Divine.

We can call the aesthetic paradox that confronts the black artist "Caliban's dilemma." History has lost its coherence, producing what Du Bois described as "the contradiction of double aims" (11), which has a paralyzing effect on the psyche of the black artist or intellectual.

> The would-be black *savant* was confronted by the paradox that the knowledge his people needed was a twice-told tale to his white neighbors, while the knowledge which would teach the white world was Greek to his own flesh and blood. The innate love of harmony and beauty [the sublime and beautiful] that set the ruder souls of his people a-dancing and a-singing raised but confusion and doubt in the soul of the black artist; for the beauty revealed to him was the soul-beauty of a race which his larger audience despised, and he could not articulate the message of another people. (11–12)

Through his mastery of language, Du Bois penetrates symbolically the boudoir of Western culture; he lifts the veil. He scores points with his academic language while simultaneously showing how Caliban blackens the orthodox text in his cultural productions. This is Caliban's revenge; he turns the language against itself from his position at the margin of civilization, on the cusp between night and day, savage and civilized. He destabilizes the "slash" that separates him from meaningful participation or holistic worship.

Any theory of life must begin with a theory of the sublime and beautiful, the ultimate cultural capital, for they are closely tied to our perception of as well as relationship with the Divine. Our morality informs our aesthetics. And our aesthetics is linked to our construction of the sublime, an authorizing narrative. Du Bois seeks to replace this authorizing narrative premised on European norms with one that is congruent with the lived reality of black people in the modern Western world.

Du Bois understood that the notion of identity is always "up for grabs." He therefore contests "culture" as an ideologically charged field. This contestation is heightened in a rigidly segregated society organized around race as an immutable category. The sublime is supreme. It is about image making. It functions at a metasymbolic level as a narrative of coherence and as a narrative of power. The sublime is the meaning beyond the meaning. It normalizes the various semiotic systems of a culture—religion, politics, economics. The sublime lies at the heart of the West's crisis of representation and stands in the way of Du Bois's desire to recenter Africa.

In a world of imaginative possibilities, it was hardly possible for post-Enlightenment writers and thinkers to imagine the African as imaginative, much less capable of the sublime in the grand sense of the term. To have savages (the uncivilized) participating in civil society is a repulsive idea.

But these savages not only lived in a civil society in the New World, they also altered the texture of a civil society that did not recognize their humanity. Du Bois crosses the Rubicon of the imagination and boldly asserts that Africans are made in the image of God. Thus, one begins to discern the full weight of Du Bois's aesthetic calibration when he places the sorrow songs on a par with European classical music.[33] The songs carry a critique of the metanarrative called civilization.

Du Bois signifies on the trope of civilization. He boldly asserts that it was the despised Africans who brought beauty to America; they reconceptualized the sublime and the beautiful. He skillfully places snippets of spirituals in dynamic tension with European classical music to challenge any notion of a sublime deficiency on the part of blacks in the New World:

> Little of beauty has America given the world save the rude grandeur God himself stamped on her bosom; the human spirit in this new world has expressed itself in vigor and ingenuity rather than in beauty. And so by fateful chance the Negro folk-song—the rhythmic cry of the slave—stands to-day not simply as the sole American music, but as the [sublime and] most beautiful expression of human experience born this side of the seas. It has been neglected, it has been, and is, half despised, and above all it has been persistently mistaken and misunderstood; but notwithstanding, it still remains as the singular spiritual heritage of the nation and the greatest gift of the Negro people. (155)

Du Bois locates the sublime in black religion in general and the sorrow songs in particular. Du Bois does this to reverse the idea that black people were aesthetically impoverished and incapable of using symbolic language. Through their religious expression, New World Africans challenge an Anglo-European conception of the sublime. They transmute their experience in America into black oral expressive culture, the sublime in a "blue note" of black cultural productions, and they produce a sublimity and a beauty that is congruent with their reality, thereby deconstructing the social text called America. For Du Bois, the sorrow songs are the perfect metaphor for the sublime. They reflect man's innate longing to be connected to the Divine, they contain the widest range of human expression, and they harmonize the incongruities of the New World experience. In another era, unfiltered by racism, this genius that captures the grandeur of the human experience would be called sublime. In bringing black religion into the formation of the New World, Du Bois provides us with a mode of reading that examines the ways in which the perspective of aesthetics and ideology and color and class, and their interrelationships, structure the discourse of race.

33. Long, "Primitive/Civilized: The Locus of a Problem," in *Significations*, 81–85.

"Nobody Knows de Trubble I Sees."

Because of the long, previous history of degradation of the African, it was easy to be dismissive of his cultural production and the mores of his aesthetic community. Most cultivated whites tended to look upon blacks, whose "appearance was uncouth, their language funny" (155) as quaint relics on a lower rung of the Great Chain of Being. Accordingly, they tended to "ridicule the shout or describe it [and, by extension, black cultural expression] as savage and uncivilized,"[34] at the opposite end of the aesthetic scale from the Divine. Against the background of a Christian context, this "barbarous music" was viewed as an affront to their God, constructed as distant, imperial, and white.

In her trenchant social history, *Sinful Tunes and Spirituals,* Dena J. Epstein provides an account of how African music and dance spread throughout the world. We see how aesthetics colored the encounter between Africa and Europe, setting the stage for a later, more rigid, racial hierarchy. When the black population was relatively small, many commentators, such as Ulrich Bonnell Philips, thought they "had by far the best opportunity which any of their race had been given in America to learn the white men's ways," and, of course, give up their own culture. The music that arrived in the New World with the African slaves survived with them the traumas of exile, forced labor, and alienation. In their new environment, Africans from various linguistic communities were transformed into something now called Afro-Americans.[35] The authentic product of their experience was the sorrow songs, for they could have been produced only in America; as Du Bois reminds us: "They are the music of an unhappy people, of the children of disappointment; they tell of death and suffering and unvoiced longing toward a truer world, of misty wanderings and hidden ways" (157). The Civil War introduced white America to the "unvoiced longing" of the enslaved blacks.

The Port Royal experiment after the fall of Hilton Head Island, South Carolina, Du Bois notes, provided the setting where "perhaps for the first time the North met the Southern slave face to face and heart to heart with no third witness" (155); there was no white Southern interpreter for the slaves. For the first time on a large scale, the country was introduced to the music of the slaves, whose "hearts were human and their singing stirred men with a mighty power" (155).

A southern-born white clergyman living in Worcester, Massachusetts,

---

34. Epstein, *Sinful Tunes,* 278.
35. Ibid., 16, 21; Ulrich Bonnell Phillips, *American Negro Slavery* (1918; reprint, Baton Rouge: Louisiana State University Press, 1969), 75. See also Le Roi Jones, "Hunting Is Not Those Heads on the Wall," in *Home: Social Essays* (New York: William Morrow, 1966), 176–77.

expressed his disapproval of the blacks' "native songs" in 1863, equating them with the ignorance of slavery:

> We have heard these long enough, and we hope the good taste of the re-
> fined young ladies at Port Royal will substitute others more sensible and el-
> evated in language. Northern people love to hear these songs as specimens
> of negro ignorance.[36]

The sorrow songs represent a center of consciousness, which observers often failed to comprehend because of their moral superiority. Blinded by
their imperial position, the observers could not see their subjective attitudes and the inflexibility of their rational morality.

A visitor to the Sea Islands schools in 1866, identified only as M. R. S.,
wrote of "these little barbarians . . . circling round in this fetish dance"—
meaning a shout—and concluded, "These people are receiving an education through their songs which is incalculable. Our teachers discourage the
use of the old barbaric chants, and besides our beautiful, patriotic and religious hymns teach the virtues of industry, truth, honesty and purity in
rhyme and measure."[37]

That shocked visitor, M. R. S., described the shout, which occurred on
May 15, 1866, in a school held in an old cotton-gin house in Beaufort:

> After school the teachers gave their children permission to have a "shout."
>   This is a favorite religious exercise of these people, old and young. In the
> infant schoolroom, the benches were first put aside, and the children ranged
> along the wall. Then began a wild droning chant in a minor key, marked with
> clapping of hands and stamping of feet. A dozen or twenty rose, formed a
> ring in the centre of the room, and began an odd shuffling dance. Keeping
> time to this weird chant they circled round, one following the other, changing
> their step to quicker and wilder motion, with louder clappings of the hands
> as the fervor of the singers reached a climax. The words of their hymns are
> simple and touching. The verses consist of two lines, the first being repeated
> twice. Take for example:

> > Nobody knows de trubble I sees,
> > Nobody knows de trubble I sees,
> > Nobody knows de trubble I sees,
> > Nobody know but Jesus.[38]

36. William George Hawkins, *Lunsford Lane; or, Another Helper from North Carolina*
(Boston: Crosby and Nichols, 1863), 294.

37. M. R. S., "Visitor's Account," quoted in Epstein, *Sinful Tunes*, 275, 281–82. The
last item in this string forms the foundation for the American Dream, which Du Bois
pointedly reminds his readers is the illusion of progress for many blacks who are denied
access to the American Dream.

38. Ibid., 281.

Du Bois opens *The Souls of Black Folk* with "Nobody Knows the Trouble I've Seen." It serves as the musical epigraph to "Of Our Spiritual Strivings" and sets the tone for Du Bois's meditation on history. It is no state-sanctioned reading of the social text. This master song serves as the leitmotif of the book and, indeed, of the experience of Africans in the New World. It speaks to their marginalization and loss of subjectivity. Du Bois plucks ten master songs (or statements on the sublime and beautiful) from this "forest of melody," these "songs of undoubted Negro origin and wide popular currency" (157). Among the songs from black America's corporate biography, he includes the following: "The Trumpet Sound," "Swing Low, Sweet Chariot," "Roll, Jordan, Roll," "My Lord, What a Mourning! When the Stars Begin to Fall," "My Way's Cloudy," "Wrestlin' Jacob," and "Steal Away." Du Bois advises the reader not to be seduced by the "quaint beauty of the music" (and by extension, black oral expression), for the words "conceal much of real poetry and meaning [the sublime] beneath conventional theology and unmeaning rhapsody" (159).

The people who walked in darkness created the sorrow songs. Although the cultural script of the West had reduced blacks to a position of contextual invisibility and darkness, blacks textured the darkness of America that refused to see them. Through their music, they critiqued a system whose aesthetic underpinning rendered them invisible. The sorrow songs begin with the phenomenology of the body and the trope of sight as blacks resolutely affirmed their humanity in a New World inhabited by people who were in the dark when it came to the rich diversity of the human experience.

And what did black people see in America? Briefly, what did the enslaved Africans, now transformed into blacks, see?

They saw the legal system that gave weight to the moral force (the sublime and beautiful) that led to their debasement, fixed social prejudices, and established racial hierarchy.[39]

They saw themselves defined as property and treated like animals.[40]

They saw the Planter Class (white masters) fear an alliance among the white indentured servants, Native Americans, and the enslaved. They were the only group subjected to a lifetime of servitude.[41]

They saw blacks used as pawns in the hands of the British and the Americans during the American Revolutionary War, with each side promising them freedom.

They saw the African home defiled within the shadow of the church and the "loss of ancient African chastity" as a result of the "legal defilement of Negro women" (14).

39. A. Leon Higginbotham Jr., *In the Matter of Color: Race and the American Legal Process: The Colonial Period* (New York: Oxford University Press, 1978), 21–22.
40. Ibid., 50–53.
41. Ibid., 26–30.

They saw self-evident lies, instead of the self-evident truths proclaimed in the majestic words of the Declaration of Independence.

The pledges of the Preamble to the Constitution had a hollow ring, for the American legal process did not apply to them: "We the people . . . in order to form a more perfect union, establish justice, . . . promote the general welfare, and secure the blessings of liberty to ourselves and our posterity."

From a black perspective, Higginbotham notes, "the Constitution's references to justice, welfare, and liberty were mocked by the treatment meted out daily to blacks from the seventeenth to nineteenth centuries through the courts, in statutes, and in those provisions of the Constitution that sanctioned slavery for the majority of black Americans and allowed disparate treatment for those few blacks legally 'free.' "[42]

Moreover, their historical memory told them that "We the people" did not include the sons and daughters of Africa. Their conviction was affirmed in the 1857 U.S. Supreme Court decision *Dred Scott v. Sandford*. Chief Justice Roger Taney, speaking for the majority, wrote:

> [A]t the time of the Declaration of Independence, and when the Constitution of the United States was framed and adopted . . . [blacks] had no rights which the white man was bound to respect.[43]

The corruption of Christianity that made the religion meaningful for whites but irrelevant for themselves was the one constant they saw in their American nightmare. Their skin was their sin, and conversion to Christianity did not entitle the enslaved black to freedom.[44] Yet blacks took the word, daily profaned in their midst, and made it their own. The sorrow songs make the world less alien and draw the community closer to God. In spite of the blacks' life of absurdity, they produced a body of music that spoke to the ages. The creators of the sorrow songs point out the moral bankruptcy of a philosophy of life that does not respect the rich diversity of the human experience. The sorrow songs do not exist as things in themselves, as objects of aesthetic contemplation. In his book's final essay, "The Sorrow Songs," Du Bois takes the "barbaric music" of the despised Africans and holds it in dynamic tension with European music to assert that we have the production of two world-class peoples. He thus continues a process of reversal (or overturning) begun by Douglass and Jacobs that is grounded in black oral expressive culture—spirituals, sermons, and folklore. He illuminates how blacks used music to redefine their humanity and reconceptualize America. To accept the sorrow songs is to embrace a new definition of America. As a statement on the sublime

42. Ibid., 6.
43. Ibid.
44. Ibid., 36–38.

and beautiful, the sorrow songs become an expression of the American character.

In using the sorrow songs as an organizing principle for *The Souls of Black Folk,* Du Bois employs memory as a device to redefine history, to validate both a personal and a collective identity, and to shape narrative. Simply put, the black presence in the New World acted on the social text in ways unacknowledged. To acknowledge formally the black presence (these black bodies in white space) would mean acknowledging the humanity of black people and thereby calling into question the European social construction of the sublime and beautiful. The political and cultural realities of race and ethnicity in American life—as refracted through history and memory— give a special meaning to the identity crisis of New World Africans, their "double-consciousness." Du Bois uses the trope of the veil and the rhetoric of black invisibility to symbolize this rupture of memory.

It seems to me what Du Bois is getting at by "double-consciousness" and "the souls of black folk" is to deconstruct the Euro-American construct of the sublime that privileges whites and negates blacks by privileging, first, the spiritual world of people of African descent rather than their material bodies. Before he can do this, Du Bois must first "locate" their physical bodies, their social, material essence, from the vantage point of their own cultural traditions in which they can see themselves as normal and "beautiful." Rather than constructing "blackness" through the tropes of the black body, Du Bois insists that our essence lies in our spiritual world, our souls, which is a bold assertion, given that nineteenth-century racist discourse insisted that black folks did not have souls, but were more akin to animals, as Douglass described in his *Narrative.* This is why there was no need, from the perspective of racist whites, to offer baptism, communion, church membership, Christian marriage, and burial ceremonies to black folks. They did not have souls that needed to be saved but were instead simply "hewers of wood and drawers of water." The discourse of darkness takes on a new meaning in a charged religious atmosphere: Blacks were held hostage to the Hamitic hypothesis. Du Bois signifies against the dominant hegemony that defines itself against that which is not pure or beautiful, the antithesis of the sublime.

When Du Bois begins *The Souls of Black Folk* by talking about being black as a cultural "problem" and develops the paradigm of "double-consciousness," he signifies against the discourse of difference that has generated racist discourse grounded in Kantian aesthetics. He "fixes" black identity within spirituality, and in doing so destabilizes the "fixity" of racial hegemony that privileges whites and negates blacks. Reading history, Du Bois challenges what the modern Western world defines as the cultural norm. That is to say, when white folks generated the sublime as a justification for all the dehumanizing things they were doing to black folks and other non-Europeans (the theft of history to justify the theft of labor and natural resources), they privileged themselves as "normal" and everyone else as a deviation from that norm through the discourse of difference. The slash, as in "me/other," is built around the arbitrary sign of skin color. Du Bois deconstructs this European notion of normality that is grounded in the tropes of the black body—difference by perception— and establishes difference via spirituality or religion. The reconstruction of the sublime and beautiful allows Du Bois to speak for black folks from both within and outside the veil, and for the black world, characterized by its private, delimited space. He does do through the discourse of black spiritual culture—the sorrow songs, which also share in common tenets of other groups of people who have experienced similar oppression. The discourse of difference that Du Bois constructs allows black folks to have voice and to construct identity through some means other than through the construct of blackness that was generated by the discourse of whiteness.

Rather than embrace the discourse of difference, Du Bois instead creates a dynamic relationship among the sorrow songs and the history of racial oppression. Ultimately, the sorrow songs do more than shape his narrative. They structure a new discourse of blackness that allows black people to speak in a manner other than that of a problem. They inform narrative structure. Thus, Du Bois prompts a revolution in thought. Prevoicing Ellison's *Invisible Man*, Du Bois, on "the lower frequencies," speaks for the community in much the same way as did the creators of the sorrow songs. It is in this sense that he challenges the black writer and artist to mine what Baldwin calls "our rich confusion" produced by our cultural tradition, and develop an aesthetic that is *with* and not *against* itself.[45]

Du Bois directs the black writer and artist away from fissures in the social text and toward wholeness in black cultural production, including music, song, sermons, and folklore. In spite of his own ambivalence toward evangelical piety, Du Bois, a New England Congregationalist, draws on black religion to scale the aesthetic wall of the unrepresentable that is reserved for Europeans only. He recognizes that black artists, because of their class orientation, often resist embracing the faith of their fathers and mothers. Black artists associate black religion with a culture of poverty. Standing in two worlds, they feel the full weight of the aesthetic paradox when they confront a model of the sublime and beautiful that does not recognize their

45. Ralph Ellison, *Invisible Man* (New York: Modern Library, 1952), 439; James Baldwin, "The Discovery of What It Means to Be an American," in *Nobody Knows My Name: More Notes of a Native Son* (New York: Dell, 1961), 22. In his preface to *The Book of American Negro Poetry* (New York: Harcourt, Brace, 1922), James Weldon Johnson notes that the Irish writers mined their cultural heritage for its nationalistic tendencies, and he urges black writers also to make the inward turn, if they expect to escape stereotyping by the larger society.

humanity. Du Bois's theory of black life leads us away from the proposition that the sign should efface itself.[46] Du Bois's message is clear. One cannot fully appreciate American life without first coming to terms with the cultural production of these "half-despised" African Americans, whose art "has been persistently mistaken and misunderstood." To recognize their art and consciousness is to expand the meaning of America and to add another layer to the complexity of the human experience.

For Du Bois the dialectal thinker, aesthetic contemplation does not constitute an entirely autonomous reality radically separated from life.[47] He articulates the rupture in the social text most clearly in "Of the Coming of John," an essay pitched as a short story, to reinforce the central point of *The Souls of Black Folk:* Black people labor behind a vast veil. Du Bois combines theory and critical practice in this provocative story as he signals to black writers and artists that belles lettres and other sophisticated literary forms cannot be thought of as separate from other sorts of writing, including black oral expressive literature.

"Of the Coming of John" is a metaphor for the jarring encounter between black and white men locked in blood feud with no apparent way out of the prison house of language known as the New World. Set in the American South, the story tells of two Johns, one black and one white. Both go to college in the North and return South to claim their patrimony. One is lifted up and welcomed back; the other is no longer recognizable to his community or to himself. He goes to pieces under the weight of trying to live up to the "double aims" and lashes out and kills the white John for making sexual advances toward his sister. Du Bois presents two worldviews that are now intertwined in the New World and in search of a language of reconciliation.

The black John needs a larger space in which to express himself (in which to give expression to his existential angst or pain of being black). Like Hester Prynne in *The Scarlet Letter* and Edna Pontiller in *The Awakening,* the social text provides him with no way out. Black religion, if we mean evangelical piety, will not do. In the imaginative space of the short story, Du Bois opens the cultural door to another dimension of black religion, grounded in the sorrow songs and folklore, and makes sense of the American bricolage. New World Africans redefined themselves through music. Jazz provides a larger canvas on which to give expression to the pain of being black. With the sorrow songs forming its aesthetic foundation, jazz enables Du Bois (or any black writer) to create an alternative in the face of an apparently hermeneutically sealed space. Jazz represents the acme of risk taking and

46. Gabriel Moyal, "René Descartes," in *The Johns Hopkins Guide to Literary Theory and Criticism,* 203–4.

47. Lucien Goldmann, *Cultural Creation in Modern Society,* trans. Bart Grahl (St. Louis: Telos Press, 1976), 15.

thereby the grand gesture in the reformulation of the sublime in the New World.[48]

While the two Johns struggle within the text because civil society does not give them a language in which to communicate as equals, Du Bois illuminates how music serves the black community as a healing force, thereby providing the black savant, artist, and intellectual with another way out of the madness and existential angst (the hermeneutics of memory). This is the revolutionary implication of *The Souls of Black Folk* for black artists and intellectuals.

Conclusion

It is through the process of interpretation that the souls of black folk are revealed. By this, I mean Du Bois interprets the rhythms that govern black life, adds a layer of complexity to the formation of the New World, and demonstrates that black people are active, not passive, participants in the construction of the social text called America.

These "black and unknown bards" are the unacknowledged benefactors of America's cultural gift to the world. They stand in the vanguard of American culture, leading the way with their expression of the thoughts of black America. Their songs articulate the fundamental truths of human experience.

Through their religion and music, African Americans achieved the "one quality of 'the sublime,' that cardinal excellence from which 'the greatest poets and writers have derived their eminence.'" This achievement cuts across all areas of black expression. In the final analysis, the sorrow songs—as the touchstone for the experience of blacks in America and the signature work of African American corporate biography—reflect the quality of their anonymous composers. Their excellence of expression reaffirms Longinus's observation: "Sublimity is the echo of a great soul."[49]

48. In *The Jazz Cadence of American Culture* (New York: Columbia University Press, 1998), ed. Robert G. O'Meally, a diverse collection of writers offer a wide range of eloquent statements about the influence of this art form on our world. Baker, in *Blues, Ideology, and Afro-American Literature,* shows how the "blues voice" and its economic undertones are both central to the American narrative and characteristic of the Afro-American way of telling it. In *Blues and Evil,* Spencer suggests that white blues scholars, and a fair number of black ones, I might add, have tended to overlook the religious nature of the blues partly because they have not fully understood African American culture. The religious foundation that supports this trinity of black music—spirituals, blues, jazz—humanizes a Eurocentric construction of the sublime that is antagonistic to the black presence in the modern Western world.

49. M. H. Abrams, *The Mirror and the Lamp: Romantic Theory and the Critical Tradition* (New York: Oxford University Press, 1953), 73.

A Selected Publication History
of *The Souls of Black Folk*

Compiled by M. Elaine Hughes

The Souls of Black Folk: Essays and Sketches. Chicago: A. C. McClurg & Co., 1903.

The Souls of Black Folk. 2d ed. Chicago: A. C. McClurg, 1903.

The Souls of Black Folk. 3d ed. Chicago: A. C. McClurg, 1903.

The Souls of Black Folk. 4th ed. Chicago: A. C. McClurg, 1904.

The Souls of Black Folk. 5th ed. Chicago: A. C. McClurg, 1904.

The Souls of Black Folk. 6th ed. Chicago: A. C. McClurg, 1905.

The Souls of Black Folk. London: Archibald Constable, 1905.

The Souls of Black Folk. 7th ed. Chicago: A. C. McClurg, 1907.

The Souls of Black Folk. 8th ed. Chicago: A. C. McClurg, 1909.

The Souls of Black Folk. 9th ed. Chicago: A. C. McClurg, 1911.

The Souls of Black Folk. 10th ed. Chicago: A. C.McClurg, 1915.

The Souls of Black Folk. 11th ed. Chicago: A. C. McClurg, 1918.

The Souls of Black Folk. 12th ed. Chicago: A. C. McClurg, 1920.

The Souls of Black Folk. 13th ed. Chicago: A. C. McClurg, 1922.

The Souls of Black Folk. 14th ed. Chicago: A. C. McClurg, 1924.

The Souls of Black Folk. 15th ed. Chicago: A. C. McClurg, 1928.

The Souls of Black Folk. 16th ed. Chicago: A. C. McClurg, 1929.

The Souls of Black Folk. 17th ed. Chicago: A. C. McClurg, 1931.

The Souls of Black Folk. 18th ed. Chicago: A. C. McClurg, 1935.

The Souls of Black Folk. 19th ed. Chicago: A. C. McClurg, 1935.

The Souls of Black Folk. 20th ed. Chicago: A. C. McClurg, 1935.

The Souls of Black Folk. 21st ed. Chicago: A. C. McClurg, 1937.

The Souls of Black Folk. 22d ed. Chicago: A. C. McClurg, 1938.

The Souls of Black Folk. New York: Blue Heron Press, 1953.

The Souls of Black Folk. Introduction by Saunders Redding. Greenwich, Conn.: Fawcett Publications, 1953.

Ames noires: Essais et nouvelles. Trans. Jean-Jacques Fol; notes by Sherley Graham. Paris: Presence Africaine, 1959.

The Souls of Black Folk. Reprint of 1903 ed., with introduction by Saunders Redding. New York: Dodd, Mead, 1961.

Kokujin no tamashii: Essei to suketchi. Trans. Kijima Hajime. Tokyo: Miraisha, 1965.

The Souls of Black Folk. Reprint of 1903 edition, with introduction by R. L. C. James. London: Longmans, 1965.

The Souls of Black Folk. Large print edition. New York: Magnavision Large Print Books, 1968.

The Souls of Black Folk. Reprint of the 1903 edition. The Basic Afro-American Reprint Library Series. New York: Johnson Reprint Corporation, 1968.

The Souls of Black Folk. Reprint of 1903 edition, with introductions by Dr. Nathan Hare and Alvin F. Poussaint. New York: New American Library, 1969.

The Souls of Black Folk. Reprint of 1903 edition, with introduction by Truman Nelson. New York: Washington Square Press, 1970.

The Souls of Black Folk. Reprint of the 1953 Blue Heron Press edition, with introduction by Herbert Aptheker. Millwood, N.Y.: Kraus-Thomson Organization, 1973.

The Souls of Black Folk. Fisk Diamond Jubilee edition, with introduction by L. M. Collins. Nashville: Fisk University Press, 1979.

The Souls of Black Folk. Reprint of 1903 edition, with introduction by Henry Louis Gates Jr. New York: Bantam Books, 1989.

The Souls of Black Folk. Introduction by Donald B. Gibson; notes by Monica M. Elbert. New York: Penguin Books, 1989.

The Souls of Black Folk. Reprint of 1903 edition, with introduction by John Edgar Wideman, notes by Nathan I. Huggins. New York: Vintage/Library of America, 1990.

The Souls of Black Folk. Reprint of 1903 edition, with introduction by Arnold Rampersad. New York: Knopf, 1993.

The Souls of Black Folk. Reprint of 1903 edition; Dover Thrift Edition. New York: Dover, 1994.

The Souls of Black Folk. Reprint of 1903 edition, with introduction by John Gabriel Hunt. New York: Gramercy Books, 1994.

The Souls of Black Folk. Introduction by Randall Kenan. New York: Signet Classics, 1995.

The Souls of Black Folk. Reprint of 1953 Blue Heron Press edition, with introduction by Herb Boyd. New York: Modern Library, 1996.

The Souls of Black Folk. Introduction by Robert J. Cummings. Grand Rapids, Mich.: Candace Press, 1996.

The Souls of Black Folk. Reprint of 1903 edition, with introduction by David W. Blight and Robert Gooding-Williams. Boston: Bedford Books, 1997.

The Souls of Black Folk. Reprint of 1905 Archibald Constable edition, with introduction by Bruce Kellner. Tokyo: Hon-no-Tonosha, 1997.

The Souls of Black Folk. Reprint of 1903 edition, with introduction by A. Lee Henderson and afterword by Cecil L. Murray. Las Vegas: Classic Americana, 1999.

The Souls of Black Folk. Reprint of 1903 edition, with introduction by Henry Louis Gates Jr. and Terri Hume Oliver. New York: Norton, 1999.

Las almas del pueplo negro. Trans. Ruben Casado y Francisco Cabrera, with prologue by Miguel Barnet. Havana: Fundacion Fernando Ortiz, 2001.

Contributors

Christopher A. Brooks is Associate Professor of African American Studies in the College of Humanities and Sciences at Virginia Commonwealth University in Richmond. He holds a doctorate in anthropology/ethmusicology from the University of Texas at Austin. He has numerous publications focusing on the African continental and diasporan experience and has recently done field research on women's rights organizations in southern Africa. A recent project has been his coauthoring of the autobiography of Shirley Verrett, the celebrated African American opera singer.

Keith Byerman is Professor of English and Women's Studies at Indiana State University and is an associate editor of *African American Review*. He is the author of *The Short Fiction of John Edgar Wideman; Seizing the Word: History, Art, and Self in the Work of W. E. B. Du Bois; Fingering the Jagged Grain: Tradition and Form in Recent Black Fiction;* and, with Erma Banks, *Alice Walker: An Annotated Bibliography, 1968–1986.*

Carolyn Calloway-Thomas is Associate Professor of Communication and Culture at Indiana University. A former Ford Fellow and Fulbright and Carnegie Scholar, she is a coauthor of *Intercultural Communication: Roots and Routes* and a coauthor of *Martin Luther King, Jr., and the Sermonic Power of Public Discourse.* Her scholarly interests include identity, change and cross-cultural communication, class and power, and the rhetoric of black Americans.

Carrie Cowherd is Associate Professor of Classics at Howard University, where she has served as Chair of Classics, Director of Humanities, and Director of the Honors Program. She holds degrees from Indiana University and the University of Chicago, and her current interests include classical influences in the writings of Charles Johnson and Toni Morrison.

Chester J. Fontenot, Jr., is the Benjamin W. Griffith, Jr., Professor of English and Chair of the English Department at Mercer University in Macon,

Georgia. He has published six books, over sixty articles, and numerous book reviews and newspaper articles. His latest book, *W. E. B. Du Bois and Race: Essays Celebrating the Centennial Publication of* The Souls of Black Folk, inaugurated the Mercer University book series "Voices of the African Diaspora," for which he serves as general editor.

Thurmon Garner is Associate Professor in the Department of Speech Communication at the University of Georgia. He graduated from the Department of Communication Studies at Northwestern University in Evanston, Illinois, in 1979. His scholarly interests include the study of rhetorical communication, with an emphasis in rhetorical criticism, African American discourse, and African American orality. His publications have appeared in *The Journal of Black Studies, The Quarterly Journal of Speech*, and *The Journal of Language and Social Psychology.*

Erica L. Griffin, a Ph.D. candidate in English at the University of Georgia, has a biographical entry on Johnson Publishing Company President Linda Johnson Rice forthcoming in *Notable Black American Women.* Her interests include black women novelists from the Civil War to World War II, the Victorian novel, and creative writing. Her most recent work is "The 'Invisible Woman' Abroad: Jesse Fauset's New Horizon," published in *Recovered Writers/Recovered Texts: Race, Class, and Gender in Black Women's Literature,* edited by Dolan Hubbard.

Shanette M. Harris is Associate Professor of Psychology in the Clinical Program Area in the Department of Psychology at the University of Rhode Island, Adjunct Assistant Professor for Community Health at Brown University, and a licensed psychologist. Her current research broadly focuses on multicultural psychology and emphasizes minority health (physical and psychological) and the psychology of African Americans. She has primarily published on body image and eating behavior, minority student retention, and African American gender role behavior.

Dolan Hubbard is Professor and Chair of the Department of English and Language Arts at Morgan State University in Baltimore. A former editor of *The Langston Hughes Review,* he is the author of *The Sermon and the African American Literary Imagination* and is a member of the editorial board for *The Collected Works of Langston Hughes,* published by the University of Missouri Press.

M. Elaine Hughes is Reference Desk Coordinator and Assistant Head of Information Services at the William Russell Pullen Library at Georgia State University. With a master's degree in Library Science from Atlanta University, her research interests include African American authors and a core list of material for African American studies.

Amy Helene Kirschke is Assistant Professor of Art History and African American Studies at Vanderbilt University. Her publications include *Aaron Douglas: Art, Race and the Harlem Renaissance* and the forthcoming "Sorrow and Joy: Art, Memory, and Identity in W. E. B. Du Bois's *Crisis* Magazine."

Barbara McCaskill is Associate Professor in the Department of English at the University of Georgia, where she teaches African American and Multicultural American Literature. Her books are *Multicultural Literature and Literacies: Making Space for Difference*, edited with Suzanne Miller, and *Running 1,000 Miles for Freedom: The Escape of William and Ellen Craft from Slavery*. She is also editor of the journal *Womanist Theory and Research*.

Reavis L. Mitchell, Jr., a native of Nashville, is Chair of the Department of History at Fisk University. Educated at Fisk, Tennessee State, Middle Tennessee State, and Harvard Universities, he is the author of *Thy Loyal Children Make Their Way: A History of Fisk University since 1866* and of twelve entries in the *Tennessee Encyclopedia of History and Culture*, as well as hundreds of historical monographs published in educational videotapes, compact discs, journals, magazines, and newspapers.

Shawn Michelle Smith is Associate Professor of American Studies at St. Louis University. She is the author of *American Archives: Gender, Race, and Class in Visual Culture*. She is currently completing a book on the photographs W. E. B. Du Bois collected for the American Negro Exhibit at the 1900 Paris Exposition.

Virginia Whatley Smith is Associate Professor of English at the University of Alabama at Birmingham. She has published on Charles Johnson, John A. Williams, and Richard Wright in journals such as *Mississippi Quarterly*, OBSIDIAN, *African American Review*, and *MLA Approaches to Teaching Richard Wright's* Native Son. She edited *Richard Wright's Travel Writings*.

James Daniel Steele is Associate Professor of Political Science at North Carolina A&T State University in Greensboro. With degrees from Morgan State University and Atlanta University, he is the coeditor of *American National and State Government: An African American View of the Return of Redemptionist Politics*. In 1994, he founded the W. E. B. Du Bois Symposium and was awarded a grant for its support by the North Carolina Humanities Council 1995.

Thelma B. Thompson is President of the University of Maryland Eastern Shore. With a Ph.D. in English from Howard University, she speaks nationally on the humanities and on the impact of new technological advancements. Her research interests include seventeenth-century English literature as well as African American and Caribbean literature. She is the author of *The Seventeenth-Century English Hymn: Sacred and Secular Concerns* and of numerous critical articles in the areas of American, African American, and Caribbean literatures.

Index

Italicized page numbers indicate photographs.